The Art of Music
and Other Essays

Hector Berlioz, by Maurin. Bibliothèque de l'Opéra, courtesy Bibliothèque Nationale.

HECTOR BERLIOZ

The Art of Music and Other Essays

(A Travers Chants)

TRANSLATED AND EDITED BY

Elizabeth Csicsery-Rónay

INDIANA UNIVERSITY PRESS
Bloomington and Indianapolis

Manufactured in the United States of America

Library of Congress Cataloging-in-Publication Data
Berlioz, Hector, 1803–1869.
[A travers chants. English]
The art of music and other essays = (A travers chants) / Hector
Berlioz ; translated and edited by Elizabeth Csicsery-Rónay.
p. cm.
Includes index.
ISBN 0-253-31164-0
1. Music—History and criticism. I. Csicsery-Rónay, Elizabeth, date
II. Title.
ML410.B5A543   1994
780—dc20   93-3752

1 2 3 4 5 98 97 96 95 94

Contents

Illustrations

Foreword
by
Jacques Barzun

The essays in this book are the last that Berlioz himself gathered, in 1862, for republication under the title *A Travers Chants*. Their varied occasions and contents, ranging from Beethoven's nine symphonies to the alarming rise in concert pitch, and from Wagner's first Paris concert to the qualifications a listener must possess to appreciate music as an art, and not solely as pleasure for the ear, bring to mind so many of the author's traits and powers that the reader will naturally want to fill out the emergent sketch. A few words about Berlioz's career and temperament will perhaps serve the purpose.

Many of Berlioz's biographers, knowing the strength and fertility of his musical genius, have regretted that he had to spend a large part of his adult life earning his living as a music critic: his free time for composing was drastically cut down. But in the Europe of his day public taste decreed that the money for music should be divided between the opera and the virtuoso, chiefly pianistic. So even though Berlioz was one of the first great orchestra conductors (he repeatedly occupied the podium in capital cities from London to Moscow), his work in that domain still left him to seek his livelihood elsewhere. Only the orchestras benefited, for he trained them—as Wagner testified—to a new standard of execution.

The "elsewhere" was writing, necessarily in Paris where, after casual beginnings in various journals and a spell as editor of the *Gazette Musicale*, Berlioz became chief critic of the influential *Journal des Débats*. For a quarter of a century he contributed a weekly *feuilleton*. That word is equivalent to our "column," but as the reader will see in these pages, it was a good deal longer than the syndicated newspaper articles we know under that name. It was also more scholarly, often skirting the technical while still accessible to the general public. Thanks to style and wit and passionate artistic convictions, Berlioz (like G. B. Shaw later) created a following for reading about music.

Normally, neither the musical nor the unmusical care much for that pastime. The former only want to listen; the latter keep away from both the sound and the talk about it. It is a tribute to Berlioz's skill that his Tuesday *feuilleton* came to be looked for; he was known as the *mardiste*, just as Sainte-Beuve was the *lundiste* for his Monday reviews of literature.

The present volume contains some thirty of these musical essays, together with shorter pieces which are either extracts from other *feuilletons* or "squibs" of separate provenance. What Berlioz preserved here gives us, together with his estimate of the masters he most admired, his unwavering conception of the art of music. He saw it as at once autonomous and expressive—a medium for drama that might be allied to words and action in opera, but which, in the symphony and other forms, needed neither—especially since Beethoven.

To minds both sensitive and trained, Berlioz believed, the purport of a piece of music and its quality were manifest without aid. Music being no mere adjunct to some other art, the thing called program music was a contradiction in terms. But not all listeners were equally sensitive and only a few were trained; so that for them, commentary, interpretation, and program notes could be helpful—provided that no suggestion, metaphor, or other imagery was taken literally. What words can convey is the character of the music, its mood or occasion, knowledge of which opens the mind of the hard of hearing. For music has a place in life and relates to it imaginatively without reproducing it. That relation is the point of titles, such as "Wedding March" or *Academic Festival Overture* or *Eroica* Symphony.

Nowadays the public benefits from over a century of this propaganda for purely instrumental music that is also dramatic and expressive. The campaign began with E. T. A. Hoffmann explaining what Mozart and Beethoven were up to. Soon, Weber, Berlioz, and Liszt followed and gave the models on which all subsequent indoctrination by way of concert reviews, program notes, commentary on recordings, and interviews with composers has been patterned. We all know how to "take" a work entitled *La Mer* or *Pictures at an Exhibition* or even *Ionisation*; but this sophisticated attitude did not come by the light of nature; and from what Berlioz finds it needful to say in these pages we may infer what a cultural revolution he helped to bring about.

For the present collection is but one of seven volumes of theory and criticism, if we include his *Memoirs* and *Treatise on Orchestration*. A half-dozen more could be made up of uncollected pieces, for Berlioz did not reprint the many reviews he had to write about run-of-the-mill operas and recitals; the worst part of his torment was having to attend them. Seeing that his large correspondence also contains more than one little page-long treatise on esthetics, one is glad that Berlioz was so articulate; one is even tempted to regret somewhat less the material necessity that made him a critic.

On yet another plane, these writings repay perusal: they reveal what Pascal in his *Pensées* called for: a man, not an author. Berlioz paints his own portrait in every line, and an unusual character is disclosed. A recent writer puts it in two words: "fiery and cool." Berlioz was something rare among composers: a highly educated man—a classicist widely read in the literatures of Europe, a scholar in the music of the past and of his own day, and an observant traveler with a retentive memory. He had also had medical training and showed a leaning toward the sciences. Thus by talent and experience he was judicious, as well as practical—he was for 40 years his own impresario. The fiery side was his genius—passionate, vehement, sarcastic, and incorruptible. In conversation he was witty and urbane and in his relations with performers and colleagues punctiliously polite. He reserved his burning arrows for those who in any manner desecrated art, whether by giving mutilated versions of masterpieces, by vulgarizing the use of music, or by defaming the great masters in any art.

In the pages ahead, the satirical sallies are few, because the subjects are mostly masterpieces. Admiration reigns unclouded. Beethoven, Weber, Gluck, Shakespeare receive the guerdon that is their due. For Berlioz's other deities, one must go to other collections, such as his *Evenings with the Orchestra*, which has also been translated. Single works that he greatly esteemed, for example, Rossini's *Barber of Seville* and *Comte Ory*, are also treated elsewhere. But here is Wagner, who belongs in a special category.

Contrary to common belief, the relations of the two men were not those of enmity. Berlioz, the older both in years and in time of maturing, helped Wagner when he came to Paris aged 26. They met again in London and got on very well. Then Wagner perpetrated one of his mean tricks to damage his "friend" abroad. Berlioz overlooked it. Next, Wagner sent Berlioz the score of *Tristan* with an effusive inscription, and shortly Wagner came to Paris to give concerts. Soon afterwards *Tannhäuser* was put on and failed at the Opéra.

By that time, factions had formed around Wagner's work (though hardly known), and Berlioz had to chart a difficult course. He liked the man despite his bad behavior and acknowledged his genius, but he did not like his music. Being a melodist, Berlioz could not accept Wagner's "reducing music to expressive accents"; he thought it destructive of musical form. And then there was Liszt, a lifelong intimate friend whom Berlioz did not want to hurt by criticizing Wagner, who had become Liszt's idol.

Finally, among the absurdities of the Wagnerites and anti-Wagnerites in Paris, Berlioz's name was frequently invoked, as saint or devil, for *his* innovations. Worst of all was the slogan "music of the future," which the Wagnerite faction maintained would make all earlier music obsolete, including Beethoven. That alone would have been enough to make Berlioz discharge a crash of thunderbolts. But he did not ascribe the notion to Wagner himself. As we see in this volume, he reviewed Wagner's concerts as fairly and temperately as he could. To please one party he should have fulminated; to please the other he should have worshiped to the point of disowning his own esthetic. He leaned to neither side, and in restating what he believed, at least did not *dis*please himself.

As for *Tannhäuser*, the work struck him as so contrary to his conception of music *and* drama that he turned over the reviewing to a colleague, rather than attack Wagner and serve his own cause.

And that, too, is part of the self-portrait.

The reader of this book comes upon Berlioz in English dress, thanks to the patient industry and research of a dedicated translator. French prose is always difficult to turn into English, in spite of the closeness of the two vocabularies, indeed, because of it. Nearly every look-alike pair of words is a trap.

In addition, Berlioz is a stylist, and one who obviously thinks in prose like a musician. The idea that informs a paragraph is not pre-packed from the start and simply unrolled in sections; rather, it grows as it goes, throwing out branches as it moves forward, while maintaining coherence and unity. This can be done more easily in French than in English, because of the signs of gender and number, which allow ample but tight-knit constructions to remain clear. Split up for English clarity, such sentences lose part of their elegance and the rhythm its impressiveness. Besides, Berlioz's wit and humor, as well as his penetration and his fervor, depend on a choice of words whose connotations are not always matched in their correct English equivalents. The French title of the present volume is a good example. The idiom *à travers champs* means "[walking] across the fields," but it suggests also a sense of freedom and a pastoral atmosphere; it is instinct with the nature poetry that is a leading feature of Berlioz's work. By substituting *chants* (songs, music at large), which is pronounced exactly like *champs*, Berlioz achieved a happy ambiguity, at once playful and apt, that suited both his critical purpose and his artistic sensibility. The turn of phrase—like music itself—is untranslatable.

Translator's Note

Berlioz commands a superb prose style—witty, graceful, ironic, lively, and impassioned. As if this were not enough of a challenge, he is also full of allusions, proverbs, and puns, which cannot be translated literally, but for which I felt equivalents must be sought in English. Alas, such problems can sometimes be insoluble; regrettably, some poetic play with words and ideas turned out to be beyond rendering. The very title, *A Travers Chants*, is a case in point.

Berlioz's irony was also difficult to reproduce, but it had to be attempted, or the tone of the writing would have been lost. At the same time, humor demands, in my view, that the translator try to achieve phrasing as tight and fast-paced as the original.

Another challenge has been the great range of Berlioz's style. His long-breathed, rhythmic sentences modulate sharply, like his music, from impassioned rhetoric that requires a similarly heightened approach, to a down-to-earth colloquial style that must be translated into conversational English.

There is a school of translating that holds it important for the original to be adhered to as closely as possible, in word order, syntax, and so on. I do not believe that this type of literal, word-for-word translation could do justice to Berlioz. I have opted rather for conveying the sense, not just the words; my aim has been to recreate the original as if it had been written in English to begin with. As to what kind of English would be appropriate for his nineteenth-century French, I have felt that, as Berlioz was modern in his own time, I should seek to render him into modern English.

There is, however, a special problem when Berlioz himself translates Shakespeare, or, more often, paraphrases a French translation. In the penultimate chapter, for instance, "To Be or Not to Be," I have tried to use the original Shakespeare as far as practicable, but I have refrained in places where it would distort Berlioz's meaning. For example, at the very end of the chapter, where Shakespeare says Hamlet knows a hawk from a handsaw, Berlioz speaks of an "aigle" (eagle) and a "buse" (buzzard, a dolt).

At first I intended simply to translate the notes by Professor Léon Guichard from the Gründ edition (Paris, 1971), but I soon discovered that they needed to be updated and adapted for the English-speaking reader. I have replaced, wherever possible, references to scores in the Paris Bibliothèque Nationale by editions more readily accessible to readers in English-speaking countries. References to books in English, such as those by Barzun or Cairns or John Warrack's biography of Weber have replaced Guichard's references to French authors, such as Boschot and Prod'homme. I sought out English translations of French works, for example, Romain Rolland's important book on Beethoven, but some of Guichard's allusions to French literature, those that seemed designed especially for French readers, have simply been dropped.

I was fortunate in having access to the recently published *Correspondance générale* (the first five volumes; the sixth and final one has yet to appear), which greatly facilitated referring to Berlioz's letters.

In the end I used the notes by Guichard as a first work of reference. He deserves special credit for the laborious and comprehensive work of tracking down Berlioz's *feuilletons*, their dates, and the journals in which they appeared. However, as the reader will see, I am equally indebted to other publications, principally *Grove's Dictionary of Music and Musicians* (1980 edition); Berlioz's *Memoirs*, as translated and edited by David Cairns; and Jacques Barzun's epoch-making biography, *Berlioz and the Romantic Century* (third, revised edition). Notes that appear at the bottom of a page of text, marked with an asterisk, are by Berlioz.

In all this work of annotation, I had the enlightened guidance of Jacques Barzun. Any errors, of course, are entirely my responsibility.

Other writings by Berlioz that have appeared in English include the following: *Grand traité d'instrumentation et d'Orchestration* (Paris, 1843–44), and *L'Art du chef d'orchestre* (Paris, 1855), translated by Mary [Novello] Cowden Clarke as *Modern Instrumentation and Orchestration* (London, 1856); *Les soirées de l'orchestre* (Paris, 1852), translated by Jacques Barzun as *Evenings with the Orchestra* (Chicago: University of Chicago Press, 1956); and *Mémoires* (Paris, 1870), translated by David Cairns as *Memoirs* (London: Victor Gollancz, 1969 and New York: W. W. Norton, 1969).

Acknowledgments

Heartfelt thanks and gratitude to Jacques Barzun, a foremost authority on Berlioz *and* surely one of the finest prose writers of our time. His assistance in editing the translation was invaluable. He was also generous in finding time to delve into his encyclopedic knowledge for advice on the annotations. I thank him in particular for graciously contributing a foreword. In short, this book would not have been possible without him. On a personal level, the experience of working with Jacques Barzun has been full of challenge and inspiration, and I also enjoyed it immensely.

Thanks to David Cairns, whose magnificent translation of the *Memoirs* first set me on the Berlioz path, and who first encouraged me to embark on this translation.

Thanks also to George Schuetze, musicologist, who contributed his knowledge of music and musical terminology, and assisted in editing large sections of the book.

Thanks also to André Philippe, David Miller, and Willy Mortier—knowledgeable, practicing musicians—for explaining difficulties in French musical terminology. Thanks to France Maca, Dominique Seytre, and Jean Tanguy for their help with thorny French words or expressions; and to Eva and Evandro Bertuccioli for their assistance in translating the Italian verses.

Last but not least, my gratitude and thanks to my husband, Clifford Smith, for his steady encouragement and patient assistance in bringing the text and notes to a condition where they were worthy of being sent to Jacques Barzun for a final reading.

The Art of Music
and Other Essays

Love's Labour's Lost
(Shakespeare)
Hostis habet muros [The enemy holds the walls]
(Virgil)

To
M. Ernest Legouvé
of the Académie Française [1]

THE ART OF MUSIC *

Music[3] is the art of combining sounds so as to touch the emotions[4] of intelligent persons endowed with special, cultivated faculties. To define music in this way is to confess that I do not believe it to be, as the phrase goes, *meant for everybody.*[5] No matter what the music is like or how it has been composed, whether it is simple or complex, gentle or energetic, a great number of people can neither feel nor understand its power. It has always seemed obvious to the impartial observer that these people were *not meant for music* and therefore *music was not meant for them.*

Music is both a felt perception and a science. It requires of those who cultivate it, whether as composer or performer, both natural inspiration and a knowledge that can be acquired only after long study and deep reflection. It is the marriage of skill and inspiration that produces the art of music. Without these two elements, a musician would be only an incomplete artist, if indeed he could be called an artist at all. The great question, whether talent without training is superior to training without talent, which Horace dared not resolve for poets,[6] seems to me equally difficult to settle for musicians. Some men who know nothing of the science of music can instinctively produce graceful and even sublime melodies, witness Rouget de Lisle and his immortal *Marseillaise.*[7] Yet these rare flashes of inspiration cast their glow only on one portion of the art, while the rest, no less important, remains in the dark. Given the complex nature of our art of music, it follows that these men in the last resort cannot be ranked among the musicians: They lack knowledge.

But more often one encounters methodical, calm, cold minds who, after patiently studying theory, amassing observations, and taking every possible advantage of their imperfect talents, manage to compose works that seem to fit the commonplace idea of music, works that satisfy the ear without beguiling it, works that speak neither to the heart nor to the imagination. Merely satisfying the sense of hearing is a far cry from providing the exquisite sensations this sense is able to experience; nor can the delights of the heart and the imagination be cheaply bought.

---

* This chapter was published about 20 years ago in a book[2] now out of print, various fragments of which appear in this volume. The reader will perhaps not be displeased to come across it again before we go on to the analytical study of some famous masterpieces of music.

[Notes marked * are by Berlioz, Tr.]

And since in true musical compositions of whatever school these delights are found combined with a most intense sensuous pleasure, I believe these impotent contrivers must also be struck from the ranks of
musicians: They lack feeling.

What we call music is a new art, in the sense that it probably bears
little resemblance to what the ancient civilizations meant by that word.
Moreover, and this should be stated at once, the word "music," far from
being restricted as it is today to the art of sound, had for them a meaning so broad that it applied also to dance, mime, poetry, oratory, and
even to the whole range of the sciences.[8] If we trace the etymology of
the word "music" to "muse," it becomes clear why the ancients gave it
such a broad meaning: music was that which was governed by the Muses.
From this fact derive the many errors of interpretation committed by
students of antiquity. Yet in our current speech there is an expression
whose meaning is almost as general. We use the word "art" in speaking
of the works created by intelligence, whether working alone or aided by
one of the senses and by such body movements as the mind has rendered poetic. Two thousand years from now, the reader who finds in our
books the title "On the State of the Arts in Nineteenth-Century Europe," which has become the commonplace title of many a disquisition,
will have to interpret it as follows: On the state of poetry, oratory, music, painting, etching, sculpture, architecture, drama, mime, and dance
in nineteenth-century Europe. One can see that, apart from the exact
sciences, to which it does not apply, our word "art" or "arts" corresponds closely to the ancients' use of the word "music."

We have only an imperfect idea of what was to them, strictly speaking, the art of sound. Some isolated facts, perhaps exaggerated in the
telling, as we see in similar matters every day, and the inflated or completely absurd ideas of philosophers—not to mention mistaken interpre-
tations of what they wrote—give the impression that music had such
immense power and influence on human behavior that legislators had
to regulate it in the public interest. Without considering what may lie
behind such distortions of the truth, but merely granting that the music
of the Greeks really did, in certain individuals, create extraordinary
impressions—impressions due neither to the ideas communicated by the
words nor to the facial features or gestures of the singer, but truly to the
music and only the music—we must admit that none of this proves that
their art had attained a high degree of perfection. Who is unaware of the
violent effect which, under certain conditions, even a most ordinary
composition can exert on a high-strung temperament? Alexander the
Great, for example, proved so impressionable that after a great feast,
being excited by the cheers of a crowd of ardent admirers; by the memory of a recent triumph, by the hope of new victories and the sight of
weapons, by the beautiful slaves that surrounded him; by ideas of sen-

sual pleasure, love, glory, power, and immortality—all these seconded by the action of food and wine—he was brought to a state of ecstasy by Timotheus' music.[9] One can easily see that the singer did not have to be an artistic genius in order to produce such an effect on Alexander's almost pathological sensibility.

Citing the more recent example of King Eric of Denmark, who was driven to such a frenzy by certain songs that he killed his best servants, Rousseau observed that these unhappy creatures must have been far less sensitive to music than their master; otherwise, he would have been equally in danger.[10] This witty irony shows again Rousseau's bent for paradox. Yes, of course, the Danish king's servants were less sensitive to music than their master! There is nothing surprising about that. Would it not be strange if it were otherwise? We know, do we not, that the musical sense is developed by training. We know that certain mental capacities, very strong in some persons, are much weaker in others; we know that nervous sensibility somehow belongs to the upper classes of society, whereas the lower classes, either because of the manual labor they perform or for some other reason, are virtually deprived of it. It is because this uneven distribution is indisputable and, in fact, undisputed, that I have so narrowly defined the number of people on whom music produces its effect.

Rousseau may ridicule the stories of miracles wrought by ancient music, but elsewhere in his writings he seems to give them enough credence to place this ancient art, of which we barely know anything and of which he knows no more than we, many notches above its modern forms. He, of all people, should not belittle our present-day music, for he speaks everywhere else with such enthusiasm as to prove its intense effect on him.

Be that as it may, if we but look around us, we can readily find facts that argue for the power of our music, facts at least equal in value to the dubious anecdotes told by the ancient historians. While listening to the masterpieces of our great composers, how many times have we seen members of the audience convulsed by fierce spasms, laughing and crying at the same time, and showing all the symptoms of delirium and fever![11] A young Provençal musician, carried away by the passionate feelings that Spontini's *Vestale* had aroused in him, could not bear the idea of returning to our prosaic world from the poetic heaven which had just been opened to him. He wrote to his friends of his resolve, and one night, after hearing once more the masterpiece that was the object of his ecstatic admiration and, understandably convinced that he had reached the peak of happiness allowed to earthly beings, he blew out his brains at the door of the Opéra.[12]

On hearing Beethoven's C-minor Symphony for the first time at the Conservatoire, the famous singer Mme Malibran[13] was seized with such convulsions that she had to be carried from the hall. In similar cases, dignified men have often been forced to leave, so as to hide the turmoil of their emotions from the public gaze.

As for the emotions that music arouses in the present writer, he maintains that nothing can give a true idea of their effect to anyone who has never had a similar experience. Leaving aside the intellectual perceptions that the art has developed in him and referring only to the impressions and feelings he has experienced during the performance of the works he admires, he can say in all honesty that:

On hearing certain compositions, my vital forces seem to be doubled in strength, I feel a delicious pleasure in which reason plays no part; next, the habit of analysis engenders the pleasures of admiration; my emotion grows more intense in direct proportion to the vigor or nobility of the composer's ideas and causes a strange agitation in my blood circulation: my arteries beat violently. Tears, which normally herald the end of the paroxysm, occasionally betoken an intermediate stage soon to be surpassed. When this happens, my muscles contract spasmodically, a trembling overtakes my limbs and a numbness my hands and feet, while the nerves of sight and hearing are partially paralyzed; I can no longer see, I can barely hear, I become dizzy and fall into a half-faint. As one might guess, such violent sensations are rather rare. And they are matched by their opposite: bad music produces the reverse of wonder and delight.

No music is more likely to cause this result than that whose main character seems to me platitude combined with falseness of expression. I blush as if with shame, I am overcome by indignation; anyone looking at me might think I had just been dealt an unpardonable insult. I feel a general upheaval, an effort at rejection by my entire organism, akin to that of the stomach when it spews out a nauseating liquid. It is the extreme of disgust and hatred; I am incensed by what I hear and try to expel it through all my pores.

Of course, the habit of masking and controlling my feelings rarely allows these symptoms to be revealed in full, and if once past early youth I have on occasion given them free rein, it was only when I was taken by surprise and had no time to counteract.

Thus, it is clear that modern music has no cause to envy the power of the ancients. Let us therefore ask, what are the means at the disposal of the art of music today? The following are the ones available at present; they make quite a list, but this does not preclude the possibility that yet others may be discovered in the future:

Melody: The musical effect produced by various sounds heard *successively* and organized in more or less symmetrical phrases. The art of linking these diverse sounds in a pleasing way or of making them expressive cannot be learned; it is a natural gift, modified in a thousand ways by the knowledge of existing melodies and the characteristics of individuals and nations.

Harmony: The musical effect produced by various sounds heard *simultaneously.* No doubt, only natural gift can make a great harmonist; but the craft of how to group sounds to make *chords* that are generally perceived as pleasant or beautiful and the art of linking them in a logical sequence is taught everywhere to good effect.

Rhythm: The symmetrical division of time by sounds. A musician cannot be taught to find beautiful rhythmic forms. The ability to invent them is among the rarest. Of all the elements of music, rhythm seems to me the least advanced.

Expression: [14] The quality through which music is directly related to the feelings it wants to convey or the passions it seeks to arouse. The ability to perceive this relation is extremely rare. At the opera one often sees an entire audience, people who would be upset at once by a dubious note, listening without dissatisfaction and even with pleasure, to passages whose expression is completely false.

Modulation: Nowadays this word designates the passages or transitions from one key or mode to a new key or mode. Training can greatly assist the musician in the art of changing key and in the way to modify its makeup appropriately. Folk and popular songs generally do not modulate much.

Instrumentation: [15] It consists in giving each instrument a part to play that best suits its nature and the effect to be produced. It is also the art of grouping instruments so as to modify the sound of some by that of others and thus obtain a particular sound that could not be produced by any single instrument or by its playing together with others of its own kind. Instrumentation is to music precisely what color is to painting. Today it is a splendid and powerful musical means, though often overdone. It was hardly used before the end of the last century. Here too, as with rhythm, melody, and expression, I believe that the study of great models can set the musician on the path that leads to mastery, but one cannot succeed without special talent.

The point of origin of sounds: By placing the listener closer to or farther away from the performers and, on certain occasions, placing instruments at a distance from each other, one can bring about changes in musical effect that have not yet been adequately studied.

Degree of intensity of sounds: Some phrases, when played or sung softly or with restraint will produce no effect whatever, yet can be very beautiful if given the projecting power they need. The opposite procedure leads to an even more conspicuous fault: too much power imparted to a gentle idea yields only the ridiculous or the overblown.

Multiplicity of sounds: This is one of the most powerful principles of musical emotion. When many instruments or voices occupy a vast space, an enormous mass of air is set vibrating, and its waves take on a character they do not ordinarily possess. So true is this that if out of a large church choir a single voice is given a theme that is simple and slow but not in itself very interesting, it will produce only a mediocre effect, however strong and beautiful the voice and accomplished the singer; whereas that same theme, sung in unison by all the voices, even without much art, will take on an incredible majesty.

Of the various constituent elements of music that I have just listed, almost all seem to have been known to the ancients.[16] Only harmony is generally denied them. Yet it is now forty years since a learned contemporary composer, M. Lesueur,[17] stood forth as the dauntless challenger of this view. Here are the arguments of his opponents:

That the ancients were not acquainted with harmony is shown in various passages from their historians and a mass of other documents. They used only the unison and octave. It is also well known that harmony is an invention that can be traced back no farther than the eighth century. The scale and tonal system used by the ancients were not the same as ours, which were invented by an Italian, Guido d'Arezzo.[18] The ancient system resembled that of plainsong, itself a remnant of Greek music. It is obvious to anyone versed in the science of harmony that this sort of melody defies harmonic accompaniment and lends itself only to the unison and the octave.

One could reply that the invention of harmony in the Middle Ages does not prove that it was unknown in earlier centuries. Much human knowledge has been lost and rediscovered. Gunpowder, one of the most important inventions to which Europe lays claim, was made centuries earlier in China. It is, moreover, extremely doubtful that Guido d'Arezzo's inventions were really his, for in his own writings he mentions several as universally known. As for the difficulty of adapting our harmony to plainsong, there is no denying that harmony is by nature better suited to our modern melodic forms, but the liturgical chants are nonetheless often performed in multipart counterpoint and, in addition, accompanied in all our churches by chords on the organ.

Now let us see on what M. Lesueur based his opinion:

"The ancients," he wrote, "were acquainted with harmony, and the works of their poets, philosophers, and historians establish the fact decisively at many points. These historical passages, though very clear, have been mistranslated. Thanks to our knowledge of Greek notation, entire compositions for several voices, accompanied by various instruments, are extant to prove the point. Duos, trios, and choruses by Sappho,[19] Olympus,[20] Terpander,[21] Aristoxenus,[22] and others, reproduced faithfully in our musical notation, will be published in due course. There you will find a clear and simple harmony that uses only the gentlest chords. Their style is identical with that of certain pieces of religious music composed today. Their scale and tonal system were the same as ours. It is a serious error to believe that plainsong—that ungainly legacy of the barbarous hymns chanted by Druids as they danced around the statue of Odin while offering hideous sacrifices—is a remnant of Greek music. True, some of the hymns used in the Catholic Church are Greek; but these are visibly conceived in the same system as modern music.

"Moreover, even if concrete evidence were lacking, reasoning alone would be sufficient to demolish the notion that the ancients lacked the knowledge or use of harmony. Would you have it that the Greeks— those inventive and civilized sons of the land that gave birth to Homer, Sophocles, Pindar, Praxiteles, Phidias, Apelles, and Zeuxis, these artistic people who raised marvelous temples that time has not yet destroyed, whose chisels carved marble into human forms worthy of representing the gods, this people whose monumental works serve as models for poets, sculptors, architects, and painters to this day—can it be that these people had only a music as imperfect and as coarse as that of the barbarians? Really? What about the thousands of singers of both sexes gathered in their temples at great expense, with a great variety of instruments that they called, when stringed: Lyra, Psalterium, Trigonium, Sambuca, Cithara, Pectis, Maga, Barbiton, Testudo, Epigonium, Simmicium, Epandoron, etc.; when winds: Tuba, Fistula, Tibia, Cornu, Lituus, etc; and when percussion: Tympanum, Cymbalum, Crepitaculus, Tintinnabulum, and Crotalum, etc.[23]

"Would the Greeks have used all these only for cold and sterile unisons and miserable octaves? Would they have made the harp and the trumpet march together to the same step, forcing into a grotesque unison two instruments whose character and style are so vastly different? To say so is an undeserved insult to the intelligence and musical sensibility of a great people. It is to accuse the whole of Greece of barbarism."

Such were M. Lesueur's arguments. As to his evidence, there is no arguing against it. Had the celebrated master published his great work on ancient music,[24] including the fragments mentioned above; had he cited his sources and the manuscripts he consulted; and had the sceptics been able to see with their own eyes that the harmonies which he attributed to the Greeks were in fact their legacy to us, then M. Lesueur no doubt would have won the cause for which he had fought so long with unshakable perseverance and conviction.

Unfortunately, he did not do so, and as the issue is still very much open to doubt, I shall discuss below the case for M. Lesueur's belief with the same care and impartiality as I have used in examining the ideas of his opponents. My reply to him is as follows:

The plainsong that you deem barbarous is not judged so severely by most musicians today. On the contrary, in their view, some of it is marked by a rare and austere grandeur. The modal system in which these hymns are composed and which you condemn can often be used with admirable results. Many traditional songs, naïve and full of expression, lack the leading tone and are thus composed in the modal system of plainsong. Others, such as Scottish airs, employ a still stranger scale, lacking as it does both the fourth and the seventh degree of ours. Yet what can be fresher and more vigorous than these mountain melodies? To call barbaric art forms that are unfamiliar to us is not a proof that an education different from our own might not alter our estimate of their worth.

Besides, there is no need to go so far as to charge the Greeks with barbarism in order to concede that their music, compared with ours, was still in infancy. The contrast between the imperfect state of one special art and the splendid flowering of other arts that have no link or relation with it is not at all beyond belief. Arguments based on the idea that this kind of anomaly is impossible are not new; but as is well known, conclusions based on them have later been harshly contradicted by irresistible facts.

As for the argument based on the musical absurdity of forcing instruments as dissimilar as the lyre, trumpet, and timpani to sound together in unison and octaves, it is really without force. One should rather ask, "Is such a combination of instruments feasible?" Of course it is; modern musicians can use it whenever they like. Hence, it is not at all strange that it was practiced among a people the very nature of whose music did not enable them to use any other.

Now as to the superiority of our music over theirs; it seems to be more than probable. Whether the ancients were acquainted with harmony or not, we can put together the notions of their art that the two opposing factions have brought out and on their evidence come to the following conclusion:

Our music encompasses that of the ancients but theirs did not encompass ours; that is to say, we can easily reproduce all the effects of ancient music and in addition create an infinite number of other effects that the ancients never knew and could not have produced.

I have not said anything about the art of sound in the Orient. The reason is that until now, all that travelers have told us on the subject has been limited to childish crudities that bear no relation to the ideas we associate with the word "music." Barring new information contradicting what we have been told, I must consider music among the Orientals to be a grotesque noise similar to that made by children playing games.*

---

* Since these lines were written I have had the opportunity in France and in England to hear Arab, Chinese, and Persian musicians, and these experiences of their songs and instruments, together with their answers to the questions I have asked some of those who speak French, have only confirmed my opinion.[25]

A CRITICAL STUDY OF
BEETHOVEN'S NINE SYMPHONIES [1]

It is now thirty-six or thirty-seven years since music by Beethoven, whose works were then totally unknown in France, was first played at the Concerts spirituels given at the Opéra. Today it is hard to believe the condemnation with which most musicians greeted this wonderful music. It was considered grotesque, incoherent, long-winded, bristling with harsh modulations and primitive harmonies, devoid of melody, extravagant in expression, noisy, and horribly difficult. To satisfy the men of taste who ruled the Académie royale de musique [2] at that time, M. Habeneck [3] was forced to make dreadful cuts in the very symphonies he later directed with such care at the Conservatoire, [4] cuts which could at most be allowable in a ballet by Gallenberg [5] or an opera by Gaveaux. [6] Without these *corrections*, Beethoven would never have been granted the honor of appearing on the program of these Concerts spirituels between a bassoon solo and a flute concerto. At the first rehearsal, when Kreutzer [7] heard the passages marked later in red pencil, he ran out covering his ears. He had to muster all his courage during the other rehearsals to force himself to listen to *what was left* of the Symphony in D.

Rest assured that in those days 99 percent of the musicians in Paris shared Kreutzer's opinion of Beethoven. If it had not been for the sustained effort of a tiny fraction that felt otherwise, perhaps the greatest composer of modern times might scarcely be known to us even today. Moreover, without the performance of these fragments of Beethoven's music at the Opéra, the Société du Conservatoire might never have been founded. This excellent institution owes its existence to that small number of intelligent men and also to the public—the real public that *does not belong to any clique,* that judges according to its own impressions and not by narrow ideas or ridiculous esthetic theories. This public, which is often mistaken in spite of all (as is evident from its frequent changes of mind) was struck from the outset by some of Beethoven's outstanding qualities. It did not ask whether this or that modulation was relative to another, whether certain harmonies were permitted by the schoolmasters, or whether certain novel or unfamiliar rhythms were permissible. It perceived only that these rhythms, harmonies, and modulations, adorned by a noble and passionate melody and clothed in a powerful instrumentation, made a strong and completely new kind of impression. What more could have been needed to arouse its applause?

François-Antoine Habeneck, by Lange. Bibliothèque de l'Opéra, courtesy Bibliothèque Nationale.

Only rarely does our French public experience the intense and ardent
emotions that music can evoke. But when this public is truly moved,
nothing can equal its gratitude to the artist, whoever he may be.

The famous A-minor *Allegretto* of the Seventh Symphony, which had
been inserted into the Second *to make the rest of it palatable,* was appreciated at full value by the audience from its very first appearance at
these Concerts spirituels. The pit rose in a body with vociferous cries
for a repeat performance, and this won almost as great a success for the
first movement and the scherzo of the Symphony in D, which had been
little applauded the first time. From that time on, Beethoven's champi-
ons were strengthened by the interest the public began to show in his
works, and this reduced most of his detractors to inaction, if not to
silence. Gradually, thanks to these first rays of light, which showed the
clear-sighted where the sun was about to rise, the small core of admirers
grew and the magnificent Société du Conservatoire, virtually unrivaled
in the world today, came to be founded, almost expressly for Beethoven.

We shall now attempt to analyze the symphonies of this great master,

Ludwig van Beethoven. Courtesy Bibliothèque Nationale.

beginning with the first of them, which the Conservatoire[8] performs so rarely.

I. Symphony in C Major

In form, melodic style, harmonic restraint, and instrumentation, this work is markedly different from Beethoven's later compositions. When writing it, the composer was still obviously under the spell of Mozart's ideas, which he sometimes expanded and everywhere imitated with ingenuity. From time to time in the first and second movements there appear rhythmic patterns which, it is true, had been used by the composer of *Don Giovanni*, but only rarely and much less strikingly. The principal theme of the first *Allegro* is a six-measure phrase, not very distinctive in itself but made interesting by the skill with which it is treated. A transitional melody of no particular distinction follows, and by means of a half-cadence repeated three or four times, we reach a short passage of imitation by the woodwinds at the fourth above.[9] Its appearance here is all the more surprising, as the same formula had already been used in the overtures to several French operas.

The *Andante* contains a soft accompaniment for timpani which seems quite ordinary today, but in which one should see an intimation of the startling effects Beethoven was later to produce with this instrument[10]—an instrument that was for the most part rarely or badly employed by his predecessors. This movement is full of charm; its theme is graceful and lends itself well to the fugal development, which device the composer exploits ingeniously and with piquancy.

The Scherzo is the first-born of that family of delightfully playful pieces of banter (scherzo = joke or play) whose form and tempo Beethoven invented and with which he replaced in almost all his instrumental works the much slower and significantly different minuets of Haydn and Mozart. This scherzo has an exquisite freshness, agility, and grace. It is the only real novelty in this symphony, which quite lacks the poetic idea that so richly and grandly informs most of the works that came later. Here is admirably wrought music, clear and lively, but rather bland, at times cold and even small-minded, as in the final rondo, which is musically childlike. In short, this is not yet the true Beethoven. But we shall soon find him.

II. Symphony in D

This symphony is all nobility, energy, and pride. The introductory *Largo* is a masterpiece, wherein the most beautiful and unexpected effects follow one another without creating confusion. The melody is touchingly solemn from the outset; it inspires respect and sets the stage emotionally. Soon the rhythm grows bolder; the orchestration becomes richer, more sonorous, and more varied. This wonderful *Adagio* leads into an *Allegro con brio* of irresistible spirit. The *gruppetto* [turn] which is played in unison by the violas and cellos in the first measure of the theme reappears on its own to establish either progressions in crescendo or imitations between the winds and strings—all this as original as it is full of life. In the middle of the movement, a melody begun by the clarinets, horns, and bassoons[11] is concluded by a *tutti* from the rest of the orchestra; its virile energy is enhanced by a felicitous choice of accompanying chords.

The *Andante* is quite unlike that of the First Symphony. Instead of a subject developed by canonic imitation, the theme is a pure and ingenuous song, presented first simply by the quartet of strings and then embellished with rare elegance by delicate runs that are always in keeping with the feeling of tenderness which characterizes the main theme. This *Andante* is a lovely image of innocent happiness, scarcely clouded by a few melancholy accents.

The Scherzo is as openly cheerful and playful in its fantasy as the *Andante* was happily serene, for this symphony is cheerful throughout. Even the warrior-like verve of the first *Allegro* is entirely free of violence; one can sense only the youthful ardor of a noble heart that keeps intact the finest illusions of life. The composer still believes in immortal glory, love, and self-sacrifice. What gay abandon! What flashes of wit! What high spirits! To hear the instruments challenging each other over fragments of a motif which none plays in its entirety, each portion shimmering with a thousand colors as it passes from one instrument to the other, you would think you were watching Oberon's graceful sprites at play. The finale belongs to the same world: it is a second scherzo, in duple meter, perhaps even more subtle and piquant in its playfulness.

III. The Eroica Symphony[12]

It is a mistake to abridge the inscription that the composer put at the head of his Third Symphony. Its title is: *Heroic Symphony to Celebrate the Memory of a Great Man.*[13] Hence there is no question here of battles or triumphal marches, as the truncated title might lead people to expect, but of deep and serious thoughts, melancholy memories, and ceremonies impressive in their grandeur and sorrow. In short, the funeral rites of a hero. I know of few examples in music where the expression of grief is so steadily sustained and in forms so pure and noble.

The first movement is in three-quarter time; its tempo is more or less that of a waltz. Yet what could be more serious and dramatic than this *Allegro*? The vigorous theme that forms its foundation is not presented in its entirety at the start; contrary to custom, the composer begins by giving us only a partial glimpse of his melodic idea; only after some introductory measures is it displayed to full effect.

The rhythm is extraordinarily remarkable both for its frequent syncopations and for the way that duple meter is thrown, by the stressing of weak beats, on top of the triple meter.[14] When rough dissonances are added to these conflicting rhythms—as we hear in the middle of the development section, where the first violins play a high F against an E-natural appearing as the fifth of the A-minor triad[15]—one can barely restrain a shudder at this spectacle of uncontrollable fury. Here is the voice of despair, almost of rage. One may wonder, why this despair, why this rage? The cause is not revealed. In the next measure, suddenly, calm comes over the orchestra as if, exhausted by the outburst to which it has just given way, its strength suddenly fails. Now come softer phrases that recall to us those painful, helpless feelings that memory can evoke in the soul.

It is impossible to describe or even to suggest the myriad aspects, both melodic and harmonic, in which Beethoven presents his treatments of the theme. I shall confine myself to mentioning one which is exceedingly strange, which has been the subject of much controversy, and which in fact the French publisher corrected in the score, thinking it a misprint; it was restored later, after further inquiry. The first and second violins, alone, are sounding a major-second tremolo, B-flat–A-flat (part of the dominant-seventh chord of E-flat), when a horn, coming in apparently four measures early,[16] rashly plays the beginning of the main theme, consisting of the notes E-flat, G, E-flat, and B-flat. It is not hard to imagine what strange effect this melody, built on the three notes of the tonic chord, produces when set against the two dissonant notes from the dominant chord, even though the parts are sufficiently far apart to soften the discord. But just as the ear is about to rebel against this anomaly, a vigorous *tutti* cuts off the horn and, by ending *piano* on the tonic chord, allows the cellos to take up the theme again, now in its full form and its proper harmony. Viewed with detachment, it is difficult to find any serious justification for this musical whim.* Yet the composer was said to value it highly. It is said that at the first rehearsal of this symphony, Mr. [Ferdinand] Ries[17] stopped the orchestra, shouting, "Too soon, too soon, the horn has come in too soon!" As a reward for his zeal, he was given a vigorous dressing-down by the enraged composer.

The rest of the score contains no eccentricities of this kind. The highly tragic funeral march is like a translation into music of Virgil's beautiful lines on the funeral procession of young Pallas:

> Multaque praeterea Laurentis praemia pugnae
> Adgerat, et longo praedam jubet ordinet duci.
> Post bellator equus, positis insignibus, Aethon
> It lacrymans, guttisque humectat grandibus ora.[18]

> Many trophies from the battle of Laurentis are borne,
> and the spoils of war are brought in a long line.
> Then the warhorse, Aethon, stripped of his trappings,
> follows weeping, great tears rolling down his face.

The end, especially, is deeply moving. The march theme reappears,[19] but in fragments, interrupted by rests and accompanied by a few strokes, pizzicato, in the double-basses. As the bare, broken, solitary shreds of this mournful melody fall one by one into the tonic, the winds shout a cry, a last farewell of the warriors to their comrade-in-arms, and the entire orchestra fades away on a sustained organ point, *pianissimo.*

The third movement has the customary title, Scherzo, the Italian word for play or badinage. At first sight it is none too clear why music of this

---

*No matter how you look at it, if this is really what Beethoven intended, and if there is an iota of truth to the stories circulating about it, we are forced to conclude that this whim is absurd!

kind should be included in this epic work. It must be heard to be understood. It has indeed the rhythm and tempo of a scherzo, and sure enough, these are games, but they are funeral games repeatedly darkened by thoughts of mourning; in short, games such as those with which the warriors of the *Iliad* celebrated their leaders at the graveside.[20] Here, even in the most playful orchestral developments, Beethoven keeps a dark and solemn tone and the deep sadness fitting for the subject.

The finale is nothing but a further development of the same poetic idea. A very curious instrumental passage in the opening section[21] shows the effects that can be produced by contrasting timbres. The violins play a B-flat, which is echoed immediately by the flutes and oboes. Though the sound is played with equal force, on the same note of the scale and in the same rhythm, the difference between these identical notes is so great that one could compare it to the difference between blue and purple. It is to Beethoven that we owe such refinements in tone, which were unknown before his time.

This finale, though greatly varied, is based entirely on a very simple fugue theme. In addition to a thousand ingenious details, the composer superimposes on it two other themes, one of them very beautiful. It is not readily seen from the shape of the line that this melody is, so to speak, mined from another. For its expressive quality is by contrast much more touching and incomparably more graceful than the original, which rather resembles a harmonic bass line and indeed serves as such very well. This singing theme reappears just before the end[22] in a slower tempo and with another harmony, intensifying its sadness. The hero calls forth many tears. After these final lamentations, the poet abandons the elegiac mood and strikes up an enraptured hymn to glory. Though somewhat terse, it is a brilliant peroration, a worthy crown to a musical monument.

Beethoven may have written music more striking than this symphony, and several of his other works make a stronger impression on the public; yet it must be acknowledged that the *Eroica* Symphony is so powerful in conception and execution, its style so sinewy, so consistently elevated, and its form so poetic, that it must be ranked with the composer's noblest inspirations.[23]

Whenever I hear this symphony, I am overcome by a solemn and, so to speak, ancient sorrow. The public seems much less moved. It is really deplorable to see how a creator fired with such enthusiasm is unable to make even an elite audience understand him, to make it rise to the level of his inspiration. This is all the sadder since, in other circumstances, this very audience does catch fire, quiver, and weep with him. But although some of his other compositions, which arouse the public to a genuine, lively passion, may be as admirable as this one, they are not more beautiful. The *Allegretto* in A minor of the Seventh Symphony, the *Allegretto Scherzando* of the Eighth, the finale of the Fifth, and the

Scherzo of the Ninth are appreciated at their true value. Even in the *Eroica*, the audience seems greatly moved by the funeral march, but let us have no illusions about the first movement. For over twenty years, I have noticed that the public listens to it coolly, seeing in it only a skillful composition of considerable energy, nothing more. For this lack there is no consolation. In vain, you tell yourself that it has always been so, that the loftiest works of the spirit suffer the same fate, that the springs of poetic emotion are hidden and inscrutable, that the masses totally lack the feeling for certain kinds of beauty, and that it cannot be otherwise. None of this makes you feel any better, none of this soothes the indignation—instinctive, involuntary, and, if you will, absurd—which fills the heart at the sight of a marvel unnoticed, of a masterwork that the crowd looks at without seeing, listens to without hearing, and allows to pass by virtually without turning its head, as if it were something commonplace or mediocre. Oh, it is dreadful to have to tell yourself with pitiless certainty: what I find beautiful is beauty for me, but may not be so for my best friend, whose tastes I usually share; he will be affected in a completely different way; a work that overwhelms me, throws me into a fever, brings tears to my eyes, may leave him cold, may even annoy or bore him.

Most great poets have no feeling for music, or like only trivial and childish melodies. Many great minds who think they love music have no idea of the emotions it can arouse. These are sad truths, but palpable and obvious. Only a pig-headed adherence to certain esthetic theories keeps them from being recognized. I once saw a bitch howl with pleasure at the sound of a major third played as a double-stop on the violin; but she produced a litter on which thirds, fifths, sixths, octaves, and consonant and dissonant chords never made the slightest impression. The public, however constituted, is like this bitch and her pups when it comes to great works of music. It has nerves that vibrate to certain resonances, but this sensitivity, incomplete as it is, is unevenly distributed and subject to infinite variation. Consequently, it would be folly for a composer to rely on particular artistic means rather than others. He had better follow blindly his own sentiments and resign himself in advance to all the hazards which chance may have in store.

I was leaving the Conservatoire with three or four *dilettanti* after hearing a performance of the Choral Symphony.

One of them asks: "What did you think of it?"

"Tremendous! Magnificent! Overwhelming!"

"How odd! I found it dreadfully boring. What about you?" he asks, turning to an Italian.

"Oh, I couldn't make head or tail of it; or rather, it was unbearable; it has no melody. But wait, here are some reviews from the papers. Listen:

" 'Beethoven's Choral Symphony is the apex of modern music. Art has produced nothing comparable in nobility of style, grandeur of structure, and perfection of detail.' "

Another review: "Beethoven's Choral Symphony is an abomination."

Another: "The work is not altogether devoid of ideas, but they are so badly organized that the general effect is incoherent and lacking in charm."

Yet another: "Beethoven's Choral Symphony contains many remarkable passages, yet it is obvious that the composer is short on ideas. When his imagination is exhausted, he wears himself out trying, albeit often successfully, to make up for lack of inspiration by sheer artistic craft. The work's few themes are treated with a high level of skill and arranged in an order that is perfectly clear and logical. In short, it is a very interesting work by a *tired genius.*"

Where is the truth? Where the error? Everywhere and nowhere. Everyone is right. What is beautiful for one is not for another, on the sole basis that one has been moved, and another left cold; the one deeply enjoyed it, while the other was bored. What to do about it? Nothing—and that is dreadful. For my part, I would rather lose my mind and be able to believe in absolute beauty.

IV. *Symphony in B-Flat* [24]

Here Beethoven abandons ode and elegy and returns to the style of his Second Symphony, less solemn and elevated but perhaps no less difficult. This score is generally lively, brisk, and cheerful, or else imbued with a heavenly sweetness. Save perhaps for the contemplative *Adagio* introduction, the first movement is full of joy. The staccato motif that opens the *Allegro* is merely a frame on which the composer hangs other melodies more worthy of the name, so that what seemed initially to be the main theme turns into an accessory idea.

This device yields curious and interesting results; it had already been used by Mozart and Haydn with equal felicity. But in the development section of the same *Allegro* there appears a truly new idea, which captures one's attention from the first few measures and, after drawing the listener into its mysterious developments, surprises him with an unexpected ending. What happens is this: after a rather energetic *tutti*, the first violins break the first theme into fragments with which they have a playful *pianissimo* conversation with the second violins; this ends in sustained dominant-seventh chords of the key of B-natural.[25] Each of these chords is cut off by a rest of two measures, filled only by a delicate roll of the timpani on B-flat, that is, the enharmonic major third of the F-sharp triad. After two such appearances, the timpani fall silent to let the strings gently murmur other fragments of the theme and arrive via a new enharmonic modulation at a B-flat six-four chord. The timpani, entering again on B-flat—now a true tonic instead of a leading tone, as it was the first time—continue the tremolo for about twenty measures. The tonal strength of this B-flat, barely perceptible at first, grows more audible as the tremolo continues. Then the other instruments come into play, tossing incomplete bits of phrases into their progression above the continual growl of the timpani, reaching a climax on a general *forte* as a majestic B-flat triad is sounded by the full orchestra. This marvelous crescendo is one of the most ingenious musical inventions that I know. It scarcely has a rival besides the crescendo that ends the famous Scherzo of the C-minor Symphony. And the latter, in spite of the tremendous effect it makes, is conceived on a smaller scale, starting out *piano* and ending in a final explosion without leaving the tonic pedal, while the one just described starts *mezzo-forte,* dies away for a moment in a *pianissimo* that drifts under harmonies of vague, indefinite coloring, then reappears with chords of a more settled tonality and explodes only when the cloud veiling this modulation has been wholly dissipated. It reminds one of a river whose peaceful waters suddenly vanish, only to emerge from their subterranean bed as a furious foaming cascade.

As for the *Adagio,* it defies analysis. Its forms are so pure, its melody so angelic and so irresistibly tender, that the consummate art of the structure is entirely concealed. From the first few measures, one is gripped by feelings that finally become painful in their intensity. Only in one of the giants of poetry is there anything to compare with this sublime page by this giant of music. Indeed nothing resembles more closely the impression produced by this *Adagio* than one's experience of reading in the *Divine Comedy*[26] the touching episode of Paolo and Francesca, which Virgil [in the poem] cannot hear without sobbing and whose last line causes Dante to "collapse in a dead faint." This movement seems like a sigh breathed by the Archangel Michael when, overcome by an attack of melancholy, he stood on the threshold of the empyrean contemplating the cosmos.

The Scherzo consists almost entirely of rhythmic phrases in duple time that are made to fit into the movement's measures in triple. This device, which Beethoven often uses, gives the style much of its sinew. It makes the melodic accents more piquant, more unexpected. Besides, these syncopated rhythms have a real charm of their own, though it is difficult to explain. One gets pleasure from hearing the meter thus broken become whole again at the end of each unit, and the interruptions of the musical discourse lead to a satisfying conclusion, a complete solution. The melody of the trio, given to the winds, is of a delicious freshness. Its tempo is slower than that of the rest of the Scherzo, and its elegant simplicity is enhanced by contrast with the little phrases that the violins toss off like so many teasing sallies. The finale—gay and sprightly—returns to conventional rhythmic forms; it is a ceaseless chatter of sparkling notes, interrupted by some wild, rasping chords, angry outbursts like those we have pointed out elsewhere in the composer's work.

V. Symphony in C Minor[27]

This, the most famous of all his symphonies, is also the one in which I think Beethoven first gave free rein to his vast imagination, without recourse to any idea but his own to guide him. In the First, Second, and Fourth symphonies, he used more or less familiar forms, enlarging and investing them with all the poetry and brilliance and passionate inspiration of his vigorous youth. True, the form of the Third *(Eroica)* is more expansive, and the idea rises to great heights; yet one cannot fail to recognize in it the influence of one of those divine poets to whom the great artist had long ago erected a shrine in his heart. Faithful to Horace's precept,

> [Vos exemplaria Graeca]
> Nocturna versate manu, versate diurna.[28]
>
> You must read [your Greek models] night and day,

Beethoven was in the habit of reading Homer,[29] and in his own magnificent musical epic, which rightly or wrongly is said to have been inspired by a modern hero, memories of the *Iliad* evidently play a beautiful role.[30]

By contrast, the C-minor Symphony seems to spring solely and directly from Beethoven's own genius. It is his intimate thoughts that he means to develop, his secret sorrows, his pent-up anger, his dreams full of dejection, his nocturnal visions, and his outbursts of enthusiasm. Melody, harmony, rhythm, and instrumentation take forms as individual and original as they are noble and powerful.

The first movement depicts the chaotic feelings that overwhelm a great soul when prey to despair. It is not the calm, concentrated despair that shows the outward appearance of resignation, nor is it Romeo's dark and mute grief on learning of Juliet's death, but Othello's terrible rage on hearing of Desdemona's guilt from Iago's poisonous lies. At times it is a frenzy that explodes in a terrifying outcry, at times an extreme dejection that expresses itself only in regrets and takes pity on itself. Listen to the gasps in the orchestra, to the chords in the dialogue between winds and strings that come and go, sounding ever weaker, like the painful breaths of a dying man. Then their place is taken by a phrase full of violence, as if the orchestra were revived by a flash of anger. Note this trembling mass as it hesitates for a moment, then dashes headlong, splitting into two fiery unisons like two streams of lava; and then say whether this impassioned style is not beyond and above any instrumental music hitherto written.

There is a striking example in this movement of the effect produced in some contexts by the excessive doubling of parts, and also of the untamed quality of the six-four chord above the supertonic, otherwise known as the second inversion of the dominant chord. Often it is neither prepared nor resolved; once it even occurs without the leading tone and on an organ point, a solitary high G in the winds sounding dissonant against the low D in the strings.

The *Adagio*[31] shares several traits with the A-minor *Allegretto* of the Seventh Symphony and the *Adagio* in E-flat of the Fourth. It has something of the melancholy of the former and also something of the touching grace of the latter. The theme, first presented in unison by the cellos and violas with a simple *pizzicato* accompaniment by the double-basses, is followed by a phrase given to the winds that keeps returning unchanged and in the same key throughout the movement, no matter what transformations are undergone by the first theme. This stubborn recurrence of a deeply sad and simple phrase gradually produces in the listener's soul an impression impossible to describe, and surely the most intense of its kind I have ever experienced.

Among the most daring harmonic effects in this sublime elegy may be mentioned: (1) the high pedal-point in the flutes[32] and clarinets[33] on the dominant note, E-flat, while the low strings stir restlessly through the first inversion of the chord, D-flat, F, B-flat, to which the high sustained note does not belong; (2) the incidental phrase performed by flute and oboe with two clarinets moving against them in contrary motion,[34] thus producing from time to time unprepared dissonances of the second between G, the leading tone, and F, the sixth degree of A-flat major. This third inversion of the seventh chord on the leading tone is forbidden by most theoreticians, as is the high pedal just mentioned; the result achieved is not any the less delightful. And then there is the last entry of the first theme in a canon in unison[35] between the violins and, one measure apart, the flutes, clarinets, and bassoons. If it were possible to hear this imitation in the winds, it would confer new interest on the melody. Unfortunately, the whole orchestra right then is so loud as virtually to drown it out.

The Scherzo is a singular composition. Its first measures have nothing alarming about them, yet they produce unaccountable sensations like those that one feels under the magnetic gaze of certain individuals. Everything is mysterious and dark; the rather ominous interplay of instruments seems akin to the range of ideas created in the famous Blocksberg scene in Goethe's *Faust*.[36] Shadings of *piano* and *mezzo-forte* predominate. The middle section, or trio, is based on a running figure bowed with full force in the basses, whose lumbering roughness sets the music stands shaking and resembles nothing so much as the frolicking of a tipsy elephant. But the monster soon moves off, and the noise of its mad flight gradually dies away. The Scherzo motif reappears *pizzicato;* little by little, silence is restored until nothing is heard but a few notes plucked lightly by the violins and the odd clucking noises produced by the bassoons playing a high A-flat, which is jostled in the same range by an octave G, the root of the dominant minor ninth chord.[37] Then, interrupting the cadence, the strings gently bow the chord of A-flat and seem to fall into slumber while holding it. The timpani alone keep the rhythm alive by light strokes from sponge-covered sticks, a faint pulse beating against the immobility of the rest of the orchestra. The notes the timpani play are all Cs, and the key of the movement is C minor; but the A-flat chord, held for a long time by the other instruments, seems to introduce another key, while at the same time the lone throbbing of the timpani on C tends to maintain the feeling of the original key. The ear hesitates, it cannot tell where this harmonic mystery is going to end. As the muffled beating of the timpani grows more intense, the violins come back to life, changing the harmony to the dominant-seventh chord—G, B, D, and F—while the timpani stubbornly continue their tonic C. Then the entire orchestra, reinforced by the trombones, now appearing for the first time,[38] bursts into a triumphal march theme in the major mode, and the finale begins.

The effect of this thunderclap is well known—no need to say more about it. Critics have nevertheless tried to disparage the composer for using this device by declaring it vulgar, that is, for making the brilliance of the major emerge in a grandiose way from the shadows of a *pianissimo* in the minor. They also complain that the triumphal theme lacks originality, and that the level of musical interest falls off, instead of increasing all the way to the end. This is my answer: Is the man who created such a work any less a genius, because moving from *piano* to *forte* and from minor to major is a commonly used device? Many other composers have indeed chosen to do the same things; how can their results be compared with this immense song of victory, in which the soul of the musician-poet, freed from earthly fetters and sufferings, seems to spring up radiant toward the heavens? It is true that the first four measures of the theme are not particularly original, but the forms of a fanfare are naturally limited, and I do not believe that new ones can be found without giving up its proper character of simple, grandiose pomp. Beethoven wanted a fanfare only to open his finale, and he returns very quickly—even in what follows the opening phrase—to the lofty and original style from which he does not depart for a moment in the rest of the movement.

As for the reproach that he did not heighten the level of interest all the way to the dénouement, here is what one may say: music—at least as we know it today—cannot produce a stronger effect than this transition from scherzo to triumphal march. It was therefore impossible to increase it as the movement went on. Merely to keep the level at such a height is a prodigious effort. Beethoven was up to it, despite the breadth of the musical developments he designed. This very evenness between the beginning and the end is enough to suggest a decrease in interest, because the opening causes such a terrifying shock to the listener's senses; the violent paroxysm of the emotions makes its increase thereafter all the more difficult. In a long row of columns of equal height, optical illusion makes the farthest appear smaller. Possibly, our feeble senses would be better adapted to a more laconic peroration, such as Gluck's "Our general calls you,"[39] where the listener would then not have time to go cold, and Beethoven's symphony would be over before sensory fatigue prevented the mind from following any further in the composer's wake. Be that as it may, this observation applies only to what might be called the staging of the work, and does not detract from the magnificent richness of the finale, beside which very few works could be put without being crushed.[40]

VI. Pastoral Symphony[41]

This astonishing landscape seems as if composed by Poussin and drawn by Michelangelo. The creator of Fidelio and the Eroica now sets out to depict the peace of the countryside and the gentle ways of shepherds. But let there be no mistake: these are not the beribboned, pink-and-green shepherds of Florian, much less those of Lebrun,[42] the composer of Le rossignol [The Nightingale], or those of Rousseau, composer of Le devin du village [The Village Soothsayer].[43] On the contrary, this is Nature as she really is. Beethoven entitles his first movement "Pleasant sensations inspired by a cheerful landscape."[44] Shepherds begin to make their nonchalant way about the fields; the enchanting melodies of their reed pipes come from far and near to caress you like a fragrant morning breeze. Flights, rather flocks, of birds pass chattering overhead; at times the air seems heavy with moisture. Great clouds appear and hide the sun, then suddenly they disperse and let fall floods of dazzling light on the woods and fields. This is what I imagine for myself when I hear this movement, and even allowing for the indefiniteness of instrumental music, I believe many listeners may have had the same impression.

Further along we come to a "Scene by the brook." Contemplation. Surely, when he created this wonderful Adagio, the composer must have been lying on the grass, gazing at the sky and listening to the wind, entranced by thousands of soft impressions of reflected sound and light, watching and listening to the sparkling waves of the brook that break gently on the pebbles of the bank. It is a delight.

Beethoven has come in for some sharp criticism for imitating, at the end of the *Adagio*, three kinds of bird song, separately and together.[45] Since, in my view, the wisdom or absurdity of this kind of venture is to be decided in the main by its success or failure, I would reply to these critics that they are right about the nightingale, whose song is no better conveyed here than in Lebrun's celebrated flute solo, the reason being simply that the nightingale's song consists of indeterminate or variable notes that cannot be imitated by instruments of fixed pitch. But it is not the same, it seems to me, in the case of the quail and the cuckoo, whose calls consist of only one and two notes respectively. These notes are fixed in pitch and can thus be imitated exactly.

If, however, Beethoven is to be accused of childishness for giving us a direct imitation of the song of birds in a scene where all the peaceful voices of heaven and earth and waters are naturally to be found, I would reply that the same objection can be raised when he imitates just as closely the wind, thunder and lightning, and the lowing of cattle in a storm. And God knows, it has never occurred to a critic to find fault with the storm in the *Pastoral* Symphony.

But let us go on: The poet takes us to a "Merry Gathering of Peasants." There is laughter and dancing, restrained at first; the bagpipe sounds a cheerful refrain, accompanied by a bassoon capable of only two notes.[46] Beethoven, no doubt, wanted to depict a good old German peasant standing on a barrel and playing some dilapidated instrument from which he wrings with difficulty the two main notes of the key of F, the tonic and the dominant. The old bassoon blows its two notes whenever the oboe, like a young girl dressed in her Sunday best, starts to sing a naive and cheerful musette.[47] But if the melody modulates, the bassoon falls silent, quietly counting his rests until the original key returns, when he can come in again with his imperturbable F, C, F. This detail, so splendidly grotesque, seems to escape the public's notice almost completely.

Now the dance quickens, becomes raucous and a little mad. The rhythm changes; a coarse air in duple meter[48] announces the arrival of mountaineers in heavy wooden shoes. The reprise in triple time comes back livelier than ever. The crowd mingles and grows more excited; the women's hair flies loose about their shoulders; the merry mountaineers become noisily tipsy; people clap their hands, shout and rush about—it is wild, a frenzy—until a distant thunderclap strikes dismay into the dancers and puts them to flight.[49]

The storm breaks, the lightning flashes. I despair of giving an idea of this stupendous movement; you must hear it to appreciate the degree of truth and sublimity that descriptive music can reach in the hands of a man like Beethoven. Listen to these gusts of wind heavy with rain, the muffled roaring of the basses and the shrill whistling of the piccolos, warning of a dreadful storm about to break. The tempest comes nearer; a tremendous chromatic run,[50] starting from high up, plunges into the lowest depths of the orchestra, seizes the basses and drags them along in its wake as it rises again, shuddering like a whirlwind that sweeps all before it. Next the trombones explode,[51] and the thunder of the timpani redoubles in violence. No longer mere wind and rain, it is a terrifying cataclysm, a universal flood, the end of the world. It makes one dizzy, and many of those listening to this storm can hardly tell whether they are feeling pleasure or pain.

The symphony ends with "The peasants giving thanks for the return of fair weather."[52] Everything becomes cheerful again; the shepherds reappear on the mountain, shout to one another and call their scattered flocks. The sky clears, and the torrential rain gradually stops. Calm returns and with it the rustic songs whose sweet melodies soothe the soul, shaken and dismayed by the magnificent terror of the preceding scene.

After all this, is it absolutely necessary to discuss the stylistic oddities that are found in this tremendous work? For instance, the groups of five notes played by the cellos against groups of four in the double-basses,[53] jostling one another without ever being able to merge into a true unison? Is it necessary to draw attention to the horn call in arpeggios on the C chord while the strings hold an F chord?[54] I cannot do it. For such a task, you must be able to reason coldly, and how can you steel yourself against intoxication, when your mind is full of such a work? One would far rather sleep, sleep for months, and in one's dreams keep living in the unknown realm that a genius has allowed us to glimpse.[55] If, after experiencing such a concert, you are unlucky enough to have to attend some comic opera or a soirée with fashionable cavatinas and a flute concerto, you will doubtless act stupid, distracted, and if someone asks you:

"How did you find that Italian duet?"

You will reply seriously, "Very nice."

"And the variations for clarinet?"

"Superb."

"And the finale of the new opera?"

"Wonderful."

And any artist of repute who overhears your answers without knowing the reason for your absence of mind, will not fail to inquire, "Who is that idiot?"

Poems of the ancient world, beautiful and justly admired as they are, seem pale next to this miracle of modern music! Theocritus and Virgil were great singers of natural beauty. Theirs is a sweet music in such lines as:

> Te quoque, magna Pales, et te, memorande, canemus
> Pastor ab Emphryso; vos Sylvae amnesque Lycaei,[56]

We sing of you, great Pales, never to be forgotten, and you, Shepherd of Emphryso; and you, forests and streams of Lycae, especially if they are not recited by barbarians like us French, who pronounce Latin so that it sounds like Auvergnat.

But this poem of Beethoven's! These long phrases full of color! these speaking images! these perfumes! this light! this eloquent silence! those vast horizons! those enchanted forest glens! those golden harvests! those wandering patches of pink cloud! that vast plain dozing beneath the noontime sun! Man is absent! Nature alone, unveiled, displaying her charms for herself. The deep repose of all that lives! And the delightful life of all that is in repose! The little brook that runs babbling like a child toward the river! the river, father of waters, which winds its way in majestic silence toward the open sea! Then man intervenes, man working in the fields, robust and religious, his joyous revels interrupted by the storm, its terrors his hymn of thanksgiving.

Cover your faces, ye great poets of old, ye poor immortals. Your conventional language with all its harmonious purity cannot compete with the art of sounds. You are glorious in defeat, but defeated nonetheless! You never knew what today we call melody, harmony, the combination of various timbres, instrumental color, and modulations, the masterly clash of discordant sounds that battle one another only to embrace later, the surprises to the ear, the uncommon accents that reverberate in the deepest unexplored recesses of our souls. Of all this, the stammerings produced by the childish art you used to call music could never give you any idea. For the cultivated spirits of your time, you were the sole melodists, harmonists, masters of rhythm and expression. But in your languages, these words had a meaning totally different from that which we give them today. The art of sounds, rightly so-called, was born yesterday. It is barely mature—only twenty years old. It is beautiful and all-powerful. It is the Pythian Apollo of modern days. We owe to it a world of feelings and sensations that were closed to you. Yes, ye great and beloved poets, you are vanquished: *Inclyti sed victi.**

VII. Symphony in A[57]

The Seventh Symphony is famous for its *Allegretto.*** Not because the other three movements are less wonderful, far from it. But since the public usually judges according to the effect produced and measures this effect by the volume of applause, it follows that the movement receiving the loudest applause[59] is always regarded as the finest (even though there are works of infinitely great beauty that are not of the kind to arouse noisy admiration). The remainder of the work is then sacrificed to the enhancement of the favorite movement. This, at least in France,

---

* Glorious but defeated.
** Still [mistakenly] called *Adagio* or *Andante.*[58]

is the invariable custom. And so with regard to Beethoven, people say: "Ah, the Storm of the *Pastoral* Symphony, the Finale of the Symphony in C minor, the *Andante* of the Symphony in A," and so on.

There is, I believe, no proof that this symphony was composed after the *Pastoral* or the *Eroica*.[60] Some people think that it was written some time earlier. If this view is correct, the number seven merely indicates the order of publication.

The first movement opens with a broad, majestic introduction, in which the melody, the modulations, and the instrumental design successively vie with one another for attention. It begins with one of those orchestral effects of which Beethoven is unquestionably the inventor. The entire orchestra strikes a strong, staccato chord; in the silence that follows, an oboe is exposed—its entrance was drowned out earlier by the orchestral attack—and it now develops the melody in sustained notes.[61] A more original opening could not be devised. At the end of the introduction, after several excursions into neighboring keys, the note E, dominant of the tonic A, is brought back and becomes the subject of an interplay of tone colors between the violins and flutes,[62] similar to the one that opens the finale of the *Eroica*. For six measures the E comes and goes, unaccompanied, changing aspect each time it passes from strings to winds. Taken over finally by the flute and oboe, it serves to link the introduction to the *Allegro [Vivace]* and becomes the first note of the main theme, whose rhythmic form it gradually shapes. I have heard this theme ridiculed for its rustic naïveté. Had the composer, as in the *Pastoral* Symphony, written "Peasant Dance" in large letters at the head of his *Allegro*, the accusation that it lacks nobility probably would not have been made. This only shows that while some listeners dislike being told what the composer's subject is, others are, on the contrary, ever ready to reject any musical idea a bit out of the ordinary—unless the reason for the anomaly is given in advance. If he is unable to decide between these divergent opinions, the artist should perhaps trust his own feelings rather than chase madly after the phantom of universal approval.

The musical phrase in question has a strongly marked rhythm, which recurs in myriad guises as it passes into the harmony, keeping its rhythmic drive right to the end. Never has the device of an ostinato rhythm been attempted with such success. This *Allegro*, whose substantial developments are all based on the same idea, is handled with incredible skill; the changes of tonality are so frequent and so ingenious, and the chords form such new clusters and progressions, that the movement is over before the fascination and enthusiasm aroused in the listener have lost any of their intensity.

The harmonic effect most criticized by the guardians of the school doctrine, and at the same time the most felicitous, is the resolution of the dissonance in the six-five chord above the subdominant note [A] in the key of E-natural.[63] The dissonant second—a very loud tremolo in the first and second violins—is resolved in a completely new way: the E could have been sustained and the F-sharp raised to G, or else the F-sharp continued and the E lowered to D. Beethoven does neither. Without changing the bass, he joins the two dissonant notes in an octave on F-natural, lowering the F-sharp a semitone and the E a major seventh. The chord of the fifth and major sixth has thus become a minor sixth without the fifth, which has vanished into the F-natural. The abrupt shift from *forte* to *piano,* at the precise moment of this remarkable harmonic transformation, heightens its distinct character and redoubles its charm.

Before going on to the next movement, I must not forget to mention the singular crescendo with which Beethoven restores his favorite rhythm, momentarily abandoned: it is produced by a two-measure phrase (D, C-sharp, B-sharp, B-sharp, C-sharp)[64] in the key of A major, repeated eleven consecutive times in the low strings and violas, while the winds hold an E in quadruple octaves (high, low, and in between) and the violins play like a chime the notes E, A, E, and C [-sharp], repeating them faster and faster and always combining them so as to present the dominant when the basses attack the D or B-sharp, and the tonic or its third when the basses intone the C [-sharp]. That is absolutely new, and I believe that, by good luck so far, no imitator has put this lovely invention to wasteful use.

It is rhythm again, a rhythm as simple as that of the first movement but different in form, that is the chief source of the incredible effect produced by the *Allegretto.* It is merely a dactyl followed by a spondee, struck without cease, sometimes in three parts, sometimes in one, then in all parts together. Sometimes they serve as an accompaniment; often they hold center stage; now they furnish the first theme of a short episodic fugue with two subjects in the strings.[65] The rhythm first appears *piano* in the lower strings, and is soon repeated in a *pianissimo* full of sadness and mystery. It then passes to the second violins, while the cellos sing a kind of lament in the minor mode.[66] The rhythmic phrase keeps rising from octave to octave until it reaches the first violins; they transmit it by way of a crescendo to the winds in the upper regions of the orchestra, where it explodes with full force. Thereupon the songful lament, now stated more energetically, becomes a convulsive wail, and incompatible rhythms compete harshly one against the other. These are tears, sobs, entreaties; they express a boundless sorrow, an all-consuming anguish. But after these heartrending strains a glimmer of hope appears: a nebulous melody, pure, simple and sweet, sad, resigned *like patience smiling at grief.*[67] The basses alone keep up their inexorable rhythm beneath this melodious rainbow. To borrow again from English poetry:

One fatal remembrance, one sorrow that throws
Its black shade alike o'er our joys and our woes.[68]

After alternating several times between anguish and resignation, the orchestra, as if exhausted by its arduous struggle, is reduced to playing
only fragments of the main theme; then it collapses and dies away. The
flutes and oboes take up the theme again but in a faint voice;[69] they are
too weak to complete it. It is the violins who do so with a few barely
audible pizzicato notes, after which the winds, reviving suddenly like
the flame of a dying lamp, breathe a deep sigh over an indecisive harmony and—*the rest is silence.*[70]

The plaintive cry that begins and ends the movement is created by a
tonic six-four chord that tends always toward its resolution; its harmonic incompleteness is the only way of concluding so as to leave the
listener in uncertainty and increase the impression of dreamy sadness
inevitably produced by all that precedes.

The theme of the Scherzo *[Presto]* modulates in a totally new way. It
is in F major but, instead of concluding the first section in C or B-flat
or D minor, or A minor or A-flat or D-flat, as in most movements of
this kind, it moves to the third above, to the key of A major. The Scherzo
of the *Pastoral* Symphony, also in F, modulates down a third, to D major. These two key relations show a certain resemblance in color, and
indeed other affinities between the two works can be noted. The trio of
the Seventh Symphony *(Presto meno assai),* in which the violins hold
almost constantly to the dominant, while below the oboes and clarinets
play a cheerful rustic melody, is quite in keeping with the feeling of an
idyllic countryside. One also notes a new kind of crescendo, contrived
by means of the second horn in its low register,[71] whispering the two
notes A and G-sharp in duple rhythm (though the measure is in triple
time) and stressing the G-sharp (though A is the key note). Audiences
always seem astounded by this passage.

The finale is at least as rich as the earlier movements in new combinations, piquant modulations, and enchanting flights of fancy. The theme
has some similarity with that of the overture to *Armide,*[72] but it is only
in the order of the opening notes and exists more for the eye than for
the ear; in performance the two are as dissimilar as can be. One would
better appreciate the freshness and coquettishness of Beethoven's phrase,
so different from the knightly *élan* of Gluck's theme, if the high chords
in the winds did not dominate so strongly the melody in the first violins
playing in their medium range, while the seconds and violas accompany
it from below with a double-stop tremolo. Throughout this finale, Beethoven creates by the sudden key transition from C-sharp minor to D
major, effects that are as graceful as they are unexpected. One of his
happiest strokes of harmonic boldness is, without doubt, to embellish
the great pedal-point on the dominant E by a D-sharp of equal length.[73]

The seventh chord is sometimes brought in above in such a way as to make the D-natural of the upper parts sound precisely with the D-sharp of the lower strings. One might think this would result in a dreadful dissonance, or at least in harmonic muddle. But nothing of the kind happens, for such is the tonal strength of the dominant that the D-sharp does not adulterate it in any way; one hears only the insistent humming of the E. Beethoven did not write his music *for the eye*.

The coda, ushered in by this menacing pedal-point, is extraordinarily brilliant, a worthy end to this masterpiece of technical skill, taste, imagination, knowledge, and inspiration.[74]

VIII. Symphony in F[75]

This symphony is in F, like the *Pastoral*, but its dimensions are smaller than those of the preceding symphonies. Indeed, in breadth of form it barely surpasses the First Symphony in C major, though it is far superior to it in orchestration, rhythm, and melodic style.

The first movement is based on two themes, both calm and gentle. The second,[76] in my opinion the more remarkable, seems continually to avoid the perfect cadence first by modulating in a completely unexpected way (the phrase begins in D major and ends in C major) and then by vanishing without a cadence on the diminished-seventh chord of the subdominant.[77] Listening to this melodic caprice, one might say that the composer, though ready to feel cheerful, is suddenly deflected by a sad thought that cuts short his joyous song.

The *Andante scherzando*[78] is one of those works of art that have neither model nor counterpart; they fall into the composer's head full-blown from heaven. He writes it down as if dictated at one stretch, and we can only listen in amazement. The woodwinds here play a role quite opposite to their usual one: they strike *pianissimo* chords eight times in each measure to accompany a light *punta d'arco* dialogue between the violins and basses. The effect is gentle, innocent, and gracefully indolent, like a tune two children sing while gathering flowers in a meadow on a fine spring morning. The main phrase is in two sections, each of three measures, the symmetry being upset by a rest after the reply given by the low strings. Thus, the first section ends on the weak beat, the second on the strong beat. However, the harmonic tapping effects created by oboes, clarinets, horns, and bassoons are so engaging that the listener does not notice the lack of symmetry in the strings produced by the extra [half] measure of rest. This rest evidently exists only to prolong the sound of the delightful chord upon which the cool melody is again about to flutter. This example shows once again that the rule of phrase symmetry can sometimes be happily infringed.

Would anybody believe that this exquisite idyll ends with the cliché for which Beethoven professed the greatest aversion, the Italian [feminine] cadence? Just when the instrumental conversation between the two small orchestras, woodwinds and strings, is at its most captivating, the composer seems as if suddenly compelled to end the movement. He gives the violins a four-note tremolo motif—G, F, A, B-flat (submediant, dominant, leading tone, and tonic)—repeats it rapidly several times, for all the world like the Italians when they sing *Fe-li-ci-tà*,[79] and stops short. I have never been able to account for this piece of willfulness.

Here a minuet of the shape and tempo of Haydn's replaces the scherzo in quick triple time that Beethoven himself invented and that he put to such adroit and striking use in his other symphonies. To tell the truth, this movement is rather commonplace: the old-fashioned form seems to have stifled the composer's inventiveness. The finale, by contrast, fairly sparkles; its ideas are new, brilliant, and lavishly developed. There are diatonic progressions of two voices in contrary motion by means of which the composer creates a vastly extended and most effective crescendo for his peroration. The harmony contains only a few harsh moments, produced by passing tones that do not resolve quickly enough, and that sometimes even end on a rest.

It is easy to explain away these momentary discords by stretching the letter of the law, but in performance they always more or less bruise the ear. It is a different thing when a high pedal for flutes and oboes on F[80]— the same note being pounded out below by the timpani tuned in octaves—greets the theme as it reappears (the violins playing C, G, and B-flat of the dominant-seventh chord preceded by a fragment of the tonic chord, the third F–A). This sustained high note, I say, may be theoretically incorrect, since it does not always belong to the harmony, but it is in no way shocking to the ear—far from it: thanks to the skillful instrumentation and to the character of the theme itself, the combination of sounds produces an excellent and remarkably sweet effect.

Before closing, I cannot resist mentioning an orchestral effect in this finale which may perhaps cause the listener a greater surprise than any other. I mean the C-sharp, attacked *forte* by the entire orchestra in unison and octave after a diminuendo that has just come to an end on a C-natural. The first two times that it occurs,[81] this sonic roar is immediately followed by the return of the theme in F, and it becomes clear that this C-sharp was really an enharmonic D-flat, that is, a lowered submediant of the principal key. But on its third appearance this strange blast of sound takes on quite another aspect:[82] after modulating to C as before, the orchestra this time plays a genuine D-flat, followed by a fragment of the theme in that key. Then comes an equally genuine C-sharp, followed by another fragment of the theme in C-sharp minor. Finally, this same C-sharp is given out three times with redoubled force and the entire theme reappears in F-sharp minor. Thus, the sound that at first figured as a minor sixth becomes successively a tonic major in flats, a tonic minor in sharps, and finally, the dominant.

It is curious indeed.

IX. Choral *Symphony*[83]

The analysis of a work such as the *Choral* Symphony is a task fraught with difficulty and danger, a rash endeavor that I undertake only after long hesitation; the only excuse for so doing is that I have worked long and hard to see things from the composer's point of view, to penetrate the inner meaning of his work, to experience its effect, and to observe the impression it makes on certain exceptional persons as well as on the public at large. Among the divergent opinions that have been expressed on this score, perhaps no two are identical. Certain critics consider it a monstrous folly; others can only see in it the last glimmers of expiring genius. Still others, more cautious, confess that they are baffled by it now but do not despair of coming to appreciate it—at least to some extent—later. Most artists consider it an extraordinary work, of which some parts nevertheless remain obscure or without apparent purpose. But there is a small minority of musicians, whose nature inclines them to consider carefully whatever may broaden the scope of art; these few, after reading the score and listening to it several times, have pondered the structure of the *Choral* Symphony, and they assert that this work is the most magnificent expression of Beethoven's genius. As I remarked on an earlier page, that is the view I share.

Without inquiring what ideas personal to himself the composer may have wished to express in this immense musical poem—a field of conjecture open to all—let us see whether its novelty of form is not justified by a purpose independent of all philosophical or religious thought, and thus equally full of meaning and beauty for the fervent Christian as for the pantheist or atheist—in short, a purpose that is purely musical and poetic.

Beethoven had composed eight symphonies before this one. To go beyond the point he had reached with the orchestra's resources alone, what means were available?—the addition of voices to his instruments. But in order to observe the law of crescendo and set off the power of this additional force, was it not necessary to let the instruments by themselves occupy the foreground of the panorama he proposed to unfold? Once this premise is accepted, it is easy to see that the next step was to look for a mixed type of music to link the two great sections of the symphony; instrumental recitative was the bridge he ventured to build between chorus and orchestra, whereby the instruments crossed over to join the voices.

Having built this passageway, the composer felt obliged to justify the fusion he was about to create by announcing it through the voice of a soloist. Using the same notes just sounded in the instrumental recitative, he cries out: "Friends, let us have no more chords like these: rather let us sing songs more pleasant and joyful!" Here then, he concludes, as it were, a treaty between the chorus and the orchestra; the same phrase of recitative, uttered by the one and by the other, seems like an oath cementing an alliance. Now the musician was free to choose the text of his choral composition. It is to Schiller that Beethoven turned.[84] He took the poet's *Ode to Joy*, invested it with a thousand nuances that poetry alone could never convey, and steadily enhanced to the end its splendor, grandeur, and brilliance.

So much may be said, more or less plausibly, of the general plan of this vast composition. Its parts I shall now examine in detail.

The first movement, full of dark majesty, is unlike any Beethoven had written up to then. The harmony is bold, sometimes excessively so. The most original patterns, the most expressive passages press in on each other, cross and intertwine in all directions, yet without producing obscurity or overcrowding. On the contrary, it all yields a perfectly clear effect; the many voices of the orchestra which complain or threaten each in its own distinctive way, seem to form one whole, so great is the emotional force that gives them life.

This *Allegro maestoso* is in D minor, beginning however on the chord of A without its third, i.e., on sustained fifths consisting of A and E, themselves arpeggiated above and below by the first violins, violas, and double-basses. The listener does not know whether he is hearing A minor, A major, or the chord of the dominant of D. This prolonged tonal ambiguity lends great power and strong character to the *tutti* entrance of the D-minor chord. The peroration contains deeply moving accents; it is difficult to imagine anything more profoundly tragic than this song of the woodwinds, as below it, a chromatic tremolo in the strings gradually swells and rises, roaring like the sea at the approach of a storm.[85] It is magnificently inspired.

We shall have more than one opportunity to observe in this work groups of notes that are sounded together but cannot possibly be called chords; and I must confess that the reason for these anomalies escapes me completely. Thus, on page 17 of this splendid movement there is a melodic passage in the key of C minor for clarinets and bassoons[86] which is accompanied as follows: the bass first strikes an F-sharp supporting a diminished-seventh chord; then an A-flat supporting a third, a fourth, and an augmented sixth, and finally a G, above which the flutes and oboes play the notes E-flat, G, and C, that is, a six-four chord. This would be an excellent resolution of the preceding chord if the second violins and violas did not come in with two additional notes, F-natural and A-flat, which denature the harmony and produce an unpleasant confusion, fortunately very brief. This passage is scored lightly and is completely free of roughness. That is why I cannot understand this quadruple dissonance, which is oddly brought about and unmotivated. One might think it a misprint, but close examination of these two measures and those that precede clears up any doubt and convinces one that such was really the composer's intention.

The *Scherzo vivace* that follows contains nothing of this kind. True, there are several tonic pedals, both high and middling, which are held through the chord of the dominant, but I have already declared my creed on the subject of sustained notes alien to the harmony, and there is no need of this new example to demonstrate how effective they can be when they arise naturally from the musical sense.

It is mainly by means of rhythm that Beethoven makes this charming *badinage* so full of interest. The theme makes a lively impression, its fugal answer joining in after four measures; but the next time it fairly sparkles with verve as the answer comes in a measure sooner, thus forming patterns in triple rhythm instead of the original duple.[87]

The middle of the Scherzo is taken up by a duple-time *Presto* of rustic joviality, whose theme unfolds over a pedal, now on the tonic, now on the dominant, and is accompanied by a countersubject that harmonizes equally well with either of the sustained notes, dominant or tonic. This melody is introduced on its last appearance by a ravishing phrase for the oboe,[88] which, after hovering for a time over the dominant-ninth chord of D major, blossoms out into F-natural in a manner as graceful as it is unexpected. Here is a reflection of those gentle impressions evoked by Nature that were so dear to Beethoven—its smiling and serene aspects—the purity of the air, the first rays of a spring dawn.

In the *Adagio cantabile,* the principle of unity is so little observed that it might be regarded as two distinct movements rather than one. The first melody, in B-flat and in common time, is followed by one in D major, absolutely different from the first, and in triple meter. The first theme, slightly changed and varied by the first violins, makes a second appearance in the original key, bringing back the melody in triple time without change or variation, but in the key of G major. After this, the first theme becomes solidly established and no longer allows the rival phrase to share the listener's attention.

One must hear this splendid *Adagio* several times to get used to its unusual structure. As to the beauty of all these melodies, the infinite grace of their adornment, the feelings of tender melancholy, passionate dejection, and religious meditation that they express, if my prose could even come close to intimating all this, Music would have found in the written word a rival that the greatest of poets himself will never be able to fashion. The movement is a truly magnificent creation. Once one has come under its powerful spell, one can only answer the critic who reproves the composer for having violated the law of unity: "Too bad for the law!"

We have now come to the moment when the voices are about to join the orchestra. The cellos and double-basses utter the recitative I have mentioned above, this after a *ritornello* in the winds as harsh and violent as a cry of rage. The tonic six-three chord—F, A, D—that opens this *Presto* is disfigured by a simultaneous B-flat appoggiatura on the flutes, oboes, and clarinets. This sixth note of the scale of D minor grates horribly against the dominant and creates an exceedingly harsh effect. It depicts very well a furious anger, but I still do not see what could arouse such a feeling here, unless the composer, before saying through his soloist, "Let us sing more pleasant songs," wanted in some strange way to give instrumental harmony a bad name. If so, he soon seems to regret it, for between successive phrases of the recitative in the basses, he brings back fragments of the three earlier movements, like so many memories dear to his heart. Moreover, after this recitative, it is in the orchestra that he introduces, surrounded by exquisite chords, the beautiful theme which the voices will soon sing to Schiller's *Ode.* This serene and gentle song grows lively and brilliant as it moves from the basses, where it is first heard, to the violins and winds. Then, after a sudden interruption, the entire orchestra takes up the furious *ritornello* mentioned above, and which now heralds the vocal recitative.

The first chord is again built over an F that should normally underpin a six-three chord and does so. But this time the composer does not content himself with the B-flat appoggiatura; he adds G, E, and C-sharp, so that *all the notes of the minor diatonic scale* are struck simultaneously and produce a terrible cacophony of sounds: F, A, C-sharp, E, G, B-flat, and D.

Forty years ago, the French composer Martin, known as Martini,[89] wanted to produce a similar orchestral howl in his opera *Sapho* by using all the diatonic, chromatic, and enharmonic intervals at the moment when Phaon's lover flings herself into the sea. Without troubling about the advisability of his endeavor, or considering whether it infringed the dignity of art, one certainly cannot mistake his intention. But as for understanding Beethoven's intention here, I am utterly baffled. I perceive a formal plan—a calculated and thought-out project—to produce discords at the two moments preceding the successive appearances of the recitative in the instruments and in the voice. But though I have long sought the reason behind this idea, I confess I cannot find it.

After the soloist has sung his recitative—the words, as I have pointed out, are Beethoven's own—he sings alone the theme of the *Ode to Joy,* with a light accompaniment of two wind instruments and the strings playing pizzicato. This theme is now in command to the very end of the symphony and is always recognizable, though its aspects change continually. These various transformations are all the more engrossing that each variation brings out a new and distinct nuance of one and the same feeling: joy. This joy at first is full of gentleness and peace; it becomes a little more lively when the women's voices make themselves heard. The meter changes; the phrase sung at first in 4/4 time reappears in 6/8 and in constant syncopation; it takes on a stronger character, more agile, more martial. It is now the farewell song of a hero, departing for battle and confident of victory; you can almost see his armor flashing and hear the rhythmic sound of his step. A fugal theme, in which the original pattern is still present, serves for a while as material for orchestral revels. It is like a crowd milling about, full of ardor. But the chorus soon returns to sing the joyful hymn with vigor, in all its pristine simplicity, supported by the wind instruments, who strike their chords in step with the melody, while being criss-crossed in all directions by a diatonic passage from the whole of the string section in unison and in octaves.

The *Andante maestoso* that follows is a kind of chorale, first intoned by the tenors and basses of the chorus, joined by one trombone, the cellos, and double-basses. Joy has become religious, solemn, and boundless; the chorus, silent for a moment, takes up its great chords again, but less forcefully, after a passage for orchestra alone that produces an organ-like effect of great beauty. This imitation of the majestic instrument of the Christian church is produced by low flutes, clarinets in their *chalumeau* register,[90] low bassoons, violas divided in two parts, high and middle range, and cellos playing on their open G and D strings or on their C string and its octave, double-stopped. This section begins in G, goes to C, then to F, and ends on a pedal-point on the dominant-seventh of D. There follows a great *Allegro* in 6/4 time, where from the outset the first theme, which has already been varied in so many ways, is brought together with the chorale of the preceding *Andante*. The contrast between the two melodic ideas is heightened by a fast variation on the "Joy" song, played above the long notes of the chorale not only by the first violins but also by the double-basses. Now it is impossible for the basses to play a series of notes so rapidly, and it is a mystery how a man as skilled as Beethoven was in the art of instrumentation could be so careless as to write such a rapid passage for this ponderous instrument.[91]

There is less passion, less grandeur, and more lightness of style in the next section. It relies on a naïve gaiety, first expressed by the four solo voices and then in warmer colors through the addition of the chorus. Twice, passages religious and tender alternate with the joyful melody; then the movement accelerates, the whole orchestra bursts forth; the percussion instruments—timpani, cymbals, triangle, and bass drums—pound ruthlessly on the downbeat of the measure; joy triumphs again, the boisterous joy of the people, which would resemble an orgy if toward the end the voices did not all stop once more on a solemn rhythm to offer an ecstatic shout—their last manifestation of love and devotion to religious joy. The orchestra concludes alone, but not without flinging out in its blazing path fragments of that first theme, which no one can weary of listening to.

A translation, as exact as possible, of the German poem set by Beethoven will show the reader what called forth this array of musical combinations, learned handmaids of an unflagging inspiration, docile agents of a powerful and tireless genius. Here it is:

> Joy, bright spark of divinity,
> Daughter of Elysium,
> Fire-inspired we tread
> Thy sanctuary.
> Thy magic power reunites
> All that custom has divided,
> All men become brothers
> Under the sway of thy gentle wings.
>
> Whoever has created
> An abiding friendship,
> Or has won
> A true and loving wife,
> All who can call at least one soul theirs,
> Join in our song of praise;
> But any who cannot must creep tearfully
> Away from our circle.
>
> All creatures drink of joy
> At nature's breast.
> Just and unjust
> Alike taste of her gift;
> She gave us kisses and the fruit of the vine,
> A tried friend to the end.
> Even the worm can feel contentment,
> And the cherub stands before God!
>
> Gladly, like the heavenly bodies
> Which He set on their courses
> Through the splendour of the firmament;
> Thus, brothers, you should run your race,
> As a hero going to conquest.
>
> You millions, I embrace you.
> This kiss is for all the world!
> Brothers, above the starry canopy
> There must dwell a loving Father.
> Do you fall in worship, you millions?
> World, do you know your Creator?

Seek Him in the heavens,
Above the stars must He dwell.[92]

Of all the symphonies by Beethoven, this is the most difficult to perform. It requires many rehearsals, patient, thorough, and above all well conducted. It also requires a large number of singers, for in many places the chorus must overtop the orchestra. Moreover, the music is set to the words in such a way, and certain vocal parts are so excessively high, that singers find it difficult to project their voices, and the volume and force of the sound they make is greatly reduced.

Be that as it may, when at the end of his work Beethoven contemplated the majestic dimensions of the monument he had just erected, he must have said to himself: "Let Death come now, my work is done."

A FEW WORDS ABOUT THE TRIOS
AND SONATAS OF BEETHOVEN [1]

There are many people in France for whom Beethoven's name evokes ideas only of orchestras and symphonies. They do not know that this tireless Titan composed masterpieces in all musical genres—almost all of them are equally wonderful.

He wrote *Fidelio*, an opera;[2] *Prometheus*, a ballet;[3] *Egmont*, a melodrama;[4] overtures to the tragedies *Coriolan*[5] and *The Ruins of Athens*,[6] and six or seven other overtures on miscellaneous subjects; two great masses;[7] *Christ on the Mount of Olives*, an oratorio;[8] eighteen string quartets; several other quartets and quintets for three or four wind instruments and piano;[9] trios for piano, violin, and cello; a large number of sonatas for piano solo or for piano with a string instrument, cello or violin; a septet for four string instruments and three wind instruments; a concerto for violin; four or five concertos for piano and orchestra; a fantasia for piano, orchestra, and chorus; many sets of variations for diverse instruments; romances and songs with piano accompaniment; a book of hymns for one or more voices; a cantata or lyric scena with orchestra; choruses with orchestra as settings to various German poems; two volumes of studies on harmony and counterpoint;[10] and, of course, the nine famous symphonies.

But it should not be supposed that Beethoven's productivity has anything in common with that of Italian composers who count their operas by the fifties—witness Paisiello's 160 scores. No, indeed. Such an opinion would be manifestly unjust. If we except the overture to *The Ruins of Athens* and perhaps two or three other pieces unworthy of their composer's great name and written during those rare moments of inattention that Horace, with a touch of irony charges against "the *good* Homer" himself,[11] everything else by Beethoven is in that noble, lofty, bold, expressive, poetic, and always innovative style that makes Beethoven indisputably the vanguard of musical civilization. Among the thousands of phrases that give his music splendor and life, one can find, at the very most, a few fleeting similarities. This astounding ability to be constantly original without ever straying from the path of truth and beauty we can understand to some extent in the fast movements. There, the musical thought, aided by the power of rhythm, can with its capricious leaps leave more easily the well-trodden paths. But where this power eludes our grasp is in the *adagios*, those more-than-human meditations in which Beethoven's pantheistic genius loves to dwell. In these, no more passion, no more earthly landscapes, no more hymns to joy, love, or glory, no more childlike songs, no more sweet nothings, no more flashes of wit whether caustic or comical, no more terrifying outbursts of rage or cries of hatred, such as are often wrung from him in the throes of secret pain. No longer does he even have contempt in his heart; he is no longer one of our species; he has forgotten us; serene and solitary, he floats in ethereal space. Like those eagles of the Andes that soar at heights where other creatures suffocate and die, his eyes pierce the void; he flies toward all the suns, singing of nature unbounded. Is it credible that the genius of this man could thus take flight whenever (so to speak) he wanted to? Yet it was obviously so, as one can verify from the abundant evidence he has left, perhaps less often in the symphonies than in his compositions for piano. There and only there, he seems to write for himself alone. No longer having a big audience in mind, he composes with a majestic abandon that the crowd cannot understand and that is bound to be impaired whenever the requirement is to arrive quickly at what we call an *effect*.

In these piano works, too, the performer's task is made overwhelming, not so much by technical difficulties as by the deep feeling and the musical intelligence that the works demand. The virtuoso must absolutely efface himself before the composer, just as the orchestra does in the symphonies. There must be complete absorption of the one by the other; and it is precisely in this identifying himself with the thought he conveys that the performer rises to the greatness of his model.

There is a composition of Beethoven's known as the Sonata in C-sharp minor,[12] whose *Adagio* is poetry of the kind that no human language can describe. Technically, it is very simple: the left hand plays soft broad chords full of a solemn sadness and that last long enough to allow the piano's vibrations to fade gradually upon each of them. Above, the lower fingers of the right hand play an ostinato accompaniment in arpeggios that hardly varies from the first measure to the last, while the other fingers play a sort of lament, a melodic expansion of this dark harmony.

One day thirty years ago,[13] I was present when Liszt played this *Adagio* for a small gathering of friends. Following the custom he had adopted to win the applause of the fashionable public, he distorted the music: instead of playing those long sustained notes in the bass, instead of maintaining the severe uniformity of rhythm and tempo I have just referred to, he added trills and tremolos; he accelerated and slowed down the tempo, thus making passion intrude into the sad tranquillity. He made thunder growl in a cloudless sky, where the only source of darkness consists in the sun's vanishing. I suffered cruelly, I confess, even more than I had suffered when hearing our wretched singers embroider the great aria in *Der Freischütz*.[14] For added to this torture was my distress at seeing such an artist as Liszt fall into the bad habits usually displayed only by the second-rate. But what could one do? At that time Liszt was like one of those children who, without crying, pick themselves up after a fall—a fall one pretends not to have seen—and who burst into tears if one gives them a helping hand. Liszt picked himself up, proudly. Anyhow, a few years later it was no longer he who pursued success, but success which breathlessly pursued him. They had traded roles.

But to return to our sonata. Recently, one of those men with a mind and heart,[15] whom we artists are fortunate to meet, had gathered together a few friends; I was one of their number. Liszt joined us later in the evening, and finding the conversation concerned with a composition by Weber that the public had received badly at a recent concert, either because of the performer's inadequacy or for some other reason, sat down at the piano to reply in his own way to Weber's detractors. His argument was unanswerable, and we were forced to admit that a work of genius had been misjudged. As he came to the end, the lamp lighting the room seemed about to go out. Someone got up to trim it for more light.

I said: "Don't do it, please. If Liszt will only play Beethoven's C-sharp minor *Adagio*, this semidarkness won't spoil a thing."

"Gladly," said Liszt, "but turn the light down altogether, and cover the fire, too, so the darkness will be complete."

Then, after a pause to collect his thoughts, out of the darkness emerged the noble elegy that he had once so perversely distorted. It was now heard in its sublime simplicity; not a single note, not an accent, was added to the composer's notes and accents. It was the shade of Beethoven himself, his great voice that we heard, called forth by the virtuoso. Each of us felt the characteristic *frisson* in silence and, after the last chord died away, we were still silent—we were weeping.

A considerable portion of the French public is still unaware of the existence of these marvelous works. To be sure, the B-flat Trio in its entirety, the *Adagio* of the trio in D, and the Cello Sonata in A must have proved to those who know them that the great composer certainly did not lavish the wealth of his genius only on the orchestra. But his last word is not there; it must be sought in the sonatas for solo piano. Perhaps the time is at hand when these works, which are ahead of all that is most advanced in art, can be played with a good chance of being understood, if not by the crowd, at least by an elite public. It is an experiment worth trying; if at first it does not succeed, it can be tried again later.

The great sonatas of Beethoven will become the yardstick by which we can measure the development of our musical intelligence.

FIDELIO

Opera in Three Acts by Beethoven. Its Performances at the Théâtre-Lyrique[1]

On the first day of Ventôse in the year VI,[2] the Théâtre Feydeau performed *Léonore or Conjugal Love, historical event in two acts* (such was the title of the piece), libretto by Jean-Nicolas Bouilly,[3] music by Pierre Gaveaux.[4] In spite of the talent shown by the two leading actors, that is, Gaveaux, the composer, and Mme Scio,[5] a great actress of the period, the work struck people as only second-rate.

Several years later, Paër[6] composed a graceful score to an Italian libretto in which Bouilly's Léonore was again the heroine. It was after seeing a performance of Paër's *Leonora* that Beethoven, with his usual rough humor, told the composer: "I like your opera, I'd like to set it to music."[7]

Such was the origin of the masterpiece I want to discuss now. The first appearance of Beethoven's *Fidelio* on the German stage[8] gave no sign of its eventual fame; it apparently had only a short run.[9] A short time later, it reappeared with changes in both text and music and introduced by a new overture.[10] This second attempt was a complete success.[11] The audience demanded Beethoven with loud shouts, and he was hoisted to the stage after the first act and again after the second, whose finale aroused an enthusiasm hitherto unknown in Vienna. The music of *Fidelio* nonetheless had to endure a great deal of more or less acerb criticism.[12] But from that time on, the opera has been performed in all the theaters of Germany, where it is part of the classic repertory.

It was similarly honored a little later in the theaters of London;[13] and in 1827, a German troupe performed it in Paris.[14] The two leading roles were sung with rare talent by Haitzinger[15] and Mme Schroeder-Devrient,[16] and the opera was acclaimed enthusiastically.

Fidelio has just been staged at the Théâtre-Lyrique; a fortnight earlier, it was being performed again at Covent Garden in London, while at the present moment, it is being played in New York. You would look in vain for a house where you can hear Gaveaux's *Léonore* or Paër's *Leonora*. Only scholars know that these two operas exist. Indeed, they are no longer with us; they have passed on. The reason is that of the three scores, one is extremely weak; the second is, at most, a work of talent; and the third a work of genius.

There can be no doubt; the more I listen to Beethoven's work, the

Wilhelmine Schroeder-Devrient, by Vigneron. Bibliothèque de l'Opéra, courtesy Bibliothèque Nationale.

more I read the score, the more I find to admire. It seems to me as fine in detail as it is beautiful as a whole. Everywhere it displays vigor, grandeur, originality, and feelings as deep as they are true.

Fidelio belongs to that sturdy species of works which, though attacked with the most inconceivable prejudice and the most flagrant lies, are still so vital that nothing can prevail against them. They are like those robust beech trees that grow among rocks and ruins and end up splitting the rocks and pushing through the masonry; they rise up proud and green, all the more solidly rooted because of the obstacles they have had to overcome; whereas willows that grow with ease along the riverbank fall into the mud and die there forgotten.

Beethoven wrote four overtures for his one opera.[17] After finishing the first,[18] he started rewriting it for no apparent reason. He kept the same structure and themes, but linked them by different modulations, gave them a different instrumentation, and added a crescendo and a flute solo. This solo, in my opinion, does not reach the lofty heights of the rest of the work. But the composer seems to have preferred this second version, for it was published first.

The manuscript of the original remained in the hands of Beethoven's friend Schindler and was published only ten years ago by the firm of Richault. I have had the honor of conducting it some twenty times, at Drury Lane Theatre in London[19] and at a few concerts in Paris: it produces a grandiose and stirring effect. The second version, however, has now firmly established the popularity it won under the title *Leonore* Overture. Most probably it will keep it.

This superb overture, perhaps the finest Beethoven ever wrote, shared the fate of several numbers of the opera that were dropped after the first performances. Another, in C major like the other two,[20] was no luckier. It is a charming and gentle piece, but its ending did not seem suited to arousing applause. Finally, for the revival of his rewritten opera, Beethoven composed the one in E major, known as the *Fidelio* Overture;[21] this was the one ultimately settled on in preference to the three others. A masterly work, incomparable in verve and brilliance, it is truly a symphonic masterpiece, though not related either in character or in themes to the opera it introduces. The other overtures, by contrast, are rather like abridged versions of the opera itself. They have the tender accents of Leonora, the pitiable plaints of the prisoner dying of hunger, the delicious melodies of the third-act trio, and the distant fanfare announcing the arrival of the minister who will free Florestan. Everything in these overtures quivers with dramatic tension; they are indeed true introductions to *Fidelio*.

The directors of the principal theaters of Germany and England perceived, after 30 or 40 years, that the second great overture, *Leonore* (the first published) [i.e., *Leonore* No. 3], was a superb work and they now have it played as an entr'acte before the second act of the opera. The *Fidelio* Overture in E is kept to introduce the first act. It is a pity that the Théâtre-Lyrique did not see fit to do likewise. I should even like to see the Conservatoire take the risk some day of following Mendelssohn's example of conducting all four overtures at one of the Gewandhaus concerts in Leipzig.

Perhaps it would be far too bold a venture for Paris. Why so? Well, because boldness, as is well known, is not the chief fault of our musical institutions.

The story of *Fidelio* (a few words about the play being now in order) is both sad and melodramatic. This fact has contributed not a little to the prejudice of the French public against the opera. It is the story of a political prisoner whom the governor of a fortress has thrown into a dungeon and intends to starve to death. The prisoner's wife, Leonore, having disguised herself as a boy and taken the name Fidelio, has insinuated herself as a servant into the good graces of the jailer, Rocco. Marcellina, Rocco's daughter and the promised bride of Jaquino the turnkey, is soon captivated by Fidelio's good looks and loses no time in abandoning her vulgar swain for him. Pizarro, the prison governor, eager to see his victim dead, and, finding that hunger is acting too slowly, decides to cut the prisoner's throat himself. He orders Rocco to dig a hole in a corner of the dungeon, into which the prisoner's body will soon be thrown.

Rocco chooses Fidelio to help him in this dismal task. Picture the poor woman's anguish at thus finding herself near her husband, whom she dares not approach and who is about to be killed. Soon the cruel Pizarro arrives; the prisoner rises in his chains, recognizes his executioner, and defies him. Pizarro advances, dagger in hand, but Fidelio thrusts herself between them, pulls a pistol from her breast and aims it at Pizarro, who recoils in terror.

At that very moment they hear the sound of a distant trumpet. It is the signal to lower the drawbridge and open the gate. The Minister is announced. Pizarro cannot finish his bloody work; he rushes from the dungeon; the prisoner is saved. For when the Minister appears, he recognizes Pizarro's victim as his friend Florestan. Whence general rejoicing—and much embarrassment for poor Marcellina, who learns that Fidelio is a woman and goes back to her Jaquino.

The Théâtre-Lyrique has felt it desirable to transfer these situations of M. Bouilly's drama to a fresh setting, which is Milan in the year 1459, the main characters being Ludovico Sforza; Jean Galeas; his wife, Isabella of Aragon; and King Charles VIII of France. Thus, it has been possible to create at the dénouement a brilliant tableau, and in costumes less gloomy than those of the original work. Such was the motive, however inadequate, that led M. Carvalho,[22] the theater's able director, to make the substitution[23] while Fidelio was in rehearsal. In France it is not thought acceptable merely to translate a foreign opera. The changes in Fidelio, it is true, were carried out without too much damage to the score. The music still goes with situations similar in character to those for which it was written.

What stands in the way of this music for the Paris public is its chaste melody, and the composer's supreme disdain for sonorous effects that are not justified, for routine closes and predictable phrases. It is also the rich soberness of his instrumentation and the boldness of his harmony; it is above all—I am not afraid to say it—the depth of his power to express emotion. One has to give ear to everything in this complex score; everything must be heard if one is to understand it. The orchestral parts—sometimes the principal ones, sometimes the more hidden—contain the expressive accent, the passionate outcry; in short, the ideas that the composer could not embody in the vocal line. This does not mean that the voice no longer predominates, as is claimed by those tiresome bores who keep on repeating the objection Grétry made to Mozart: "He put the pedestal on the stage and the statue in the orchestra."[24] This same criticism had already been made about Gluck, and was later leveled at Weber, at Spontini, at Beethoven, and will always be leveled at anyone who refuses to write platitudes for the voice and who—while exercising a wise moderation—gives interesting parts to the orchestra.

As a matter of fact, the very people who are so quick to criticize the true masters for supposedly making the instruments usurp the role of the voice do not set great store by their own precept. Every day, more than ever during the past ten years, we have seen the orchestra turned into a military band, a blacksmith's forge or a workshop for boilermakers—all this without the critics becoming indignant or even taking the slightest notice of such atrocities. As things are now, the orchestra can be noisy, violent, brutal, insipid, revolting, destructive of both voice and melody, and the critics utter not a word. But when the orchestra is subtle, delicate, intelligent, if at times it attracts attention by its liveliness, grace, or eloquence, while also adhering to its role of serving the needs of the drama and the art of music, then it is censured. By contrast, the orchestra is readily excused for saying nothing at all—or nothing but stupid and vulgar things.

Without counting the four overtures, the score of *Fidelio* consists of sixteen numbers. There were more in the original version, but several were dropped for the second performance of the work in Vienna;[25] many cuts and changes were also made in those that were kept. A publisher in Leipzig undertook (I think it was in 1855) to publish the original work complete, indicating the cuts and changes inflicted upon it.[26] Studying this curious score gives one an idea of what torture it must have been for the impatient Beethoven to submit to these alterations. No doubt he raged as he did so, and compared himself to the fate of Alfieri's slave:[27] "Servo, si, ma servo ognor fremente" (I serve, yes, but never without grumbling).

In Germany, as in Italy, as in France, as everywhere in the theater, everybody knows better than the composer, everybody without exception. The composer is a public enemy, and if some apprentice stagehand asserts that a piece is too long, everyone hastens to take his side against Gluck, Weber, Mozart, Beethoven, or Rossini. Speaking of Rossini, look at the insolent cuts made in his masterpiece *William Tell*,[28] both before and after its first performance. For poets and musicians, the theater is a school of humility; the poets find themselves being instructed by persons ignorant of grammar, the musicians by people who do not know their scales. All these Aristarchs,[29] moreover, harbor a bias against anything that reveals a trace of boldness or novelty; they are filled with an invincible love for safe banalities. In the opera theaters especially, everyone assumes the right to follow Boileau's precept: "Ajoutez quelquefois et souvent effacez" (You should sometimes add but more often erase).[30] This practice is observed so well and so variously—copy editors of one theater invariably seeing black where others see white—that should a score go traveling unprotected from theater to theater, the handiwork of all the correctors would leave barely ten pages intact.

The sixteen numbers of Beethoven's *Fidelio* are almost all noble and beautiful in countenance. But they are beautiful in different ways, which is precisely what gives them their outstanding worth. The first duet between Marcellina and her fiancé is distinctive for its familiar, cheerful style and piquant simplicity; the character of the two people is revealed at once. The aria in C minor for Marcellina seems in its melodic form to approach Mozart's best style. Beethoven, however, handles the orchestra with more meticulous care than his illustrious predecessor ever did.

After this lovely piece comes a quartet [for Marcellina, Fidelio, Jaquino, and Rocco]. Its exquisite melody is treated in canon at the octave; each voice enters with the theme, first as a solo accompanied by a small orchestra of cellos, violas, and clarinets; then as a duet; then a trio; and finally as a complete quartet.[31] Rossini wrote a host of ravishing things in this form; one is the canon "Mi manca la voce" in *Mosè*.[32] But the canon in *Fidelio* is an *andante*, not followed by the usual *allegro* with its *cabaletta* and noisy coda. So the audience, though enchanted by the graceful *andante*, remain at a loss when they do not get their final *allegro*, their cadence, their lash of the whip. Come to think of it, why not give them a lash of the whip?

Rocco's couplets on the power of gold, as Gaveaux wrote it for his French score, should be compared with those in Beethoven's German score. Of all the numbers in Gaveaux's *Léonore*, it is perhaps the one that can best stand the juxtaposition. Beethoven's song charms by its frank cheerfulness, though a modulation and an abrupt change of meter in the middle somewhat modifies its energetic simplicity. Gaveaux's song, though of a more ordinary style, is no less interesting in its melodic frankness, excellent adaptation to the words, and pungent orchestration.

In the trio that follows, Beethoven begins to use larger forms, with extensive developments and a richer, more stirring orchestration. One senses the approaching drama; its high emotions are prefigured by distant flashes of lightning.

Next comes a march; the melody and modulations are felicitous, though its mood is bleak, as a march of prison guards must be. The opening two notes of the theme, struck with a hollow sound by the timpani and a pizzicato in the double-basses, from the outset contribute to the gloom. Neither this march nor the preceding trio has a counterpart in Gaveaux's opera. The same is true of many other numbers in Beethoven's opulent score.

Pizarro's aria is one such. Although it received absolutely no applause in Paris, I nevertheless ask permission to consider it a masterpiece. In this fearsome aria, the ferocious joy of a scoundrel eager to wreak vengeance is depicted with appalling realism. In his opera, Beethoven has closely followed Gluck's precept that instruments be used only as required by the *degree of importance and of passion.* Here for the first time he unleashes the whole orchestra, launching it with a crash on the minor-ninth chord of D minor. Everything shudders, vibrates, cries aloud, and flails about. True, the vocal part is nothing but declamation, but what a declamation! And how true its accents, which develop a savage intensity when, after establishing the major mode, the composer brings in the chorus of Pizarro's guards; their voices accompany his words, murmuring at first, then bursting into full force at the conclusion. It is wonderful! In Germany I heard Pischek[33] sing this aria with stunning power.

The duet for two basses (Rocco and Pizarro) does not quite reach the same heights. Even so, I cannot approve the liberty taken by the Théâtre-Lyrique in dropping it. A similar kind of liberty was taken in Vienna—but at least it was done more or less with the composer's consent—in dropping the charming duet for sopranos sung by Fidelio and Marcellina. In it a solo violin and cello, aided by a few phrases from the orchestra, accompany the two voices with elegance. This duet, recovered thanks to the Leipzig score mentioned above, was reinstated at the Théâtre-Lyrique production. It would seem as if the experts of the Paris theater do not share the view of those of the Vienna theater! What a good thing it is, else we would have been deprived of this musical dialogue, so fresh, so sweet, so elegant! They say it is to the prompter at the Théâtre-Lyrique that we owe its reinstatement. Worthy prompter![34]

Fidelio's great aria[35] is made up of a recitative, an *adagio cantabile,* and a final *allegro* with obbligato accompaniment of three horns and a bassoon. Now I find the recitative charged with fine dramatic impetus, the *adagio* sublime in its tenderness and saddened grace, the *allegro* stirring in its noble enthusiasm, superb, and fully worthy of being the model for Agathe's aria in *Der Freischütz.* I know there are excellent critics who do not share my opinion; I am glad that I do not share theirs.

The *allegro* theme of this admirable aria is introduced by the three horns and bassoon playing nothing more than the five notes of the tonic chord: B, E, G [#], B, and E. Out of these are formed four measures of incredible originality. You could ask any musician who does not know *Fidelio* to make a hundred different combinations of these five notes and I wager that not one would produce the proud and impetuous phrase that Beethoven fashioned, so unexpected is its rhythm. For many people, this *allegro* is seriously flawed because it does not contain a little tune that is easy to remember. These *dilettanti,* insensitive to the many striking beauties of the music, wait for their little four-measure phrase like children expecting to find the little king hidden in their Twelfth

Night cake,[36] or like provincials waiting for the high B-natural from the tenor making his debut. The cake may be delicious, the tenor may have the most delightful voice, yet neither will have any success without the precious accessory! How could they? There is no king in that cake! The tenor hasn't the high note! Agathe's aria in *Der Freichütz* is almost popular; it has the note. But how many arias, even by Rossini, that prince of melodists, have been neglected for want of the note!

The four wind instruments that accompany Fidelio's aria upset most listeners by being too insistent in drawing attention to themselves. Yet these instruments make no display of pointless difficulties. Beethoven has not used them as solo instruments, in the ostentatious sense of the word, as Mozart did several times with the basset horn.[37] In *La Clemenza di Tito*, while the prima donna sings "I can see death approaching," Mozart gives the basset horn a kind of concerto to perform.[38] This contrast between a character who is prey to the saddest emotions, and a virtuoso who, under pretext of accompanying her song, thinks only of showing off the agility of his fingers, is one of the most childish and unseemly. It is contrary to dramatic sense and even to good musical effect. Such is not the role Beethoven assigned to his four wind instruments. It is not a matter of making them shine, but of obtaining a kind of accompaniment in perfect keeping with the feelings of the character, together with a special sound that no other orchestral combination can produce. The veiled, slightly grating timbre of the horns goes perfectly with the painful joy and anxious hope that fills Leonore's heart; it is as sweet and gentle as the cooing of doves. About the same time, Spontini, without having heard Beethoven's *Fidelio*, wrote a similar passage for horns to accompany the beautiful aria in *La Vestale*, "Toi que j'implore" (Thee, whom I beseech).[39]

Since then, several masters—Donizetti among others, in his *Lucia*[40]— have done the same thing with equal felicity. All this is evidence of the special expressive quality of the horns when used by composers familiar with the musical language of the passions and their nuances. It was indeed a great and tender soul that found utterance in this moving inspiration.

The emotion aroused by the prisoners' chorus is no less deep for being less intense. A wretched band of unfortunates emerges from their dungeon for a breath of air in the prison yard. Listen, as they come on stage, to the opening measures of the orchestra, to the radiant bloom of these soft, rich harmonies, to the timid voices as they slowly come together to reach an expansive harmony, which is like a sigh of happiness issuing from all these oppressed breasts. And what a melodious line in the winds that accompany them!

Some might say here again: "Why did the composer not give the melody to the voices and the vocal parts to the orchestra?" Why? Because it would have been an obvious blunder. The voices sing exactly what they should sing; one note added to the vocal parts would damage their expression, so right, so true, and so deeply felt. Melodious though it is, the instrumental line is only an ancillary idea; it is especially suited to the winds, and it could not set off with greater perfection the softness of the vocal harmonies so ingeniously designed above the orchestra. I cannot think that any composer endowed with common sense, no matter what his school, would criticize Beethoven's idea.

The prisoners' rejoicing is disturbed momentarily by the entrance of their guards. Instantly, the musical coloring changes; everything becomes dull and leaden. But the guards finish their rounds: their suspicious eyes no longer bear down on the prisoners. Now the tonality of the choral episode moves closer to the main key, hints at it, touches it; then a brief silence—and the first theme reappears in the original key, with a naturalness and charm I shall not even begin to describe. It is light, it is air, it is sweet liberty, it is life restored to us.

Some listeners, as they dry their eyes at the conclusion of this chorus, may be outraged by the silence in the hall when it should be echoing with thunderous applause. Yet it is possible that the greater part of the audience is genuinely moved; certain kinds of beauty, though apparent to all, may not be of the kind to arouse applause.

In Gaveaux, the chorus of prisoners: "What a splendid sky, how green the earth!" tries to express the same feeling. Alas! compared with Beethoven's chorus, it seems flat and prosaic indeed! Notice, too, how the French composer, until then circumspect in his use of the trombone, brings it in at this precise moment as if it were a mild and suave instrument. Let who can, explain this odd idea.

In the second part of the duet, in which Rocco tells Fidelio that they are going to dig the prisoner's grave, Beethoven has written a curious syncopated figure for the winds, but its moaning accent and restless rhythm are perfectly adapted to the situation. This duet and the following quintet contain very fine passages, some of which, in their writing for voices, suggest Mozart's manner in the *Marriage of Figaro*.

A vocal quintet with chorus closes this act. It is dark and somber, as it should be. Midway through, there appears a brusque, rather dry modulation, and a few voices stand out rhythmically from the mass, without giving a clear indication of what the composer had in mind. Indeed, it is the mystery hovering over this finale that makes it so intensely tragic. It ends in a *piano* expressing consternation and fear. The Paris public does not applaud; it cannot applaud a conclusion so alien to its habits.

Before the curtain rises for the next act, the orchestra plays a slow and lugubrious prelude, full of anguished cries, of sobbing and trembling, of heavy pulsating sounds. We are entering the realm of pain and tears. Florestan is stretched out on his straw mat. We are about to witness his suffering and hear his voice in delirium.

Gluck's orchestration for Orestes' dungeon scene in *Iphigénie en*

Tauride is fine indeed,[41] but how Beethoven surpasses him here! Not only because he is a powerful symphonic composer and because no one can make the orchestra speak more eloquently than he, but also because—it cannot be denied—his musical conception is stronger, grander, and incomparably deeper in its expressiveness. From the very first measures, we sense that the unhappy wretch locked up in this cell must, on entering it, have *abandoned all hope*.[42]

There he is. His heart-rending recitative, interspersed by the principal phrases of the preceding prelude, is followed by a *cantabile,* desolate and harrowing, of which the accompaniment in the woodwinds steadily increases the sadness. The prisoner's pain becomes more and more intense. His mind wanders; he has been touched by the wings of death. Seized by a sudden hallucination, he thinks he is free; he smiles and tears come to his dying eyes. He thinks he sees his wife; he calls to her, and she replies. He is drunk with love and the joy of freedom.

Let others describe this sobbing melody, this quivering orchestra, this unbroken song by the oboe accompanying Florestan like the voice of his beloved wife, whom he believes he can hear. Let others describe the stirring crescendo and last cry of the dying man. I cannot. Let us only acknowledge here the masterly skill, the burning inspiration, the incandescent flight of genius.

After his feverish attack, Florestan collapses and falls back on his mat. Enter Rocco and the trembling Leonore (Fidelio). The horror of this scene is weakened in the new libretto, where they merely clear out a cistern instead of digging the grave of a prisoner who is still alive. (You see what all these "improvements" lead to.) Nothing is more sinister than this famous duet, in which Rocco's cold impassivity contrasts with Fidelio's heart-rending asides, where the dull murmur of the orchestra is comparable to the hollow sound of dirt falling on a coffin. One of my fellow music critics has very aptly compared this scene to that of the gravediggers in *Hamlet.* Can there be higher praise?

Beethoven's gravediggers finish their duet without a coda, without a *cabaletta,* without any vocal outburst; the people in the pit also keep a strict silence. Too bad, isn't it?

The following trio is more fortunate; it gets applauded, even though it too ends quietly. Moved by tender sympathy, the three characters sing dulcet melodies, supported naturally and effortlessly by the most harmonious accompaniment. Nothing could show more elegance and at the same time sound more touching than the beautiful twenty-measure theme sung by the tenor. It is a song of the most exquisite purity; an expression of what is most true, most simple, and most penetrating. Later this theme is taken up again, sometimes whole, sometimes in fragments, and after some bold modulations, it is led back into the original key with incomparable grace and skill.

The quartet with pistol is one long roll of thunder whose threat of violence keeps growing until it ends in a series of explosions. From the moment that Fidelio cries out: "I am his wife!" the musical interest merges with the dramatic. One is moved, carried away, overwhelmed without knowing whether these powerful emotions are being aroused by the voices, the instruments, or the miming of the characters and the action on stage, so complete is the composer's identification with the situation—a situation he has depicted with stunning lifelikeness and prodigious energy.

The voices, calling to each other in burning challenges, always stand out above the orchestral tumult and cut through the rapid figurations in the strings, which are like the clamor of a crowd stirred by a thousand passions. It is a miracle of dramatic music to which I know no counterpart in any master ancient or modern.

This splendid score has suffered enormous, lamentable damage from the change in the libretto. Because the action was taken back to the time before the invention of the firearm, Fidelio could not be equipped with a pistol; the young woman has to threaten Pizarro with an iron bar. This is a less dangerous weapon, especially for such a "man," than the little tube with which her frail hand could strike him dead at the slightest move. Besides, the sight of Fidelio aiming the pistol at Pizarro's face is a most effective piece of stage action. I can see Mme Devrient now,[43] her arm trembling as she points the pistol at Pizarro, her face distorted by convulsive laughter.

There again, you see the result of all this tinkering with plays and scores to make them fit the supposed *demands* of a public that in fact demands nothing and would be well enough pleased if works were put before them just as the authors and composers had written them.

After the wonderful quartet, the couple—now left alone—sings a no-less wonderful duet, in which boundless passion, joy, amazement, and exhaustion by turns find expression in music that cannot be described to anyone who has not heard it. What love! What ecstasies! What embraces! With what ardor these two beings cling to each other! Passion makes them stammer. Words tumble out of their trembling lips, they stagger, they are breathless—they love each other! Do I make myself clear? They love each other. What can this impetuous love have in common with those insipid duets of couples joined in a *mariage de convenance?*

The last finale is a great choral ensemble in march rhythm, interrupted at first by episodic passages in slow tempo. The *allegro* then returns, growing ever livelier and richer in sonority until the end. Even the coldest and most uncooperative listeners are dazzled and swept along, first by the majesty, and then by the verve of this peroration. They approve with a grudging air and say: "Well now, that's better!" Seeing them applaud, I say likewise to them: "That's better!" But the other parts of the score, which move them so little, are no less admirable on

that account; without wishing to depreciate the value of this giant finale, I must say that several of the preceding pieces are greatly superior.

Still, who knows but that the light may dawn sooner than we think,
even for those whose hearts are now closed to this magnificent work of
Beethoven's, as they are also closed to the marvels of the Ninth Symphony, the last quartets, and the great piano sonatas of this same match-
lessly inspired man. It sometimes seems, when we look at the artistic
heavens from a certain angle, as if a thick veil is covering the *mind's
eye*[44] and keeps it from seeing the great stars that make the heavens
bright. Then all at once, by unknown causes, the veil is torn, we see,
and we blush to have been blind for so long.

This reminds me of poor Adolphe Nourrit.[45] He confessed to me one
day that, of all Shakespeare's works, he admired only *Macbeth,* and found
Hamlet in particular to be absurd and incomprehensible. Three years
later he came to me and said with intense enthusiasm: "*Hamlet* is the
masterpiece of the greatest philosopher-poet that ever lived. Now I understand it. My heart and my head are full of it, intoxicated with it. You
must have taken a dim view of my brains and my feeling for poetry.
Please let me again have a place in your good opinion."

Alas, poor Yorick!

BEETHOVEN IN THE RINGS OF SATURN[1]

Mediums

The musical world is in uproar just now, the philosophy of art in total disarray. Only a few days ago, it was generally believed that in music, beauty was absolute, and so was the mediocre and the ugly. In other words, what was beautiful, ugly, or mediocre, for those who consider themselves connoisseurs—people of taste—would be no less beautiful, mediocre, or ugly for everyone, and thus for people without knowledge or taste. This comforting view meant that a masterpiece able to bring tears to the eyes of a resident of No. 58 rue de la Chaussée d'Antin in Paris, or which managed to bore or revolt him, must needs produce the same effect on an Indo-Chinese, a Lapplander, a pirate from Timor,[2] a Turk, or a street porter on the rue des Mauvaises Paroles.[3]

When I say it was generally believed, I mean believed by scholars, academics, and the simple of heart, for in these matters, great and small minds meet, and birds not of a feather flock together.

As for me, I am neither scholar, nor academic, nor simple. I have never known quite what to think about these deep controversial subjects. All the same, I used to think that I believed in nothing. Now I am sure of it. My mind is made up, and I believe in absolute beauty rather less than I believe in the horn of the unicorn. For, I ask you, why not believe in the horn of the unicorn? It has now been proved beyond the shadow of a doubt that unicorns flourish in several parts of the Himalayas. The adventure of Mr. Kingsdoom[4] is well known. The famous English explorer, astonished to find one of these animals, which he had believed to be mythical (you see the perils of belief), stared at it with a curiosity that must have offended the elegant quadruped. Thus angered, the unicorn charged at him, nailed him to a tree, and as proof of its existence left a long piece of its horn in his chest. The unfortunate Englishman never did get over it.

Now I must tell why I have recently become certain that I do not believe in absolute beauty in music. Ever since the marvelous discovery of table-turning (tables of the right kind of pine) and the advent of psychic mediums, the calling up of spirits and thereby the record of *spiritistic* conversations,[5] a revolution had to take place in philosophy, and it has taken place.

Music could not stay untouched by such a tremendous event, or isolated from the world of spirits—music, the science of the intangible, the imponderable, the unseizable. Many musicians, therefore, have thus established relations with the spirit world—they ought to have done it long ago.

With a reasonably priced pine table on which to put one's hands, and which, after a few moments of reflection (on the part of the table, that is) begins to lift a leg or two in a manner that unfortunately offends the sensibilities of English ladies, one can not only invoke the spirit of a great composer but even begin to have a regular conversation with him and force him to answer all kinds of questions. Even better, if one handles it right, one can compel the spirit of the great master to dictate a new work, a whole composition that leaps like fire from his brain. It has been agreed, just as for the letters of the alphabet, that the table, by lifting its legs and letting them fall, will tap so many times for a C, so many for a D, so many for an F, so many for an eighth note, so many for a sixteenth note, so many for an eighth-note rest, so many for a sixteenth-note rest, and so on. Yes, I know, someone will ask, "It has been agreed, you say? Agreed with whom?" The spirits, of course. "But then, before this agreement, how did the first medium get in touch with the spirits to see if they would agree to it?" I cannot tell you; what is certain is that it is certain. And, anyway, in great questions like this, one must trust absolutely one's inner sense and above all not strain at a gnat.

Now already therefore (as the Russians say), the spirit of Beethoven, who lives on Saturn, was recently summoned. Mozart, as everyone knows, lives on Jupiter, and one might have thought that the composer of *Fidelio* would have chosen the same planet for his new abode. But Beethoven is known to be something of a recluse, not very sociable; perhaps he even harbors a secret aversion to Mozart. The fact remains that he lives on Saturn, or at least on one of its rings. On Monday last, a medium who is intimate with the great man and who is not afraid of irritating him by making him take such a long journey for no earthly reason, lays his hands on the pine table and issues Beethoven the order to leave Saturn's ring immediately and come speak with him. Immediately, the table begins to make unseemly movements, raises its legs, and shows—well—that the spirit is nigh.

These poor spirits, you will admit, are remarkably obedient. Beethoven while alive would not have bothered to go as far as from the Carinthian gate to the imperial palace[6] if the Emperor of Austria had asked him to call; and now he interrupts his lofty thoughts and leaves Saturn's ring to obey the order (note the word), the order of anyone at all who happens to own a pine table. It's amazing how death changes one's character! And how right Marmontel was in his opera *Zémire et Azor*,[7] when he said:

Les esprits dont on nous fait peur,
Sont les meilleurs gens du monde.[8]

The spirits that we're told to fear
Are the nicest people in the world.

That's the way it is. As I have already said, in these matters one should not haggle over trifles.

Beethoven arrives and causes the feet of the table to say: "Here I am!" The medium, delighted, nudges him in the ribs.

"Come now," you will say, "you are talking nonsense!"

"Not at all."

"Yes, yes, and a moment ago you mentioned the brain in talking about a spirit. Spirits don't have bodies."

"Perhaps not, but as you know very well, they have what might be called semibodies. It's all been thoroughly explained. Don't interrupt with pointless remarks; let me get on with my sad story."

The medium, who is himself half spirit, half slaps Beethoven on the back and without further ado asks the demigod to dictate a new sonata. No need to tell him twice; the table begins at once to frolic about while the medium takes down the dictation. The sonata written, Beethoven is off back to Saturn. The medium, surrounded by a dozen dumbfounded spectators, goes to the piano and plays the sonata, and the dumbfounded spectators turn into a disconcerted audience as they perceive that the sonata is not a half platitude, but a total platitude, an absurdity, sheer nonsense.

How then can one believe in absolute beauty? Certainly Beethoven, in going to live in a higher sphere, could only have improved himself as a composer; his genius must have become greater and more elevated, and, in dictating a new sonata, must have wanted to give earthly residents an idea of the new style developed in his new home—an idea of his *fourth* period,[9] an idea of the kind of music played on the Erard pianos of Saturn. Now it turns out that this new style is exactly what we infinitely small musicians of an infinitely small sub-Saturnian world would call the flat style, the stupid style, the unbearable style. Far from transporting us to seventh heaven, it irritates us and makes us feel sick. The whole affair is enough to make us lose our minds—if such a thing were possible.

It follows therefore (since one is forced to conclude that the beautiful and the ugly are not absolute and universal) that many creations of the human spirit that are admired on Earth will be scorned in the spirit world. And I find myself justified in concluding, as I have long suspected, that the operas performed and applauded daily—even in those of our theaters that can be named without indecency—will be booed on Saturn, Jupiter, Mars, Venus, Pallas,[10] Sirius, Neptune, Orion, and the

Big and Little Dippers, being for the infinite universe nothing but infinite platitudes.

Now this way of thinking is not such as to encourage our great creators. Indeed, several of them, depressed by the dismal discovery, have fallen ill and, it is said, could well pass over to the condition of a spirit. Fortunately that will take them a long time.

THE EMOLUMENTS OF SINGERS [1]

In contrast to Robert Macaire's famous coffers,[2] which were always open *to receive*, those of the opera houses are always open to pay out. What the tenors, sopranos, and baritones eat up is beyond belief. The world has never seen such Gargantuan appetites. The public does not pay in more than before, on the contrary; so the demigods of the stage have quickly transformed the wretched directors' cash box into the barrel of the Danaïdes,[3] into which buckets of gold are poured but never a coin is left inside. Even so, Paris can no longer pay for exceptional voices. As soon as a singer is sure he is a god, he begins to look down on those who pay him some few tens of thousands in Paris; he begins to sing in Italian (more or less), and asks his hundred thousand[4] from the directors in London and St. Petersburg. A singer at the top of his voice and who earns less than one hundred thousand francs a year considers himself a booby. Unwilling to let him entertain such a bad opinion of himself, and dead set on holding on to these musical Grandgousiers [Great-throats],[5] England and Russia will pay him that sum. Who is to blame? Well, nobody exactly. Let us look after the cash box. Art is but a dream.[6] Let us learn to do without it.

THE CURRENT STATE OF THE ART OF SINGING

In the Lyric Theaters of France and Italy and the Causes That Have Brought It About

The Large Halls, the Claque, the Percussion Instruments [1]

Common sense would say that in the establishments known as lyric theaters, the singers are there for the operas; the fact is just the other way around—the operas are there for the singers. A score must continually be fitted, recast, patched up, lengthened, or shortened to put it into a state (and what a state!) in which it can be performed by the artists to whom it is delivered. One singer finds his part too high, another too low; this one has too much to sing, that one not enough. The tenor wants every phrase to end with *i*, the baritone wants *a*.[2] One singer finds an accompaniment bothersome; his rival complains of a chord that rubs him the wrong way. One aria is too slow for the prima donna, another too fast for the tenor. In short, if a wretched composer took it upon himself to write the scale of C in the middle register, to a slow tempo and without accompaniment, he could not be sure of finding singers who would sing it *without making changes*. Most would still insist that the scale *does not fit their voice*, not having been composed expressly *for them*.

Given the system of singing in Europe now in force (the word is apt), of ten persons who call themselves singers, it would be hard to find two or three at most who could sing a simple romance well, really well, could sing it correctly, in tune, expressively, with a sense of style and a pure, attractive voice. If we choose a singer at random and say: "Here is an old song, quite simple and touching. Its lovely melody does not modulate; it stays within the modest range of an octave. Sing it for us." It is most likely that our singer—and he might be a famous one—would destroy the poor little musical flower, and that as you listened, you would long for the voice of that honest village girl you once heard humming the old song.

No musical thought, no musical form, no expressive accent can survive the dreadful style of interpretation that is spreading everywhere

SÔIRÉE MUSICALE.

Ardore!! Amore!! Mio padre!! Ma figlia!!

"First there is the innocently stupid, the plain dull; then comes the pretentiously stupid . . . criminal singing, villainous singing. . . ." Gustave Doré, "Soirée musicale." Courtesy Bibliothèque Nationale.

today. Would that it were always the same style! But there are several varieties of antimelodic singing. First, there is the innocently stupid, the plain dull; then comes the pretentiously stupid—singing that is embellished with *all* the stupidities a singer can think of contributing. This is bad enough; but next comes the depraved style of singing that corrupts the public and lures it along false musical ways by means of a certain brilliant and capricious style of execution, which is revolting to both good taste and common sense. Finally, there is criminal singing, villainous singing, which adds to its villainy an inexhaustible fund of obtuseness; it proceeds by way of bawling, while it revels

> Aux bruyantes mêlées,
> Aux longs roulements des tambours,[3]

> In noisy frays
> And in the long roll of drums,

in dark dramas, the slitting of throats, poisonings, curses, anathemas—
in short, in all the theatrical horrors that give the most opportunities
for *letting the voice go.* This last style, they tell us, now rules like a
tyrant over the musical life of Italy. What is the cause, the cause?[4] one
may ask. The cause or causes are easy to find. It is the cure that is
hardly known or, to speak frankly, never applied, even when it is known
and its effectiveness long since proved.

The causes are both moral and physical and mutually dependent. If
theatrical ventures were not always and almost everywhere in the hands
of greedy men ignorant of art and its needs, these causes would not
exist. They are: the inordinate size of most opera houses; the practice
of applause, paid or unpaid;[5] the dictatorship that has been allowed to
prevail of performance over composition, of the larynx over the brain, of
matter over spirit; and all too often the cowardly submission of genius
to mediocrity.

The opera houses are too large. It is a proven fact that for sound to
act *musically* on the nervous system, the listener must not be too far
from its source. Whenever the acoustics of an opera house are mentioned, people are given to replying: *Everything can be heard easily.*
Well, from my room I can hear well enough the cannon shots from the
Invalides. And yet this noise, which in any case is not musical, does not
in any way strike or move me, does not stir my nervous system. Even
the most powerful voices and instruments, when they are too far away,
will fail to deliver this stroke, this emotion, this shock that the organ
of hearing absolutely must receive in order to be moved musically.

Some scientists believe that the electrical impulse *(fluide électrique)*
cannot travel through space more than a certain number of thousands
of miles. I do not know whether this is true, but I am sure that the
musical fluid (if I may so describe the mysterious source of musical
emotion) is without force or warmth of life when it has to travel too
great a distance. We may *hear,* but we *do not vibrate.* And one *must*
vibrate *with* the instruments and voices and *because* of them in order
to have genuine musical sensations. Nothing is easier to demonstrate.
Put a few people endowed with sensitivity and some knowledge of music in a fairly small drawing room, not too heavily furnished or hung
with draperies. Play them a true masterpiece by a true composer, one
who is clearly inspired, a work that is free of those unbearable conventional "beauties" that the pedagogues and fanatics so insistently rec-
ommend. Play just a trio for piano, violin, and cello, the B-flat Trio by
Beethoven, for example. What happens? The listeners will gradually feel
themselves invaded by a kind of disquiet; they will then experience a
deep and intense joy that now disturbs them and now plunges them into

a state of serene delight or of veritable ecstasy. At the third or fourth recurrence of the sublime and passionately religious theme in the middle of the *Andante,* one of them may no longer be able to restrain his tears, and once he begins to let them flow, he will end up (I have witnessed this phenomenon more than once) weeping violently, fiercely, and convulsively.[6] That is what you may call a musical effect. Here is a listener overwhelmed and intoxicated by the art of sound, a human being lifted to heights immeasurably far above the plane of ordinary life. Such a one adores music, that is all. He has no idea how to express his feelings, or put his wonderment into words, but his gratitude for the great poet-composer who has thus ravished him is equal to his admiration.

Now suppose that while this same work is being played by the same virtuosos, the room where it is performed is gradually enlarged and the audience little by little pushed away from the performers, on and on, until our room is now the size of an ordinary theater. Our listener, overcome by emotion a moment ago, begins to regain his composure. He still *hears* but he has virtually stopped *vibrating;* he admires the work, but rationally, not any longer carried away by irresistible feeling. Enlarge the room even more, so that the listener is still further removed from the musical center. He is now as far away as he would be if the three performers were playing in the middle of the Opéra stage and he were sitting in the first tier. He still *hears,* he does not miss a note, but the *musical fluid* no longer reaches him. His inner stirrings disappear, he grows cold; he even feels a sort of unpleasant anxiety, all the more intense that he has to strain so as not to lose the thread of the music. But his efforts are in vain; he is paralyzed by indifference, overcome by boredom and fatigue. The great master bores him. The masterpiece is now a ridiculous little noise, the giant a pygmy, his art a disappointment. Impatient, he stops listening.

Another example: A military band is playing a brilliant march in the rue Royale. You listen with pleasure, you follow it, marching gaily in step. The rhythm carries you along, the warlike fanfare stirs you, and soon you are dreaming of combat and glory. The military band enters the Place de la Concorde; you can still hear it, but the sound reflectors are no longer there; its power vanishes, you are no longer vibrating; you let it go its way, paying no more attention to it than if it were a barrel organ.

But let us return to the heart of the matter. When the Opéra had the great goodness to perform the works of Gluck[7]—not too badly, I must admit—how often, while hearing the first act of *Orphée,* was I left cold, yet at the same time irritated by my coldness. I knew, I was certain all the while, that it was a marvel of expressiveness and poetic melody; no essential quality was lacking in the performance. But the set representing a sacred grove was open on all sides; the sound was lost through the back and the wings, there were no walls to reflect the sound, and consequently no effect. Orphée really seemed to be singing in the plains of Thrace. Gluck had got it wrong. A few days later, Orphée was again sung by Adolphe Nourrit,[8] with the same choruses sung by the same choristers, and the same pantomime air performed by the same orchestra; but this time it was in the hall of the Conservatoire: the work regained all its magic. One fell into ecstasy; one was infused with the ancient poetry. Gluck was absolutely right.

Beethoven's symphonies, when played in the Conservatoire, overwhelm everybody. They were performed several times at the Opéra—they created no effect at all. Beethoven's fault. Mozart's *Don Giovanni*, so ardent, passionate, and exciting when well done at the Théâtre-Italien, is, as everyone agrees, glacial at the Opéra. Done there, the *Marriage of Figaro* would seem even colder. At the Opéra therefore, Mozart is at fault.

Rossini's masterpieces in his first manner—the *Barber, La Cenerentola*, and so many others—lose their provocative wit at the Opéra. They can still be enjoyed, but coldly and from *afar*, like a garden seen through a telescope. So the early Rossini, too, got it wrong.

And *Der Freischütz*, a musical drama so full of life and wild energy, see how it drags and languishes at the Opéra. Is Weber, too, at fault?

I could easily multiply the examples. What kind of theater is it in which Gluck, Mozart, Weber, Beethoven, and Rossini are all in the wrong, if not a theater built on wrong musical principles? True, it is not "acoustically bad." It is not that: rather, like all theaters of that size, the Opéra is too big. Though *sound* fills it easily, the *musical fluid* radiated by ordinary methods of performance does not. No doubt I shall be told that some beautiful works do produce the effect there that they should, and that a clever singer with the ability to capture and hold the audience's attention will be able to sing a gentle song successfully. I would reply that in a smaller hall this remarkable singer would make an even greater impression. And the same would hold true for the fine works composed expressly for the Opéra. Of twenty splendid ideas contained in these exceptional scores (even scores written today with the Opéra in mind), barely four or five survive; the rest are lost. The surviving qualities themselves are diminished and obscured by the distance; they never disclose their true splendor, vivacity, and brilliance.

Hence the need—so often derided but nonetheless real—to hear a fine opera several times, if one is to appreciate it and discover its true worth. At the first performance, everything seems confused, vague, colorless, formless, and feeble; it is a half-erased picture whose contours must be looked for, one line at a time. Listen to the comments during the interval at the first performance: to hear the critics tell it, the new work is invariably "boring" or "dreadful." I have been listening to them for twenty years, and not once have I heard them express a favorable opinion. It is much worse at dress rehearsals, when the hall is only half full: then nothing survives, everything is engulfed. Neither melodic grace, harmonic skill, nor instrumental color makes any difference; neither love nor anger; the work is but a vague, wearisome noise that irritates or bores one to death; one leaves cursing the work and its composer.

I shall never forget the dress rehearsal of *Les Huguenots*.[9] When, after the fourth act, I ran into M. Meyerbeer on stage, all I could say was, "There is a chorus in the next-to-last scene which *it seems to me* should be very effective." I was referring to the monks' chorus, the scene with the blessing of the daggers, one of the most overwhelming inspirations in music. It *seemed to me* that it ought to produce an effect; it had not "come across" more vividly than that.[10]

The composition of dramatic music is a dual art: it is the fruit of a combination, an intimate union between poetry and music. Melodic phrases no doubt command their own special interest and cast a spell entirely derived from music itself; but their force is doubled if they work together with a poem worthy of the name to express noble feelings or a great passion. Thus joined, the two arts reinforce each other. Now this union is to a great extent destroyed by halls that are too large, where no matter how hard he tries, the listener can scarcely understand one line in twenty and can barely see the features of the actors. It is consequently impossible for him to perceive the delicate nuances of melody, harmony, and instrumentation, or their justification through linkage with the dramatic contents of the text, since he cannot hear the words of this text.

Music, I repeat, must be heard up close. At a distance its spell disappears or at least is strangely altered and weakened. Would we find any pleasure in the conversation of the wittiest people in the world if we had to listen to them at a distance of thirty paces? Sound coming from beyond a certain distance, though still audible, is like a flame that can be seen but whose warmth is no longer felt.

The advantage of small halls over large ones is manifest. It was on this account that a director of the Opéra used to say with agreeable candor and a touch of bad temper: "Oh, in your Conservatoire, everything creates an effect." Is it so? Just try to play the vulgarities, the brutish platitudes, the nonsense, absurdities, discords, and cacophonies that we endure patiently enough at the Opéra, and see what kind of effect they produce.

Now look at another side of the question, the side of the singer's and the composer's art.[11] We shall quickly find evidence to support my earlier contention that the excessive size of the halls has turned the art of singing into the art of screaming. We shall also find that this has given rise to other excesses equally degrading to the art of music.

The theater of La Scala in Milan is vast; that of La Cannobiana[12] is also very large. The San Carlo in Naples and many others I could mention are huge, too. Now, where is the birthplace of the school of singing so openly and rightly criticized today? In the great musical centers of Italy. During performances the Italian public habitually speaks as loudly as we do at the stock exchange.[13] As a result, the singers, and the composers as well, have been compelled to do whatever they can to lure and hold the attention of a public that professes to love its music. Volume has become the primary aim. To obtain it, nuances must be left out. Head tones, the lower notes of each voice, and voices that can span parts of two registers have all had to be given up. For tenors, only the so-called high chest tones have survived; the basses now sing only in the upper end of their range and have become baritones. Men's voices, which do not really gain in the upper register what they lose in the lower, have deprived themselves of one-third of their range.

In turn, when composers write for the voice, they keep within an octave, and thus limited to no more than eight notes, produce melodies that are of a disheartening monotony and vulgarity. The highest and most piercing of women's voices are the most favored. These tenors, baritones, and sopranos who utter all their notes full force, regardless of everything, are the only ones applauded. Composers assist them by composing so as to second their stentorian ambitions. Duets in unison, trios, quartets, choruses in unison have proliferated. This way of composing, being moreover easier and speedier for the maestros and more convenient for the performers, has come to prevail. And so now, with the help of the bass drum, the type of dramatic music that we enjoy today has taken hold through most of Europe.

I say *most* of Europe advisedly, because this system does not in fact exist in Germany. There, the halls are not caverns; they are not inordinately large, not even that of the Berlin Grand Opera. People say the Germans sing badly; that may seem to be true in general. I do not wish to raise here the question whether or not their language is the cause, or whether Mme Sontag,[14] Pischek,[15] Tichatchek,[16] and Mlle Lind[17] (who is practically German), and a few others, are not magnificent exceptions. But by and large the vast majority of German singers sing; they do not howl. They do not belong to the screaming school; they make music. How to account for this? No doubt their feeling for music is more refined than that of their counterparts in other countries. But also their theaters are smaller, which allows the musical fluid to fill every corner. Besides, the public always listens silently and attentively, which makes it pointless to write awkward vocal and instrumental contortions; they would seem even more hateful there than they are with us.

This amounts, you will say, to the indictment of large halls. Henceforth, no box office receipts of 11,000 francs, no chance to attract 1,800 people for one evening at the Opéra, Covent Garden, La Scala, San Carlo, or elsewhere, for fear of incurring the displeasure of musical connoisseurs. We reply without hesitation: "Just so." You have uttered the key

word: *box office;* you are speculators, we are artists—and we are not
talking about the art of making money, the only art that interests you.

True art is defined in terms of power and beauty. Speculation, which
I am careful not to confuse with industry, has its own aim, which is to
arrive at success, more or less ethically. In the last analysis, art and
business speculation loathe each other. Their antagonism is universal
and eternal; it lies in the very nature of things. Talk to the director of
an opera house, ask him what is the best opera house, and he will reply,
or will think it if he doesn't dare say it, the house that brings in the
biggest take. Talk to a reputable musician or a knowledgeable architect
who loves music, and he will tell you: "If the essential qualities of the
art of sound are to be appreciated, an opera house must be a *musical
instrument.* And it will not be one unless certain well-known physical
laws have been taken into account in its construction. No other consideration has any force or authority over that fact. You can stretch metal
strings over a packing crate, fit a keyboard to it, and you will not have
a piano. Stretch gut or silk over a wooden shoe, and you will not have a
violin. The skill of pianists and violinists will be powerless to transform
these absurd contraptions into musical instruments, even if the crate
were made of rosewood and the wooden shoe of sandalwood. Make a
windstorm blow through a stovepipe; the sounds emitted, though full of
impetus, will not make it an organ, a trombone, a tuba, or a horn. In
building an opera house, all the arguments imaginable—arguments of
perspective, or splendor, or money—collapse before the laws of acoustics and of the transmission of the musical fluid. These laws do exist.
Such are the facts, and the stubbornness of facts is proverbial." That is
what the artists will tell you. But they want to make music, while you
want to make money.

As for the effectiveness of an orchestra playing in an oversized hall, it
is under par, incomplete, and falsifying, in the sense that the result produced differs from what the composer imagined when writing his score,
even if he intended it to be played in that very hall. Since instruments
vary in their power to project, it follows that powerful instruments will
be audible out of proportion to the importance the composer had in mind,
and the weaker ones will be blotted out or will fail to carry out the role
he assigned to them. For the musical action of the voices and instruments to be complete, all sounds must reach the listener at the same
time and with an equal strength of vibration. In other words, the sounds
written in the score must reach the ear—musicians will understand what
I mean—"as in score."

Another consequence of the inordinate size of opera houses, a consequence I hinted at a moment ago when I mentioned the present-day use
of the bass drum, is the introduction into ordinary orchestras of all the
violent instrumental auxiliaries. This abuse, now pushed to extremes,

spoils the power of the orchestra itself and simultaneously forces the singers to a trial of strength with the instruments, thus contributing more than a little to bringing about the system of singing whose prevalence I deplore.

Here is how the percussion instruments have come to dominate. (Will readers who are lovers of music forgive my launching into such a long digression? I hope so. The others I am not afraid of boring; they will not be reading this anyway.)

The bass drum appeared for the first time, if I am not greatly mistaken, at the Paris Opéra in Gluck's *Iphigénie en Aulide*. But there it was used alone, without cymbals or any other percussion instrument, in the last chorus of the Greeks (a chorus in unison, let me note in passing), whose first words are: "Let us depart, let us fly to victory!"[18] The chorus, in march time and *with repeats*, accompanies a parade of the Thessalian army. As in all vulgar marches, the bass drum strikes the downbeat of each measure. This chorus was deleted, however, when the ending of the opera was changed, and the bass drum was not heard again until the beginning of our century.

In the Scythian chorus of *Iphigénie en Tauride*, Gluck also introduced with admirable effect the cymbals alone, without the bass drum, which conventional minds everywhere believe to be inseparable from them. In one of the ballets of the same opera he used with rare felicity the triangle by itself, and that was all.

In 1808 Spontini[19] used the bass drum and cymbals in the triumphal march and gladiators' dance of *La Vestale*.[20] Later, he used them again in Telasco's processional march in *Fernand Cortez*.[21] Up to that point, the use of these instruments, if not particularly adroit, was at least apt and restrained.

Then Rossini gave his *Siege of Corinth*[22] at the Opéra. He had noted, not without regret, the drowsiness of the audience in our large theaters, even during performances of the most beautiful works, a drowsiness induced much more by the physical causes inimical to music that I have just been pointing out, than by the style of the masterpieces of that period. Rossini vowed to himself not to endure the insult. "I know how to keep you people from falling asleep," said he, and he put the bass drum everywhere—and the cymbals and the triangle, and the trombones and ophicleide, making them blare out clumps of chords and play headlong rhythms with all their might. He brought out of the orchestra such brilliant clusters of sounds, if not of harmony, and created such thunderclaps that the audience, rubbing their eyes, enjoyed this new sensation, the most vivid if not the most musical they had ever experienced.

Encouraged by success, he pushed this abuse still further in composing *Moïse*, where in the celebrated finale of the third act the bass drum, cymbals, and triangle strike all four beats of the measure *forte*. They have as many notes as the voices, which compete in the way one can guess with this kind of accompaniment. Even so, by being put together in this way, the sonority of the voices and the instruments is so over-powering that the music survives the din, and the musical fluid, pro-jected in floods to all corners of the hall in spite of its huge dimensions, grips the audience, shakes it up, makes it *vibrate,* and thus creates one of the most memorable effects ever obtained at the Opéra. But do the percussion instruments really contribute to this effect? They do if one thinks of them as furiously stimulating the other instruments and voices. But not if one considers only the part they play in the musical action, for they overwhelm the orchestra and the voices, and substitute their madly violent noise for an otherwise splendid and energetic sonority.

In any event, from Rossini's arrival at the Opéra,[23] one can date the instrumental revolution in theater orchestras. Great noise came to be used in and out of season, in any and all works, regardless of the style required by the subject. And soon the timpani, bass drum, cymbals, and triangle were no longer enough. First a side drum joined the percussion, then two cornets were added to the trumpets, trombones, and ophi-cleide. An organ was installed in the wings next to a set of bells. Then military bands walked on stage full strength, and finally came Sax's big instruments,[24] which are to the others in the orchestra what a cannon is to a gun. Finally, Halévy in *La Magicienne*[25] added the tamtam[26] to all these instrumental means of violence. The new composers, angered by the impediment resulting from the vastness of the hall, felt that they must overcome it under pain of death. But now, when they are overcom-ing it with these extreme methods, are the demands of high art or wor-thy art still being met? No longer, surely; exceptions are rare.

The art of music is compatible with the judicious use of the most vulgar, even the coarsest of instruments; they can in fact add to its rich-ness and power. None of the means available today is to be disdained, but the instrumental horrors we now witness thereby become only more detestable. I believe I have demonstrated their role in the emergence of the vocal excesses that have prompted these overlong and, I fear, all too useless reflections. Let us add that these excesses are being gradually introduced by the spirit of imitation into the Opéra-Comique, where due to the particular conditions of that house—its orchestra, its singers, and the general tone of its repertory—the results are even more repel-lent.

I believed it my duty to meet head on, for the first time, this question on which the life of dramatic music obviously depends. The truths of the matter may be displeasing to great artists and men of excellent and powerful minds, but I believe that in their hearts they know them to be truths. I pointed out at the beginning the moral causes of this vast dis-order, whose physical causes I went on to describe. The influence of applause and of what the performers still have the astonishing naïveté to call "success" play a dominant role. The ridiculous importance granted to performers who are or are deemed to be indispensable, and the authority they have usurped, should not be overlooked, either. But this is not the place to examine such questions. They would fill a book.

GOOD SINGERS AND BAD
The Public and the Claque[1]

I have already said that a singer who is able to sing even sixteen measures of good music in a natural and engaging way, effortlessly and in tune, without distending the phrase, without exaggerating accents to the point of caricature, without platitude, affectation, or coyness, without making grammatical mistakes, without illicit slurs,[2] without hiatus or hiccup, without making insolent changes in the text, without barks or bleats, without sour notes, without crippling the rhythm, without absurd ornaments and nauseating appoggiaturas—in short, a singer able to sing these measures simply and exactly as the composer wrote them—is a rare, very rare, exceedingly rare bird.

Such a singer will become even rarer if the public continues to show aberrations of taste, as it now does with zest, enthusiasm, and hatred of common sense.

Should a man with a powerful voice, but lacking the most elementary notion of how to use it and completely ignorant of the art of singing, force a note violently, the audience will violently applaud the *sonority* of that note.

Should a woman with a voice whose only quality is its exceptional range sing, whether appropriate or not, a low G or F more like the groan of a dying man than a musical note or a high F about as pleasant as the yelp of a dog whose paws are being stepped on,[3] the hall will resound with applause.

Should this singer, who cannot sing the simplest melody without making you wince in pain, whose soul is about as warm as a Canadian iceberg but whose voice is agile and quick like an instrument, let out her snakelike roulades and fiery rockets at a rate of sixteen sixteenth notes per measure, should she bore a hole in your eardrum with her infernal, fiercely insistent trill without taking breath for an entire minute, you can be sure you will see:

> bondir et hurler d'aise
> Les claqueurs monstrueux au parterre accroupis.[4]

> Jump up and shout for joy
> The egregious hired-clappers squatting in the pit.

Should a high-flown singer get the notion that emphasis, whether correct or not, but exaggerated in any event, is everything in dramatic music; that it can take the place of sonority, measure, and rhythm; that it can replace lilt, form, melody, movement, and tonality; then, to meet the demands of a turgid, inflated, and bloated style loaded with bombast, he thinks it right to take the strangest liberties with the most admirable compositions. He can be sure, when he puts this system into practice before certain audiences, that the most intense and sincere enthusiasm will reward him for having butchered a great composer, ruined a masterpiece, shredded a beautiful melody, and torn to tatters a sublime passion.[5]

These people do have a degree of talent, though not enough to make singers of them, and which their exaggerating has made into a fault, a repellant vice. It is no longer a beauty mark, but a wart, a polyp, a wen on a face that is otherwise perfectly insignificant, unless it be perfectly ugly. Such performers are a scourge to music; they demoralize the public, and it is an evil deed to encourage them.

As for the singers who have a voice, a human voice, and can sing, who know how to vocalize and can sing, who know music and can sing, who know French and can sing, who know how to emphasize with discernment and can sing, and who, in singing, respect the work and the composer, whose work they perform in an attentive, faithful, and intelligent way, the public all too often greets them with nothing but haughty contempt or lukewarm applause. Their regular features have no beauty mark, no wen, not even the smallest wart. They do not wear cheap finery; they do not do a jig on the phrase. They are nonetheless true singers, useful and pleasing. Their singing is musical, and they deserve the recognition of people of good taste in general and the gratitude of composers in particular. Through them art survives; with the others it perishes. But, you may say, do you dare assert that the public does not also give warm applause to great singers, masters of all the resources of true dramatic and musical singing, gifted with sensitivity, intelligence, virtuosity, and that rare quality called inspiration? Undoubtedly, the public sometimes applauds them *as well*. The public is then like the sharks that follow ships and are caught by fishermen: they swallow everything, both the bait and the hook.

GLUCK'S *ORPHÉE*
At the Théâtre-Lyrique [1]

In November 1859, M. Carvalho, the director of the Théâtre-Lyrique, had the audacity to revive Gluck's *Orphée;* by this bold act he achieved one of the greatest triumphs I have ever witnessed. He had to be daring indeed, and absolutely convinced of the work's beauty, to brave the prejudices of conventional minds and of the frivolous who rose up on all sides against his venture. He also had to close his ears to the recriminations of people with an interest in being hostile to the revival of masterpieces which, if once heard by the intelligent public, would elicit highly unflattering comparisons with their current productions. What is more, with the limited resources at his disposal, Carvalho had to produce the sort of performance—faithful, energetic, living—without which so many splendid works are all too often libeled, disfigured, and destroyed.

In Paris, when one wants and knows how to choose wisely, one can find an excellent orchestra and a quite satisfactory chorus, as well as a group of lesser soloists who can sing passably the lesser roles in an opera. But when an artist of the first rank is needed for one of those great roles that can tolerate nothing imperfect or shabby, the difficulties are nearly always insurmountable. *Orphée* requires such artists. Where is the tenor who can combine the special qualities the part demands: deep knowledge of music, skill in *chant large;* [2] complete mastery of a simple and austere style; a strong and noble voice; deep sensibility, expressive features, beauty, and natural grace; and, finally, a perfect understanding and hence a reasoned love of Gluck's music? Fortunately, as it happened, the director of the Théâtre-Lyrique knew that the role of Orphée was originally written for contralto. He knew that if he could persuade Mme Viardot [3] to accept it, he would ensure the success of the enterprise. Once apprised of the great singer's cooperation, he commissioned a special task to be done on the score, which I shall now describe:

Orfeo ed Euridice, azione teatrale per la musica, del signor Cavaliere Cristoforo Gluck, was originally an opera in three very short acts with an Italian libretto by Calzabigi. It was performed for the first time in Vienna in 1764, [4] soon afterwards in Parma, [5] then in a host of other Italian theaters.

In Vienna the roles were distributed as follows: Orfeo: Signor Gaetano Guadagni [6] (contralto castrato); Euridice: Signora Marianna Bianchi; Amore [Cupid]: Signora Lucia Clavarau. Even the names of the ballet master,

Léon Carvalho, by Guth. Courtesy Bibliothèque Nationale.

Gasparo Angiolini, and the stage director, Maria Quaglio,[7] have been preserved.

Later, when Gluck came to France to present *Orphée* at the Académie royale de musique,[8] he had Calzabigi's libretto translated by M. Moline.[9] He also transposed[10] the role for the *haute-contre* [high tenor] Legros,[11] added many new numbers to the score, and made numerous and important changes in the old ones. Among the new numbers, I shall point out only Cupid's first aria: "Si les doux accords de ta lyre" (If the sweet chords of your lyre); Eurydice's aria with the chorus: "Cet asile aimable et tranquille" (This pleasant and calm retreat); the bravura aria which Gluck inserted at the end of the first act: "L'espoir renaît dans mon âme" (Hope revives in my soul); the pantomime air for solo flute in the first scene of the Elysian fields; and several highly developed *airs de ballet.*

Gluck also added six measures to Orphée's first song in the Underworld scene, three to his second song, three to the peroration of the aria "Che faro senza Euridice," and a single one to the chorus of the Happy Shades, "Torna o bella al tuo consorte." (He had noticed quite late that the absence of this measure destroyed the regularity of the last phrase.) He reorchestrated virtually from top to bottom the delightful "descriptive symphony" that accompanies the song Orphée sings as he enters the Elysian fields: "Che puro ciel! che chiaro sol!" (What a pure sky! What brilliant sunshine!). He also deleted more than 40 measures in the recitative that begins the third act and entirely recast a later one.

These changes, together with some I do not mention here, all improved the score. Unfortunately, other alterations were made, perhaps by a different hand, which mutilated certain passages in a barbarous manner. These distortions were preserved in the engraved French score and were included in the performances of *Orphée* that I heard at the Opéra so often between 1825 and 1830.[12]

When Gluck composed *Orfeo* in Vienna, he wrote for an instrument he called a cornetto, a wind instrument still in use to accompany chorales in some German churches. It is made of wood, is pierced with holes, and is played with a brass or horn mouthpiece similar to that of a trumpet. Gluck combined the cornetto with three trombones to accompany his four-part chorus during the funeral rites around Eurydice's tomb in the first act. Since it was unknown at the Paris Opéra, the cornetto was left out, and as it was not replaced by another instrument, the sopranos of the chorus, whose melodic line it doubles in the Italian score, were deprived of their instrumental support. In the third stanza of the first act romance: "Piango il mio ben cosi" (I regret my happiness), the composer introduced two English horns. The orchestra of the Paris Opéra, not having English horns, used two clarinets instead.

The contralto voices which Gluck used in *Orfeo,* like all the Italian and German masters in their operas, and which produce such a fine effect in choral music, were replaced by the strident *haute-contres.* Worse, in the chorus of the Elysian fields, "Viens dans ce séjour paisible" (Come to this tranquil land), at the passage, so effective in the Italian score, where the leaders of the chorus sing: "Eurydice va paraître" (Eurydice is about to appear), this *haute-contre* part was altered for no reason one can imagine, producing not once but *four times* the most insipid mistake in harmony that can be made.

As to the printing errors in the two scores (Italian and French), the indispensable directions omitted, and the details misplaced—I cannot even begin to list them all.

Gluck seems to have been extremely lazy and careless in editing even his finest compositions. Not only did he neglect to correct the harmony with the precision expected of a master; he was not even as careful as a good copyist. Often, in order not to bother writing out the viola part, he indicated it with the words *col basso*, without troubling to reflect that this could lead the violas, which are two octaves above the basses, to climb above the first violins. In several places, for example, in the last chorus of the Happy Shades, he even wrote out all the notes of this part too high, thus producing octaves between the two outer voices, a childish mistake as surprising as it is distressing.

Finally, one of the former conductors of the Opéra orchestra added trombones to certain parts of the Underworld scene where the composer had not included them. This, of course, weakens their effect when they enter at the famous response of the demons, "Non!" which is where the composer did want them to be heard.

One can now imagine the type of labor required to restore order in this opera. The recitatives and new arias that Gluck added to the principal part in Paris now had to be adapted for the contralto; the trombones added by an anonymous hand had to be deleted; the wooden cornetto, an instrument that no one plays in Paris but which is needed to double the sopranos of the chorus when they are accompanied by the trombones in the first and second acts, had to be replaced by the modern brass cornet.

In addition, several of M. Moline's verses had to be corrected, as their silliness would have been dangerously unacceptable even to an audience accustomed to the style of the Molines of today. For example, how could one allow Eurydice to say, when she imperiously demands that her husband look at her: "Contente mon envie!" (Gratify my desire!) and other such happy turns of phrase?

After this long, though doubtless necessary, preamble, I shall find it easier to discuss Gluck's *Orphée* and the way it has been revived at the Théâtre-Lyrique.

M. Janin[13] wrote recently: "We do not revive masterpieces, masterpieces revive us." And indeed here is *Orphée* reviving us, those of us who are game for revival. As for the others, the Poloniuses who find everything too long and who need a dirty story or a stupid parody to keep them awake,[14] no masterpiece would want to have anything to do with them, and *Orphée* should take care not to revive them.

All this is obvious enough, yet it wrings the heart to listen to the opinions of the crowd whenever an important work of art is subjected to its judgment. One feels one's gorge rise when, after experiencing noble emotions oneself, one hears talk about what the work will probably earn, by way of the crass question: "Will it make money?"

But let us drop these matters of profit and trade to which nowadays everything is reduced.[15] Let us go straight to things that stir us to the depths, and let us not take trouble to prevent our enjoying ourselves.[16]

What is genius? What is glory? What is beauty? I do not know, and neither do you, Sir, nor you, Madam, any better than I. Only, it seems to me that if an artist has been able to create a work that in all ages can inspire sublime emotions and rouse lofty thoughts in the hearts of people whom we believe to be superior by the refinement of their senses and the cultivation of their minds, then it seems to me that this artist has genius, that he is worthy of glory, that he has created beauty. Gluck was such an artist.

His *Orphée* is almost a hundred years old and, even after a century of evolutions, revolutions, and every kind of turmoil in the arts and everywhere else, his work has deeply touched and charmed the public of the Théâtre-Lyrique. Does it really matter then, what opinion is held by people who need, like Shakespeare's Polonius, a titillating story to stay awake? The feelings and passions of art are like love: one loves because one loves, with no thought of the more or less disastrous consequences of loving.

In truth, the vast majority of the audience at the first performance of *Orphée* felt sincere admiration for the many brilliant strokes of genius embodied in this venerable score. They found the introductory choruses somber and thus perfectly in keeping with the drama, deeply moving in the slowness of their tempo and the sad solemnity of their melody. Orphée's sorrowful cry, "Eurydice," which several times interrupts the chorus's lamentation, is wonderful, everybody said. The music of the romance,

> Objet de mon amour,
> Je te demande un jour
> Avant l'aurore,
>
> O you whom I love
> I ask of you but one day
> Before sunrise,

is a worthy reflection of Virgil's verse:

> Te dulcis conjux, te solo in littore secum,
> Te veniente die, te decedente canebat.[17]
>
> Sweet wife, who were with him on these solitary shores,
> He sang of you at sunrise and sunset.

The recitatives which frame the two stanzas have a lifelikeness and elegance of form that are extremely rare. The distant orchestra in the wings echoes each phrase of the grieving poet, intensifying its painful charm. Cupid's first aria has a certain mischievous grace that befits the god of Paphos; the second contains many formulas in bad taste, which now seem old-fashioned. The bravura aria is even more dated. I hasten to say that it was not composed by Gluck. This aria, whose presence in the score of *Orphée* is unexplained, was taken from the opera *Tancredi* by an Italian named Bertoni.[18] I shall refer to it again in a moment.

In the act set in the Underworld, the instrumental introduction, the pantomime air of the Furies, the chorus of Demons, who at first are threatening then gradually touched and finally tamed by Orphée's song, his heartrending and yet melodious entreaties—everything is sublime.

What a marvel is the music of the Elysian fields! These vaporous harmonies, these melodies as melancholy as happiness, this soft and gentle instrumentation that conveys so well the idea of infinite peace! All this is caressing and enchanting. One begins to detest the coarse sensations of life, to wish for death so as to be able to listen forever to these divine murmurs. How many people, who blush to reveal their emotions, have shed tears in spite of their efforts to restrain them, on hearing the final chorus of this act, "Près du tendre objet qu'on aime" (Near the tender object of one's love), or during Orphée's honeyed soliloquy describing the regions of bliss: "Quel nouveau ciel pare ces lieux!" (What new skies adorn this land!). Finally comes a duet full of desperate agitation, then the tragic accents of Eurydice's great aria, and the melodious theme of Orphée's aria "J'ai perdu mon Eurydice" (I have lost my Eurydice), interrupted by slow, poignantly expressive episodic passages, and followed by the short but wonderful *largo*, in which is expressed the feeling of ecstatic joy of the lover about to die so that he can rejoin his beloved: "Oui, je te suis, cher objet de ma foi" (Yes, I am following you, dear creature I worship).

All this the public took as the crowning glory of the splendid old poem that Gluck bequeathed to us. Ninety-five years have not dimmed its expressiveness and grace. I believe I have already said that the instrumentation was untouched except to restore exactly what Gluck had set down.

Mlle Marimon[19] is graceful in the role of Cupid, yet she occasionally shows a tendency to slow the tempo, as to which I would advise her to be watchful. It will not do to forget that she is playing the winged god of Paphos and Gnidus, not the goddess of wisdom.

Mlle Moreau (the Happy Shade) was made to encore the aria "This pleasant and tranquil retreat,"* which calls for a high soprano and chorus, and which she sings with great purity of tone. Mlle Sax[20] put a good deal of energy, perhaps too much, into the role of Orphée's beloved. Eurydice is a sweet and timid young woman, and her role hardly requires brilliant vocal outbursts. However, Mlle Sax sang "Fortune ennemie" very well.

---

* In the score this aria belongs to the role of Eurydice.

Pauline Viardot as Orphée, by D. Philippe. Courtesy Bibliothèque Nationale.

As for Mme Viardot, her performance is worthy of a study by itself. Her gifts are so complete and so varied, they touch on so many aspects of music and combine such fine technique with irresistible spontaneity, that they inspire both amazement and deep emotion. Her art is at once impressive and moving, awesome and convincing. Her voice, which is of exceptional range, goes with a mastery of vocal control and of phrasing in *chant large* which is rare today.[21] She fuses an indomitable verve, thrilling and commanding, with a deep sensibility and an almost shattering ability to express great sorrow. Her gestures are sober, as noble as they are true, and the expressive quality of her features, always powerful, is even more so in the mute scenes than when called on to heighten the nuances of the vocal part.

At the beginning of the first act, her pose near Eurydice's tomb is reminiscent of certain figures in Poussin's landscapes, or rather, of certain bas-reliefs that Poussin used as models. The virile, ancient costume, moreover, could not suit her better.

From her first recitative,

> Aux mânes sacrés d'Eurydice
> Rendez les suprêmes honneurs,
> Et couvrez son tombeau de fleurs,
>
> To the sacred shade of Eurydice
> Render the supreme honors
> And cover her tomb with flowers

Mme Viardot captured the audience. Each word, each note carried. The great and lovely melody "Objet de mon amour," sung with a peerless breadth of style and a deep and calm sorrow, was interrupted several times by cries from the more impressionable listeners. Nothing could have been more graceful than her gestures, more moving than her singing, when she turned toward the back of the stage and, contemplating the trees of the sacred grove, sang:

> Sur ces troncs dépouillés de l'écorce naissante
> On lit ce mot, gravé par une main tremblante,
>
> On these trunks of nascent bark stripped
> Can be read this word, by a trembling hand inscribed,

Such is the elegy, the antique idyll; it is Theocritus, it is Virgil. With the cry "Implacables tyrans, j'irai vous la ravir!" (Implacable tyrants, I will take her from you!), everything changes; reverie and sorrow give way to enthusiasm and passion. Orphée takes his lyre, he will descend into the Underworld—"Les monstres du Ténare ne l'épouvantent pas" (The monsters of Tenarus do not frighten him). He will bring back Eurydice. It is impossible to describe what Mme Viardot did with this bravura aria. Listening to it, one no longer thinks of the style of the piece. One is carried away by the flood of impetuous vocalizations warranted by the situation.[22]

Mme Viardot's performance of the Underworld scene is well known; she has sung it often in London and Paris. Yet never before—quite understandably—has she put such ardor in her entreaties, such tremors in her voice, such dying sounds, which make her successful appeal to the ghosts, specters, and diabolical monsters seem credible.

Yet it was in the land of eternal peace that the actress made her talent

most manifest. Moved by Orphée's song, the diaphanous shades, simu-
lacra devoid of life and as numerous as a thousand birds hidden among
the leaves, rise from the depths of Erebus.[23]

> Matres, atque viri, defunctaque corpora vita
> Magnanimum heroum, pueri, innuptaeque puellae[24]
>
> Mothers and men, lifeless bodies of
> high-minded heroes, boys, and unmarried girls

Here the great artist had to scale the heights of Virgil's poetry, and she
proved equal to the task.

Nothing could be more noble than her entrance to the region of Ely-
sium, which the shades have just left; nothing could be more sweetly
solemn than these beautiful contralto sounds, uttered soft and solitary
from the depths of the stage, while the waters and leaves murmur in
harmony: "Quel nouveau ciel pare ces lieux!" (What new skies adorn
this place!). But the beloved does not appear. Where can she be? Orphée
is filled with anxiety. The smile that lit up his face has vanished. "Eurydice! Eurydice! Where are you?" The young shades, young beauties,
lovers, virgins—the *innuptae puellae*—all come in groups of twos and
threes, arm in arm, heads slightly tilted, eyes full of curiosity, silently
encircling the mortal being. His anxiety growing, Orphée moves from
group to group examining the lovely pale faces, hoping to recognize Eurydice's, but in vain. Overcome by discouragement and dread, he is about
to succumb to despair when the voices rising from a nearby grove sing
this ineffable melody:

> Eurydice va paraître
> Avec de nouveaux attraits.
>
> Eurydice is about to appear
> More alluring than ever.

Orphée is joyful again; his smiling face is wet with those tears that
only the greatest ecstasies provoke. The shades finally bring him his
sweet wife, *dulcis conjux*. Now he stands with his back to her, unable
to see her, but warned of her approach by an unfamiliar rapture, the
feeling of great love. Orphée starts to tremble. Eurydice's hand is put
into his. At the touch of the beloved, we see him overwhelmed, gasping,
and about to faint. Nonetheless, he takes a hesitant step, leading Eurydice, still cold and wondering, up the hill to the sky of the living, while
the silent motionless shades raise their arms in farewell toward the two
lovers. What a scene! What music! And what acting by Mme Viardot! It
is grace in sublimity. It is ideal love. It is divinely beautiful.

Oh, heartless Polonius who feels none of this, you are truly to be pitied.

There is yet more to admire. Not to mention the aching excitement with which Mme Viardot sang the great duet "Viens, suis un époux qui t'adore" (Come, follow the husband who adores you), her stance and accents in the asides of the other duet, where these words are sung in a heartrending chromatic progression: "Que mon sort est à plaindre!" (O my fate is pitiable!).

There is yet to be noted the masterly, crowning moment in this great artist's *creation* of the role of Orphée. I mean her performance of the famous aria "J'ai perdu mon Eurydice" (I have lost my Eurydice).

Gluck said somewhere:[25] "Change the least nuance of tempo or accent in this aria and it will become a dance tune." Mme Viardot made it what it was meant to be, one of those miracles of expression that are virtually beyond the understanding of ordinary singers and which are, alas! so often desecrated.[26] She sang the theme in three different ways: first with restrained grief in a slow tempo and then, after the episodic adagio:

> Mortel silence!
> Vaine espérance!
>
> Deathly silence!
> Futile hope!

she sang *sotto voce, pianissimo*, in a trembling voice, muffled by a flood of tears. Finally, after the second *adagio*, she took up the theme again in a faster tempo as she rose from kneeling beside Eurydice's body, and rushed mad with despair to the other end of the stage, weeping and sobbing. I shall not attempt to describe the feelings of the audience during this overwhelming scene. Several loutish admirers got carried away and shouted "encore" before the sublime passage "Entends ma voix qui t'appelle," (Hear my voice calling you), and they were hushed up with difficulty. Some people would shout "encore" during Priam's scene in Achilles' tent or Hamlet's soliloquy "To be or not to be."

But why did Mme Viardot give cause for reproach by introducing a deplorable change toward the end of this aria, where she keeps holding the high G? It not only stops the orchestra where Gluck would have it rush impetuously toward the close but also alters the harmony, substituting a dominant chord for that of the sixth on the subdominant B-flat—in short, it does *the opposite of what Gluck intended*.

Again, why does she incur the reproach of making other changes in the text and adding vocal flourishes that are out of place in the recitative? Alas!

The staging, as I have already said, is worthy of the music. One could not conceive of anything more artfully designed, more in keeping with the subject, especially for the scene in the Elysian fields and the Underworld. The costumes, moreover, are charming and the dances adequate. This revival of Gluck's poetic score reflects great credit on M. Carvalho and has earned him the gratitude of all the friends of art.

LINES WRITTEN SOON AFTER THE FIRST PERFORMANCE OF *ORPHÉE*[1]

At the Théâtre-Lyrique

Orphée is beginning to be disquietingly popular.[2] One hopes that Gluck does not become à la mode. That the house should be full every time this masterpiece is performed is all to the good; that M. Càrvalho should make a lot of money, good again; that the musical taste of the Parisians should undergo refinement, that their narrow ideas should enlarge and become loftier, is better still; that the artistic public should take pleasure in an uncommon source of joy, better and better—a thousand times better. But that these Poloniuses (Polonius is the new name for Monsieur Prud'homme[3]) should feel obliged now to stay awake during the performances of *Orphée*, that they should have to sneak off to see their favorite parodies in a theater whose name is unmentionable,[4] that they should pretend to find Gluck's music *delightful*—that is too bad, too bad, and worse! Drive out nature with a pitchfork and it comes back double strength.

When one is a respectable M. Prud'homme, a Polonius with or without a beard, why not speak one's native tongue, why pretend to understand and feel, why not say openly like so many others, "It's a bore! A crashing bore!" (I will not quote the word that the Poloniuses use; it is too unliterary.) Why lower one's voice to say, as I have overheard it loud enough, "Please pardon me, Madame, for compelling you to endure this rhapsody, forcing you to attend this long funeral service. To make up for it, we shall go to see Punch and Judy tomorrow on the Champs Elysées; for we've been robbed, in the full sense of the word, robbed as it doesn't happen even in a dark wood.[5] It was those crazy journalists who led us by the nose into this ambush."

Or again: "It is very learned music, very learned; but if we have to study counterpoint in order to enjoy it, you will agree, I'm sure, dear Mme Prud'homme, that it is not for us."

Or: "There aren't two measures of melody in it. If we young musicians wrote such music, people would pelt us with rotten apples."

Or: "It's music made by calculation and only mathematicians can appreciate it."

" 'It's beautiful, but it's too long,' Or: 'It's long and it's not beautiful.' " Honoré Daumier, "L'orchestre pendant qu'on joue une
tragédie." Lithograph, courtesy Musée Carnavalet. © 1993 ARS,
New York/SPADEM, Paris.

Or: "It's beautiful, but it's too long."
Or: "It's long and it's not beautiful." And other such wonderful aphor-
isms.

Yes, it would be worse, much worse, if a new kind of hypocrisy began
to spread, because nothing is more delightful or flattering for people endowed with a certain kind of mind than to see the things they love and
admire being insulted by persons with a different kind of mind. It adds
to their pleasure. And in the contrary case, they are always tempted to
paraphrase the aside of an ancient Greek orator thus:[6] "The Poloniuses

are delighted; can it be that what we're admiring is a platitude?" Rest assured, it will never come to pass. Gluck will not become à la mode. The take at the Punch and Judy Show has recently shown a great upsurge; so many people go there to make up for their pain.

One of the reasons for the splendid success of Gluck's work at the Théâtre-Lyrique is the small size of the hall, which allows one to hear both the words, so intimately linked with the music, and the nuances of the instrumentation. I believe I have shown that huge houses are fatal to expressive music, to the delicacy and the most intimate pleasure afforded by the art.[7] It is these huge halls that have led opera librettos to include absurdities and shameless idiocies that *are not heard* (so say the cynics who write them). As I shall never tire of repeating, it is oversized halls that seem to give certain composers an excuse for senselessly brutish orchestration. Have they not thus helped produce the school of singing we enjoy today, the school where instead of singing, one shouts; or in order to project the sound more forcefully, the singer takes a breath after every three or four notes, breaking up, shredding, dismembering, and destroying every well-turned phrase, every noble melody, eliminating verbal elisions, lengthening each verse into lines of thirteen or fifteen feet—to say nothing of dislocating the rhythm, inserting hiatuses, and a hundred other misdeeds that change melody into recitative, poetry into prose, and the French language into gibberish? These halls, huge caverns that benefit the box office, have always made for the howling and screaming of tenors, basses, and sopranos at the Opéra, where the best-known singers have come to deserve the name of bull, peacock, strutting hen, or braying ass, which are bestowed on them by ill-mannered people who call a spade a spade.

There is in fact a sally of Gluck's on the subject. During the rehearsals of *Orphée* at the Académie royale de musique, Legros persisted as usual, as he entered Tartarus, in screaming the phrase, "Let yourselves be moved by my tears!" One day, angered at last beyond endurance, the composer cut him off in mid-phrase and fired this salvo at him: "Monsieur! Monsieur! Kindly cut down your shouting! What the devil! They don't shout like that in hell."

> Comme avec irrévérence
> Parlait aux dieux ce maraud![8]
>
> How irreverently
> This villain spoke to the gods!

Still, this reproof was nothing to what went on in the days when Lully broke a violin over the head of an inept musician, or when Handel threw a refractory prima donna out the window.[9] Gluck was protected by his gracious pupil the queen of France.[10] When Vestris,[11] "the god of the dance," dared to say that Gluck's ballet music was not for dancing, he was ordered by Marie-Antoinette to apologize to Chevalier Gluck. The interview, it seems, was rather boisterous. Gluck was tall and strong; when he saw the diminutive "god," he ran up to him, lifted him by the armpits, and, humming a dance tune from *Iphigénie en Aulide,* swung him willy-nilly around the room. After depositing him breathless on a chair, Gluck cackled: "You see, you *can* dance to my ballet music. You only have to hear me hum it and you can't keep from leaping about like a mountain goat!"

The Théâtre-Lyrique is exactly the right size for a work such as *Orphée.* Nothing is lost, neither the sound from the orchestra nor the voices, nor the expression on the actors' faces.

Speaking of *Orphée,* let me mention one of the boldest acts of plagiarism in the history of music; I discovered it a few years ago while glancing through a score by Philidor.[12] We know that this learned musician had access to proofs of the Italian edition of *Orfeo,* which was being published in Paris during its composer's absence. Philidor saw fit to borrow the melody "Objet de mon amour" and to adapt it, after a fashion, to words in his own opera *Le Sorcier*[13] [The Wizard], which he was composing at the time. He changed only measures 1,5,6,7, and 8, and turned Gluck's first section (three phrases of three measures each) into two four-measure phrases; he had to fit the makeup of his verses. But beginning with the words

> Dans son coeur on ne sent éclore
> Que le seul désir de se voir,
>
> In their hearts all they can feel
> Is the sole desire to meet again.

Philidor copied Gluck's melody, his bass line, his harmony, and even the echoes of the oboe in his small backstage orchestra, at the same time transposing the whole thing to A. I had not heard any mention of this barefaced theft, which is obvious to anyone who looks at Bastien's romance "Nous étions dans cet âge" (We were at an age), on p. 53 of *Le Sorcier.*

I have now learned, however, that M. de Sévelinges[14] had already pointed it out in his article on Philidor in Michaud's *Bibliographie universelle,* and that M. Fétis[15] tried to defend the French musician. Since *Orfeo* was supposed to have opened in Vienna sometime in 1764 and *Le Sorcier* opened in Paris on January 2 of that year, Fétis thought it impossible for Philidor to have been acquainted with Gluck's work. But M. Farrenc has recently proved[16] on the basis of authentic documents that *Orfeo* was performed for the first time in Vienna in 1762, that Favart was given the score to publish in Paris in 1763, and that Philidor *offered* at that time to correct the proofs and *to oversee the engraving of the work.*[17]

It is conceivable that after pillaging Gluck's romance, the officious proofreader may have changed the date on the title of the *Orfeo* score from 1762 to 1764 and so made plausible the argument that this incorrect date suggested to M. Fétis: "Philidor could not have plagiarized Gluck since *Le Sorcier* was performed before *Orfeo.*"[18] The theft itself is beyond doubt. With but a little more audacity, Philidor could have made it appear that Gluck was the thief.[19]

Now to return to the bravura aria that concludes the first act of the French version, *Orphée.* I had heard some people say that it was not composed by Gluck, though he had written several similar arias in some of his Italian scores. I wanted to make certain. After vainly searching the Conservatoire library for the score of Bertoni's *Tancredi*, from which the aria was said to be taken, I finally found it in the Imperial Library. Browsing through the first act of this work I recognized the piece in question at first glance; it is impossible to mistake it; only a few notes were added to the *ritornello* in its *Orphée* version. How was this aria introduced into Gluck's opera and by whom? That is what I do not know. In a pamphlet entitled "Entretiens sur l'Etat actuel de l'Opéra de Paris," [Conversations on the Current State of the Paris Opera], published in Paris in 1779 by a certain Coquéau,[20] an enemy of Gluck's, the great composer was violently attacked and accused of various acts of plagiarism, and in particular of lifting an entire aria from Bertoni's score. When Gluck's adherents denied it,[21] Coquéau wrote to Bertoni. The Italian sent him the following reply, which Coquéau published in a supplement to his pamphlet, entitled "Suite des entretiens sur l'état actuel de l'Opéra de Paris, ou Lettres à M.S. [Suard]."[22] Despite Bertoni's wariness and embarrassment, and his comical fear of being compromised, the truth nonetheless emerges very clearly in this letter, which I owe to the courtesy of M. Anders[23] of the Imperial Library:

London, September 9, 1779

Monsieur:

I am very much surprised at being challenged in the letter you have done me the honor of writing to me, and I should very much like to stay clear of a musical quarrel which, judging by the heat with which you speak of it, could have serious consequences. You assure me besides that fanaticism is involved, which is yet another reason for me to avoid it. So I beg you to let me simply reply that I composed the melody of *So che dal ciel discende* in Turin for Signora Girelli;[24] I do not remember the year. I could not even tell you if I really wrote it for *Iphigénie en Tauride*,[25] as you assure me. I think rather that it belongs to my opera *Tancredi*,[26] but that does not prevent the aria from being mine. That is what I can and must assert with all the truthfulness of a man of honor, full of respect for the works of great masters, but also full of affection for his own. With my assurance of deep obligation, I am, sir, your very humble and very obedient servant,

Ferdinando Bertoni

Tancredi was performed in Venice during the carnival of 1767,[27] and the French version of *Orfeo*, retitled *Orphée*, was not performed in Paris until 1774. It is probable that the singer Legros who created the role of Orphée in Paris was dissatisfied with the simple recitative that Calzabigi and Gluck wrote for the end of the first act and demanded a bravura aria, which Gluck refused to write. Finally yielding to insistent demands, Gluck may have given him Bertoni's aria, saying: "Take that, sing it, and leave me alone." Gluck, however, had no right to let Bertoni's aria be published in his score without indicating where and from whom he took it. Nor is it clear why he apparently kept silent when the author of the pamphlet I have cited denounced him for plagiarism.

I must add that this Bertoni, who is so obscure today, also set Calzabigi's *Orfeo* to music, and his opera was performed in 1766[28] at the theatre of San Benedetto in Venice.

In publishing his score (which I have read), he thought he ought to excuse himself for committing such a bold act. "I neither claim nor hope," he said in his preface, "to have a success for my *Orfeo* equal to that which greeted M. Gluck's masterpiece throughout Europe, and I shall consider myself only too happy if I can deserve the encouragement of my own compatriots."[29]

He was right to be modest, because his music is, as it were, a tracing of Gluck's. In several places, especially in the Underworld scene, the rhythmic forms of the German master are so faithfully imitated that if one looks at the score from a little distance, the way the notes are grouped creates the illusion of seeing Gluck's *Orphée*.

Is it not possible that, on hearing the aria from *Tancredi*, the latter said to himself: "This Italian has stolen enough from me for his own *Orfeo;* now it is my turn to take one of his arias"? Though possible,[30] it is so unworthy of such a man as to make it hard to believe. That is all I know of the matter.

When Adolphe Nourrit came to sing *Orphée*,[31] he left out the bravura aria, either because he did not like it or because he was aware of the fraud. He replaced it with a splendidly turbulent aria from Gluck's *Echo et Narcisse:*[32] "O transport, ô désordre extrême" (O ecstasy, o extreme disarray).[33] The words and music happen to fit Orphée's situation, and I think that is what should always be done.

THE *ALCESTE* OF EURIPIDES
And Those of Quinault and Calzabigi
Scores by Lully, Gluck, Schweitzer, Guglielmi, and Handel on This Subject[1]

Alceste, a tragedy by Euripides, has been the subject of several operas: one by Quinault set to music by Lully;[2] another by Calzabigi with music by Gluck;[3] a third by Wieland,[4] music by Schweitzer;[5] and several others. Gluck's opera, first written to an Italian text for Vienna was later translated into French[6] for the Paris Opéra, where it was performed after several important changes and additions by Gluck himself. None of these operas follows the Greek tragedy exactly. Now that Gluck's great work is being revived,[7] it might be worth looking at the original play which inspired these modern versions.

Nowadays, Euripides' tragedy would shock the customs, ideas, and feelings of all civilized peoples. Mores have changed so much, on the one hand, and literary education (especially in France) has, on the other, made such a point of creating contempt for what is natural and genuine, that—on superficial reading—one can imagine how a professor of rhetoric had the daring to say to his students, "It is a farce by Bobêche!"[8] Yet the Athenians were neither barbarous nor stupid, and it is highly improbable that they would have admired or applauded ignoble or scandalous works. We seem to expect Euripides, as we do Shakespeare, to take our habits, prejudices, vices, and even our religious beliefs into account, so that we have to muster all our critical honesty and common sense to acknowledge that a Greek poet, who lived in Athens two thousand years ago and wrote for a people whose language and religion we know imperfectly, had no obligation to seek the approval of the Parisians living in 1861.

But this has to do only with the question of substance. It must be added that the great Greek poets, who used what is perhaps the most harmonious language that was ever spoken, are inevitably and fatally destined to be misrepresented by unfaithful translators who are often incapable of understanding them. In any case translators always find themselves in the impossible situation of trying to carry over the harmony of style, the imagery, the very ideas of the original into our modern languages, which are so colorless and full of a prudery that does not allow certain notions to be truthfully rendered. It is more or less the same case with the Latin poets. Who today would dare to make a faithful French translation of Queen Dido's naïve and touching words:

> Si quis mihi parvulus aula
> Luderet Aeneas, qui te tamen ore referret;[9]

> If only some little Aeneas were playing in my court
> Whose face would remind me of you;

Such a translation would make people laugh. "A little Aeneas," people would say, "a little Aeneas playing in my court!" What is he playing with? A hoop? A top? But what is truly ridiculous is that in certain literary circles there are persons who honestly believe that they can know these ancient poems through our modern translations and imitations. They would be surprised to learn that Bitaubé[10] gives no better an idea of Homer than Abbé Delille[11] does of Virgil, or Racine of Greek tragedy.

With these reservations in mind about translators, who are of necessity the most treacherous people in the world, let us take a look at what Father Brumoy,[12] for example, enables us to see of Euripides' *Alceste*—or at least of that series of scenes, virtually devoid of what today we call action, that makes up the Greek tragedy.[13]

Admetus, king of the city of Phères in Thessaly, is on his deathbed. Apollo, who was banished from heaven by Jupiter's anger and who has been guarding Admetus' sheep while in exile, outwits the Fates and snatches the young king from their clutches. But the goddesses consent to let Admetus live only if another victim can be found who is willing to die in his stead. No one volunteers, so the queen, Alceste, offers to die for her husband. From the rather lively argument between Apollo and Orcus, the spirit of death, that takes place at the beginning of the play, it appears that Admetus already knows about the queen's sacrifice and has accepted it. Although he loves Alceste passionately, he loves life even more and agrees, however reluctantly, to being saved at this price. Hence a scene of mourning, everyone bowed in grief. Alceste's children utter heartrending cries, the people weep, and the young, devoted queen is terrified of what her sacrifice entails. There is a moving scene in which the dying queen begs the broken-hearted Admetus to remain faithful and not take another woman to the altar. Admetus gives his word and—comforted—the queen dies in his arms. Funeral preparations are made; people bring the gifts and emblems that are to be placed with Alceste in her tomb. Now comes Phérès, Admetus' old father, and a scene takes place which, though atrocious according to our ideas and our morality, is nonetheless sublime. I leave the responsibility for the following text to the translator:

PHÉRÈS: "I feel for you in your grief, my son. The loss you have suffered is great—all would agree; you have lost an excellent wife. But no matter how terrible your pain, you must endure it. I give you these precious robes to be put in her tomb. One cannot honor too highly a wife who has sacrificed herself for you. It is to her that I owe the joy of having a son preserved *for me* (the translator has mistakenly added the italicized words). She could not bear the thought of a disconsolate father having to drag out his old age in mourning."

ADMETUS: "I did not invite you to this funeral, and, to keep nothing from you, I must tell you that I find your presence here not at all agreeable. Take these clothes away; they shall never be put on Alceste's body. I shall see to it that she does without your gifts in her tomb. You saw me on the point of death; that was the time for you to weep. But what were you doing then? Is it becoming to shed tears now, after running away from the danger that threatened me, after allowing Alceste to die in the bloom of youth, while you are bent under the weight of many years? No, I am no longer your son and do not acknowledge you as my father. . . . You must be the most cowardly of men, since, being near the end of your life, you had neither the will nor the courage to die for your son; you were not ashamed to let an outsider fulfil this duty."

PHÈRÈS: "To whom are you speaking in this arrogant way, my son? Do you think you are addressing a slave from Lydia or Phrygia? Since when have Nature and Greece laid it down that a father must die for his children? You accuse me of cowardice, but you were not ashamed to sacrifice your wife so as to prolong your own days beyond their fated time. What a clever device for henceforth escaping death, to persuade one's wife to die for her husband!"

There follows a rapid, headlong dialogue in which the speakers heap abuse on each other in this vein:

ADMETUS: "Old age has lost all shame."

PHÈRÈS: "Why not marry several women, so as to keep extending your days?"

ADMETUS: "Go, go, you and your unworthy wife, drag out your miserable old age without children, even though I am still alive; that is the reward for your cowardice. I want nothing more to do with you, not even to share a house. I wish I could with propriety forbid you to enter the palace! I would not scruple to do so in public."

Nobody can read these exchanges without shuddering. Shakespeare himself never went further. Those two poets seem to have plumbed the deepest secrets of the human heart, dark caverns that ordinary minds dare not explore, where only the burning eyes of genius can penetrate without fear, to drag out into the light the incredible monsters that lurk there. Incredible, but all too real; for where are the men who would refuse to sacrifice even the most beloved wife so that they might live? No doubt such men exist; but surely they are as rare as the woman capable of such a sacrifice. Each of us may say, "I think I am one of those." But the philosopher-poet would answer, "Alas! You may be deceiving yourself; you would rather mourn than die."

Phérès is right: "Everyone here on earth is for himself. The light of day is precious and sweet to you; do you think it is any the less so for me?" Twenty centuries later, Molière had one of his most honest characters say of his own body: "Guenille si l'on veut, ma guenille m'est chère" (Call it an old rag, if you will, but my old rag is dear to me).[14] And La Fontaine used almost the same words as Euripides' Admetus: "Le plus semblable aux morts meurt le plus à regret" (It is those who are nearest death who die most reluctantly).[15]

Amid these dreadful scenes, in which the young king is driven by grief to the impious wish of parricide, a stranger now appears. "O citizens of Phérès," he asks, "shall I find Admetus in this palace?" It is Hercules, the knight-errant of antiquity. Obeying the orders of Eurystheus, king of Tiryns,[16] he is on his way to encounter Diomedes,[17] the son of Mars, and capture the man-eating horses which, until then, only Diomedes himself could tame. While passing through Phérès on this dangerous mission, the brave son of Alcmene[18] asks to see his friend. Admetus steps forth and invites Hercules to enter the palace. But the shattered look on the young king's face shocks Hercules, who stops on the threshold.

"What grief is yours? Have you lost your father?"

"No."

"Your son?"

"No."

"Alceste then? I have heard she promised to die for you."

Admetus, still secretive, assures Hercules that the woman they are mourning was a foreigner reared in the palace. He is afraid that if he tells the truth, his friend will decline hospitality in a grief-stricken house, and that would be one more source of grief. Finally, Hercules enters and is taken to the quarters set aside for him, where slaves prepare a sumptuous feast. The king adds these touching words: "Close the doors of the entrance hall. It would not be decent to disturb a feast with weeping and tears. We must spare our guest the sad sights and sounds of our funeral ceremonies." More or less reassured, Hercules sits at the table, puts a crown of myrtle on his head, eats, drinks, gets a bit drunk, and makes the palace echo with his singing. Suddenly noticing the dazed condition of the slaves who serve him, he questions them and finally learns the truth. "Alceste is dead! Ye gods! How could you think of entertaining me at such a time?" (Similarly, Shakespeare has Cassius say to Brutus, whom he has just insulted, "Portia is dead! Why didn't you kill me?"[19])

HERCULES: "Alceste is no more. And wretch that I am, I have been carousing here at this feast. I crowned my head with flowers in the house of a friend in despair. But it is you who are guilty of this crime. Why did you conceal the fact? Where is the tomb? Speak up. Which way am I to go?"

OFFICER: "Take the road for Larissa. You will see the tomb as soon as you're out of the city."

Hercules goes to the royal tomb, waits in ambush nearby and, as Orcus comes to drink the blood of his victim, leaps upon him and compels him by main strength to bring back Alceste alive. Returning to the palace, he presents her, wearing a veil, to Admetus. "You see this woman. I entrust her to your keeping and expect you, as my friend, to look after her until I return triumphant after killing Diomedes and seizing his chargers."

Admetus pleads with him not to ask this favor; the mere sight of a woman reminds him of Alceste and would break his heart.

Hercules insists so much that Admetus dare not refuse, and the king extends his hand to the veiled woman. Satisfied, Hercules lifts the veil from the woman's face and Admetus, dumbfounded, sees that she is Alceste. But why does she stand there mute and still? Having been consigned to the gods of the Underworld, she must undergo three days of purification before she can return to the love of her joyful husband. Public festivities are ordered, Hercules sets off on his dangerous journey, and the tragedy ends with this moral from the chorus:

"The gods resort to extraordinary means to obtain their ends! Through their mysterious powers they bring about great events contrary to the expectations of mortals. Such miracles command our joy and wonderment."

Now, the talents of our hack playwrights are far superior to those of Euripides. As can be seen from this brief outline of the Greek poem, *Alceste* has so little in common with their work that they are quite justified in saying, "There is nothing here for a play." Let us see what Quinault has done with this theme of wifely devotion. As we know, he was not a particularly skillful maker of plays.[20]

The opera begins with a prologue, like most of the works of its time that were written for the Académie royale de musique, the Paris Opéra. In this prologue, the nymphs of the Seine, the Marne, and the Tuileries sing of their desire for the king's return, and reproach Glory for having kept him away so long.

> Tout languit avec moi dans ces lieux pleins d'appas.
> Le héros que j'attends ne reviendra-t-il pas?
>   Serai-je toujours languissante
>   Dans une si cruelle attente?
>
> Everything pines like me in this place so charming.
> The hero whom I await, will he never return?

Shall I always yearn
With such cruel longing?

After the nymphs of the Seine, the Marne, and the Tuileries, after
Pleasure and Glory and the French naïads and dryads have sung enough
insipid songs, the play begins.

Alceste has just married Admetus. Two rejected suitors are burning
for her: Hercules and Lycomedes, who is the brother of Thetis and king
of the island of Scyros.[21] On the pretext of taking her to a nautical display, Lycomedes lures Alceste onto one of his ships. Hardly has the un-
wary princess gone aboard without her husband, when the treacherous
Lycomedes weighs anchor and, aided by his sister Thetis, who sends
him favorable winds, carries Alceste off to Scyros—the scheme has succeeded. But Lycomedes' two rivals pursue the abductor. Hercules and
Admetus reach Scyros, lay siege to the city, break down the gates, and
put everything to fire and sword while they sing:

> Donnons, donnons de toutes parts.
> Que chacun à l'envi combatte,
>   Que l'on abatte
> Les tours et les ramparts.
>
> Smite, smite, on all sides smite
> Let each of us vie in the fight,
>   We must overpower
> The ramparts and the towers.

Alceste is rescued and Lycomedes is probably killed, as we hear no more
about him. But Admetus is seriously wounded in the battle and will
succumb unless someone volunteers to die in his stead. The stage shows
a large structure with an *empty* altar, which is to bear a likeness of the
person who will be the victim[22]—the sacrifice for Admetus. No one
comes forward, so Alceste offers herself. The altar opens up, and we see
the likeness of Alceste, who stabs herself in the heart.[23] She is now
down in the darkling depths. Everyone grieves. Hercules, who was on
the point of leaving *to overthrow some tyrant or other,* changes his mind
and holds forth to Admetus in this strange speech:

> J'aime Alceste; il est temps de ne m'en plus défendre;
> Elle meurt; ton amour n'a plus rien à prétendre.
> Admète, cède-moi la beauté que tu perds;
> Au palais de Pluton j'entreprends de descendre;
>   J'irai jusqu'au fond des enfers
>   Forcer la mort à me la rendre.
>
> That I love Alceste, I can no longer deny;
> But your love has no claim on one who must die.

Admetus! Yield to me the beauty whom you lose;
To Pluto's palace I go, death to defy;
    To the ends of hell, no means I refuse
    To force death to let her be mine.

Admetus agrees to this odd bargain and answers:

Qu'elle vive pour vous avec tous ses appas
Admète est trop heureux pourvu qu'Alceste vive.

Let her then live for you with all her charms
Admetus will be happy if Alceste lives unharmed.

The great Alcides[24] arrives on the banks of the Styx. He finds Charon
beating back with great strokes of his oar the wretched Shades that have
no money to pay the ferry.

A Shade without the wherewithal: "Alas, Charon, alas!"

CHARON:

Crie hélas! tant que tu voudras!
Rien pour rien en tous lieux est une loi suivie;
    Les mains vides sont sans appas,
Et ce n'est point assez de payer dans la vie,
Il faut encor payer au-delà du trépas.

Cry alas as much as you like!
Nothing for nothing, the law is everywhere the same;
    'Tis not enough to pay during one's life,
Empty hands here can nothing obtain.
All must pay, even after they've passed away.

Hercules jumps into the ferry, which splits beneath his weight and lets
in water everywhere. He nonetheless reaches the other side. As he nears
Pluto's palace, Alecton[25] sounds the alarm. The furious Pluto shouts:

Qu'on arrête ce téméraire;
Armez-vous, amis, armez-vous
Qu'on déchaîne Cerbère,
Courez tous, courez tous.

Arrest this rash intruder
To arms, my friends, to arms.
Let loose Cerberus, set Cerberus free,
Run, one and all, run one and all.

Cerberus can be heard barking.
    But Proserpina [Pluto's wife] is moved by Alcides' love for Alceste and
persuades Pluto to hand her over to him.

> Il faut que l'amour extrême
>   Soit plus fort
>   Que la mort
>
> The power of so great a love
>   Must prove stronger
>   Than Death itself,

Alceste, once more in the land of the living, weeps upon learning that she has become the property of her liberator. Nor is Admetus very jolly. Hercules notices all this distress: "Vous détournez les yeux! Je vous trouve insensible!" (You turn your face away! I see you do not care!).

> ALCESTE:
> Je fais ce qui m'est possible
> Pour ne regarder que vous.
>
> I am doing what I can
> To look at none but you.

This is not exactly what Hercules wanted to hear, but after all, this demigod is a decent sort. Turning over Alceste to her husband, he masters his feelings and sings:

> Non, vous ne devez pas croire
> Qu'un vainqueur des tyrans soit tyran à son tour.
> Sur l'enfer, sur la mort j'emporte la victoire;
>   Il ne manque plus à ma gloire
>   Que de triompher de l'Amour.
>
> No, I don't want you to think
> That he who has defeated tyrants can sink
> To be tyrant, too. Both death and Hades conquered,
>   One thing only is missing from my glory;
>   To win, over love, this victory.

And that is why this curious opera is called *Alceste or the Triumph of Alcides.* There are many other characters in this lyric tragedy whom I have not mentioned—among them a fifteen-year-old minx, one of Alceste's maids-in-waiting, beloved of both Lycas and Straton, who are confidants of Hercules and Lycomedes. When her two suitors urge her to choose between them, she retails moral lessons of this order:

> Je n'ai point de choix à faire:
> Parlons d'aimer et de plaire,
> Et vivons toujours en paix.
> L'hymen détruit la tendresse
> Il rend l'amour sans attraits:

Voulez-vous aimez sans cesse?
Amants, n'épousez jamais.

I have no choice to make
Let us speak of love and pleasure
Let us live in peace forever.
Hymen destroys affection
Deprives love of its attraction:
Do you wish to love forever?
Then lovers, never marry, never.

Boileau[26] certainly made no mistake when he lambasted this versifying of pastry cooks and wigmakers:

Et tous ces lieux communs de morale lubrique
Que Lulli réchauffa des sons de sa musique.[27]

And all these platitudes of lewd morality
That Lully warmed up with the sounds of his music.

Only, he should have said, "which Lully chilled," for there is nothing so glacial, bloodless, dull, and poverty-stricken as this music, which is at once old-fashioned and childish.

That excellent singer, Alizard,[28] earned some success in several concerts by singing Charon's scene with the Shades. Its rhythm gives this piece a certain comic jollity that the audience applauded and laughed at, without knowing whether it was the words or the music that amused them. The vocal part is genuinely expressive and the words:

Il faut passer tôt ou tard,
Il faut passer dans ma barque,

You must come to me late or early,
You are bound to use my ferry,

could not be better suited to the half-grotesque character of Quinault's boatman.

If, nowadays, one wants to get a fair idea of Lully's musical style, one should go to the Théâtre Français and hear the music he wrote for Molière's comedies. His music for *Alceste* has the coloring, the mood, and all the features of that which he wrote for *Le Bourgeois Gentilhomme*.[29]

Lully had original ideas only infrequently, and he used for all genres the only procedures that he knew. It could not be otherwise for most musicians at a time when the art was in its infancy. Palestrina, for example, in a very different style, composed madrigals that resemble his masses, and many others composed masses that resemble their madrigals.

Many people think that the monotony of the works of early composers is due to the meagre resources at their disposal; people say: "The instruments in use today had not yet been invented." This argument is clearly mistaken. Palestrina wrote solely for voices, and the singers of his time were very likely capable of performing music other than his counterpoint in five or six parts. As for the instrumental players, though they were less proficient in Lully's time than in ours, a modern composer of talent could nevertheless use them to very good effect. Too much importance should not be attributed to the material means of performance. A Beethoven sonata played on a spinet would be no less a miracle of inspiration, whereas many other works that I could name would still be absurd platitudes even if played on the most magnificent Erard or Broadwood piano.[30]

The arts in their infancy do not know all the words of their language, and they are moreover kept from learning them by a swarm of prejudices which they are slow to shed. If a man endowed with true genius—that is, a grouping of faculties which unites creative power with common sense in its highest form, with power, intellect, courage, and a certain disdain for the crowd's opinion—appears in those early times, he will in spite of many obstacles cause a sudden leap forward in his art, even if he cannot liberate it completely by himself. Gluck was such a man, and we shall now look at his great work.[31]

We have seen what happened to Euripides' *Alceste* at the hands of Quinault, and the curious "poetry" that Lully "chilled with the sounds of his music."

In the course of time, there came a man who, unlike the Florentine composer [Lully], was not *equerry, councillor, secretary to the king, his household, the crown of France and its finances*,[32] who was not even the *superintendent of music* for some highness or other, but who had a powerful mind, a heart full of the love of beauty, and a bold, courageous spirit. That man was Gluck. He cast his eyes on Euripides' *Alceste* and chose it as the subject for an opera. His intention was to compose that opera in a radically new style that would set off a revolution in dramatic music. Gluck was then living in Vienna after a long stay in Italy. During this Italian sojourn, he had developed a deep disdain for the method of composition which then prevailed exclusively in the lyric theaters, and which was contrary to both common sense and the noblest instincts of the human heart. According to this method, an opera was mainly a pretext for showing off singers who came on stage *to play their larynx* as a virtuoso of the clarinet or oboe comes there to play his instrument in a concert.

He saw that music possesses a power far greater than that of tickling the ear with pleasant vocal pyrotechnics, and he wondered why this expressive power, which is unmistakable in melody, harmony, as well as in instrumentation, could not be made use of to produce works that are rational, moving, and worthy of the attention of a serious audience endowed with good taste. Without denying the sensory appeal, he wanted the claims of feeling acknowledged also. And without regarding poetry as the center of interest in opera, he thought that verse should be so combined with music that the expressive power of the resulting union would be incomparably greater than that of either art by itself. Living in Vienna at the time was an Italian poet with whom he frequently discussed his subject, who shared his views with warmth and conviction, who helped him plan his much-needed reform and soon became, as we shall see, his astute collaborator.

Still, one must not think that Gluck decided all of a sudden to make *Alceste* the vehicle that should bring expressive and dramatic music to the stage. *Orfeo*, which was composed earlier, tells us otherwise. He had been working up to this bold move for a long time, led to it by instinct. Already in his Italian scores[33]—written in Italy for Italians—he had dared to compose numbers in the most austere, expressive, and beautifully noble style. The proof of their merit is that he himself later found them worthy of inclusion in his most celebrated French scores. It is believed—wrongly—that they were composed for these new scenes, so carefully and adroitly have they been fitted in.

Telemaco's aria "Umbra mesta del padre" (My father's gloomy shade), in the Italian opera of that name,[34] was transformed into the now-famous duet in *Armide*, "Esprits de haine et de rage" (Spirits of hatred and fury). Other parts of this Italian score were also plundered for his French operas: one of Ulysses' arias serves as the introductory theme of the overture to *Iphigénie en Aulide;* a large section of another of Telemaco's arias reappears in Orestes' aria "Dieux qui me poursuivez" (O gods who pursue me) in *Iphigénie en Tauride;* the entire scene where Circe calls on the infernal spirits to change Ulysses' comrades into animals became that of the character Hatred in *Armide;* Circe's great aria was turned, by developing its orchestration a little, into the A-major aria "Je t'implore et je tremble"[35] (I beseech you and tremble) in the fourth act of *Iphigénie en Tauride;* and the overture itself, with the enrichment only of one episodic theme, came to introduce the opera *Armide*. One is inclined to regret that Gluck did not complete his pillage of *Telemaco* by reusing the enchanting aria of the nymph Asteria, "Ah! l'ho presente ognor"[36] (Ah, ever-present to my eyes), which is a marvel. The grief of love disdained that is expressed in this elegy has never since been clothed in such beautiful form by any other master, not even by Gluck himself, nor has its heartbreak been rendered with such melodic poignancy.

Finally, to conclude the list of borrowings he made from his Italian scores, and where I find clear evidence that Gluck wrote dramatic music long before he composed *Alceste*, let me add further: the immortal aria "O malheureuse Iphigénie" (O unhappy Iphigenia), in *Iphigénie en Tauride*, which was taken complete from his Italian opera *Tito;*[37] the charming chorus in the French *Alceste*, "Parez vos fronts de fleurs nouvelles"

(Adorn your brows with fresh flowers), and the final chorus of *Iphigénie en Tauride,* "Les dieux longtemps en courroux" (The gods long outraged), the last two from the score of *Elena e Paride.*[38]

Once the subject of *Alceste* was chosen, Calzabigi set to work. He was then court poet to Maria Theresa, and he understood Gluck's genius and intentions. He prudently set aside what today we would call faults in the Greek poem and brought out some new dramatic situations which, everyone will agree, could not be more suitable for the development of an opera. He left out only the character of Hercules—a serious mistake, I think, for he could have been put to good use. In Calzabigi's poem, the action begins with the Thessalians gathered in front of Phérès's palace, waiting for news of Admetus, who is seriously ill. A herald announces to the appalled multitude that the king is at death's door. The queen appears with her children and invites the people to come with her to Apollo's temple and pray to the god for Admetus' life.

The scene changes, and a religious ceremony takes place at the temple. The priest consults the sacrificial entrails and, awestruck, announces that the god is about to speak. All bow down, and in the solemn silence, the oracle utters these words: "Il re morrà s'altro per lui non more."

> Le roi doit mourir aujourd'hui
> Si quelque autre au trépas ne se livre pour lui.

> Today the king shall die
> If none will die for him.

The priest asks the horrified crowd, "Who among you will offer himself in sacrifice? No one? Then your king shall die!" The people disperse in confusion, leaving the unhappy queen half-fainting at the foot of the altar. But Admetus is not going to die. In a sublime gesture of heroic love, Alceste goes up to the statue of Apollo and solemnly swears to give her life for her husband. The priest returns and tells Alceste that her sacrifice has been accepted, and that the emissaries of the god of the dead will await her at nightfall by the gates of Hell. This first act is full of action and arouses intense emotions.

In the second act we find the whole city of Phères in ecstatic celebration. Admetus has been restored to health, and we see him joyfully accepting the congratulations of his friends. But Alceste does not appear, and this makes the king anxious. She has gone to the temple, he is told, to thank the gods for restoring her husband. Alceste returns, and although she tries to join in the public rejoicing, she cannot hold back painful sobs. Admetus begs her, at first, then orders her to tell him why she is weeping. The unhappy woman confesses the truth. The king is in despair. Refusing to accept this dreadful sacrifice, he swears that if Alceste persists in her vow, he too will die.

The hour draws near. Alceste has escaped from the king's watchful eye and has reached the gateway to Tartarus. "What do you want?" shout invisible voices. "It is not yet time; wait for night to take the place of day; it will not be long." These strange and lugubrious cries and the dim glimmering lights that come from the pit make Alceste feel she is losing her mind. Desperate and half-mad with horror, she staggers about the altar of death, yet she does not falter in her purpose. Admetus runs to her and redoubles his pleas to thwart it. The hour strikes while they dispute in this heart-rending way; an infernal deity springs out of the abyss, swoops down onto the altar of Death, and summons the queen to keep her promise.

From the banks of the Styx, the grim boatman Charon calls Alceste, blowing his conch shell three times with hoarse and hollow sounds. Yet the god of Hell allows Alceste one more chance to give up her dreadful resolve. He can release her from her vow; but if she accepts, Admetus dies on the instant. "Let him live!" she cries, "and show me the path to the infernal regions!" At once a horde of demons seizes the queen and, ignoring Admetus' shouts, drags her down to Tartarus.

In Calzabigi's play it is Apollo, appearing soon afterward in a cloud, who returns Alceste alive to her husband. This ending was at first retained in the French version; but a few years after the first performance, Marie-François du Rollet, who had translated *Alceste* from the Italian, decided to introduce Hercules abruptly into the action, and so it is he who now descends into Hell and brings back Alceste. Apollo still appears, but only to congratulate the hero for his brave deed and to tell him he now has a place in the ranks of the gods.

As we can see, Calzabigi adapted his play to modern tastes and mores: there is a plot, there is action, and there are the requisite surprises. Admetus, far from accepting the queen's sacrifice, falls into despair when he hears of it. The temple scene, which is not—and could not be—in Euripides, is striking and majestic. Alceste is well drawn as a woman who has a noble though not a fearless heart; she quails at carrying out a vow that she nevertheless fulfils. The public celebration when the king is restored to health provides a most dramatic contrast with the grief of the queen, who has to be present but cannot restrain her tears.

But despite what Gluck says in his letter of dedication to Archduke Leopold, the Grand Duke of Tuscany, there is not much variety in the libretto of *Alceste*.[39] The opera public is bound to grow weary of the scenes expressing pain, horror, and despair that follow one another virtually without interruption. This is the cause of the criticisms leveled against Gluck's music in Paris and Vienna, though these criticisms are deserved only by the libretto. In the score itself, on the contrary, one can hardly admire enough the wealth of ideas, the unflagging inspiration, the expressive vehemence with which Gluck succeeds as far as was possible in overcoming that regrettable monotony.

Over twenty years ago,[40] I discussed in some detail Gluck's credo and his exposition of it in the dedication that prefaces his Italian *Alceste*. I venture to return to it now, in order to add a few comments. Gluck says:

> When I undertook to set *Alceste* to music, I proposed to avoid all the excesses which the misguided vanity of singers and the excessive deference of composers had introduced into Italian opera and which turned the most splendid and beautiful of spectacles into the most ridiculous and wearisome. I tried to reduce music to its true role: that of seconding poetry so as to enhance the expression of feeling and the drama of the situations without interrupting or damping the action with useless ornamentation. I believed that music should add to poetry that which is added to a well-composed drawing by vivid colors and the felicitous harmony of light and shade, in such a way that the figures are brought to life without changing their contours.
>
> I took good care not to interrupt an actor in the heat of dialogue and hold him back till the end of a *ritornello;* nor did I have him stop his utterance on a suitable vowel, whether to show off at great length the agility of his fine voice, or to let the orchestra give him time to catch his breath before launching into a cadenza. I did not think that I should rush through the second part of an aria, when in fact it might be the more impassioned and important, or conclude the aria when its meaning is not concluded, so as to give the singer an opportunity to show how well he can make every kind of capricious variation. In short, I tried to eliminate all the abuses against which common sense and reason have long protested in vain.
>
> I thought that the overture should give the audience a foretaste of the type of action that would unfold before their eyes, and indicate its subject. I believed that the instrumentation should be kept in proportion to the degree of excitement and passion, and that one should avoid too sharp a contrast between aria and recitative, as well as any contradiction between the end of the musical phrase and the meaning of the words. For this can interrupt the forward motion and emotional pitch of the scene. I also considered it my primary goal to seek a noble simplicity and to refrain from technical displays that undermine clarity. I put no value on novelty, unless it flowed naturally from the situation and was expressive. Finally, there was no rule that I did not deem worth sacrificing for the sake of a desired effect.

This confession of faith seems by and large wonderfully rational and frank. Its fundamental doctrine, which for some years now has been so absurdly, so monstrously misapplied, nonetheless rests on solid reasoning and a deep feeling for true dramatic music. Aside from a few points that I shall discuss below, Gluck's principles are so excellent that they have been followed in the main by most great composers in every country. In promoting his theory, however—a theory that to anyone with the least feeling for art or even with simple common sense must have seemed called for in Gluck's day—did he not at times exaggerate its implications? On impartial examination one can hardly fail to see that he did. He himself did not apply it rigorously in his works. Thus, in the Italian *Alceste,* we find recitatives that are accompanied only by a figured bass, probably chords played on the *cembalo* [harpsichord], as was customary in Italian theaters. This sort of accompaniment to a vocal recitation results in a *sharp contrast* between aria and recitative.

Several of his arias are introduced by a fairly long instrumental solo. At such times, the singer must keep silent and *wait for the end of the ritornello.* Moreover, Gluck often uses a type of aria that his theory of dramatic music should have proscribed; I mean arias with repeats, in which each section is sung twice without any motive for the repetition—quite as if the audience had shouted "encore." Such is Alceste's aria:

> Je n'ai jamais chéri la vie
> Que pour te prouver mon amour;
> Ah! pour te conserver le jour,
> Qu'elle me soit cent fois ravie!

> I never treasured life,
> Save to prove my love for you
> Oh, to preserve your days
> I'd lose my own a hundred times!

Why, when the melody comes to a cadence on the dominant, does he begin again with "Je n'ai jamais chéri la vie," without making the slightest change in the vocal part or in the orchestration?

This kind of repetition is certainly shocking to the dramatic sense, and if ever there was a composer who should have refrained from committing this fault, which is contrary to nature and truth, it was Gluck. Yet he committed it in virtually all his works. No instances of it will be found in later music; composers after Gluck were more demanding, at least in this respect.

When Gluck says that in an opera the sole purpose of music is to add to poetry what color adds to drawing, I believe he is altogether wrong. It seems to me that an opera composer's task is far more important. His work contains both line and color, and, to continue Gluck's analogy, the words form the *subject* of the painting, hardly more than that. Nor is expressiveness the sole aim of dramatic music. It would be misguided as well as pedantic to scorn the purely sensuous pleasure that is found in certain effects of melody, harmony, rhythm, and orchestration, quite independently of the way they depict the sentiments and passions in the drama. What is more, even if one should want to deprive the hearer of this source of enjoyment and not allow him to revive his interest by a diversion from the main concern, there would still be a great many occasions when the composer alone has to sustain the interest of an operatic work. For example, in dances, pantomimes, marches—wherever, in short, instrumental music claims attention and there are no words, what does the poet contribute? Here music by itself must necessarily supply both line and color.

Apart from some of those brilliant sonatas for orchestra in which Rossini so gracefully displayed his genius, most of the instrumental potpourris of thirty years ago that the Italians honor with the name of overture were grotesquely devoid of sense. But how much more comical must such things have been a hundred years ago, when we see that Gluck himself, impelled by bad example, did not scruple to write the incredible inanity called "Overture to Orfeo"! He did better in the overture to *Alceste* and still better for *Iphigénie en Aulide*. It must be acknowledged that Gluck was not nearly so great a musician, in the strict sense of the term, as he was a composer for the stage. His theory of expressive overtures spurred later composers to produce overtures that are symphonic masterpieces—works which, despite the fall from favor or the deep oblivion that has overtaken the operas themselves, still stand on their own, like magnificent peristyles of temples fallen in ruins.

But here again, by exaggerating a good idea, Gluck left truth behind—this time not through limiting the power of music but through attributing to it a power it can never possess. He says that the overture should "indicate the subject" of the drama. The expressiveness of music cannot go that far. It can indeed reflect joy, grief, solemnity, and playfulness. It can express the marked difference between the joy of a pastoral people and that of a warrior nation, between the grief of a queen and the sorrows of a simple village girl, between calm, sober meditation and the ardent reverie that precedes an outburst of passion. By drawing upon the musical styles characteristic of various nations, music can suggest the difference between the serenade of a brigand of the Abruzzi[41] and that of a Tyrolean or Scottish huntsman, between a nocturnal march of pilgrims given to mystical reflection and that of a band of cattle dealers returning from market.[42] It can contrast the extremes of brutishness, vulgarity, and grotesqueness with angelic purity, the noble mind, and the candid soul. But if it wishes to go beyond this broad domain, music must of necessity resort to words, whether sung, recited, or simply read, to fill the gap left by its expressive powers in works that aim simultaneously at the mind and the imagination.

Thus, the overture to *Alceste* may foreshadow scenes of sorrow and of love, but it can indicate neither the object of this love nor the cause of this sorrow. It can never inform the listener that Alceste's husband is king of Thessaly and condemned by the gods to die unless someone undertakes to die for him. And that is the *subject* of the drama.

Readers may be surprised to find the present writer expounding such principles, because some people believe, or pretend to believe, that in his conception of the expressive power of music he has gone as far beyond the truth as they themselves have fallen short of it. They have consequently ascribed to his views—most generously—the absurdity that was theirs. This said in passing and bearing no grudge.

The third tenet in Gluck's theory that I take the liberty of challenging is his professing to attach no importance to the *discovery of novelty.* Already by his time, composers had blotted many a sheet of music paper, and any musical discovery, however remotely linked to dramatic expression, was not to be despised. As to the rest of Gluck's maxims, they cannot, I think, be disputed with any hope of success, even the last, which proclaims his indifference to the rules, an indifference that many professors will find blasphemous and heretical. Even though as I have said, Gluck was not strictly speaking a musician of the caliber of some of his successors, he was nonetheless enough of one to have earned the right to answer his critics in the way that Beethoven once dared to: "Who is it that forbids this harmony? Fux,[43] Albrechtsberger,[44] and a dozen other theorists? Well, I allow it."[45] Or to repeat the terse reply of one of our greatest poets[46] when he was reading his play to the committee at the Théâtre Français, and one of the members of this high court ventured to interrupt him:

"What is it, sir?" asked the poet with icy calm.

"Well, it seems to me . . . I think . . ."

"What?"

"That expression is not good French."

"It will be, sir, it will be."

Such proud self-confidence befits the musician even better than the poet, for the musician is more justified in believing that his innovations will come to be accepted, his language not being a language of convention.[47]

These, then, were Gluck's principles of dramatic music. *Alceste* certainly, and especially the French version, is one of the most splendid examples of his theory put into practice. During the years between the composition of this work in Vienna and its performance in Paris, the composer's genius seems to have grown and gathered strength. The opposition he encountered among the Italians seems to have redoubled his powers and given his mind deeper penetration. Hence the wonderful transformation of the Italian *Alceste.* Several numbers, it is true, were kept intact in the French version. They are so fine that it is hard to see what changes the composer could have made. But many others (with a single exception that I shall mention) were notably improved when adapted to our language and performed on our stage. The melodic curve became broader and clearer, certain accents became subtler, the instrumentation was enriched while also growing more inventive; besides which, several new numbers—arias, choruses, and recitatives—were added to a score whose composer seems to have kneaded the musical matter like a sculptor molding clay for his statue.

In rereading what I wrote earlier about the music of *Alceste,* I find in it criticisms that no longer seem to me just. I had of course been vivdly struck by all the beauties it contains, and I certainly shall never forget the impression it made upon me at the dress rehearsal I attended in 1825, when Mme Branchu returned in the leading role.[48] But at that time I had conceived so violent a passion for the work that I became anxious not to fall into blind fanaticism, and I tried to avoid it by raising objections to several things that in truth I admired. Today I no longer have any such fear; I am sure that my admiration is not at all blind, and I do not want to weaken its expression by misguided scruples.

The overture, though not particularly rich in ideas, contains many touching accents of pathos. A dark coloring prevails; the orchestration shows neither the brilliance nor the forcefulness of the instrumental compositions of our time, yet it is fuller and stronger than Gluck's other overtures. Trombones are scored from the beginning; only trumpets and timpani are left out. A propos of this omission, I might point out a peculiarity that has few parallels: there is not a single note for either trumpet or timpani in the entire opera, except for the two trumpets onstage ushering in the herald who is about to address the people.

Let me add, in order to correct certain fairly widespread misconceptions, that in this score Gluck used clarinets, bassoons, horns, and trombones, as well as flutes and oboes. In several places in the Italian *Alceste* he also relied on English horns.[49] But as these instruments were unknown in France when he arrived there, he very adroitly substituted clarinets. Nor are there any piccolos in the work; he excluded everything shrill, piercing, or harsh, so as to confine the sound to what is gentle or majestic.

The overture to *Alceste,* like those of *Iphigénie en Aulide, Don Giovanni,* and *Démophon,*[50] does not end before the curtain goes up. It is linked to the first number by a harmonic progression by means of which a suspended cadence never comes to a close. In spite of its use by Gluck, Mozart, and Vogel,[51] I fail to see the advantage of this incomplete form of overture. True, it binds the opening music more to the action, but the listener, disappointed at being deprived of an ending to the instrumental preface, feels a moment of discomfort which is damaging to what precedes without benefiting what follows. The opera gains little by it, and the overture loses much.

As the curtain rises, the chorus enters (on a chord that interrupts the harmonic cadence in the orchestra) with the words: "Dieux, rendez-nous notre roi, notre père!" (O gods, give us back our king, our father!). This exclamation in the very first measure calls for a comment applicable to the vocal texture of all Gluck's other choruses. As is well known, the natural classification of human voices is soprano and contralto for women, tenor and bass for men. Women sing an octave above the men and in the same proportional relation among themselves, the contralto's range being a fifth below that of the soprano, just as the bass is a fifth below the tenor. As recently as thirty years ago, it was believed at the Opéra that France did not produce contraltos. As a result, there were only sopranos on the female side of French choruses, the contralto part being taken by a shrill, strained, and rather uncommon voice called *haute-contre*,[52] which is nothing but a very high tenor.

On arriving in Paris, Gluck had to abandon the excellent scoring for chorus used in Italy and Germany and conform to French usage. He disarranged the contralto part and adapted it for *haute-contre*. Sixty years later, it was discovered that nature produces contraltos in France just as elsewhere. As a result, there are now many of these low female voices at the Opéra and very few *haute-contres*. Quite rightly, therefore, the natural vocal order that Gluck followed in his Italian score has now been restored almost everywhere in *Alceste*. I say *almost* everywhere, because it cannot be carried out completely; Gluck has choruses for male voices exclusively, in which the alto part must necessarily stay with the high tenors.

The chorus "O dieux, qu'allons nous devenir?" (O gods, what shall become of us?), which follows the herald's proclamation, is full of a noble sadness whose grave mood brings out forcibly the agitation of the following *stretta*, "Non, jamais le courroux céleste" (No, never shall the divine wrath). The principal melodic lines of this *stretta* are as fittingly rhetorical and as truly accented as one finds in the most skillful recitative. The same is true of the chorus-with-dialogue, "O malheureux Admète" (O unhappy Admetus), whose last phrase, "malheureuse patrie" (unhappy homeland) is poignantly expressive.

As Alceste enters, the whole soul of the young queen is revealed in just a few measures of recitative. The fine aria "Grands dieux, du destin qui m'accable [suspende la rigueur]" (Great gods, [withhold the rigor] of the fate which overwhelms me) is in three movements: a slow movement in four-four time, another in three-four time, and an agitated *Allegro*. It is in this *agitato* that one finds the lovely orchestral phrase, taken up again by the voice, "Quand je vous presse sur mon sein" (When I clasp you to my bosom). A musician once remarked on hearing it: "It is the *heart of the orchestra* that palpitates!" This aria presents difficulties that most singers do not suspect—difficulties of diction, of phrasing and melodic continuity, and of artful control of the dynamics up to the final climax.

The third scene opens in the temple of Apollo. The high priest enters with the celebrants of the sacrifice carrying flaming tripods and their instruments for the ordeal. Alceste follows, leading her children; then come the courtiers and the people. Here Gluck uses local color if anything ever deserved the name. It is ancient Greece that he reveals to us in all its majestic and splendid simplicity. Listen to the instrumental music on which the procession enters; listen (if you do not have a pitiless chatterbox sitting next to you) to this gentle melody—soft, veiled, calm, resigned—this pure harmony, this rhythm, barely perceptible in the basses, whose sinuous line seems to hide beneath the orchestra like the feet of the priestesses beneath their white robes. Let your ear follow the unusual sound of the flutes in their low register and the interlacing of the two violin parts making a dialogue of the melody, and then say if there is anything in music more beautiful, in the ancient sense of the word, than this religious march. The orchestration is simple, but exquisite; it is scored only for strings and two wind instruments. This passage, like so many others in his works, reveals the composer's instinct; he finds exactly the tone colors that he needs. Use oboes instead of flutes and you ruin everything.

The ceremony begins with a prayer whose first words, solemnly uttered by the high priest alone, "Dieu puissant, écarte du trône . . . " (Great god, avert from the throne . . .) are cut into by three broad C chords *mezza-voce*, which the brasses turn into a swelling *fortissimo*. Nothing is more impressive than this dialogue between the voice of the priest and this ceremonial band of "sacred trumpets." After a brief pause, the chorus takes up the same words in a rather lively 6/8 tempo, whose strange form and melody create surprise. One naturally expects a prayer to be slow and in any meter other than 6/8. Why does this chorus, without losing any of its solemnity or its tragic disquiet, display at the same time such brilliant orchestration and strongly marked rhythms? I strongly suspect that Gluck was aware of the ritual leaping and dancing that are said to have been part of certain religious ceremonies in antiquity, and he wanted to give his music characteristics in keeping with this supposed custom. The impression made by this chorus in performance seems to prove that, despite the ignorance of even our best choreographers about ancient sacrificial rites, the composer's poetic instincts did not mislead him.

The high priest's recitative, "Apollon est sensible à nos gémissements" (Apollo is moved by our plaints), is clearly the most ingenious and striking application of the composer's principle of proportioning the number of instruments to the "degree of excitement and passion." Here the strings begin alone, in unison, their theme growing in vigor throughout the scene. At the prophetic ecstasy of the priest, "Tout m'annonce du dieu la présence suprême" (Everything declares the supreme presence of the god), the second violins and violas begin a *tremolando* in arpeggios. If properly bowed hard near the bridge, it produces a sonority resembling that of a waterfall, broken now and again by the crash of single notes from the basses and first violins. One after the other, the flutes, oboes, and clarinets enter in the pauses between the outbursts of the inspired priest; horns and trombones are still silent. But on the words,

Le saint trépied s'agite,
Tout se remplit d'un juste effroi!

The holy tripod stirs
All are filled with a righteous fear!

the brasses let loose their volley so long held back; the flutes and oboes utter their feminine cries; the violins redouble their shuddering; and the terrifying tread of the basses shakes the entire orchestra. "Il va parler" (He [the god] is going to speak!). Then a sudden silence:

Saisi de crainte et de respect,
Peuple, observe un profond silence.
Reine, dépose à son aspect
Le vain orgueil de la puissance!
  Tremble! . . .

Possessed by fear and reverence,
People, maintain a deep silence.
Queen, give up before his presence
The vain pride of power!
  Tremble! . . .

This last word, uttered on a single sustained note as the priest casts a distraught glance on Alceste and directs her to the altar where she should rest her royal brow, crowns this extraordinary scene in a sublime manner. It is magnificent, the music of a giant, music of a kind whose possibility no one had ever suspected before Gluck.

After a long pause—whose duration the composer fixed with a precision unusual for him by marking a rest of two and a half measures for both voices and instruments—one hears the voice of the oracle:

Le roi doit mourir aujourd'hui,
Si quelque autre au trépas ne se livre pour lui.

Today the king shall die,
If none will die for him.

Both this declamation, given out almost entirely on a single note, and the dark chords of the accompanying trombones were imitated, or rather copied, by Mozart in *Don Giovanni* in the few words uttered in the cemetery by the statue of the Commendatore.[53]

The whispered chorus that follows is in the grand style; it marks the bewilderment and dismay of a people whose love of their king does not go so far as to sacrifice themselves for him. The composer deleted from his French version a second choral ensemble which, in the Italian *Alceste*, stood behind the scenes murmuring "Fuggiamo, fuggiamo!" (Let us flee, let us flee!), while the first chorus, aghast, repeated with no thought of flight, "Che annunzio funesto! (What a fateful prophecy!).

Instead of this second chorus, Gluck now has the high priest speak in a completely natural and dramatic manner, a propos of which let me point out an important tradition. Failure to follow it weakens the peroration of this wonderful scene. At the end of the *Largo* in triple time, which comes before the agitated coda, "Fuyons, nul espoir ne nous reste!" (Let us flee, there is no hope for us), the score has the high priest intone the words "Votre roi va mourir!" (Your king is about to die!) on the notes C, C, D, D, D, F in the middle register and sounding with the penultimate chord of the chorus. In performance, however, the high priest waits for the chorus to fall silent, and in the middle of this deathly stillness, he utters his "Votre roi doit mourir!" an octave higher. It is a cry of alarm signaling the horrified people to take flight. This change, it is said, was made at rehearsals by Gluck himself, who then neglected to have it noted in his score.

Everyone then scatters in confusion to a wonderfully terse chorus and leaves Alceste fainting at the foot of the altar.

Jean-Jacques Rousseau criticized this *Allegro agitato* because the confusion it expresses could just as well be of joy as of terror.[54] One might reply that the composer found himself at the edge or at the dividing line between the two emotions, and that it was thus almost impossible to avoid incurring such a reproach. Obviously, when a crowd is rushing about and shouting, a distant observer cannot know, unless he has been told, whether the mob is excited by fear or by joy. The composer can indeed write a chorus whose joyful mood is unmistakable, but the converse does not hold. When translated into music, the excitement of a crowd, unless provoked by hatred or vengeance, will always come close, at least in tempo and rhythm, to the expression of riotous joy.

A more valid objection could be raised against this chorus by invoking the needs of staging: it is too short, and its terseness also lessens the musical effect; for during a mere eighteen measures the chorus cannot easily exit without curtailing the end of the number.

The queen, left alone in the temple, expresses her anguish in one of those recitatives that Gluck alone knew how to compose. Her monologue, already very fine in Italian, is sublime in French; it is as wonderful as the most superb aria; I do not think one can find anything comparable, for truth and force of expression, to the music of the following words:

> Il n'est plus pour moi d'espérance!
> Tout fuit . . . tout m'abandonne à mon funeste sort;
> De l'amitié, de la reconnaissance
> J'espérerais en vain un si pénible effort.
> Ah! l'amour seul en est capable!

Cher époux, tu vivras; tu me devras le jour;
Ce jour dont te privait la Parque impitoyable
Te sera rendu par l'amour.

There is no more hope for me
They all have fled . . . they leave me to my fatal destiny;
From friendship, from gratitude
It would be vain to hope for such fortitude.
Ah! only love is capable of such a sacrifice!
Dear husband, you shall live, to me you shall owe your life;
That life the pitiless Fates would take away
My love shall give you back.

At the fifth line, the orchestra begins a crescendo, the musical image
of that noble idea of sacrifice which has now begun to grip the soul of
Alceste; it excites, it inflames her, and she rises to a state of rapture and
pride, "Ah! l'amour seul en est capable!" (Ah! love alone is capable of
such a sacrifice!). After this, the vocal line rushes forward with so much
passion that the orchestra seems to give up trying to follow it; it stops,
panting, and does not reappear until the end, when it blossoms out on
the last line with chords full of tenderness. All this belongs solely to
the French version, as does the following aria, "Non, ce n'est point un
sacrifice!" (No, it is not a sacrifice!).

In this number, which is at once an aria and a recitative, the conductor and the singer must have an intimate knowledge of the Gluck tradition and style if they are to do justice to the music. The frequent
changes of tempo are difficult to foresee, and some are not even marked
in the score. Thus, after the last marked pause, when Alceste says, "Mes
chers fils, je ne vous verrai plus!" (My dear sons, I shall not see you
again!), the tempo must slow down by rather more than half, so as to
make the quarter notes equal in value to the dotted half notes of the
preceding section. Another passage, the most striking one, can lose all
meaning if the tempo is not handled with extreme care; it comes at the
second appearance of the theme:

Non, ce n'est point un sacrifice!
Eh! pourrai-je vivre sans toi,
Sans toi, cher Admète?

No, it is not a sacrifice!
How could I live without you,
Without you, dear Admetus?

At this repetition, just as she ends the phrase, Alceste is struck by a
chilling thought and stops short on "Sans toi." A memory wrenches her
maternal heart and cuts across the heroic impulse that was bearing her

toward death. Two oboes raise their plaintive voices in the brief silence left by the sudden interruption of the voice and the orchestra. Then Alceste sings, "O mes enfants! O regrets superflus!" (O my children! O vain regrets!). She thinks of her sons, imagines she can hear them, and, distracted, looks about for them. Beside herself and trembling, she answers the fitful lament of the orchestra with mad and convulsive lamentations of her own, wrung as much from delirium as from grief. It is extraordinarily moving to see the unhappy mother resist these dear imagined voices and repeat for one last time with unshakable resolve, "Non, ce n'est point un sacrifice!" Truly, when dramatic music attains such poetic heights, one has to pity the performers charged with interpreting the composer's thought. Talent is barely enough for this overwhelming task; it needs something akin to genius.[55]

The vigorous and imposing recitative "Arbitres du sort des humains" (Masters of human fate), in which Alceste, kneeling before Apollo's statue, makes her awesome vow, was not in the Italian score (nor was the preceding aria). The instrumentation of this recitative is peculiar in that the voice is almost continuously accompanied in unison and octaves by six wind instruments (two oboes, two clarinets, and two horns) above a *tremoto* by all the strings. This word *tremoto*[56] (trembling) in Gluck's scores does not indicate the orchestral quivering called *tremolo,* which he often used elsewhere and which is an extremely rapid repetition of a single note by many short and quick strokes of the bow. Here it is only a matter of the finger of the left hand trembling while it presses the string; it thereby gives the sound a sort of undulation. Gluck marks it by the sign 〜〜〜〜〜 above the held notes and sometimes also by the word *appoggiato* (pressing). There is yet another kind of trembling that he uses to extremely dramatic effect in recitatives. He marks it by means of dots above a held note with a slur over the dots: ⌒......... This symbol means that the strings should repeat the same note, not fast, but in an irregular way. Some play four notes to the measure, others eight, still others five, or six, or seven, thus producing a variety of different rhythms whose incoherent blurring affects the whole orchestra and imbues the accompaniment with a vague trepidation suited to many situations.

In the recitative just mentioned, an effect of incomparable grandeur is created by this mode of orchestration by *tremoto appoggiato,* together with the solemn sound of the wind instruments that follow the voice, and the imposing bass line descending diatonically during rests in the vocal part.

Note also the unusual series of modulations that connect the two great arias that Alceste sings at the close of the first act. The first is in D major; the recitative that follows, which I have just discussed, also begins in D but ends in C-sharp minor. The high priest, who returns to announce that Alceste's vow has been accepted, does so in a *ritornello* in C-sharp minor which leads into an aria in E-flat, and the queen's last aria is in B-flat.

The priest's number, "Déjà la mort s'apprête" (Already death waits in readiness), is in two movements, the second of which sounds almost menacing. It is based on Ismène's aria "Parto ma senti" (I leave but listen) from the Italian *Alceste*, but enlarged and transfigured by the composer's utmost skill when he changed it to fit the new lyrics. In the French version, the *Andante* is shorter, the *Allegro* longer, and a rather interesting bassoon part has been added to the orchestra. Otherwise, the original idea has been kept almost throughout. Once again I must point out a very important nuance which is missing in the engraved French score as well as in the Opéra manuscript, but which was marked with the greatest care in the Italian score. The second violins, which accompany the entire *Allegro* with their *ostinato*, should play the first half of each measure *forte* and the second *piano*. Despite the oversight of copyists and engravers, it is clear that this double nuance is too striking to be ignored, as it is at the Opéra, where I have heard the entire passage played *mezzo-forte* from beginning to end.

It is probably another of those editing mistakes that Gluck put right at rehearsals, but since the corrections were not marked in the parts or in the score, later performers could not help being misled when the *maître-soleil* had long since departed.

I have now reached the aria "Divinités du Styx." Alceste is alone again; the high priest has left her, saying that the ministers of the god of the dead will be waiting for her by the gates of Tartarus at nightfall. All is over. She has barely a few hours left. But now the frail woman, the trembling mother, is replaced by a being whom the frenzy of love has filled with supernatural strength, a being who feels that from now on she will be above fear and able to knock without blanching at the gates of Hell.

In this paroxysm of heroic fervor, Alceste apostrophizes the gods of the Underworld, to taunt them. A hoarse and terrifying voice answers, the exultant shouts of the infernal hordes and the dreadful fanfare of the cataracts of Tartarus resound for the first time in the ears of the beautiful young queen who is about to die. Her courage is not shaken; on the contrary, with redoubled energy she upbraids these greedy gods whose threats she scorns and whose pity she disdains. She does falter for a moment, but then recovers her nerve, and her words rush on: "Je sens une force nouvelle" (I feel new strength). Her voice rises gradually and grows more passionate: "Mon coeur est animé du plus noble transport" (My heart is stirred by the noblest emotion). After a brief pause, she again takes up her challenge. Deaf to the barking of Cerberus and the threatening voices of the shades, she repeats "Je n'invoquerai point votre pitié cruelle" (I shall not appeal to your cruel pity) in such tones that the unearthly sounds from the abyss fade away, vanquished by this last outburst of frenzy mingled with anguish and horror.

This prodigious scene, in my opinion, is the most complete proof of Gluck's various powers, which perhaps were never again to be combined to the same degree in the composer: an enthralling inspiration; superior reasoning; grandeur of style; a wealth of ideas; a thorough knowledge of the art of "dramatizing" the orchestra; deeply moving melodies; an expressiveness that is always natural, exact, and picturesque; a gift for fashioning a seeming disorder which is only a more masterly order; simplicity of harmony; clarity of line; and, above all, a tremendous strength, which must awe any imagination capable of appreciating it.

This monumental aria, this *climax* to the tremendous crescendo, for which the entire second half of the first act has been preparing, never fails to transport the listeners when it is well performed; it inspires feelings that it would be futile to try to describe. To achieve a fully adequate performance, Alceste's part must be given to a great actress who also has a powerful voice with a certain agility, not in vocalizing, but in the production of sounds. She must be able to sing *swiftly*, that is, not take time to "settle" every note. Lacking this ability, the episodic *prestissimo*, "Je sens une force nouvelle," is more or less lost. Notice the liberty that Gluck takes in this passage, as in many others, to flout squareness and even symmetry. The *prestissimo* is made up of five phrases of five measures each, coupled with four additional measures. This irregularity, far from shocking the listener, first arrests his attention and then thrills him.

Again, to do justice to this aria, the singer must also choose her tempo shrewdly at the outset so as to express a kind of dark majesty, and then change it delicately to suit the final, touching melody,

> Mourir pour ce qu'on aime est un trop doux effort,
> Une vertu si naturelle!
>
> To die for the beloved is so sweet a task
> So natural a virtue!

where each measure draws blood and tears.

In addition, the orchestra must absolutely be as inspired as the singer, so that its *fortes* terrify and its *pianos* sound now threatening and now melting. The brass instruments must give their first two notes a thunderous sound by first attacking them energetically and then sustaining them without flinching throughout the whole measure. In this way, a result is achieved of a kind that up to now the art of music has rarely afforded.

Now, can one conceive that Gluck, in order to conform to the demands of French prosody or the incompetence of his translator, agreed to spoil, indeed ruin, the marvelous structure of the beginning of this incomparable aria, the remainder of which he adapted so expertly? Yet that is exactly what happened. The first line of the Italian text goes as follows: "Ombre, larve, compagne di morte"[57] (Shades, phantoms, companions of death).

The first word of the aria, "ombre," is sung on two long notes, the first of which can and must swell in volume, so as to give the voice time to gain strength and also to make more conspicuous the reply of the infernal gods, which is given by the horns and trombones; the voice stops at the moment the instrumental clamor erupts. The same applies to the two notes written a third higher for the second word, "larve." But instead of turning the two Italian words into French by simply adding an s, we find "Divinités du Styx." Now, instead of a short phrase extremely well suited to the voice and a complete meaning enclosed within one measure, we have five pointless repetitions of the same note on the five syllables di-vi-ni-tés du, the word "Styx" coming in the next measure just as the winds enter, and being drowned out by the orchestral *fortissimo*. Since the meaning is incomplete in the measure where the singer can be heard, the orchestra seems to come in too soon and to give an answer to an unfinished question. What is more, to omit the Italian phrase "compagne di morte," which is so well suited to the voice, and to replace it in the French version with a rest, leaves an unaccountable gap in the vocal part. The composer's splendid conception could be restored in full if, instead of the words I have singled out, the following were inserted: "Ombres, larves, pâles compagnes de la mort!" (Shades, phantoms, pale companions of death!).

The translator-poet possibly was bothered by the form of this quasi-verse, and so, rather than violate the metrical rule, he mutilated, disfigured, and destroyed one of the most stunning inspirations of dramatic music. M. du Rollet's lines must of course take precedence! Mme Viardot, being on this occasion a compromiser, and not daring to omit the words "Divinités du Styx," which have become famous and which all music lovers expect to hear in this aria, keeps one part of M. du Rollet's mutilation, but reinstates the second phrase of the Italian aria with the words "Pâles compagnes de la mort." That is something at least.

What a proud pleasure must the singer feel in her heart when, as she begins to sing this aria, sure of herself and seeing at her feet an audience quivering with expectation, she feels lifted on the wings of the genius she is interpreting! It must be something like the joy an eagle feels when leaving its mountain peak to soar freely in space!

In all his scores, but especially in *Iphigénie en Tauride*, Gluck often resorted to accompanying his recitatives with a series of four-part chords sustained without a break by all the stringed instruments. This static harmony gives inattentive listeners—and there are a great many of them—

an irresistible feeling of numbness and torpor that finally makes them sink into somnolence. They become impervious to the most original means the composer uses to move them. It would indeed be hard to find anything more repellent to French ears than this slow, persistent humming. No wonder that many of them find Gluck's works as boring as they are admirable. What is surprising is that a genius should so underestimate the importance of details as to use a technique that a moment's thought should have made him reject as inadequate or harmful. This is the unrecognized cause of the cruel disappointments that this genius all too often has had to endure, regardless of the merits of his magnificent compositions.

Another source of the disconcerting monotony of Gluck's orchestration is the simplicity of the bass line, which is almost never interesting. It limits itself to sustaining the harmony by monotonously marking the beat or following the rhythm of the melody note for note. The skilled composers of today do not neglect any section of the orchestra, but strive to make each part interesting and to vary the rhythm as much as possible. Gluck's orchestration is generally lacking in brilliance when compared, not to offensively noisy scores, but to the well-written works of the true masters of our century.

Gluck's deficiency is due to his continual use of the sharp-timbre[58] instruments in their middle register, a fault made more glaring by the harshness of the basses that results from the opposite error: they frequently play at the top of their range and thus unduly dominate the other harmonic elements.

The reason for this practice, which was not Gluck's alone, is not hard to find: it was the lack of proficiency among the instrumentalists of his time. The violins were frightened by a high C, the flutes by an A, and the oboes by a D. The cellos, moreover, were considered (as even today in Italy) a luxury that opera houses tried to do without; the double-basses were left almost alone to carry the lower parts of the harmony, so that a composer who wanted closer harmony but had a shortage of cellos had perforce to write the double-bass part higher than its usual very low range so as to bring it closer to the violins.

Since that time, the absurdity of this practice has been acknowledged in France and Germany. Enough cellos have been added to the orchestra to outnumber the basses, whereby Gluck's basses in a good many passages are now in a situation essentially different from that of his own time. He should not be blamed for the exuberance his double-basses have acquired, through no fault of his, at the expense of the rest of the orchestra. Again, he refrained so consistently from using the low registers of the clarinets, horns, and trombones that he seems not to have been aware of their existence. A thorough analysis of his instrumentation would take us too far afield. Let me simply say that he was the first in France to use—though only once—the bass drum (without cymbals), in the final chorus of *Iphigénie en Aulide;* the cymbals (without bass drum), the triangle, and the tambourine in the first act of *Iphigénie en Tauride.*[59] All these instruments today are stupidly misused and over-used in a revolting manner.

The second and third acts of *Alceste* are regarded by some superficial critics as inferior to the first. The dramatic situations are less striking and tend to detract from each other by their similarity and their unfortunate monotony. But the composer's inspiration does not flag for a moment; his inventiveness seems even to redouble in order to overcome the handicap. To the very last moment he shows the same power. With unremitting strength, he finds new ways of depicting grief, despair, fear, pity, anguish, and amazement. He drowns you in heartrending melodies and sorrowful accents—in the voices, in the high parts of the orchestra, in the middle parts—everything implores, everything weeps and groans. And yet these tears do not cease to move us, so irresistible is the beauty of the poet-musician's inspiration.

Moreover, during the second act, the celebration of the king's recovery is the occasion for the most enchanting music, the most gladsome melodies, whose charm is enhanced by their contrast with the rest. The choruses "Que les plus doux transports" (Let the sweetest excitement) and "Livrons-nous à l'allégresse" (Let us give way to joy) may lack the glitter that some listeners desire, but I find a special merit in the tender and naïve gaiety that they express. It is the joy of a people who love their king; their hearts are still aching from the anguish of which they have just been relieved. And, as Admetus says when he appears, the Thessalians are not so much his subjects as his friends. The aria:

> Admète va faire encore
> De son peuple qui l'adore
> Et sa gloire et le bonheur,
>
> Admetus is still
> to his adoring people
> Both glory and joy,

is entirely imbued with this feeling.

During the same aria, with its dance rhythm, the queen—walking among her people—cries out, "Ces chants me déchirent le coeur!" (These songs are breaking my heart!), and the celebration becomes yet more joyful.

In a study such as the present one, in which criticism speaks nearly always in admiration, one must point out the composer's weaknesses, if only to show that he belongs to the human race. In the midst of the first chorus of the Thessalian people, whose gentle joy is, I repeat, expressed with such charm and truth to life, there is an absurd bit of instrumentation, one horn part making octave leaps and diatonic runs that are unplayable in so lively a tempo. The least-adept musician, on seeing this slip of the pen, might well have said to Gluck: "Come, come, my lord, what do you think you are doing? You know perfectly well that these octave arpeggios and this kind of rapid phrasing are difficult enough for the cellos and quite unplayable on a wind instrument such as the horn, especially a horn in G! And you cannot be unaware that even if a performer somehow managed to play this impossible passage, the effect, far from being good, would be to make people laugh." This kind of lapse in a great master is absolutely inexplicable.

A third joyous chorus seems to me even more fully charged with the affectionate feelings of the people for their king; this is "Vivez, coulez des jours dignes d'envie!" (Live, spend your days in enviable bliss!).

It is in *da capo* form like those arias whose incompatibility with dramatic truth I have already pointed out. But here the defect of the form is not visible, because the first part of each section is sung by the attendants alone and then repeated by the large chorus, as if the people were joining in the feelings first expressed by Admetus' closest friends. Thus, the repetition of each section is perfectly justified. The melody for the two lines,

> Ah! quel que soit cet ami généreux
> Qui pour son roi se sacrifie . . .

> Ah! this generous friend, whoever he may be,
> Who sacrifices himself for his king . . .

is of a rare beauty; the words *son roi* form a sort of outburst in which the affection is coupled with a sort of admiration. Then comes another chorus with dancing, full of melodic seductiveness and grace. They sing:

> Parez vos fronts de fleurs nouvelles,
> Tendres amants, heureux époux,
> Et l'hymen et l'amour de leurs mains immortelles
>   S'empressent d'en cueillir pour vous.

> Adorn your brows with fresh flowers
> Tender lovers, happy couples,
> Both Hymen and Love, the immortal pair
> Hasten to gather them for you.

and the orchestra accompanies with a soft pizzicato. All is smiling voluptuousness and charm. One imagines oneself transported to some ancient gynaeceum and beholding the beautiful women of Ionia waving their arms to the sound of the lyre and swaying their divine forms worthy of Phidias' chisel.

Gluck borrowed the theme of this delightful chorus, as I said, from his score of *Elena e Paride*. He added two stanzas for a young Greek maiden that reintroduce the principal melody with uncommon felicity. Next comes a flute solo in the minor mode to which the people dance while Alceste, weeping and turning her head aside, speaks the heart-rending words:

> O dieux! soutenez mon courage,
> Je ne puis plus cacher l'excès de mes douleurs.
> Ah! malgré moi des pleurs
> S'échappent de mes yeux et baignent mon visage.

> Oh gods, come give me courage,
> No longer can I hide my boundless grief
> Ah! in spite of myself, from my eyes
> Tears flow and bathe my cheeks.

Then it is sunshine once more, divine sunshine, as the chorus takes up again in the major, "Parez vos fronts de fleurs nouvelles," with its pizzicato accompaniment.

A great poet once said, "Les forts sont les plus doux" (The strong are the most gentle).[60] Admetus' aria "Bannis la crainte et les alarmes" (Banish fears and alarm) is full of tender serenity; the joy of the young king restored to life is as sincere as his love for Alceste is deep. The melodic line of this number seems to me of exquisite elegance; the violin accompaniment enfolds it as with chaste and delightful caresses. Note in passing the effect of the two oboes playing in thirds and the breathless sobs of the stringed instruments during the following two lines:

> Je cherche tes regards, tu détournes les yeux;
> Ton coeur me fuit, je l'entends qui soupire.

> I seek your glance, but you avert your eyes,
> Your heart flees from me, I hear it sighing

and this splendid cry by the queen: "Ils savent, ces dieux, si je t'aime" (The gods must know how much I love you). Here the repetition that Gluck permitted himself of the first words—"Ils savent, ces dieux"—far from being the insipid nonsense which in commonplace scores too often occurs in such a situation, in fact redoubles the expressive power of the phrase and the intensity of the feeling.

The melody of the aria "Je n'ai jamais chéri la vie" (Life was never dear to me) is as suave as it is noble; its accent is that of ardent love bursting forth, most emphatically at the line "Qu'elle me soit cent fois ravie!" (I would lose it a hundred times!). The words "cent fois" could not be better stressed to show the boundless love of a faithful heart. One is struck by the vision created in the passage "Jusque dans la nuit éternelle (Into eternal night), whose solemnity is enhanced by the horns playing an octave below the voice. But this is not because the phrase covers the interval of a tenth from treble to bass; it is not because the voice *goes down* to the words "nuit éternelle." I think I have shown elsewhere that there are in reality no sounds that go *up* or *down,* and that the terms high and low have been used only because the eye sees notes up and down *on paper.* The beauty of this passage and the musical image it creates are due to the voice taking on a darker resonance as it moves from treble to bass; this effect is increased by the shift from major to minor and by the ominous chord at the entry of the double-basses on the word "éternelle." Nor is it for the childish pleasure of a play on words that Gluck has used this dark coloring, made even darker by the fermata on the penultimate syllable; it is because it is natural that on the verge of death Alceste is unable to restrain her terror in speaking of the fate she feels is so near.

This aria, as I have already said, is in two parts, and each is repeated without plausible justification. The ear takes to this quite well, because one does not tire of listening to such splendid music; but one's dramatic sense is shocked, and Gluck here is in obvious contradiction with himself.

The tremendous recitative in which Admetus' earnest entreaties finally wring from Alceste the secret of her sacrifice is one of the most marvelous in the score. Every word is telling, every motive is shown in high relief. The urgent questions of Admetus, the painful asides of Alceste, the growing intensity of the dialogue, the furious outburst of the orchestra as the king in despair cries out, "Non, je cours réclamer leur suprême justice" (No, I rush to demand their high and just decree) almost make this scene a match for the priest's recitative in the first act. The aria at the end crowns it magnificently. One would not suppose that by means so simple music could attain such an intensity of expression, such heights of pathos. The problem here was to blend the expression of reproach with that of love, to combine rage with tenderness, and the composer performed the feat.

> Barbare! Non, sans toi je ne puis vivre,
> Tu le sais, tu n'en doutes pas!

> Cruel one! No, without you I cannot live.
> You know it, you do not doubt it!

exclaims the unhappy Admetus. Interrupted for a moment by Alceste, who cannot keep from crying out, "Ah! cher époux!" (Ah, dearest husband), he repeats more vehemently than before, "Je ne puis vivre, tu le sais, tu n'en doutes pas!" and rushes distractedly offstage, leaving the spectator with barely enough strength to applaud.

The recitative that follows shows the queen in a calmer mood. But her resignation will not last long.

The chorus speaks up in its turn:

Tant de grâces! tant de beauté!
Son amour, sa fidelité,
Tant de vertus, de si doux charmes,
Nos voeux, nos prières, nos larmes,
Grands dieux! ne peuvent vous fléchir,
Et vous allez nous la ravir!

So many charms! so much beauty!
Her love, her faithfulness,
So many virtues, such sweet appeal,
Our vows, our prayers, our tears,
Great gods, cannot bend you from your purpose,
And you are bent on taking her from us.

One lone voice answers another, then the two join together, and finally the entire chorus cries out and laments. When all the voices have
died away in a pianissimo, the orchestra left by itself brings this concert
of sorrows to a close with four measures full of grave resignation which,
in the mysterious language of the orchestra, seem to say much more to
the heart and the mind than do the words of the poet.

"Dérobez-moi ces pleurs, cessez de m'attendrir" (Conceal these tears
from me, cease moving me to pity), cries Alceste, as she rises from the
seat on which she had collapsed during the preceding lamentation. After
that moment of calm resignation, despair is again about to overwhelm
her soul. She falls silent. From the orchestra comes a melodious lament
played by one instrument,[61] soon accompanied by others in a sort of
slow, stubborn arpeggio of which the fourth note is always accented.
This constant return of the same stroke in the same place with the same
degree of intensity is the very image of Alceste's grief; her every heart-
beat renews her implacable obsession. The queen weeps for her fate and
invokes the pity of her friends in this immortal *Adagio*, which surpasses
in grandeur of style everything we know of its kind in music: "Ah! malgré moi mon faible coeur partage . . . " (Ah, against my will, my feeble
heart . . .).

What a web of melody! What modulations! What gradations in the
relentless orchestral accompaniment!

Voyez quelle est la rigueur de mon sort!
Epouse, mère et reine si chérie,
Rien ne manquait au bonheur de ma vie,
Et je n'ai plus d'autre espoir que la mort!

Behold my fate, its pitiless rigor!
Beloved queen, wife, and mother,
Naught but joy filled my life,
Now I have no other hope but that to die!

And now the fit is upon her again; she is once more the slave of despair and distraction, more enfevered than ever. The orchestra shudders in quick tempo:

> O ciel! quel supplice et quelle douleur!
> Il faut quitter tout ce que j'aime!
> Cet effort, ce tourment extrême,
> Et me déchire et m'arrache le coeur!

> O heaven! What torture and what pain!
> I must abandon all that is dear to me!
> This struggle, this exceeding torment
> Both rends me and tears out my heart!

Her words become broken: "Il faut—quitter—tout ce—que j'aime." Here an error in prosody (tout ce . . .) (all th . . .) turns out to be a fine touch: Alceste sobs and can no longer speak. Finally, her voice, which has reached high A-flat, strains upward to A-natural on the words "m'arrache le coeur."

Let us do justice here to the French translator.[62] He has found a wording that is incomparably stronger and better matches the musical image than does Calzabigi's line in the Italian *Alceste:* "E lasciar li nel pianto così" (And leaves them crying so).

Again Alceste falls onto her seat in a half-faint. The chorus comes in again, moralizing in the ancient Greek manner:

> Ah! que le songe de la vie
> Avec rapidité s'enfuit!

> Ah, how the dream of life
> quickly flies!

Toward the end of this number there is a very fine passage sung by all the voices in octaves and unison:

> Et la Parque injuste et cruelle
> De son bonheur tranche le cours.

> And the unjust and cruel Fates
> Cut off her span of happiness.

It is all the more effective that Gluck rarely resorts to this device, which today is so commonplace.

The act ends with Alceste alone. Her children are brought to her, and, pressing them to her breast, she repeats with redoubled anguish, her *agitato*, "O ciel! quel supplice et quelle douleur!" while the chorus, dismayed at this grievous sight, stays silent. This scene is one of those that led a contemporary of the composer to say rightly that Gluck had "rediscovered antique grief."[63] To which the Marquis de Caraccioli[64] replied that he "preferred modern pleasure." Lord, how stupid can a wit be, and how ridiculous when it tries with its little teeth to bite a diamond.

Listening to music such as this, one's heart swells, one wants something to hug tight. Were Niobe's marble statue near by, I feel as if I would crush it in my arms.

In the third act, the people crowd into Admetus's palace. They know that the queen is headed toward the gates of Tartarus to fulfil her vow. Dismay is at its height: "Weep, oh weep," wails the crowd over broad minor chords,

> Pleure ô patrie!
> O Thessalie!
> Alceste va mourir!

> Weep, o my country!
> O Thessaly!
> Alceste is about to die!

Gluck now achieves another sublime effect through a splendid idea of musical staging, of which the poet had not given even a hint in the libretto. He has put way upstage a second group of voices marked *coro di dentro* (inside chorus), which on the last syllable of the first chorus repeats the phrase "Pleure, ô patrie" like a mournful echo. The palace resounds with cries of mourning; there is thus lamentation everywhere—inside, outside, in the courtyards and great halls, on the balconies, everywhere. To accompany this group of distant voices the composer uses for the first time the low C of the bass trombones, a note lacking on our tenor trombones and for which the Opéra now uses a large trombone in F. The sound is majestic, lugubrious.

At this point, Hercules arrives. He has a lusty recitative followed by an aria that also begins with splendid energy. But after a few measures, it becomes dull, redundant; and the winds utter phrases of a vulgar turn. This aria is not by Gluck. Hercules, as is well known, does not appear in Calzabigi's *Alceste* and was not present, at first, in the French *Alceste*, as translated and arranged by du Rollet.

After the first four performances—so the newspapers of the time tell us—Gluck heard of the death of a niece[65] whom he loved dearly. He went to Vienna for the funeral. As soon as he had left, *Alceste*, which the regular patrons of the Opéra were talking down more and more, was taken off the boards. To "indemnify the public," the management staged a new ballet at great expense. The ballet was a fiasco. Not knowing which way to turn, the Opéra had the daring idea of reviving Gluck's opera, but with the addition of a part for Hercules. Coming near the end of the drama in this way, it contributes nothing of interest and serves absolutely no purpose; the dénouement can be handled perfectly well by Apollo acting alone, just as Calzabigi conceived it. With Hercules, moreover, there is a ridiculous scene, which has been unfairly attributed to Euripides by people who have not read the Greek tragedy.

In Euripides, Hercules does not come on, grotesquely naïve, to chase the Shades away with his club; he does not even make his way down to Hades. He forces Orcus, the spirit of death, to give Alceste to him alive; and this struggle takes place offstage, near the royal tomb.

It was therefore an unfortunate idea that was urged on du Rollet for that revival, and it seems probable that Gluck, who was presumably consulted by letter while in Vienna, was reluctant to fall in with it, since he stubbornly refused to write an aria for the new character. Thereupon, the Opéra asked a young French musician named Gossec[66] to compose it. How did Gluck allow this music by another hand[67] to figure in his score and be published as part of it? I cannot fathom why.

The scene changes: we are on the borders of Tartarus. Gluck here demonstrates that he is almost as great a master of the descriptive style as he is of the expressive and passionate. The orchestra is listless, immobile; it lets silence speak:

> Tout de la mort, dans ces horribles lieux
> Reconnaît la loi souveraine.

> All acknowledge in these dreadful haunts
> The sovereign law of death.

A long murmur traverses the depths of the orchestra, while in the higher instruments arise the calls of nocturnal birds. Alceste gives way to panic. Her terror, her distraught mind, her unsteady steps are wonderfully rendered in the music, and her supreme struggle is still more vivid when she exclaims:

> Ah! l'amour me redonne une force nouvelle;
> A l'autel de la mort lui-même me conduit,
> Et des antres profonds de l'éternelle nuit
> J'entends sa voix qui m'appelle!

> Ah! Love gives me new strength;
> He leads me to the very altar of death,
> And from the deepest pit of eternal night
> I hear his voice calling me.

In place of this wonderful recitative, which ends with such tenderness, the Opéra has recently reinstated an aria from the Italian *Alceste*, "Chi mi parla! che rispondo?" (Who speaks to me? What do I answer?), which had been deleted by du Rollet. It should have been possible to restore this number without the dreadful cutting of the other. The music of these pieces is so full of interest that we would have been happy to hear both. In the [Italian] one, Gluck wanted particularly to portray the fears of the unhappy woman. It is not an aria, since it has no rounded musical phrases; nor is it a recitative, since the rhythm is commanding and headlong. What we have are apparently disordered exclamations: "Who is that speaking?... What am I to answer?... What is this I see?... How fearful?... Where can I flee?... Where can I hide?... I am burning up... I am freezing... My heart fails me... I feel it—in my breast—slow—ly—beat—ing. Ah! I have barely—enough—strength—to bewail—and—tremble..." Exalted devotion and love are now far from Alceste's heart; the urge to self-sacrifice that led her to this frightful den is now broken. The instinct of self-preservation has prevailed. Totally undone, she runs to and fro, while the orchestra, weirdly agitated, plays a rushing rhythm in the muted strings, across which is heard a kind of death rattle in the lower winds. It could be taken for the voice of the ghostly inhabitants of the dark abode. This merges seamlessly with a chorus of invisible shades, "Malheureuse, où vas-tu?" (Unhappy wretch, whither are you bound?). This is sung on a repeated note accompanied by horns, trombones, clarinets, and strings. Sinister chords from the orchestra hover round this desolate pedal-point in the voice, sometimes jostling it, sometimes swamping it, without its ceasing to be part of the harmony. It has a dreadful rigidity, creating an icy terror. Alceste replies at once with humility in an aria where resignation predominates through a melodic design of incomparable beauty:

> Ah! divinités implacables,
> Ne craignez pas que par mes pleurs
> Je veuille fléchir les rigueurs
> De vos coeurs impitoyables.
>
> Ah, relentless gods,
> Do not fear that with my tears
> I want to bend the rigor
> Of your pitiless hearts.

Notice the sagacity here that led the composer to see that this aria did not need a *ritornello*, or even an introductory chord. As soon as the infernal gods end their monotonous phrase "Tu n'attendras pas longtemps" (You shall not have long to wait), Alceste gives her reply. Obviously the least delay here, by any musical means whatever, would have been a gross error. This aria, whose painful appeal I cannot possibly describe, also has repeats, but only of the first section; for in the second, though the words are repeated, the music changes. The lines that are sung twice are these:

La mort a pour moi trop d'appas
Elle est mon unique espérance!
Ce n'est pas vous faire une offense
Que de vous conjurer de hâter mon trépas.

Death is to me most enticing
It has become my only hope!
It is not to give you offense
That I beg you to hasten my passing.

In its second musical setting, this prayer becomes more urgent, the
entreaty more intense. The line "Ce n'est pas vous faire une offense" is
sung almost timidly, but then the voice rises more and more on the
words "que de vous conjurer" and falls again with solemnity on the
final cadence, "de hâter mon trépas."

One would have to be a great writer, a poet with an ardent heart, to
do justice to such a masterpiece of sorrowful grace, such a model of
classical beauty, such a striking example of musical philosophy united
with so much noble sensibility. I wonder: would even the greatest of
poets succeed? Such music cannot be described; it must be heard and
felt. As for those who have little or no feeling for it, what can one say?
They are unfortunate and should be pitied.

It is the same with Admetus' great aria "Alceste, au nom des dieux!"
(Alceste, in the name of the gods), for if Beethoven has rightly been
called a tireless Titan, Gluck in his own genre has as good a claim to
the same title. When he has to express a passion or give voice to the
human heart, his eloquence is inexhaustible. His ideas and the force of
his conception are as great at the end of a work as they were at the
beginning. He goes as far as the edge of the world. When listening to
Beethoven, one feels it is Beethoven singing; in listening to Gluck, one
feels that it is the characters themselves; Gluck has simply noted down
their utterance. After expressing so much grief, he can still find for Admetus' great aria new melodies, new harmonies, new rhythms, new *cris
de coeur*, and new orchestral effects. There is even a daring modulation
from C minor to D minor, which produces a magnificently sorrowful
impression. It is totally unexpected, so unusual is this shift in tonality.
Beethoven often moved with great felicity from the tonic of a minor key
to that of the key below; for example, from C minor to B-flat minor. At
the beginning of his *Coriolan* overture,[68] this sudden modulation im-
parts to the phrase a fine, almost primitive fierceness. But I cannot remember anyone other than Gluck using the *rising* modulation (from C
minor to D minor).

This aria is one of those in which the use of an ostinato bass makes
the orchestra into a character. One might say that the instruments do
not accompany the voice so much as speak and sing at the same time
as the singers; they suffer his sufferings, they shed his tears. Besides the

ostinato line, the orchestra also plays a melodic phrase that recurs continually, reinforcing the expressive power of the vocal phrase which it precedes or follows. Yet this vocal part hardly needs assistance to make it stand out; it is so full of striking details, for instance on the words: "Je pousserais des cris que tu n'entendrais pas" (I could cry out without your ever hearing); and in another passage where at the words: "Me reprocher ta mort" (To reproach me for your death), the voice abruptly leaps a minor tenth, from low F to high A-flat, and ends with a desolate conclusion on the line "Me demander leur mère" (To ask me for their mother). In the rising progression,

> Au nom des dieux
> Sois sensible au sort qui m'accable
>
> In the name of the gods
> Take pity at the fate that crushes me

the same short phrase is repeated four times with growing urgency and seems to depict Admetus sobbing and prostrating himself at his wife's feet. Anyone who has a feeling for this kind of musical beauty and who has heard this aria well performed will remember it all his life. There are things one can never forget.

Although the next number does not equal Admetus' aria, it is nonetheless remarkable for its special texture. It is the only duet in the score. In his other works the composer has not kept to such strict logic, but in this one he does not allow his voices to sing together except when one of the characters becomes so impatient that he must interrupt the other. Hence the end of the duet finds Admetus singing alone, Alceste having already finished. The effect is rather odd.

One of the most famous arias in the score is that of the infernal god emerging from Hades to tell Alceste that her hour has struck and that Charon is calling her. Its psychological makeup is altogether special. Although the inner development, beginning with the line "Si tu révoques le voeu qui t'engage" (If you cancel the vow that binds you) has a note of menace, which is intensified by the timbre of the three trombones accompanying in unison and at half strength, the general mood of the aria is one of awe-inspiring calm. Death is strong and effortless in seizing its prey. The theme "Caron t'appelle, entends sa voix!" (Charon is calling you, hearken to his voice!) is sung on a monotone like the chorus of the infernal gods, "Malheureuse, où vas-tu?" (Unhappy wretch, whither are you bound?). It is given out three times, first on the tonic, then on the dominant, and a last time on the tonic, each time introduced and followed by three calls from the horns on the same note as the voice, but sounding mysterious, hoarse, and cavernous. It is the conch shell of the old boatman of the Styx reverberating in the depths of Tartarus. The natural (so-called open) notes of the horn cannot even come close to producing the strange and dismal sound that Gluck had in mind for Charon's call. It would thus be a serious mistake and an egregious want of accuracy to let the horns simply play the notes as written.

Gluck did not at first find a way to produce this astonishing orchestral effect.[69] To represent Charon's shell in the Italian *Alceste,* he had used three trombones and the two horns playing a rather high note, the D above the bass staff. It was too sonorous, almost violent—it was vulgar. In the new version, he changed the rhythm of the distant summons and left out the trombones. But the two horns in unison with their tonic and dominant notes, both open, did not produce at all what he wanted, either. Finally, he hit on the idea of joining the two horns bell to bell, so that they act as mutes for each other. As their sounds collide randomly upon emission, they create the extraordinary timbre he was looking for. This procedure has disadvantages that the horn players never fail to point out when they are asked to use it. To play in this way, the performer must sit in an unnatural position, which can disturb his embouchure and make his attack on the note wavering. That is why some performers who play this piece refuse to change their old habits and thereby ruin a remarkable effect. The same thing was about to happen at the Opéra, when someone thought of replacing Gluck's risky method by another whose effect is even more striking.

The infernal god's aria was transposed down a whole tone, so that it is now sung in C. The horn players were then told to play instruments in E-natural instead of C, and to play the notes A-flat and E-flat, which on these transposing instruments sound C and G for the listener. These two notes being what are called *stopped* notes—meaning that the right hand stops two-thirds of the bell for one note and half for the other—they produce exactly the timbre Gluck intended. The composer probably knew the effect of such stopped notes, but the players' lack of proficiency in his day would have kept him from using it.[70]

The chorus of infernal spirits coming to fetch Alceste ably fulfils one's ideas of what it might be like—the colossal roar of the miserly Acheron[71] demanding his prey. The mighty chords blasted out by the trombones and the violent tremolo in the strings recurring at irregular intervals heighten the sense of savagery. Admetus' last solo, "Aux enfers je suivrai tes pas!"[72] (To hell itself, I will follow your steps!), is a splendid, desperate impulse. The only trouble, and here again it is not the composer's fault, is that it goes on too long. Admetus, left by himself, instead of rushing into the pit of Hell after Hercules, keeps repeating "Que votre main barbare porte sur moi ses coups! Frappez! Frappez!" (Let your barbarous hand rain its blows on me! Strike! Strike!) to demons who are no longer there. It is not plausible, and he cuts a ridiculous figure, despite the power and truth of the music given him by the composer.

But "the son of Jupiter triumphs over Hell," and Alceste is restored to

life. Apollo comes down from heaven when his help is no longer needed
and goes back there after congratulating the couple on their good fortune and praising Hercules for his courage. These three then sing a short
trio in a not very lofty style, which could well be by Gossec, too. It was
thought best to omit it at the Opéra's recent revival of *Alceste*.[73] Also
left out was the final chorus, "Qu'ils vivent à jamais, ces fortunés époux!"
(Let them live forever, this happy pair!). Not that there was the slightest
doubt about the authenticity of this number—it is indeed by Gluck—
but it would have looked like want of respect toward the great genius
to perform something so unworthy of him at the end of his masterpiece,
after so much marvelous music. For it is in truth commonplace, small
and shabby, dreadful from every point of view. "C'est le choeur des banquettes,"[74] they said at the rehearsals. Not wanting to take the trouble
of composing it, Gluck must have said to his valet, "Fritz, when you've
finished blacking my boots, write me the music for this final chorus."

This explanation, however, is inadmissible; not only is the number
really by Gluck, but he himself never considered it a "choeur des banquettes," as is shown by the fact that in the Italian *Alceste*, it serves as
the finale of the *first* act. What is more, in the French version, where
the addition of a few measures required by the versification at times
twists the melody out of shape and makes it limping and incoherent, it
is at least not at cross-purposes with the feelings of popular jubilation
expressed by the text. However, in the Italian score, this music, which
is suitable only for a chorus of drunken revelers capering about as they
leave a tavern, is an appalling irrelevance; it contradicts in the most
shocking way the sense of Calzabigi's lines, which point out a moral
about the vicissitudes of human life. Those verses, which follow the
scene with the oracle and Alceste's vow, are sung by courtiers who have
just acknowledged their inability to sacrifice themselves for their king.
Here is the exact translation of this capering chorus:

> Qui sert et qui règne
> Est né pour les peines;
> Le trône n'est pas
> Le comble du bonheur,
>   Douleurs, soucis,
> Soupçons, inquiétudes,
> Sont les tyrans des rois.
>
> He who serves and reigns
> Is born to pain;
> The throne is not
> The peak of happiness.
>   Sorrows, worries
> Suspicion and anxiety,
> Are tyrants over kings.

One had to hear it to believe it. Near the end of the number, a clownish crescendo of jollity in the voices and orchestra reiterates these words:

> Vi sono le cure
> Gli affani i sospetti
> Tiranni de' re.
>
> Worries, suspicion,
> and anxiety
> Are tyrants over kings.

One cannot believe one's eyes. This is surely a case for amending the words of Horace. Homer is not nodding here; he is raving. What is going on at such moments within these great minds? One could weep at such a spectacle.

I have not said anything about the dance music in *Alceste*. Most of it is graceful and full of lively charm. Yet it does not seem to me to be of the same musical quality as the ballet music in *Armide* or the two *Iphigénies*.

I must now say something about the three other operas composed on the subject of *Alceste*. I begin with Guglielmi's. If in analyzing Gluck's score, I often found myself unequal to the task and at a loss when trying to vary the terms of my admiration, here I have no less a problem in expressing the opposite of praise. There are three Guglielmis,[75] and *Alceste* is not mentioned in the catalogues of any of their works. It is lucky for all three. Would you believe it possible that the wretched man who wrote the score I have before me took the very same text by Calzabigi that Gluck set to music? This pigmy dared to take on the giant in hand-to-hand combat, as Bertoni did with *Orfeo*.

In the history of art there are several examples of a libretto being set by several composers, but we remember only the victorious scores with which composers slew their predecessors. Rossini, in resetting the *Barber*, killed Paisiello;[76] Gluck in remaking *Armide* did away with Lully.[77] In such cases, only murder justifies the theft. This is true even when a composer deals with the same subject as one of his predecessors without using precisely the same text. Thus Beethoven in composing *Fidelio*, whose subject was borrowed from M. Bouilly's *Léonore*, killed with one blow both Gaveaux and Paër,[78] each the composer of a *Léonore*. Grétry's *William Tell*[79] also seems to me quite ill since the birth of Rossini's.

Guglielmi, whichever he be, the composer of this other *Alceste*, has no murder to reproach himself with. His score is well written in the style that was fashionable at the beginning of this century. It resembles everything that was produced then in the opera houses of Italy. The melody is generally commonplace; the harmony is pure, correct, and also commonplace. The instrumentation is decently negligible. As for expressiveness, it is virtually nil throughout, except where it is absolutely false. The work as a whole is without character. Alceste sings arias with vocal flourishes rich in ascending scales and trills, but very poor in musical and dramatic feeling. Several scenes are so devoid even of pretense to these qualities that they are comical. In the temple scene, the priest's recitative,

> l'altare ondeggia
> Il tripode vacilla,
>
> The altar is swaying
> The tripod is shaking,

cannot be set alongside the sublime recitative of Gluck's priest,

> Le marbre est animé
> Le saint trépied s'agite
>
> The marble is alive
> The holy tripod stirs,

without causing laughter on reading it. What would happen on hearing it?

For this impressive scene, Guglielmi refrained from composing a religious march. That was shrewd of him. Nor did he write an overture. On the other hand, he treats us to a monumental piece of silliness in the form of the people's chorus that comes after the oracle:

> Che annunzio funesto!
> Fuggiamo da questo
> Soggiorno d'orrore!
>
> What a baleful prophecy!
> Let us flee from this
> Haunt of horror.

Here the Italian composer seized on what he thought a wonderful opportunity to show off his knowledge of counterpoint. As the action is that of a crowd *fleeing* in dismay, and as the word "fuga" means flight (that is, the flight of the vocal parts, which, coming in one after the other, seem to flee and pursue each other), he had the idea of writing a long fugue, extremely well made indeed. But what it exhibits is the art of handling a theme by means of an *exposition,* a *counterexposition,* a *stretta* on the pedal, of bringing in episodes of canonic imitation, and so on; and not at all the art of expressing the terror of the people. In Gluck, the crowd first sings "Quel oracle funeste" slowly in low tones of dismay; then the mob quickly disperses, as it repeats in a brisk tempo and a visibly disordered manner, "Fuyons, nul espoir ne nous reste!" This wonderfully terse *Allegro* lasts only eighteen measures. Guglielmi's fugue lasts 120. As a result, the chorus stands still for quite a while, as they sing "Fuyons" in perfect tranquillity.

The contrast between the two scores is even more amusing in the aria that follows. At the words

> Ombre, larve, compagne di morte
> Non vi chiedo, non voglio pietà,
>
> Shadows, phantoms, companions of death
> I do not ask, I do not want your pity,

a pleasant cheerfulness enlivens Guglielmi's theme; in addition, in the middle of the aria, there is a vocal run on the words "Non v'offenda si giusta *pietà*" (Take not offense at so just a pity), which flies straight as an arrow to high C and which must have made the audience enthusiastically applaud the prima donna who took the role of Alceste. The final chorus of the first act,

> Qui servi e chi regna
> E nato alle pene,
>
> He who serves and he who reigns
> Is bound to suffer.

is more brilliant and just as jovial as Gluck's and, I must confess, not so dull. It would appear that the evils of human life must be dealt with cheerfully.

In the second act, the famous aria "Chi mi parla? Che rispondo?" of Alceste, who is distracted with terror, is entitled *cavata*. It is in fact a type of *cavatina*, quite regular and particularly calm, calmer even in the orchestra than in the voice. Guglielmi's Alceste is brave; unlike Gluck's, she is not given to feeling terror when she hears the infernal gods or sees the dimly glowing lights of Tartarus. Her composure rises to the highest level of comedy toward the end of the statement:

> Il vigor mi resta a pena
> Per dolermi e per tremar,
>
> I have just enough strength
> to grieve and to tremble,

where the composer, to make sure of his cadence, repeats three times, "E per tremar, e per tremar/E per tremar," as used to be done for words like "felicità."

The chorus of the infernal spirits, "E vuoi morire o misera!" (And you want to die, unhappy one!), which Gluck composed on a single note surrounded by terrifying harmonies, is here written in two parts and is gracefully melodic. The third act contains, among other buffooneries, a long bravura aria for Admetus and a duet in which the couple try to console their children to the accompaniment of a thoroughly consoled orchestra. I hope I may be excused from going on with this analysis.

Schweitzer's *Alceste* [Alkestis] was composed to a German text by Wieland. This play differs in many ways from Calzabigi's libretto. There are only four characters: Alceste, Admetus, Parthenia,[80] and Hercules. It contains two choruses, two duets, two trios, and many arias in multiple sections consisting of a little *Andante* leading into a little *Allegro*, each including a long vocalise. All of this is written correctly according to the conventions and usages of that modest German-Italian school, which has long been held in esteem in Germany. The vocal part is heavier but no more expressive than in Guglielmi. One is subjected in all the arias to the same vocal flourishes, though a little stiffer and just as ridiculous. The small orchestra is treated with care; Schweitzer deserves praise for a certain skill in weaving the harmony and linking the modulations. It is the work of a good schoolmaster who has taught counterpoint for a long time, who is respected by everyone in his neighborhood, who is greeted affectionately as Herr Doktor or Herr Professor or Herr Kapellmeister; who has many children, all of whom know a little music and even some French. At six o'clock in the evening, this little company gathers in the paternal house and sits around a large table. The Bible is piously read aloud; half the audience knits, the other half smokes while sipping from time to time at a glass of beer. And all these honest folk go to sleep at 9 o'clock with the consciousness of having had a well-filled day, certain also that they have not written or struck on the harpsichord any dissonance that was ill prepared or ill resolved.

It may be that this Schweitzer, whose music conjures up in me such a patriarchal picture, was a bachelor and did not possess any of the domestic qualities I attribute to him, except that of thoroughly knowing counterpoint and of being fond of smoking and drinking. Be this as it may, he was Kapellmeister to the Duke of Gotha,[81] and his *Alceste* (a worthy housewife, if ever there was one) was successful enough in the Duke's domain to make the rounds in Germany, where the various opera houses put her onstage during a span of years when Gluck's *Alceste* was hardly known there. Such is the tremendous advantage of music that is economical, uses small means to convey small ideas, and is undeniably mediocre.

There is an overture in this score, a proper overture in the style of Handel, which begins with a slow and solemn movement containing the requisite basso continuo and progressions of sevenths. Then comes a fugue in moderate tempo on a single subject. It is clear and pure, but flavorless, too, and cold as water from a well. It is no more an overture to *Alceste* than to any other opera; it is music in good health without any evil passions, and which can bring neither disgrace nor honor to the good man who put it together.

I shall not say as much about one of Alceste's arias in the first act, where a vocalise that ends on a trill to the words "mein Tod" [my death] would have made Gluck collapse from indignation. La Parthenia carries on even worse in *her* arias; at the drop of a hat, she hurls at you runs and arpeggios that reach up to D and F above high C and are adorned with staccato notes rhythmically akin to the cackling of hens and in a timbre suggestive of a yelping puppy whose tail has been stepped on.[82] These vocal runs imitate all too closely those that Mozart had the misfortune to write for the Queen of the Night in the *Magic Flute* and for Donna Anna in *Don Giovanni*.

Hercules is also pretty good at gurgling and warbling. He runs all the way from the high F of the bass voice to the lowest C of the cello—two and a half octaves. It seems there was in Gotha in those days a husky fellow endowed with an exceptional voice.

Admetus alone does not indulge in excessive pyrotechnics. His runs and trills are only there to point out the lineage of this work, which belongs, as I said, to the Germanized Italian school. It is hardly worth mentioning the two choruses. They are only there to say . . . that they have nothing to say. (This *bon mot* belongs to Wagner; I do not want to steal it from him.)

There remains only Handel's *Admetus*[83] to talk about. I used to know but one number; I was just recently able to obtain the full score. Despite its Latinized title, it is another Italian opera for the London stage by the famous German master who became a naturalized Englishman. It is one of a large number of works of this kind from Handel's tireless pen; he wrote one each year for the Italian singers hired for the season, as one writes albums for New Year's Day. *Admetus,* a lyric outline on the subject of Alceste, is actually nothing more than a large collection of arias, as are *Julius Caesar, Tamerlano, Rodelinda, Scipio, Lotharius, Alexander,* and others by this composer.[84] So are the operas of Buononcini,[85] his would-be rival, and those of many others.

The first act of *Admetus* contains nine arias, the second twelve, and the third nine plus a duet and a small "choeur des banquettes."[86] There is also an overture and a *sinfonia* serving as introduction to the second act.[87] The recitatives, probably accompanied on the harpsichord according to the custom of the time, were not judged important enough to be included in the full score, and one may venture to think that Handel did not take the trouble to compose them. There were in those days clever copyists whose job it was to write, according to a regular formula, the music for the dialogue that preceded the airs, and thus give to this species of concert in costume the appearance of a drama.

From a perusal of these 30 arias, it is impossible to ascertain the plot of this story of *Admetus*. There is never any indication of action or the names of any of the characters. Each aria is designated only by the name of the singer or prima donna who sang the role. There are seven for Signor Senesino,[88] eight for Signora Faustina,[89] seven for Sra Cuzzoni,[90] four for Sr. Baldi, two for Sr. Boschi, and one each for poor Sra Dotti and the unfortunate Sr. Palmerini. These last two, no doubt, came on just long enough to sing their little numbers and give the others, the well-provided gods and goddesses, time to breathe. The only duet is sung shortly before the end of the *concert* by Sr. Senesino and Sra Faustina, who must be Admetus and Alceste.[91] The words indicate nothing more than two lovers happy to have found each other again:

> Alma mia
> Dolce ristoro
> Io ti stringo,
> Io t'abbrachio,
> In questo sen.

> My soul
> Sweet consolation
> I clasp you,
> I embrace you
> Against this breast.

This duet is accompanied by two sections of the orchestra only—the violins and the basses. The vocal parts show a hint of feeling, a few attempts at passion, all the more welcome as these qualities are so rare in the 29 arias that precede this duet. Unfortunately, the orchestral *ritornellos* before and after the vocal passages have a hearty and slightly grotesque gaiety that weans the listener away from any poetic impression and takes him back to the heavy prose of the contrapuntist. As for the 30 arias, they are almost all cut to the same pattern. The orchestra, now in four string parts, now in two or three, sometimes enriched by two oboes or by two flutes or by two horns and two bassoons, begins by unfolding a *ritornello*—usually rather lengthy—after which the voice states the theme. This theme, melodically not very graceful, is often accompanied by the double-basses bowing heavy phrases akin to the singer's. After a few measures of development (built on a system of sections that are more or less similar in rhythm), the voice almost always seizes on some one syllable—whether well suited or not to vocalising—cuts the word in two, and launches into a long passage on half the word. Often this cadenza is interrupted by rests, without the word's being completed on that account. It is stuffed with trills, with syncopated and repeated notes that would be much better suited to an instrumental than to a vocal display. The whole is as stiff and heavy as the anchor chain of a ship. In addition, an orchestral instrument often doubles the voice in unison or at the octave, and by this pairing increases the stiffness of the vocalise. The oddest of all these cadenzas is to be found in an aria for Sra Faustina (whom I take to be Alceste) on the second syllable of "risor-ge,"

> In me a poco a poco
> Risorge l'amor.
>
> Little by little
> Love revives in me.

The composer seems to have tailored the length of his vocal ornamentations to the fame of the *dio* or *diva* singing the part. The cadenzas for Faustina the goddess, pupil of Marcello[92] and wife of Hasse,[93] are interminable. Those written for Cuzzoni are somewhat shorter, others for Sr. Baldi are still shorter; the *povera ignota*[94] Dotti in her only aria has none at all.

When these indispensable passages reach their final cadence, a second section of the aria takes the vocal part into a related key; and a new cadence, almost always accompanied by the double-basses alone, is performed in this new key, after which everything is repeated once again until the final pedal-point.

One can only conclude that a composer continually subjected to this system could scarcely pay much attention to truth of expression and character. In the event, Handel hardly thought about these things, and his singers would have rebelled if he had.

I have not said anything about the overture or the *sinfonia* that introduces the second act. No analysis I could make would give an idea of such instrumental music. Handel's *Admetus* preceded Gluck's Italian *Alceste* by several years.[95] Perhaps it was even being performed at the time when Gluck, still a young man, was composing for the London Italian theater such poor works as *Pyramus and Thisbe*[96] and *The Fall of the Giants*.[97] One is free to fancy that *Admetus* gave Gluck the idea for his own *Alceste*. Perhaps, too, it was after hearing Gluck's two bad operas that Handel remarked one day, "My cook is a better musician than that man." Surely Handel was too judicious not to do full justice to his cook. But let us acknowledge that since the day the composer of *Messiah* uttered this judgment, Gluck has made significant progress and left the culinary artist far behind.

To sum up—and keeping in mind the conditions of music in France, Germany, and Italy at the various periods during which these works were composed—Handel's *Alceste* [*sic*] seems to me superior to Lully's *Alceste*, Schweitzer's superior to Handel's, Guglielmi's superior to Schweitzer's. On the whole, these four works in my opinion resemble Gluck's *Alceste* as much as a caricature cut with a penknife in a chip of wood to amuse the children resembles a bust carved by Phidias.

THE REVIVAL OF GLUCK'S
ALCESTE AT THE OPÉRA [1]

The revival of Gluck's *Alceste,* so often announced and so often delayed for various reasons, finally took place on October 21, 1861. Its tremendous success that day gave the lie most emphatically to tiresome and malicious predictions.

The audience seemed impressed by the majestic structure of the work, by the deeply expressive melody, by the liveliness of the stage action, and by a thousand and one splendid details that it had not known and that it found original because they have so little in common with what is usually presented nowadays on our opera stage. I am inclined to think that there is now a larger segment of the public able to feel and understand such a work than there used to be. Musical education, for one thing, has made progress; and for another, people seem to have become, if only through indifference, less hostile to beauty. Contrary to their usual practice, most of the Opéra's regular audience came to listen rather than to see or to be seen. They listened, they reflected, and, as Gluck said about a child who wept at the first performance of *Alceste,* they let themselves go. There was no shortage of Poloniuses to declare, as they had done about *Orphée,* that the work was unbearably boring. But this was to be expected, and people paid no attention to their grumbling.

This revival has come, I believe, at the right time, and it cannot fail to have an excellent effect on the general taste of music lovers, as well as to remove many prejudices. The only thing to regret is that the production was not more rigorously faithful to the work. The need to transpose Alceste's role from beginning to end for Mme Viardot, and the multiple changes that this entailed, have in many places altered the form and look of the work. True, some arias do not lose much in being pitched lower, but many others are weakened in their effect, not to say destroyed. The orchestration becomes flabby and dull; the sequence of modulations is no longer the composer's because the need to prepare for transpositions and then to return to the original key after the transposed sections creates an entirely different succession of keys. This is not the place to give a course in musical composition, but it should be easy to understand that such tampering, practicable when single fragments are excerpted for concert performance, becomes disastrous when applied throughout an opera produced on the stage.

"The more one seeks perfection and truth," said Gluck in his preface

Christoph Willibald Gluck, lithograph by Maurin Aîné. Bibliothèque de l'Opéra, courtesy Bibliothèque Nationale.

to *Elena e Paride*,[2] "the greater becomes the need for accuracy and precision. What distinguishes Raphael from the crowd of painters is something hardly perceptible; slight changes in contour will not distort a caricature and make it unrecognizable, but they will disfigure the portrait of a beautiful face." This principle applies to all types of infidelity in musical performance, but it is especially true of Gluck's works.

I should hasten to add that in all other respects, the production of *Alceste* at the Opéra is generally respectful and accurate. The singers change hardly a single note of their roles; the melodies, recitatives, and choruses are performed exactly as the composer wrote them. Some people believe that winds have been added to the orchestra, but that is not so. What M. Royer[3] has done is only to add to the number of stringed instruments, in view of the fact that they play the principal role in the orchestration of *Alceste*. To give more power, the violins were increased to 28, the violas to ten, the cellos to eleven, and the double-basses to nine. One can only applaud such a procedure, which I hope will not be limited to the playing of *Alceste;* it would give the Opéra orchestra an even richer sound than that of Covent Garden in London, which is one of the most powerful orchestras in Europe. A bass trombone was also engaged to play certain low notes which the tenor trombones, the only ones in use at the Opéra, cannot play.

The 1825 revival of *Alceste* was not nearly so scrupulous, or so complete as the one we have just heard.[4] At that time several numbers were shamefully truncated and many others, including some of the most wonderful, were left out. This time, almost all have been restored to us intact. *"Almost all,"* do you say? "Yet the musical directors of the Opéra boast (very creditably) of their respect for the score. They seem to take great pride in having avoided the dishonor of perpetuating the indignities of 1825." This reminds me of those heroes of the July 1830 revolution who in the heat of their enthusiasm cried out: "Nobody can criticize the revolution this time—we are above reproach: for two days we have been masters of Paris and we haven't stolen a thing, we haven't destroyed a thing!" They were proud of not behaving like vandals. All the same, a few comments could have been made.

Still, let us give this relative probity its due. In what concerns us here, the better is, for once, not the enemy of the good. During the rehearsals of *Alceste,* the attitude of the whole Opéra staff was excellent. Everybody worked with enthusiasm and the most careful attention. And this cannot have been easy for anyone. The score and the choral and orchestral parts were in such a chaotic condition (the transpositions only adding to the confusion), that every part had to be recopied just as if it were a new opera. It was clear from the slovenliness of the old scores, the absence of indications for bowing and dynamics, the lack of markings for tempo, and the many wrong notes, how careless our ancestors were in putting on operas. As long as they had a great singer for the principal role, the rest hardly mattered. They were not going to worry whether the orchestral players knew what to do—or the conductor, who in those days was rightly called the time-beater. After all, the chorus and others would be more or less in tune, and a few wrong notes from the instruments or the voices were not enough to upset anyone.

> Les délicats sont malheureux
> Rien ne saurait les satisfaire.[5]
>
> Unhappy are the exquisite ones
> Nothing ever pleases them.

On this occasion, though, the audience did not seem unhappy.

I must admit that in *Alceste,* the errors and rough edges of past performances have largely been due to Gluck's indolence. To edit his works with care seems to have been beyond his power. All his scores were written down with incredible inattention. When they came to be engraved, the engraver added his own mistakes to those in the manuscript, and it does not look as if the composer deigned to correct the proofs. At times the first violin parts are written on the staff of the seconds; at other times, the violas, which are supposed to play in unison with the lower strings, find their parts, because of a careless *col basso* marking, written at the high double octave of the bass. As a result, they are sometimes heard playing the notes of the bass line above that of the melody. Elsewhere, the composer has forgotten to specify the key of the horns. In another place, he neglects to specify the wind instrument he wants to play an important part—is it a flute, oboe, or clarinet? Nobody can tell. In still other places, he writes some important notes for the bassoons on the double-bass line, then forgets about the bassoons, and what happens remains a mystery.

In the score of the Italian *Alceste* printed in Vienna, which is a little less messy than the French score, one still finds cause for error in the work of copyists and performers. For example, the word *Bos* occurs frequently. What is *Bos*? It is a misprint for *Pos*. But what is *Pos*? It is the abbreviation of the German word *Posaunen,* meaning trombones. Anyone would be readily excused for not guessing this solution to the puzzle, because everywhere else in the score, Gluck indicates the trombones by their Italian name, *tromboni*. I have been unable to ascertain what is meant in the Italian *Alceste* by the strange word *chalamaux*. Is it a clarinet in the *chalumeau* register? It remains in doubt.

There is no end to this chaos. In the full French score one misprint creates such a cacophony in the brass that it makes even listeners who relish the horrible in art jump up and scream in pain. It is indeed worthy of certain modern compositions, and looks at first glance as if written like its current equivalents, with the most meticulous ferocity.

In one of his letters, Gluck wrote: "My presence at the rehearsals of my works is as indispensable as the sun is to creation."[6] I can well believe it, but it would have been needed rather less had he been more careful in setting down what he meant and had he not left the performers to guess at so many of his intentions and to correct so many mistakes. One can only imagine what must happen to his works when they are performed in theaters that lack the tradition of his contemporary performances. I saw an *Iphigénie en Tauride* in Prague[7] that would have given me an attack of cholera if I had not finally burst out laughing. The staging was on a par with the rest. In the finale, the ship which Orestes and his sister were about to board to return to Greece was fitted out with a triple row of cannon.

At the Paris Opéra, neither the musical performance nor the staging of Gluck's works have anything in common with these grotesque displays. This time the great man has been given a palace peopled with intelligent and devoted servants. Everywhere else (except in Berlin) he has had to make do with a barn. To be sure, even at the Opéra the singers and players did not at once grasp the spirit of this noble style. But the more they rehearsed, the more they came under its spell, and understanding followed upon their growing feeling for a type of beauty that was new to them.

The trouble is that, for Gluck's works, nothing is further from the rendition imagined by the composer than one which is faithful but flat, which consists solely of playing the notes. What is needed besides absolute fidelity—in the singing, in the rhythm, in the accents, in everything—is to possess style in phrasing, to pay attention to nuance and clarity of diction. Without these features, the divine flower of expression which makes these works so moving loses its color and perfume, and the work as a whole perishes. Gluck was right to think his presence at rehearsals as indispensable as the sun to creation. He alone could enlighten, enliven, and suffuse everything with warmth and life. But he had to suffer cruelly from performers, and his patience was often severely tried.

In Gluck's day, choruses did not act; rooted on each side of the stage like organ pipes, they recited their lessons with a maddening impassiveness. It was he who tried to give them life, showing them what gestures and movements to make. He wore himself out in this effort and would have succumbed were it not for his robust constitution. At one of the last rehearsals of *Alceste* he had just collapsed onto a chair, drenched and steaming with perspiration as if he had just fallen into the Styx, when the ballet master's wife, who had made herself his attentive nurse, brought him a large glass of punch. "Oh my *houri*," he said, kissing her hand. "You bring me back to life. Without you, I would have been drinking from the Cocytus."[8]

I cannot say anything about the talent of Mlle Levasseur,[9] who was the first to sing the role of Alceste in Paris. She is said to have had a powerful voice that she put to rather mediocre use. Mme Saint-Huberti,[10] who succeeded her, was by contrast a true artist. It could hardly have been otherwise, since Gluck himself took charge of her musical education. Mlle Maillard,[11] the third Alceste, was tall, beautiful, and stupid.

The fourth, Mme Branchu,[12] whom I saw perform and who was neither tall nor beautiful, struck me as the incarnation of lyric tragedy. Her soprano voice was of extraordinary power but lent itself like none other to the softest accents. She had a faultless pianissimo, owing to the natural ease of her voice in the middle register. A moment later this same voice would fill the enormous hall of the Opéra and outtop the loudest orchestral *tutti*. At such times her black eyes would flash like lightning; she was possessed by her own creation; she truly believed herself Al-

Mme Branchu as La Vestale, by Favart. Bibliothèque de l'Opéra, courtesy Bibliothèque Nationale.

ceste, Clytemnestra, Iphigenia, La Vestale, or Statira,[13] as the case might be. She told me that as a young girl, vocalizing in coloratura style came to her very easily. But her teacher, Garat,[14] stopped her, warning her that if she went in for this virtuoso technique, she would never be able to master the broad, tragic *style large*.[15]

Her delivery of verse was remarkable for clarity, a prerequisite for good singing, just as it is for acting in the great dramatic genre. I was present at a benefit evening at the Opéra-Comique when she played Sylvain's wife in the opera by Grétry where the dialogue, in verse, is spoken.[16] She got a standing ovation.

At the time I was still almost a child, but I remember the dismal picture Mme Branchu painted for me of a composer's life in France. "It is not enough," she said,

to write a beautiful opera, it has to be performed. And that also is not enough, it has to be performed *well*. And even an excellent performance is still not enough, the public must be brought to understand it. Gluck could never have been what he became in Paris without the direct and active patronage of the queen, Marie-Antoinette, who had been his pupil in Vienna and who felt affection and gratitude for her teacher.[17] Yet not even this high-placed protection, or Gluck's own genius and the enormous merit of his works saved him from being the butt of insults by the Marquis de Caraccioli,[18] Marmontel,[19] La Harpe,[20] and a hundred other great wits. We're talking today of *Alceste*; well, this masterpiece was received very coldly at its first performance; the audience felt nothing, understood nothing.

In France, the greatest musical gift is virtually useless to its owner. Too few people are able to recognize it and too many have a stake in denying it or suppressing it. The men with power who hold in their hands the fate of artists are easily misled and have no way of finding out the facts for themselves. Everything in this dreadful career depends on luck. Sometimes composers discover that they have enemies even among their performers. When we first began rehearsing *La Vestale*, I myself had a hand for a couple of weeks in plotting against Spontini.[21] I found his marvelous recitatives too difficult to learn; I soon changed my mind completely, but at first they seemed impossible to sing. In short, what I know about a composer's life makes me believe that in our country it is practically hopeless. If my son wanted to be a composer, I would do everything in my power to keep him from it.

After retiring from the Opéra in 1826 or 1827,[22] Mme Branchu went to live in Switzerland. Twenty years later, I happened to be browsing in a music shop in Paris when she came in. While the clerks searched for the piece she had come to buy, she took a close look at me, then left without speaking to me. She had not recognized me. Our musical world, though, has not changed.[23]

These memories of mine, which with many others were revived by the recent performance of *Alceste*, are not unrelated to my subject; they lead me naturally to speak of the great artist who has just taken on with such success this almost inaccessible role of the queen of Thessaly.

Everyone knows what a stunning impression Mme Viardot made a few months ago when she sang a few excerpts from *Alceste* at the Conservatoire.[24] On that occasion, it was only the singer who was applauded. At the Opéra it is also the outstanding actress, the enthusiastic, inspired, and seasoned artist who arouses the emotions of the audience for the length of three long acts. She has had to struggle against the recalcitrance of her voice, as Gluck struggled against the monotony of the libretto; both came out victorious.

Mme Viardot is wonderful in her anguished tenderness, in the intensity of her despair. Her bearing and her few gestures as she enters the temple; her stricken demeanor during the festivities of the second act; her wild distraction in the third; the expressiveness of her face when Admetus compels her to answer his questions; her fixed stare during the chorus of Shades, "Malheureuse, où vas-tu?" (Unhappy wretch, where are you going?)—all this re-creation of ancient bas-reliefs, all these splendid sculptural poses aroused the liveliest admiration. In the aria "Divinités du Styx," the phrase "Pâles compagnes de la mort" aroused applause that almost drowned out the following melody, "Mourir pour ce qu'on aime" (To die for the beloved), which she sang with the deepest sensibility. In the last act, as she sang the aria "Ah! divinités implacables" (Oh, merciless gods), in the mood of sorrowful resignation that is so difficult to achieve, she was interrupted three times by applause. *Alceste*, in short, was a new triumph for Mme Viardot and one that taxed her talents to the utmost.*

Michot[26] (Admetus) surprised everyone both as singer and as actor. His high tenor, which enables him to sing everything with his chest voice, is perfectly suited to the role. He sang his arias and most of his difficult recitatives beautifully and with such accents of true emotion, as one hears all too rarely. Let me make special mention of the aria "Non, sans toi je ne puis vivre!" (No, without you I cannot live), of which the last phrase, repeated on four high notes,

> Je ne puis vivre
> Tu le sais, tu n'en doutes pas,
>
> I cannot live;
> You know, you cannot doubt it,

stirred the entire audience. He brought out very nicely the tender serenity of "Bannis la crainte et les alarmes" (Banish fear and alarm). But the last aria, which is the high point of the role and whose main passages Michot sang to perfection, especially "Je pousserais des cris que tu n'entendrais pas" (I could cry out and you would not hear me), loses half its effect when it is sung so slowly. It is marked *Andante*, but for Gluck, *Andante* does not mean *slow*. It calls for a tempo of some liveliness relative to the sentiment being expressed; *Andante* is walking, something that moves along. Here, moreover, the vocal part, the figure given to the second violins, and the texture of the piece indicate the sort of agitation that is in any case imperiously demanded by the words.

The same must be said of several recitatives that should be delivered

---

*Let me add that in this role she took none of the liberties with the text for which I had to reproach her in *Orphée*.[25]

simply and not emphatically stated, whereas in others, the passionate impetus does not allow any breadth of utterance. Thus, the lines

> Parle, quel est celui dont la pitié cruelle
> L'entraîne à s'immoler pour moi?

> Speak, who is the one whose cruel pity
> Drives her to sacrifice herself for me?

must absolutely be flung out in a kind of precipitate anxiety. The elder Nourrit,[27] who in my opinion was not Michot's equal, was tremendously effective in this role precisely because of the speed of his delivery. When asked to perform in this way, singers usually reply, "It is very difficult to pitch the voice firmly if one has to sing at this speed." No doubt it is difficult, but *art* consists in mastering difficulties. If it were not so, what would be the point of studying? The first comer with a passable voice would qualify as a singer.

As for Michot, he only needs to make a little more effort. With a faster pace he could double the effect of a role which already does him the greatest credit.

Cazaux, with his splendid voice, could not fail to shine as the priest. He was smothered with applause, both during and after his big scene, "Apollon est sensible à nos gémissements" (Apollo is not indifferent to our groans) and again at the passage,

> Perce d'un rayon éclatant
> Le voile affreux qui l'environne.

> Pierce with a blazing ray of light
> The dreadful veil that shrouds her.

He was fully up to the level of Gluck's inspiration when, with his voice like thunder, he sang.

> Le marbre est animé
> Le saint trépied s'agite.

> The marble comes to life
> The sacred tripod stirs.

I would not know how to bestow higher praise. I urge him, however, to work on his high D, where his attack is still a bit low.

For his debut in the minor role of Hercules, Borchardt received a welcome that should encourage him. His height, his robust voice, and his features suit the role perfectly. The range of his bass-baritone, moreover, enables him to reach without fear the high notes of the part, which are beyond the reach of most singers. Borchardt is a fortunate acquisition for the Opéra.

Mlle de Taisy[28] was kind enough to take on the part of the young Greek girl who sings a solo during the festivities. With exquisite grace she sang this delightful little episodic air in the middle of the chorus: "Parez vos fronts de fleurs nouvelles" (Adorn your brows with fresh flowers). In the past, this song had been entrusted to a member of the chorus who, singing shamefully out of tune in a small shrill voice, managed to spoil the charming piece and invited contempt for the whole performance. The precedent implied here should be followed. Henceforth, let us hope, every solo, short or long, will be sung by an artist. Koenig, too, does himself credit in the small role of the confidant, Evander; Coulon made the hall shake with his aria of the infernal deity, "Caron t'appelle" (Charon summons you); and Grizy's young, fresh tenor[29] is perfectly suited to the blond Phoebus, whose short recitative in the finale was at first foolishly given to a bass.

The chorus, well rehearsed by M. Massé,[30] left nothing to be desired. Those whose parts called for singing at a distance backstage accurately followed the orchestral beat though they could not hear it. Two weeks ago, this synchronization would have been impossible; the electric metronome had not yet been introduced at the Opéra.[31] As for M. Dietsch,[32] this revival of *Alceste* was a success that will be one of his titles to honor. I do not think he made a single mistake in tempo, and he brought out every nuance with scrupulous intelligence. On all sides, the house resounded with praise of the orchestra—its discreet accompaniments, its cohesion, precision, and impressive power. Never before and nowhere else has the temple scene been given such a performance. The sacred procession was applauded at three points. The audience was absorbed, rapt with contemplative emotion by this divine music. M. Dorus[33] and M. Altès[34] gave exactly the right degree of volume to the low notes of the flute which clothe the melody in such chaste colors. When long ago I heard *Alceste*, the first flutist of the Opéra, who was neither modest nor first in his art like M. Dorus, used to ruin this lovely instrumental effect. He did not want to let the second flute play with him, so he used to transpose his part an octave higher in order to be heard above the orchestra, in total disregard of Gluck's intention. And he was allowed to get away with it. He should have been dismissed from the Opéra and sentenced to six months in jail.

The short oboe solo by M. Cras in the aria "Grands dieux du destin qui m'accable" (Great gods who are fated to crush me) must not be forgotten either, although he plays the last two measures a trifle too softly. Still less should we forget the lovely *ritornello* of the clarinet in "Ah! malgré moi" (Ah, in spite of myself), played by M. Leroy with the fine tone and style of which this virtuoso has the secret.

The graceful dances were choreographed by M. Petipa,[35] and M.

Cormon[36] managed to overcome various difficulties of production with uncommon skill. Everything was set and directed with perfect awareness of the demands of the music, which directors do not usually take into consideration, and with true feeling for Greek antiquity. It was the first time at the Opéra that demons and Shades were costumed and marshalled so adroitly as to appear fantastic instead of ridiculous.

So now, at last, after over one hundred years, we have *Alceste* shown in its proper light, or nearly, and both understood and admired. People have been heard repeating Abbé Arnauld's *bon mot*.[37] Someone said at the première that *Alceste* had fallen. "Yes," he replied, "fallen from heaven."[38]

But this revival of *Alceste*, though not entirely beyond reproach, is but an exception to the rule. Usually, when a masterpiece returns to the stage after the death of the composer, it is like King Lear when no longer king: the stage belongs to the daughters Goneril and Regan; it swarms with impudent servants who insult the retinue of their illustrious guest and show disrespect even to him. If anyone complains of their shameful behavior, they are always ready to say: "Yes, we put Kent in the stocks; he ordered us about as though the master here, and we did not like it. Yes, we sent packing 25 of Lear's knights; they were in the way and made the palace too crowded. There are 25 left and that's enough. What need for 50 knights to serve the king? Why should he need 25 or twenty or ten or even one? Aren't there enough people in the palace to satisfy the whims of a stubborn, overbearing, and morose old man?"[39] Then, pushed over the brink by so many insults, Lear finally leaves in a rage. He rejects this parricidal hospitality and, alone with his faithful Kent and his fool, goes off into the stormy night on the deserted heath, and raving with grief, cries out: "Thunderbolts, roar, singe my white head! Break, you cold clouds! Blow, winds! Spout, rain! Hurricanes, tear out my hair and throw it to the winds. You may do it, I pardon you, you are not my daughters!"[40]

And we, who are faithful fools like the loyal Kent, noble Edgar, and sweet Cordelia, all we can do is groan and surround the dying king with our respect and our love. Oh Shakespeare, Shakespeare! you also were the great insulted one, who had to compete with trained bears on the London boards and to cope with the boy players of the Globe Theatre. It was on your account, but also for your heirs through all time to come, that you put into your Hamlet's mouth these bitter words: "You tear a passion to tatters, to very rags."[41] " 'Tis too long? say you. It shall to the barber's with your beard and be cut short at the same time." "Don't listen to this idiot; he's for a jig or a tale of bawdry or else he sleeps."[42] "Don't add stupid things to your part to get applause from the idiots in the pit."[43] And so much else.

Today, they rail at a great master, fortunately still alive, about the fortifications he has built around his works, about his pitiless demands, his anxious stipulations, and his continual distrust of every person and every thing.[44] How right he is, this learned composer and wise man, to exact before the performance of any new work, conditions such as these: "You must give me this singer, that musician, these many players in the orchestra, these many in the chorus. They will rehearse with me so many times. And they must rehearse nothing but my work for so many months; I shall conduct rehearsals as I see fit, etc., etc., etc., or *you shall pay me fifty thousand francs!*"

That is the only way great and complex musical works can be protected from being devoured by the rats that swarm in the theaters of France, England, Italy, and even Germany, in theaters everywhere. For one must not delude oneself, opera houses are all alike. They are the houses of ill-fame of the art of music, and the chaste muse who is dragged into them cannot enter without shuddering. Why is that? No need to ask—it is well known, it has been said so often; no need to say it again. Let me only repeat that a work like *Alceste* will never be performed as it should be *in the absence of the composer,* except under the supervision of a dedicated artist who knows it thoroughly, who has long been familiar with the master's style, who has a thorough knowledge of all aspects of music, who is deeply imbued with all that is great and beautiful in art, and who, with the authority based on his repute, his special knowledge and the loftiness of his vision, exercises that authority now gently, now with absolute inflexibility. Such a man knows neither friend nor foe; he is a veritable Brutus the Elder, who, seeing his orders disobeyed, is always ready to say:

"*I lictor, liga ad palum!* Here, lictor, bind the criminal to the post!"

"But sir, it is M——, it is Mlle——, it is Mme——."

"*I lictor!*"

"What you are asking, then, is despotism in the theater?" I reply. "Yes, in opera houses to begin with, and wherever the aim is to perform great music by means of a large number of diverse performers who are expected to work together to one end. Despotism is required; let it be supremely intelligent, by all means, but despotism it must be, military despotism, the despotism of the commander-in-chief, the admiral of the fleet in time of war. Short of that, all we shall ever have is approximation, misinterpretation, confusion, and cacophony."[45]

INSTRUMENTS ADDED BY MODERN COMPOSERS TO THE SCORES OF OLD MASTERS[1]

At a recent concert of the Conservatoire, it was noticed that in the duet "Spirits of Hatred and Fury"[2] from Gluck's *Armide*, the voices lost much of their effect because they were often drowned out by loud outbursts from the trombones. These trombones were added to the score in Paris (clumsily enough) by I do not know whom. In Berlin, still more were added to the same work. It is therefore not out of order to remark that Gluck wrote not a single note for trombone in either *Armide* or *Iphigénie en Aulide*. Nor is it to the point to reply that this omission in *Armide* was due to an absence of trombones in the Paris Opéra orchestra of his day. For they play a prominent role in *Alceste* and are also called for in *Orphée*, both of them works performed before *Armide*. There are trombones also in *Iphigénie en Tauride*.

Is it not odd that a composer, however great, is not allowed to make up his orchestra the way he wants it, and particularly that he should not be free to refrain from using certain instruments when he deems it appropriate? Even the great masters have often taken it upon themselves to revise the instrumentation of their predecessors, bestowing upon them the free gift of their skill and taste. Mozart, for example, reorchestrated Handel's oratorios. Divine justice then willed that in turn Mozart's operas should be later reorchestrated in England, where *Figaro* and *Don Giovanni* have been crammed full of trombones, ophicleides, and bass drums. Spontini confessed to me one day that he had added—very discreetly, I must admit—some wind instruments in Gluck's *Iphigénie en Tauride*. Two years later, while complaining bitterly about current excesses of this sort—the crude, abominable things added to the orchestration of the unhappy dead, who can no longer defend themselves, Spontini cried out, "It is shameful! Horrible! Shall I too be revised when I am dead and gone?" I answered sadly, "Alas, my dear master, you yourself revised Gluck."

Not even the greatest symphonic composer who ever lived has been able to escape these unspeakable insults. Quite apart from the overture to *Fidelio*, which has been trombonized from beginning to end in England—where people feel that Beethoven was too restrained in the use of trombones—elsewhere someone has already begun to correct the instrumentation of the SYMPHONY IN C MINOR.

Some day I shall disclose in a special study the names of all these ravagers of masterpieces.

HIGH AND LOW SOUNDS
The Top and Bottom of the Keyboard[1]

I noticed one day in an opera a descending scale sung as a vocal run on the words "I rolled down into the abyss." The intention to imitate in this way is something of a joke. Clearly, the composer thought that a *descending* run would express perfectly the movement of a body rolling down from a height. The notes written on the staff do in fact represent this downward movement—*for the eye.* If, however, the system of figured notes[2] were to become usual, musical notation would no longer speak to the eye in this manner. What is more, should the performer happen to hold his music upside down, the notes would seem, on the contrary, to move upward.

Is it not lamentable that there are so many examples in music of this childish nonsense, caused by a false interpretation of words? The words "go up" or "go down" are used to describe the movement of bodies that move away from the center of the earth or toward it. I challenge anyone to find another meaning for this pair of expressions. Now, how can sound, which is as imponderable as electricity or light, move away from or closer to the center of the earth by reason of its pitch?

The words "high" or "sharp" are used to describe the sound produced by a resonant body vibrating a certain number of times in a given length of time. A low or deep sound is the result of fewer vibrations in the same span, and therefore of slower vibrations. That is why the words "slow" and "grave" are more appropriate than "low," which indicates nothing to the purpose. Likewise a "sharp" sound (which pierces the ear like a sharp object), if taken figuratively, is a reasonable term, while a "high" sound is absurd. For why should the sound produced by a string vibrating 32 times a second be closer to the center of the earth than the sound produced by another string vibrating 800 times?

How can the right-hand side of the keyboard of an organ or piano be the "top" or "high" part of the keyboard, as it is usually called? Keyboards are horizontal. When a violinist playing his violin in the usual position wants to produce sharp sounds, his left hand does indeed move up as it goes toward the bridge; but a cellist, whose instrument is held in the opposite position, has to move his hand *downward* to produce the same sharp sounds that are so improperly called "high."[3]

Even the most casual reflection shows how ridiculous this misuse of words is, yet it has led even some great composers to write passages unbelievably contrary to sense. As a result, intelligent people have been so much annoyed by such silliness that they have come to condemn all musical imagery, and even to make fun of that which is acceptable to common sense and good taste and which speaks most clearly to the *auditory* imagination.

I remember the naïve sincerity with which a professor of composition had his students admire the descending scales that accompany a passage in *Alceste*, when the high priest invokes Apollo, the god of the sun, with the cry:

> Perce d'un rayon éclatant
> Le voile affreux qui l'environne.[4]
>
> Pierce, with a dazzling ray,
> The fearsome veil that envelops her.

"Please notice," he said, "this insistent scale in quarter-note triplets which goes down from C to C in the first violins. It is the ray of light, the *dazzling ray*, which *descends* at the call of the high priest." And what is even sadder to record is that Gluck himself obviously believed he was imitating the ray.

DER FREISCHÜTZ[1]

Opera-goers in France now understand and value this work, which they used to regard as an amusing curiosity. They relish it as a whole and in detail. What seemed obscure before is now seen to have a reason. Listeners perceive in Weber's work the most rigorous unity of conception and the truest feeling for the expressive and the dramatically apt—all this combined with an overflowing abundance of musical ideas, which the composer develops with judicious restraint, and with a power of imagination whose wings never carry him beyond that frontier of the ideal where absurdity begins.

It is difficult, indeed, whether we scan the old composers or the new, to find a work so flawless in every respect as *Der Freischütz*, a work so continuously engaging from beginning to end. Its melodies are so fresh, in whatever form they occur; the rhythmic and harmonic inventions so numerous and striking; and the use of chorus and instruments so effortlessly energetic and at the same time smooth without being foppish. From the beginning of the overture to the last chord of the chorus, I cannot find a single measure I would wish to omit or to change. Intelligence, imagination, and genius glow everywhere with a radiance that only an eagle's eye would not find tiring, were it not for an ever-present, yet restrained, sensibility that softens the brilliance and, as it were, shelters the listener with its friendly screen.

Der Freischütz opens with what is universally considered a queen among overtures. Nobody today would think of disputing this judgment; it is held up as a model of its genre; people all over sing the themes of its *Andante* and *Allegro*. But one other theme I must mention, because it is less remarked on, and because it moves me incomparably more than the others. It is that long wailing melody played by the clarinet above an orchestral tremolo, like a distant lament blown by the wind through the depths of a forest.[2] It goes straight to the heart. For me at least, this virginal song, which seems to breathe its shy reproach to heaven while the somber harmony shudders and threatens below, is one of the most novel, poetic, and superb contrasts in modern music.

In this inspired instrumental passage, one can readily find a foreshadowing of Agathe's character, soon to develop in all its passionate candor. Yet the passage belongs to the role of Max. It is the cry uttered by the young hunter when, perched high on a rocky cliff, he scans the depths of the hellish valley below. But when the phrase is changed slightly and given the instrumentation I have described, its tone and aspect change utterly. Its creator possessed to a superlative degree the art of melodic transformation.

It would take a book to deal individually with every facet of a work so rich in varied beauties. Its main features are more or less generally known. Everybody admires the caustic gaiety of Killian's couplets, with the refrain in which the chorus bursts out in laughter; the astonishing effect of the women's voices grouped in major seconds, and the jarring rhythm of the men's voices, which complete this bizarre concert of mockery. Who has not felt Max's utter dejection, the touching goodness that permeates the theme of the chorus in its efforts to console him, the exuberant joy of the sturdy peasants setting off on a hunt, the comic banality of the march played by the village musicians at the head of Killian's triumphal procession; Caspar's diabolical song in which laughter is a grimace; and the fierce outcry of his great aria, "Triumph, triumph!" which sets the tone of menace for the final explosion?

Everybody nowadays, whether performer or music lover, listens with rapture to the delightful duet that delineates from the start the contrasting characters of the two young girls. Once this idea of the master's is grasped, it is not hard to follow its development to the end. Agathe is always tender and dreamy, Annette always the happy child who has not yet known love and who enjoys innocent flirtation. Her happy chatter, her birdlike song inject her sparkling high spirits into the dialogue of the two lovers, who are anxious and sadly preoccupied. Nothing will be hidden from anyone who attends to those sighs of the orchestra during the prayer of the maiden waiting for her betrothed, to those strangely, gently, rustling sounds in which the attentive ear imagines for itself:

> Le bruit sourd du noir sapin
> Que le vent des nuits balance.

> The hushed sound of the black fir
> Swaying in the night wind.

The darkness suddenly seems colder and more intense at the magical modulation into C major: "Tout s'endort dans le silence" (Everything falls asleep in the silence). What a thrill of sympathy we feel further on, at the outburst "C'est lui! C'est lui!" (It's he! It's he!), and above all at the immortal cry that shakes the soul: "C'est le ciel ouvert pour moi" (Heaven has opened up for me).

No, truly, I do not know where another such beautiful aria can be found. Never has any master—German, Italian, or French—given voice successively in a single scene to devout prayer, melancholy, anxiety, meditation, the mood of slumbering nature, the silent eloquence of night, the mysterious harmony of the starry sky, the torment of waiting, and then hope, unsure assurance, joy, reeling bliss, ecstasy, and boundless love.

And what an orchestra accompanies these noble melodies for voice! What inventiveness! What ingenuity! What gems did sudden inspiration discover! Flutes in their dark register, violins in four parts, viola figures playing in sixths with the cellos, throbbing rhythms in the double-basses, the crescendo which rises and explodes at the peak of its bright ascent, the moments of silence when passion seems to be gathering strength so as to rush forward with ever greater energy. There is nothing like it! It is divine art—poetry—love itself! The day that Weber first heard this scene performed as he dreamed it could be—if indeed he ever did—that golden day must have made pale and sad all the days that followed. He should have died right then, for what could life afford after such bliss?

Wanting to push realism as far as possible, even to a point repugnant to the artistic sense, certain producers in Germany are said to contrive for the casting of the bullet a most discordant racket—animal cries, barking, yelping, howling, the sound of trees falling and splintering, and so on. How can music be heard amid this hideous din? And why, even if it could be heard, put reality next to its imitation? If I admire the hoarse bark of the horns in the orchestra, the baying of your theater dogs can only arouse my disgust. On the other hand, an actual waterfall on the stage is an effect that is not incompatible with music, but rather enhances it. The even, steady sound of water induces a mood of reverie; it is particularly effective during the long pedal-point that the composer has brought in so skillfully and that blends perfectly with the sounds of the distant bells as they slowly toll the fatal hour.

When the Paris Opéra decided in 1837 or 1838 to produce *Der Freischütz*,[3] I accepted, as is generally known, the task of setting to music the recitatives,[4] the original spoken dialogue being excluded by the rules of the house. To a German public I do not have to explain that in the strange and daring scene between Zamiel and Caspar, I refrained from having Zamiel sing. Weber's intention here is unmistakable: Caspar sings, but Zamiel speaks his brief reply. Only once does Weber set the devil's words in rhythm—each syllable on a note from the timpani. The Opéra's prohibition against spoken dialogue is not so strict as to forbid a few words when called for, and I promptly took advantage of this latitude to preserve the composer's idea. Thanks to my insistence, *Der Freischütz* was performed in its entirety, with its numbers following exactly the order prescribed by the composer. And the libretto was translated, not "arranged," by M. Emilien Pacini.

One result of the Opéra's faithfulness in performance—something that is rare at all times and places—was that the finale of the third act of this masterpiece came as a virtual novelty to the Paris public. Some had heard it fourteen years earlier during the summer season given by a German company,[5] but it was unfamiliar to the majority of listeners. This finale is a magnificent conception. What Max sings at the prince's feet is filled with shame and repentance. The first chorus in C minor, after Agathe and Caspar have fallen, is beautifully tragic in coloring and could not communicate more effectively the unfolding catastrophe. Then Agathe's return to life, her gentle cry—"O Max," the cheering of the people, the threats of Ottokar, the intercession of the saintly hermit, and the healing eloquence of his conciliatory words, the entreaties of the peasants and hunters that Max be pardoned—a noble heart momentarily led astray; the sextet in which hope and happiness are restored, the blessing of the old monk who moves all these people to bow their heads and stirs the kneeling multitude to burst forth in a mighty hymn, powerful in its brevity; and then the final chorus in which the *Allegro* theme of Agathe's aria, already heard in the overture, reappears for the third time—all this is as beautiful and worthy of admiration as what precedes, neither more nor less. Not one note is out of place, not one note could be omitted without destroying the balance of the whole. Superficial minds may disagree with this view, but for the attentive listener there can be no doubt; the more he listens to this finale, the more he will be convinced.

A few years after this production of *Der Freischütz* at the Opéra, and while I was absent from Paris,[6] Weber's masterpiece was cut, mutilated in a dozen ways, and converted into a curtain-raiser for ballets. Its performance in that guise has become an abomination, not to say a scandal. Will the work ever return? One can but hope.

OBERON

Carl Maria von Weber's Fantastic Opera
Its Première at the Théâtre-Lyrique[1]

In Paris the musical atmosphere is usually foggy, dank, dark, cold, sometimes even stormy. The seasons there show strange vagaries. On occasion it rains grasshoppers, snows mites, and hails toads. No umbrellas, whether of cloth or metal, can protect decent people from these vermin. Then suddenly the skies clear, and although manna does not actually fall instead, one enjoys warm, pure air; one finds here and there splendid flowers blooming among the thistles, brambles, nettles, and milkweed, and one runs with delight to gather them and breathe in their perfume. Right now is such a moment, when we can bask in the caress of one of these benign sunbeams; several lovely blooms of art have just blossomed and we experience the joy of their discovery. Let me mention first the greatest musical event that I have had the opportunity of announcing in a good many years: the recent production of Weber's *Oberon* at the Théâtre-Lyrique.

This masterpiece (for that is what it is, a consummate, brilliant, and unadulterated masterpiece) has been in existence for 31 years. It was first performed on April 12, 1826.[2] Weber had composed the music in Germany, the libretto being by an English author, Mr. Planché.[3] The work had been commissioned by the director of a London opera house who believed in the genius of the composer of *Der Freischütz* and counted on getting a beautiful score and at the same time doing a good stroke of business.

The principal role (Huon) was written for the famous tenor Braham,[4] who sang it, they say, with extraordinary verve. That did not keep the new work from being an almost complete failure with the British public. The Lord only knows what kind of musical education then prevailed among the *dilettanti* across the Channel. Weber had just suffered another setback in his own country, where his music for *Euryanthe* had had a chilly reception.[5] Doughty creatures who can swallow without flinching the most frightful oratorios, which are capable of changing men into stone and of congealing alcohol, took it into their heads to find *Euryanthe* boring. They were proud of discovering that they could be bored by something, thus to prove that blood did flow in their veins. It gave them an air of sprightliness, an air of being a little light, a little

French, even a little Parisian. And, to add a touch of wit, they hit upon something akin to a pun; they called *Euryanthe Ennuyante,* pronouncing it *ennyante,*[6] to mean "boring." It is impossible to measure the success of this stupid joke, which is still current; it has been making the rounds in Germany now for 33 years, for to this day no one has been able to convince the wags there that the word is not French, that a play or opera can be *ennuyeuse* but not *ennuyante,* and that in France not even the grocers' boys commit howlers like that.

Euryanthe was thus felled, for a time, by this lumpish witticism. Grieved and discouraged, Weber hesitated a while before taking on the public in another tussle. He finally made up his mind to it, but demanded eighteen months to do the work; he was not one to improvise.

Having come to London to supervise the production, he had to endure a great deal at first from the "ideas" of some of his singers; in the end, he succeeded somehow in making them see reason. In any event, *Oberon* was well performed. Weber, one of the ablest conductors of his day, had been prevailed on to conduct it himself. But the audience remained cold, serious, listless, "very grave"—again a pun—but this time the word is at least good English. *Oberon* did not make enough money to cover the impresario's outlay. He got his beautiful score but a bad piece of business. Who knows what then went through the soul of the composer, who was sure of the merit of his work? To restore his spirits through a success his friends believed he could readily obtain, they persuaded him to give a concert, for which he composed a grand cantata entitled, if I am not mistaken, the *Triumph of Peace.*[7] The concert took place, the cantata was performed to a virtually empty house, and the box office did not cover expenses.

On his arrival in London, Weber had accepted the hospitality of the honorable Master of the Royal Chapel, Sir George Smart.[8] I do not know whether it happened on Weber's return from that dismal concert, or a few days later, but one evening after chatting for an hour with his host, the dejected Weber went to bed, and there Sir George found him the next day, already cold, his head resting on his hand, dead of a heart attack.

Immediately a memorial performance of *Oberon* was announced. All the box seats were quickly sold; the whole audience came dressed in mourning. The hall was full of people in pensive mood, their attitude expressing sincere sorrow and seeming to say: "We are sorry we didn't understand his work; but we know that 'he was a man, we shall not look upon his like again. . . .' "[9]

A few months later the overture to *Oberon* was published. The Odéon Theater in Paris, which had made a fortune with its flayed and filleted version of *Der Freischütz,*[10] was interested enough to hear at least one piece from Weber's last work. The director ordered a rehearsal of this symphonic marvel. But the orchestra heard in it only a string of oddities, harsh sounds, and absurdities. I do not know whether the overture was given the privilege of being butchered in public.

Ten or twelve years later, these same musicians from the Odéon, now transplanted into the massive orchestra of the Conservatoire, played this same overture under a real conductor, Habeneck. This time they added their own shouts of admiration to the applause of the public. Eight or nine years after that, the Société des concerts du Conservatoire played the chorus of sprites from *Oberon* and the finale of the first act, both of which the audience applauded with an enthusiasm that matched their earlier welcome for the overture. Later still, two more fragments enjoyed the same good fortune . . . and that was all.[11]

One summer 27 years ago, a small German company, which had come to Paris[12] to waste its time and its money, presented just two performances of the complete *Oberon* at the Théâtre Favart (today the Opéra-Comique). The celebrated singer Mme Schroeder-Devrient[13] sang the role of Rezia.[14] But the company was entirely inadequate, the chorus too small, the orchestra wretched, the sets torn and moth-eaten, the threadbare costumes pitiable. Moreover, the musically intelligent public had left Paris for the summer; *Oberon* passed unnoticed. Only a few musicians and perceptive music lovers were there to worship this divine poem in the secret depths of their hearts, and, thinking of Weber, they repeated once more Hamlet's words, "He was a man and we shall not look upon his like again."

Germany, however, rescued the pearl, which had been created in the British oyster but scorned by the Gallic cock—always so fond of plain seed.[15] A German version of Mr. Planché's text gradually won a place in the theaters of Berlin, Dresden, Hamburg, Leipzig, Frankfurt, and Munich, and so the score of *Oberon* was saved. I do not know if it has ever been performed complete in that witty, mocking city [Vienna] that found Weber's earlier work *Ennyante*. Probably it has. Generations can follow without resembling each other.

Finally, *after 31 years,* chance having brought to the management of one of the Paris opera theaters a man who appreciates style in music, an intelligent, bold, and energetic man,[16] a man who sticks to his purpose once he has chosen it, Weber's poem has at last been revealed to us. The public has not made any nauseating puns on the composer's name or that of his work; it did not remain "grave," but gave vent to bursts of true feeling that grew ever more enthusiastic; this, even though Weber's music—with lofty disdain—disturbs, upsets, overturns the listener's dearest and most deep-rooted habits, those closest to his secret, unavowed instincts.

Oberon is indeed enjoying a great and genuine triumph at the Théâtre-Lyrique.[17] The work's successful appeal to the best minds will attract even the worst. All Paris will want to hear and see *Oberon;* admire its delightful music, its splendid sets, and rich costumes; and applaud the new tenor. For there is such a one to be heard there. M. Carvalho has discovered in Michot a genuine tenor for the role of Huon, and at every performance the popularity of this phoenix rises. And as a last reason for the current popularity of this masterpiece, let me add that the final scene has people laughing uproariously; the whole house is convulsed.

It was apparently considered inadvisable to translate Mr. Planché's English libretto as it stood; instead, a kind of adaptation was made, combining the libretto with Wieland's poem *Oberon*.[18] I cannot say whether it was right or wrong to take this liberty, but the score, at least, was left more or less intact. It was neither mutilated, nor reorchestrated, nor humiliated in any of the customary ways. All that was done was to transfer a few numbers from one scene to another, but always into situations similar to those for which they were composed.

Here is the story of this fairy play. Oberon, the king of the fairies, fondly loves his queen, Titania. Yet the couple often quarrel. Titania persists in defending the cause of wayward wives—no doubt remembering her bizarre love for a cobbler who wears an ass's head and is named Bottom. I shan't tell you what this name means in English. Look it up yourself. Read *A Midsummer Night's Dream*. In it Shakespeare's irony has outdone everything penned by the most caustic of satirists.

Oberon defends the cause of men who have been more or less unjustly betrayed. Then one fine summer night, he loses his temper and leaves Titania, vowing never to see her again. He will forgive her only if two young lovers can be found who love each other with a love so chaste and faithful that it withstands all possible trials of their virtue and fidelity. An odd stipulation that, for what do the good qualities of a human couple have to do with the bad ones of her fairy majesty, Queen Titania? I fail to see what the king will gain if he takes back his wife because virtue triumphs in two strangers. But that is the crux of the play.

Oberon has in his employ a household sprite—a small, graceful, and gently mocking imp named Puck—who is mischievous though not spiteful, who is lovable and charming, at least that is how Shakespeare has imagined him. Puck sees that his master is listless and sad. He wants to reconcile him with Titania and knows the conditions that have to be met. So he sets to work. He has come upon a handsome knight in France, Huon of Bordeaux, and in Baghdad a bewitching princess, the caliph's daughter Rezia. By means of a dream dispatched simultaneously to each of them, he makes the two fall in love. Huon is soon tramping over hill and dale in search of the princess he adores.

A kindly old woman whom he meets deep in a forest tells him that Rezia lives in Baghdad and offers to transport him there, together with his squire Sherasmin, in just one minute, if Huon will swear to be faithful to his beloved for the rest of his life and not ask the slightest favor of her until they are married. Huon takes this double oath, and at once the old woman is transformed into a charming young sprite. It is Puck, back in his own shape. Oberon appears, confirms what Puck has said, and our travelers are suddenly whisked 500 leagues away to the gardens of the Caliph of Baghdad's harem. There, Rezia is weeping for her unknown knight and in despair over the hateful marriage that her father is forcing on her. While walking forlorn in the palace garden, she encounters the new arrivals and recognizes one of them as the knight of her dreams: "O bliss, is it really you?"

"I adore you. I will save you. Come back tonight—when the imam calls the faithful to prayer, I shall be here and we shall arrange everything for our escape."

The lovers meet that evening, but the palace guards seize the two strangers and lock them up, and the caliph orders their execution. Oberon comes to their aid with his supernatural powers; they are again free. They capture the ship on which Abukan (the husband who was to be forced on Rezia) has come for his bride. Rezia reappears with her lady-in-waiting Fatima and all four leave together. "Et vogue la nacelle qui porte leurs amours."[19] (Let the skiff bearing the lovers sail away).

Alas! the flesh is weak and the trip long and boring. It is not hard to imagine how two such lovers, confined in a small boat, might find it difficult to restrain the ardor of their love. Oberon can read the knight's heart and, angered by the desires that he finds there, decides to separate him from Rezia. "Blow storm, whip up the Ocean, destroy this boat!" The winds swoop down—Eurus, Notus, Boreas, and twenty others, followed by the spirits of fire, by meteors, and what not.

Black night descends on the waters. Rezia is cast alone upon a rock. Fatima and Sherasmin are thrown upon another. Nobody knows what has happened to the knight. Nor are the castaways at the end of their troubles. Captured by Barbary pirates, they are taken to the coast of Africa and sold to the Bey of Tunis. Rezia is to be given the honors of the harem; she has aroused a violent passion in the Bey. The other two lovers (for Sherasmin and Fatima, too, have fallen in love) are luckier. They have not been separated, and their role as slaves is limited to tending one of his Highness's gardens.

The eunuch Abulifar tells them about a revolution that is about to take place in the harem: the downfall of the former favorite and the elevation of Rezia to her rank. Rezia repels the Bey's advances contemptuously; she will remain faithful until death. Skillfully turning this noble constancy to account, Puck persuades Oberon to give the knight a second chance, one last fateful trial. Oberon consents; Puck fishes up poor Huon from somewhere and deposits him in the garden of the Bey of Tunis. There we see him surrounded him by a bevy of *houris*, each more bewitching than the next. They dance, sing, clasp him in their arms, assail him with the fire of their glances, devour him with their smiles. All in vain. Huon resists all their efforts; he loves Rezia, he loves only her, and he will remain faithful. Suddenly the Bey appears and, finding a stranger among his women, orders that he be impaled forthwith. Preparations for this procedure begin, but this time the trial of the lovers has been decisive: Love has triumphed and Oberon is satisfied.

He blows his magic horn, whereupon the Bey, the head eunuch, the other guards, the entire harem give way to an irresistible impulse to dance, to whirl about like dervishes, faster and faster under the increasingly imperious sway of the pitiless horn until, with the crash of a gong, the giddy crowd falls half-dead to the ground. Oberon, his beautiful Titania, and their faithful Puck rise to heaven in a halo of light, as the King of the Fairies addresses the lovers: "You have remained faithful to each other, you have resisted all temptation, be happy! Return to France, Huon, present your Rezia to the court. My protection goes with you."

To analyze the music of *Oberon* as it deserves, one would need to write much more than an essay. One would have to go into the questions of style raised by the work and explain the methods used by the composer before one could assign the causes of the delight with which this music affects the listener—even those unfamiliar with the art of sound, though not devoid of feeling for it.

Oberon is the counterpart of *Der Freischütz*. The one belongs to the dark fantastic—violent, demonic; the other is all smiling fairyland, graceful and bewitching. In *Oberon* the supernatural is so well blended with the real world that it is hard to tell exactly where one ends and the other begins, while passion and sentiment are expressed in an idiom and accents that one feels have never been heard before.

This music is essentially melodic, but in a different manner from that of the greatest melodists. Weber's melody is given out by the voices and the instruments like a subtle perfume that one breathes in with pleasure but cannot immediately identify. A phrase whose beginning has escaped the listener takes possession of his mind before he is aware that it exists. Another, which has vanished without his noticing, continues to absorb him for some time after he has ceased to hear it. Their chief attraction is an exquisite grace and a somewhat strange loveliness. One could say of Weber's inspiration in *Oberon* what Laertes says of his sister, Ophelia: "Thought and affliction, passion, hell itself,/She turns to favor and to prettiness,"[20] except that there is no mention of hell in *Oberon*. Indeed, in Weber's hands hell is never turned to anything graceful; on the contrary, it takes on a multitude of fearsome and terrifying forms.

Weber's harmonic progressions have a coloring uniquely his, which is reflected in his melody more than one might think. Their effect is sometimes due to the alteration of a few notes in a chord, sometimes to rarely used inversions, sometimes to the omission of notes normally deemed indispensable. One example is the final chord of the sea nymph's song,[21] in which the tonic is omitted; the piece being in E, the composer lets only the G-sharp and B be heard. Hence in this ending the special quality of indeterminacy that plunges the listener into reverie.

Virtually the same thing can be said about Weber's modulations; however strange they may be, they are always managed with great art; neither harsh nor jarring—though almost always unexpected—they serve but to heighten the expression of a feeling, not to surprise the ear in a puerile fashion.

Weber believes in absolute freedom for rhythmic patterns. Nobody else is so free from the tyranny of "squareness," that symmetry based on equal numbers of measures in successive phrases which, when used exclusively, leads to such painful monotony and the sure production of platitudes. In *Der Freischütz*, Weber had already provided numerous examples of his new phraseology. French musicians, who are, next to the Italians, the squarest of melodists, were surprised to find themselves applauding (among other examples) Caspar's drinking song, the first half of which consists of a series of three-measure phrases and the second half of a series of four-measure phrases. In *Oberon*, several passages can be found where the melody moves in groups of five and five. Generally, each phrase of five or three measures has its counterpart, thus constituting the even numbers that are so dear to commonplace musicians, despite the proverb *Numero Deus impare gaudet*[22] (God rejoices in odd numbers). But Weber feels no compulsion to establish this symmetry everywhere or at all costs; quite often his odd-numbered phrases have nothing to balance them. I appeal to literary judges to decide whether the device La Fontaine used was not excellent form when he wrote a line of only two syllables to end one of his fables:[23]

> Mais qu'en sort-il souvent?
> Du vent.

> But what is often the outcome?
> Just wind.

The affirmative reply I am sure they would give explains and justifies the similar device introduced into music by a good many composers, among them Weber, Gluck, and Beethoven. It seems just as absurd to limit music to four-by-four phrasing as it is to tolerate only one kind of meter in poetry. If instead of saying so adroitly:

> Mais qu'en sort-il souvent?
> Du vent.

La Fontaine had written:

Mais qu'en sort-il souvent?
Il n'en sort que du vent.

But what is often the outcome?
The outcome is often just wind.

he would have ended his fable with a dull platitude. The analogy between this example and the musical question under discussion is striking. Only a know-nothing defense of routine can prevent its acknowl-
edgment or deny its consequences.

Now, even though it is clear that music should not and cannot follow
blindly the school that insists on the squarest of squareness at all times,
even if we believe that the absurd persistence of this prejudice is the
cause of the loose, insipid style and irritating vulgarity of a multitude
of works from every place and period, we nonetheless acknowledge that
certain irregularities can be shocking and should be carefully avoided.
Gluck (especially in *Iphigénie en Aulide*) committed a great number of
such sins against rhythmic harmony. There is no denying it.

Nor is Weber exempt; I find a regrettable instance in one of the most
delightful numbers of *Oberon*, the song of the naïads that I mentioned
earlier. After the first main vocal statement, which consists of four times
four measures, the composer wished to give the voices a brief rest. The
gap is filled by the orchestra. Believing, no doubt, that the listener would
take no account of this instrumental fragment, the composer again took
up his vocal exposition, phrased symmetrically as if the orchestral measure had never existed. In my opinion, he was mistaken. The ear is pained
by the insertion of this extra bar in the melody. It is clearly noticeable
that the swinging rhythm has been interrupted, that the music has lost
the regular oscillation which gave it so much charm. Returning to my
comparison of melody with versification, I would say that the fault here
is as obvious as would be the case if a stanza with lines of ten metrical
feet included one of eleven.

As for Weber's instrumentation, I shall say only that it is admirably
rich, original, and varied. Distinction is again its dominant quality—no
resort to methods offensive to good taste, no blatancy, nothing contrary
to sense. Everywhere the coloring is full of charm, a vivid but harmonious sound, a controlled strength, a profound knowledge of the nature
of each instrument and its characteristics, of its sympathies and anti-
pathies toward other members of the orchestral family. In short, the
closest relations are maintained between drama and orchestra; nowhere
is there a purposeless effect or an accent without motive.

Weber has been criticized for his way of scoring for voice. Unfortunately, the reproach is not without foundation. He often calls for runs
that are excessively difficult and that would hardly be manageable by
any instrument but the piano. This fault, however, does not extend as
far as people say. Indeed, it is not a defect at all when the singularity of

the vocal line is justified by a dramatic intention. It then becomes a positive quality, and at that point the composer is blameworthy only from the standpoint of the singers, who are compelled to take pains and work harder than they would in singing commonplace music. Such is the case with several truly diabolical passages for Caspar's role in *Der Freischütz*, passages which are, as I think, clear proofs of genius.

Of the twenty numbers that make up the score of *Oberon*, I cannot think of a single one that is weak. Invention, inspiration, technique, and good judgment shine in all of them. It is almost with regret that I give special mention to some among the lot: the soft, mysterious introductory chorus sung by the fairies around the flowery couch where Oberon is sleeping; Huon's courtly aria, which contains a ravishing phrase first heard in the middle of the overture; the wonderful nocturnal march of the harem guards, which ends the first act; the stark and dynamic chorus "Hail to the chief of believers!"; Huon's prayer accompanied only by violas, cellos, and double-basses; Rezia's dramatic scene on the Ocean shore; the song of the nymphs, which in this new version is given to Puck alone (in my opinion, a mistake: it should be sung in very soft unison by a few selected singers placed stage rear against the backdrop of the sea); the choral dance of the fairies that concludes the second act; Fatima's aria full of grace and high spirits, followed by the duet with the persistent orchestral phrase coming at irregular intervals; the harmonious and admirably modulated trio accompanied by *pianissimo* brass; and finally the choral ballet in the seduction scene, a piece that is unique of its kind. Never has melody been so smiling, or rhythm so irresistibly caressing. To resist the blandishments of women who sing such music, Sir Huon's virtue must have been riveted to his bodily frame.

The audience encored four numbers in addition to the overture. After three hours of absorbing with delight music of such a new flavor, people came out in a state of sheer intoxication. It was a triumph, I repeat, a great and noble triumph.

The tenor Michot has a splendid voice, with a rich and attractive timbre that practice should soon make more flexible. Night after night, the audience calls him back repeatedly to the stage. He is, as they say in the theater, "placed." He will become—he already is—an invaluable performer. Mme Rossi-Caccia,[24] after a long absence from the stage, is making her comeback in the difficult role of Rezia, which she sings with talent. Mlle Girard[25] is an excellent Fatima; if only she could control the quaver in her voice! Mlle Borghèse ably sings and acts the role of Puck the sprite, except that she is too tall. But there's no cure for that! Grillon gives a good account of himself as Sherasmin, as does Froment in the role of Oberon. As for the eunuch, Girardot, he provokes much mirth by his costume, his antics, his bizarre voice, and his wit.

Not wanting to stint in his production of Weber's masterpiece, M. Carvalho has enriched the orchestra with ten more strings, which required removing a number of seats from the hall; he also added twelve women's voices to the chorus of sprites. Great care and thought went into the staging; the grand finale, the apotheosis of Titania and Oberon, is poetically most effective.

ABU HASSAN
Opera in One Act by the Young Weber

THE ABDUCTION FROM THE SERAGLIO
Opera in Two Acts by the Young Mozart

Their First Performance at the Théâtre-Lyrique[1]

Abu Hassan is a Turkish lad in love with a young Turkish lass. He is a bit wild, but has a good heart—so they say. He gets into debt. People help him out with money, but instead of using it to pay off his debts, he buys gifts for his lady-love. Finally he has to pay up, but he cannot. Now it seems that his master, the pasha, is in the habit of contributing 1,000 piastres (I am not sure if that is the currency) toward his servants' funerals. Abu Hassan has the bright idea of pretending to be dead. His inamorata (she may be his wife) is equally eager, and she too pretends to be dead. So the pasha has to pay out 2,000 piastres, which is enough to get our lovers out of their trouble. The pasha discovers the trick. But quite disarmed, he laughs and pardons them. The lovers (or spouses) come back to life, and everyone is happy.

Weber is said to have been seventeen[2] when he wrote the music of this clever little opera. It is also said that M. Meyerbeer helped him a little in composing this work, but at the time Meyerbeer himself was not much more that sixteen and a half.[3] Consequently, the composer of *Les Huguenots* is now quite unable to recognize the numbers with which he embellished his friend's work. If some old researcher were now to tell him dogmatically: "This aria is yours," he might reply, as did the good La Fontaine when a small boy was pointed out to him as his son: "It's quite possible."

Anyhow, the score of *Abu Hassan* contains several excellent bits of youthful fun, including one aria which Meillet[4] sang superlatively well, and which was encored to much applause. Meillet sings his entire role with great verve, energy, and good taste. His success, both as singer and actor, has been complete.

The Abduction from the Seraglio is a much earlier opera than *Abu*

Hassan, and Mozart was perhaps not even seventeen when he composed it.[5] Anyone who wants to know exactly can look it up in Ulibishev's book. Mr. Ulibishev was a Russian[6] who knew the precise time of day when the composer of *Don Giovanni* wrote the last note of this or that sonata for keyboard, fell into a swoon upon hearing two clarinets play the major third (C, E) in this or that Mozart opera, but rose up full of indignation when he heard the same two clarinets play the same two notes in Beethoven's *Fidelio*. All his life, Mr. Ulibishev was prey to an anguishing doubt: he was not quite sure whether or not Mozart was God.

The *Seraglio* is introduced by a short overture in C major, of priceless naïveté, and which did not make much of an impression; the audience seemed hardly to notice it at all. That was—if I may say so—to the credit of the audience. Indeed (if the truth be told) Leopold Mozart, instead of weeping with admiration at his son's work, as he usually did, would have done better to burn it and say to the young composer: "My boy, this overture you've just written is ridiculous; I don't doubt you told your beads before you began, but now you shall compose another; and this time, go through your rosary again and pray for better inspiration."

"Outrage! Abomination! Blasphemy!" All the Ulibishevs will cry out, rending their garments and covering their heads with ashes—"Yes. Blasphemy! Abomination!" Hold on, calm down, ye venerable men, do not rend your garments. Cover your heads with wig powder if you wish, not with ashes, for there is nothing of blasphemy or abomination in what I say. It has recently been proved beyond doubt that Mozart, especially at fifteen, was not actually God. I'll have you know in addition that I admire him more and know him better than you do, and that my admiration is all the more genuine that it is not based on foolish estimates or silly preconceptions.

The Abduction from the Seraglio is yet another Turkish story. There is the ubiquitous European slave girl who resists the advances of the ubiquitous pasha. This slave girl has a pretty maidservant, and each has a young sweetheart.[7] These wretched fellows risk being impaled in order to rescue their girlfriends. They steal into the *seraglio*, bringing a ladder, even two.

But Osmin, a Turkish buffoon who is the pasha's right-hand man, foils their plan. He carries off one of the ladders, seizes all four people, and is about to hand them over for impalement when the pasha turns out to be a make-believe Turk of Spanish descent. He learns that Constanze's lover, Belmonte, is the son of a Spanish friend who had once saved his life;[8] so he loses no time before freeing our lovers and sending them back to Europe, where they will doubtless have many children.

It's as clever as that.

To claim that Mozart has written on this text a marvel of inspiration would be even cleverer, but nothing more than that. There are a host of pretty little tunes, to be sure, but also a host of formulas which one regrets finding here, especially since Mozart used them again in his later masterpieces. For us today they have become an intolerable obsession.

Generally speaking, the melodies in this opera are simple, sweet, and not particularly original; the accompaniments are discreet, pleasant, not greatly varied, childlike. The instrumentation is typical of the period, though already better managed than it is in the works of the composer's contemporaries. The orchestra often uses what was then called "Turkish music," that is, a primitive use of bass drum, cymbals, and triangle. In addition, Mozart used a small *flûte quinte* [alto flute] in G (in his day called a flute in A, while ordinary flutes were said to be in D). At times this instrument is used in a trio with the two large flutes.

If Osmin's first aria were by a contemporary composer, one would be entitled to find it rather uninteresting; and if the three stanzas sung thereupon by this same character were from the same source, they most certainly would not have been encored. The chorus accompanied by Turkish music is appropriate for its subject. The rather bland duet in 6/8 time between Osmin and the maidservant contains many high notes which the soprano has to reach at her own risk; the effect is rather unappealing. The *Allegro* of the following aria bears a regrettable likeness to the Parisian popular song "En avant, Fanfan la Tulipe!" which Mozart had certainly never heard. So the remark should be inverted, the blame changed to praise: one should say that the vulgar Parisian tune has the honor of resembling the theme of an *Allegro* by Mozart.

Belmonte's aria, on the other hand, is melodious, expressive, and charming. The quartet, which is extremely naïve in style, takes on a little life toward the *coda*, thanks to a rapid phrase in the violins. A march with muted instruments provides an effective close to the first act.[9]

The soubrette's aria[10] is unfortunately marred by grotesque runs and vocalises that Mozart used even in his most magnificent works. You will say it was the taste of the times. So much the worse for the times and so much the worse for us now. Mozart would have done better to consult his own taste. Moreover, the soprano's part here is too often at the top of her register; but the defect must have been less noticeable at a time when concert pitch was somewhat more than a half-tone lower than it is today.[11]

The very agreeable stanzas sung by Bataille and Froment[12] had the honor of being encored. Osmin's aria in D, which follows them, shows a feature most unusual in Mozart: a theme made up of three-bar phrases followed by one in groups of four. Can it be that Mozart did not think it madness to write music other than in "square" formation? His practice here upsets a whole school of thought.

Belmonte's part also contains a graceful romance; the song of the signal for eloping is piquant, with its accompaniment of pizzicato violins.[13] But in my opinion the best number in the score is the duet between Constanze and Belmonte that ends the opera.[14] The feeling is beautiful, the style loftier than all that comes before, the form broader, and the ideas developed in masterly fashion.

According to nearly all our music critics, the *Abduction from the Seraglio* was performed at the Théâtre-Lyrique with the *most scrupulous fidelity*. Only, a three-act opera was compressed into two acts, the sequence of several numbers was inverted, an important aria was transferred from Mme Meillet[15] [Constanze] to Mme Ugalde[16] [Blonde], and the famous Turkish march for piano, so well known to pianists who play Mozart, was inserted between the two acts.

Well done, friends! That is the very definition of *scrupulous fidelity!*[17]

THE METHOD DISCOVERED BY
M. DELSARTE FOR TUNING
INSTRUMENTS
Without Relying on the Ear[1]

Hear ye, hear ye, pianists, guitarists, violinists, cellists, bassists, harpists, piano tuners, and you, too, conductors! *Without using the ear!* It is a tremendous, incomparable, priceless discovery, especially for us listeners weary of pianos out of tune, violins and cellos out of tune, harps out of tune, and orchestras out of tune. M. Delsarte's invention[2] will compel you to stop torturing us, stop making us perspire with pain, stop driving us to suicide.

Without relying on the ear! Not only will it be unnecessary to rely on the ear when tuning instruments, but resorting to it will even become a danger; indeed it will be absolutely necessary *not* to rely on it. What a boon for those who have no ear! Until now, it was the other way around, and we had to forgive you for the torments you inflicted on us. In future, if your instruments or your orchestras are not in tune, you will have no excuse, and we shall single you out for public obloquy.

Without relying on the ear. Its help is so often ineffectual, misleading, pernicious! M. Delsarte's invention works only for strings. Still, that is a great deal, it is tremendous. It means that in orchestras that are tuned and conducted without the ear, the only instruments out of tune will be the flutes, oboes, clarinets, bassoons, horns, cornets, trumpets, trombones, the ophicleide, tuba, and timpani. The triangle could, in a pinch, be tuned by the new method, but it is generally held that this is unnecessary—just as with the bells; dissonance between the triangle and the other instruments is thought to *sound good.* All opera goers love it.

But what about the singers? You don't mention them, someone will say. Will it ever be possible to make them sing in tune, to agree on their intonation? The singers? Well, two or three of them do sing naturally in tune. A few more could be brought, through rigorous training and discipline, to be more or less in tune. But the rest have never been, are not, and never will be able to sing in tune, neither individually, nor together, nor with the orchestra, nor in rhythm, phrasing, expression, pitch, language, or anything suggestive of precision and common sense. For some time now, they have not even been in tune with the *claque,* the hired applause, which threatens to give them up. It would serve them right—but what a catastrophe!

M. Delsarte has made the tuning of pianos particularly easy through the use of a device he calls the *phonopticon*. It would take too long to describe it here; it is enough to say that a needle on a dial indicates the precise moment when two or more strings are in unison. I may add that, for anyone who uses it with care, the device gives a result so exact that the most practiced ear cannot equal it.

Experts in acoustics will surely take an interest in this valuable invention, and its use should soon become widespread.

ON CHURCH MUSIC

By Joseph d'Ortigue [1]

The author of this book has the literary integrity and the modesty—so rare nowadays—to state in his preface that what he offers us is not a book, but a

> collection of articles about plainsong and church music that were published in various newspapers and periodicals over the last twenty-five years. Most of these articles were written, not consecutively but from time to time, and they appeared here and there in journals of diverse character and tendencies, as well as addressed to various kinds of readers. Now thoroughly revised—some of them completely recast—the articles here brought together can be thought of as being issued for the first time. Such is this volume: though the parts are old, the whole may well offer something new. [2]

It does indeed bring us much that is new. It combines, moreover, the attraction of novelty and the interest possessed by every book that is truly useful. In addition, it is written with elegance and precision of style and perfect clarity. This last quality is highly prized by many people, and I am one of them. Nothing is so distasteful as the sort of inflated prose, where a bogus profundity does not so much obscure the author's meaning and make it difficult to follow, as conceal the fact that there is no meaning there at all—the kind of book the reader usually puts down at page 4, saying to himself: "I have no idea what the author is trying to say and probably he has none either."

I am reminded of a treatise on harmony by a learned mathematician. It was said to have been written on a most ingenious principle. I read it with enough concentrated effort to make one ill, but understood nothing. When I confessed to the author that the meaning of his work totally escaped me, he offered to explain it. We had a long conversation, but his oral explanation succeeded no better in making me understand his enigmatic treatise.

I told the author I must be temporarily in the wrong frame of mind— "Be good enough to allow me another hour of study, and I may be more intelligent at a second try." I persisted and made another appointment. I was curious to know whether I would ever manage to grasp his theory. The theorist came back and began once more to expound his doctrine, his examples, in short, his system. I made superhuman efforts to follow; my brain felt as if it were twisting in my skull. On his side, the author was sweating freely as he perceived what heroic efforts I was vainly making to understand. In the end we had to give up. I had to confess, "It's no use. I haven't the slightest idea what it is you are trying to convey. It is as if you were speaking to me in Chinese." And yet this learned man had written a huge tome to teach harmony to *people who do not know the subject!*

There is nothing of the kind, I repeat, in M. d'Ortigue's book. If I differ with him on several points, at least I know where and why these differences exist. The main purpose of his work is to analyze and explain religious music, that is, the art of sound as applied to religious worship, and the singing of sacred texts in the Catholic church. He wants to point out the mistakes of the composers who have undertaken this task without a proper understanding of its importance, as well as the reprehensible tolerance shown toward such musicians by members of the clergy—a tolerance due to ignorance of the expressive meaning of the art of sound and to a lack of taste.

M. d'Ortigue's work also aims at giving preeminence to plainsong over modern music, indeed at the expense of *music,* by declaring that plainsong alone is able to express in worthy fashion true religious feeling. On the one hand, then, the author seeks ways to remedy the countless musical abuses that have overtaken church music, and on the other, he means to rescue plainsong from the corruption into which it has fallen.

It should be said that the revolting practices of which he gives examples are not limited to our own day. Everybody knows what cynical or stupid habits some of the old contrapuntists fell into. They would take as themes for their so-called religious compositions, popular songs whose suggestive or even obscene words were familiar to all. These tunes would resound anew as the main idea of works meant for the divine service. The mass known as *L'Homme armé*[3] is a well-known example. It is part of the glory of Palestrina that he put an end to this barbaric practice.[4]

Even so, many of us remember what our missionary priests were capable of—say, up to about 35 years ago—because of their ignorant fondness for music and their zeal, both blind and deaf. During service in the church of Sainte-Geneviève, hymns were sung to tunes borrowed from the vaudevilles[5] at the Théâtre des Variétés, such as:

> C'est l'amour, l'amour, l'amour
> Qui fait le monde
> A la ronde!

> It is love, love, love
> that makes
> the world go round!

But the masterpiece of this genre was supplied more recently by a rather well known composer who even dared to publish the triumph of his art for the edification of devout souls and right-thinking people. And this is not just a story made up for the occasion: I have read this egregious score. Here is what M. d'Ortigue has to say about it:

> I wrote in an earlier article that the *Concerts spirituels*[6] of Avignon of 1835 had been outdone, far outdone, by *La Messe de Rossini*, which was brought to birth a few years ago by the witty [*spirituel*] but all too fun-loving Castil-Blaze.[7] He apparently wanted to crown his career as arranger by composing the most outrageous arrangement ever conceived, as if he were trying to challenge his own record. I shall mention only the principal sections of this "Rossini Mass." The *Kyrie* is taken from the march of Rossini's *Otello*. The *Gloria* begins with the opening chorus from that same work, which is also the source of other fragments until we come to the second half of the final verse, *Cum Sancto Spiritu, in gloria Dei patris, Amen;* these words the arranger has set to the *stretta* from the quintet in *La Cenerentola* [Cinderella], which is a comic number of irrepressible gaiety, a rapid *Allegro* in triple time. It can hardly be imagined what an insane and grotesque effect is produced when the text, *Cum Sancto Spiritu*, is delivered one syllable per eighth note in rapid tempo.
>
> The rest is in keeping. The *Credo* opens with the romance from the *Barber of Seville*, "Ecco ridente il cielo" [Behold the smiling skies]. Then come the warlike duets from *Tancredi* and *Otello*; a *Resurrexit* made up of florid runs and vocalises; and finally the *Et vitam venturi seculi* sung to the theme of Arsace's aria in the finale of *Semiramide*, "Atro evento prodigio." One last example: The *Dona nobis pacem* is hammered out by the chorus in staccato chords accompanying a *cabaletta* from *Tancredi*, the neatest and prettiest *cabaletta* in the world.[8]

Naturally, M. d'Ortigue does not hold Rossini responsible for all this madness. His blame is directed solely at the arranger. He does indeed sharply reproach the celebrated maestro Rossini—rightly it seems to me—for some sections of his *Stabat Mater*, which are on the whole more theatrical than religious. But this is not the fault of Music, the "worldly minded" art, as he calls it; and he is wrong when he lets himself drift little by little into the position of holding this great art responsible for the errors of some composers. He goes so far as to assert that "there can be no genuine sacred music other than that written in the church modes." This would mean that Mozart's *Ave Verum*, that sublime expression of ecstatic devotion, which is not modal in tonality, cannot be considered genuine religious music.

It is here that M. d'Ortigue betrays his partiality toward plainsong, a partiality that I confess I do not share. Indeed, I fail to understand how he can believe that plainsong, the offspring of Greek music, the music of pagans, is alone worthy of singing the praises of the Christian God, while *music*, a modern invention of the Christian era, is denied this privilege in spite of its various powers which plainsong lacks.

In M. d'Ortigue's view, it is precisely the simplicity, the vagueness and indeterminate tonality, the *impersonality*, the inexpressiveness that constitute the principal merit of plainsong. If that is right, then it seems to me that the ideal of religious music would be a statue reciting the words of the liturgy with cold impassivity on a single repeated note. M. d'Ortigue does not go as far as that, though his theory should bring him to that conclusion. On the contrary, he condemns the way plainsong is performed, or rather bellowed in our churches by bull-like voices, accompanied by a serpent or an ophicleide. He is certainly right about that. On hearing those ugly, menacing sounds, one feels as though one had strayed into a den of druids preparing a human sacrifice. It is horrible. But I must confess that all the plainsong I have ever heard was performed in this way and conveyed this atmosphere.

A thorough discussion of this subject and related matters would take us far. While I share the indignation of my learned friend and colleague about the perversions that have crept into church music and the shocking errors into which nearly all the great masters have fallen when composing works in this difficult genre, I still believe that it would be easy to rehabilitate *music*. Music as such is not guilty of the misuse that has been made of her riches and power. Besides, music can produce the effects of plainsong whenever desired,[9] while plainsong is of course incapable of producing those of music.

Be this as it may, *On Church Music* deserves high praise and is to be recommended to all readers who feel concerned about the dignity of religion as well as the dignity of art. The clergy, being in a position to influence directly the use of music in their churches, can only benefit from pondering the message of this book: "Nocturna versate manu, versate diurna"[10] (Turn to it by night and by day).

MUSICAL CUSTOMS OF CHINA[1]

The Chinese have been much in the news lately[2] but always in a way rather unflattering toward them. We are not satisfied with beating them in battle, smashing up their shops, putting their emperor to flight, seizing the palace of his Celestial Majesty, making booty out of his gold, diamonds, jewels and silks;[3] we must also make fun of this great people. We call them a nation of dotards, cranks, lunatics, idiots; a people in love with the absurd, the horrible, and the grotesque. We laugh at their beliefs, their customs, their arts, their science, and even their domestic customs, on the ground that they eat their rice grain by grain with little sticks, and that it takes them almost as long to learn to use these ridiculous implements as to learn to write (something they never manage completely)—as if, say we, it were not easier to eat rice with a spoon. We poke fun at their weapons, their armies, their banners painted with dragons to frighten the enemy, their old matchlock rifles, and their cannon which shoot at the moon! We deride their musical instruments, their women with deformed feet; in short, we ridicule everything.

Yet there is much that is good in the Chinese people, a great deal of good, and it is not without reason that they call us Europeans barbarians and red devils. For example: 60,000 Chinese were routed by 4,000 or 5,000 British and French troops, that is true; but when their commander-in-chief saw that the battle was lost, he sawed through his neck very efficiently with his own sword, without having to get help from his servant, as the Romans used to do; and he was not satisfied until his head was cut right off, and on the ground! Now that is very brave. Try it yourself.

The Chinese crush the feet of their women to keep them from walking about, but even more to keep them from going to balls, from dancing the polka and waltzing, from thus spending entire nights in the arms of young men who hold them close, inhale their breath, and whisper in their ears—all under the eyes of their fathers, mothers, husbands, and sweethearts.

Their music we find dreadful; to our ears, the sound of their singing is like dogs yawning, or cats coughing up a fish bone. The instruments they use to accompany the voice seem to us veritable instruments of torture.[4] But at least they respect their own music, just as it is; they protect the outstanding works produced by the Chinese genius, whereas we give no more protection to our masterpieces than we show disgust for monstrous productions. We abandon both the foul and the fair to the same public indifference.

In their country, everything is regulated—even the instrumentation of their operas—according to a fixed, immutable code. The size of the tam-tams and gongs is set according to the subject of the drama and the musical style it requires. Comic operas are not allowed to use gongs as large as those in a serious opera. With us, the most trifling work for singers has bass drums as huge as those in a grand opera. This was not true 25 years ago, which is further proof of the advantages of the fixed code that governs Chinese music.

In spite of the disastrous results of our fickle and unruly practices, our music does in certain respects excel that of the Celestial Empire. As even the mandarins who supervise melody have admitted, Chinese singers often sing out of tune, a sign of their inferiority to our singers, who so often sing in tune. On the other hand, almost all Chinese singers know their own language; they do not violate its accentuation and they respect its prosody. Twenty-five years ago we used to do likewise; today, as a result of our mania for changing everything according to individual whim, most European singers seem to be singing in Chinese.

What one cannot help admiring as truly splendid are the rules and regulations in the Celestial Empire that have been in force since time immemorial to protect the masterpieces of music. Nobody is allowed to mutilate them, to garble them in performance. There can be no alteration of the text, the feeling, or the spirit of the work. These laws are not preventive; nobody is stopped from performing a classic. But anybody found guilty of having distorted it is punished in proportion to the eminence of the composer. To us, of course, the penalties incurred by the desecrators of the works of Confucius may seem cruel, for we are barbarians accustomed to violating everything with impunity.

Confucius is called K'ung Fu-tze by the Chinese. It is another lovely custom of ours to make *arrangements* of proper names, as works are *arranged* when being translated from one language to another, or merely transferred from one stage to another. We cannot keep intact either the names of the great men of foreign nations, or those of their great cities. The French call Ratisbonne the German city that the Germans call Regensburg, while the Italians call Paris, Parigi. That extra syllable, *gi* (pronounced *dgi*), gives them endless pleasure; their ears would be shocked if they pronounced Paris as the French do. So it is not surprising that we say Confucius for K'ung Fu-tze; first, because the Latin -*us* ending is held in high esteem among the philosophical, and also because we make it a principle to suffer no hindrance when it comes to names that are difficult to pronounce. This is the reason for the much-admired precaution taken by a German musician who was afraid of finding his Teutonic name replaced by something not to his taste; he wrote on his visiting card: "Schneitzhoeffer, pronounced Bertrand."[5]

As I was saying, K'ung Fu-tze, or Confucius, or Bertrand, was a great philosopher—everybody knows this—and he combined with his philos-

ophy a great fund of musical knowledge. After composing variations on
the famous air by Li-Po, he played them on a guitar inlaid with ivory
throughout the length and breadth of the Celestial Empire, thereby moralizing its huge population. It is since that time that the Chinese people
have been profoundly moral.

But the works of K'ung Fu-tze are not limited to these variations for
guitar inlaid with ivory. No, indeed. The great musician-philosopher also
wrote a large number of moral cantatas and moral operas whose chief
merit—according to the cultured authors and musicians of China—is
the simple beauty of the melodic style, coupled with the deepest expressiveness in delineating passions and sentiments. A remarkable story is
told of a Chinese woman who was watching an opera in which K'ung
Fu-tze had depicted with touching realism the joys of motherhood. She
began to weep bitterly in the seventh act. When her neighbors asked the
reason for her tears, she replied, "Alas, I have given birth to nine children and drowned them all. Now I am sorry I didn't keep at least one. I
would have loved it so."

The Chinese lawmakers impose severe penalties, rightly, I think, not
only on theater directors who stage K'ung Fu-tze's splendid operas badly,
but also on singers who give unworthy performances of excerpts at concerts. Each week, the musical police make out a report to the mandarin
director of the arts, and if a singer is judged guilty of the offense of
desecration I have just mentioned, she is given a first warning by having
her left ear cut off. If she repeats the mistake, she loses her right ear as
a second warning. Thereafter, if she proves a third offender, the ultimate
punishment is applied: her nose is cut off. This happens very rarely; and
I must say, Chinese law seems too severe on this point, for a perfect
performance could hardly be expected from a singer who has no ears.

The punishments that certain peoples impose strike us as both comical and surprising. I remember seeing in Moscow[6] a great lady of the
Russian aristocracy sweeping the streets in broad daylight as the snow
melted. "It is the custom," a Russian told me. "She was sentenced to
sweep the street for two hours; she was caught red-handed stealing from
a fancy goods shop."

In the charming French colony of Tahiti, beautiful islanders who have
been found guilty of welcoming too great a number of men, whether
French or Tahitian, are sentenced to work with their hands at road
building, the assigned stretch being short or long, with or without cob-
blestones. Thus, amorous intrigue is turned to the improvement of the
transportation system. How many women are there in Paris who never
amount to anything, but who in that country would be sure to make
their way!

The title of Director of Arts that I used above for one of the mandarins
must sound strange. It is indeed difficult to imagine what use there can
be for such an office in our part of the world, where art is free to go

astray, where it can turn beggar, thief, assassin, or page boy in the *seraglio;* where it can starve to death or run drunkenly through the streets of our cities; where our singers all have their ears and noses intact; where the first qualification for director of an opera house is to be ignorant of music; where literary people decide the fate of musicians; where the prizes for musical composition are awarded by painters, the prizes for painting by architects, the prizes for sculpture by engravers.[7] If the Chinese only knew that! The poor Chinese!

Yes, as I have said, there is a lot of good in them. They have artistic directors who know what they are directing; they have whole institutes of mandarin-artists who exert tremendous influence for the greater good of art throughout the empire. In China, every book published on music, painting, or architecture is submitted to the mandarin-artists so that if they approve, the author can write in the second edition "Approved by the college of mandarins." Unfortunately, the esteemed members of this institution, who have the right to inflict on authors the punishment of the *cang,*[8] have always been, unlike the special directors of music, so benevolent that they usually approve whatever is submitted to them. One day they will praise an author for expounding a particular doctrine, for advocating a particular method of playing the tam-tam; the next day, another will expound the opposite doctrine, advocate the contrary method, and the college will approve that, too. They have reached such a pitch of good nature and indulgence that nowadays most authors write the formula "Approved by the college" in the first edition of their books, even before presenting it, so sure are they of getting their approval.

Ah, the poor Chinese! It is not surprising to see that their art always stays the same! But I forgive them everything for the sake of their rules about playing the tam-tam and their laws against desecrators. But, you will ask, if they cut off the ears and noses of singers who mutilate masterpieces, what do they do to those who interpret them faithfully, grandly, supremely well? What do they do to them? They shower them with honors of all kinds; they give them silver chopsticks to eat their rice; they award to some the yellow button, to others the blue button; to this one the crystal button, to that one all three buttons. In China, you will see virtuosos covered with buttons. It is not as in France, where a medal is bestowed on a singer only after he has retired from the stage or lost his voice, when he is no longer good for anything.

Chinese customs, which differ so much from ours in all that concerns the fine arts in general and music in particular, converge with ours only on a single point: It is sailors who are put in command of the fleet. If we were to continue along that line, we would end up being just like them.

LETTER TO THE ACADEMY OF FINE ARTS[1] OF THE INSTITUTE[2]

GENTLEMEN AND DEAR COLLEAGUES,

You seem to think that an account of what I am doing now in Baden might interest an audience at a public session of the Institute. I do not share your view,* but since you insist, I shall comply and write.

Do not imagine, however, that I shall go so far astray as to paraphrase the many descriptions of Baden given with uncommon talent by such writers as Eugène Guinot,[3] Achard,[4] and others. No, I shall speak only of music, of geology and zoology, of ruins, of splendid palaces, of philosophy, and of ethics. I shall evoke antiquity and the Middle Ages; I shall examine the present day; I shall quote from the Apocalypse, Homer, and Shakespeare, perhaps even from M. Paul de Kock.[5] I shall criticize this and that, from force of habit. I shall even disapprove of some of your approbations, and you will have to listen to it all. You asked for it.

"What a lot of things in a minuet!" said the great Vestris.[6] "What a lot of things in a letter!" you will say. Don't be alarmed, my letter may turn out to be as neat and clear as a printed invitation. That will depend on my state of health, which is abominable, and the whims of my neuralgia. I have dropped this hint on purpose, so that you can say when I grow too tiresome, "It's his neuralgia!"[7]

Of course, many people are devoid of wit and common sense when they are well. With me it is the opposite; my lack of wit is never so evident as when I am ill. I belong to the second category and am only too happy to know I am not in the third, people who have no common sense at any time.

And so, what am I up to in Baden?[8] I am making music, something which is absolutely forbidden me in Paris, for want of a good hall, want of money to pay for rehearsals, want of time to do them well, want of a public, want of everything.

M. Bénazet[9] is, during five months of the year, the veritable sovereign of Baden, where he exercises his power for the greater glory of art and the happiness of artists. Eight years ago, he said to me in more or less these words: "My dear sir, you know that I give many concerts in the small salons of the Palais de la Conversation. All the pianists of the

---

* This letter was indeed deemed too unlike the usual style to be suitable for a public reading at the Academy.

world come there one after the other; several come at the same time to exercise their fingers. You can hear the greatest artists and the most eccentric virtuosos. You can see violinists play the flute, flutists play the violin, basses sing soprano, sopranos sing bass, you can even hear singers who do not use voices of any kind. In short, they are fine concerts. However, even though it is said that one should leave well enough alone, Í strive for the best. So how would you like to come to Baden and organize a great music festival every year? I will let you have all the singers and musicians you want for an ensemble large enough for the great hall of the Palais de la Conversation, and above all, in keeping with the style of the works you will be performing. You can choose your programs and plan the schedule of rehearsals. Any artists you need for special occasions, you can have. Offer in my name whatever they ask. I have confidence in you, and I will have no hand in anything—except to pay!"

"O Richard, O my king!"[10] I cried, wild with delight on hearing these sublime words. Is it possible? Can there be a sovereign capable of all this? You will give me a free hand? You are actually choosing a musician to direct a musical institution, a musical enterprise, a music festival? You are abandoning the deplorable ways in use everywhere in Europe! You mean you won't take a sea captain, a cavalry colonel, a lawyer, or a goldsmith to direct your concerts? Then it must be true. As God said: 'Let there be light! And there was—light!' With you, the most hallowed traditions are thrown over. You are an ultra-Romantic; a hue and cry will be raised against you. Your windows will be smashed. You will be horribly compromised; the other sovereigns will withdraw their ambassadors.

"No matter," replied M. Bénazet. "Even if it upsets the Concert of Europe,[11] I have made up my mind. The thing is done; I am counting on you."

Every year since then, as August approaches, a certain twitching in my right arm reminds me that soon I shall have an orchestra to conduct. I begin immediately to draw up the program, if it hasn't been done the season before (which is almost always the case). After which I only have to agree with the gods and goddesses of song engaged for the festival on the choice of works that they will sing. I am careful to refrain from choosing their programs for them; I know only too well the respect that simple mortals owe to divinities. After six weeks, we generally discover that we cannot agree; the prima donnas especially have a habit of changing their minds ten times before a concert.[12]

Right now, the festival is only a few days away, and I still do not know which duet the tenor and the prima donna will be singing. For three months, I have been begging them to tell me. As for the tenor's solo,[13] we did agree at once on an admirable aria that the modesty of one of our colleagues forbids me to characterize further.[14]

I take this opportunity, gentlemen, to ask you a question. I am told that you recently approved a book on the art of singing in which the author,[15] a man of talent and intelligence, unfortunately, declared that it is not only the right but the duty of a singer to embellish expressive arias, to change passages at will, to alter them in a hundred different ways, to pose as the composer's assistant and help overcome his short-comings. Tell me frankly, what do you think the composer of this lovely aria would do if a tenor, putting into practice this egregious theory, should take it into his head, while singing in his presence, to distort all those phrases whose expression is so true, whose sentiment is so profound, and whose melodic style is so natural? In what way would his fatherly heart be stirred should the *traditore*[16] take it into his head to add ap-poggiaturas to the sublime passage where candor, innocence, and simple grace unite with a naïve terror of death? He doesn't believe in suicide, I know that. However, if he had a pistol at hand, he would surely blow the other's brains out.

Do not worry, nothing like that will happen in Baden. My tenor is a serious artist;[17] he would never dream of perpetrating such a monstrous deed. Moreover, I shall be there and if he were so forsaken by his guard-ian angel as to commit such a crime of artistic *lèse-majesté* at the dress rehearsal, I would say to the orchestra what I once said in London in a similar situation: "Gentlemen, when we get to this passage, be sure to look at me. If the singer dares to distort it as he just did, I will signal to you to stop dead—I forbid you to play; he shall sing without accompa-niment."

And yet you have approved of such displays as well as of the theory that sanctions them! You! Were you to die and come back from beyond the grave to tell me so, I should not believe it.

Now, here is a nice little anecdote in every way related to the subject. It is a true story. I call to witness another of our colleagues who fell victim to a virtuoso. In this case it was an instrumental *traditore*. For we composers have the good fortune to be assassinated by everyone—by singers without a scrap of talent; by wretched virtuosos; by mediocre orchestras; by voiceless choruses; by incompetent, lymphatic, or bilious conductors; by stage hands, producers, copyists, engravers, sellers of strings, and instrument makers; by architects who construct halls; and finally by the claque hired to applaud us. So true is this that no one attending performances in France of Mozart's *Don Giovanni* has been able to hear the beautiful instrumental phrase that ends the trio of masques; it is always drowned out by applause.

In Germany, where there are no professional clappers, the audiences know better; they do not applaud without rhyme or reason; they listen first to the music. I remember a performance of *Fidelio* in Frankfurt,[18] during which the public gave no sign of approval. With my Parisian ideas and habits, I was indignant. But after the last chord of the last act, the whole house stood up and acclaimed Beethoven's masterpiece with thunderous applause. Well done, but not a minute too soon; or rather, none too soon, but too rare.

Where was I? O Neuralgia! Yes, I was going to tell you a story about one of those brigand virtuosos who slit the throats of great composers. The one in my story did much worse. He cut the throat of a member of the Institute! I can see you tremble. Here is what happened.

Five years ago, a charming new opera entitled *Le Sylphe*,[19] composed especially for the season, was given at Baden. A harpist was brought in from Paris to accompany a very important song. Believing that a man of his stature ought to make himself talked about in Germany—after all, he had condescended to travel there—and quite sure that the composer of the opera would not write a harp solo that had no relation to the drama, our man helped himself: he secretly wrote a little concerto for harp, and at the première of *Le Sylphe*, after the *ritornello* in the orchestra that ushers in the singer's aria, the virtuoso took advantage of the pause and coolly began to play his concerto, to the great astonishment of the conductor, the musicians, the singer, and the hapless composer, who, perspiring from anxiety and indignation, thought he was having a nightmare. I was there. Now, the composer is a philosophic sort and did not visibly lose weight over the incident,[20] but I did on his behalf. Tell me, gentlemen, do you approve also of this harp concerto and the forced collaboration of virtuosos and composers?

I must add that a few days earlier this same harpist was playing in the festival orchestra. He was not far from me. Suddenly, in a *tutti* passage, I saw him stop playing. "Why aren't you playing?" I asked. "There's no point; no one can hear me." He could not entertain the idea that it was appropriate or useful to the ensemble for him to play even when his harp would not be conspicuous among the other instruments. If this doctrine were put into general practice, the second flutes, second oboes, second clarinets, third and fourth horns, and all the violas would almost always have the right to stop playing at any moment. Need I say that this noble careerist has not again, and never will, set foot in any orchestra under my direction?

This practice of deletion is in fact rather rare; that of addition is, on the contrary, extremely widespread. Let us make its disastrous results more evident by applying it to literature.

Some people who recite poetry in public get applause by overdoing their diction, exaggerating their accents, overstressing words, making bombast out of simple expressions, and so on. Let us imagine that one of these is reciting La Fontaine's "Death and the Dying Man" and introduces some verses of his own in order to enhance the effect. Let me acknowledge at once that there may be people with minds sufficiently ill constituted to forgive the insolence and even find the added lines ingenious. Imagine the reciter saying:

> La mort ne surprend point le sage:
> Il est toujours prêt à partir
> *Sans gémir.*

> Death to the sage is no surprise
> He's always ready to say goodby to life
> *Without a sigh.*

You will of course say, why on earth should he sigh? Every complaint is futile when nothing in the world can postpone the fatal moment. La Fontaine hadn't thought of that.

Once more:

> Il est toujours prêt à partir
> *Sans gémir*
> S'étant su lui-même avertir
> Du temps où l'on se doit résoudre à ce passage
> *D'usage.*

> He's always ready to say goodby to life
> *Without a sigh,*
> Having forewarned himself of the time
> When one must resign oneself to go,
> *The custom to follow.*

"Ah, but that's wonderful!" the Philintes will exclaim.[21] "Surely, nothing is more customary than death, and this little line tacked on to an alexandrine is an excellent idea; La Fontaine would surely have approved if only someone had thought of it while he was alive."

Now admit it, you *must* admit, that after hearing such a literary desecration, far from siding with those who are always ready to support the insulters against the insulted, you would provide for this garbler of La Fontaine,

> Un cabanon
> A Charenton

> A cell for his sin
> In the loony bin.

Well, this sort of thing—and worse—is what happens every day to music. True, not all composers are publicly enraged at being corrected by their performers. Rossini, for example, seems happy enough to hear about the changes, the embellishments, the thousand and one abuses singers perpetrate against his melodies. "My music isn't quite finished," the terrible cynic once said. "They're still working on it. Only when nothing of mine is left will it attain its full merit."

Heard at the last rehearsal of a new opera:

"This passage doesn't suit me," says a singer naïvely. "I shall have to change it."

"Why not?" replies the composer. "Sing something else instead: sing the *Marseillaise.*"

These ironies, bitter as they are, do not cure the evil. Composers are wrong to joke about this sort of thing, for the singers then tell themselves: "He laughed; he's disarmed." On the contrary, one must be armed—and not laugh.

Another instance, this time the reverse: a famous conductor,[22] reputed to have a deep veneration for Beethoven, nonetheless used to take deplorable liberties with his music. One day, in a state of obvious excitement, he came into a café where I happened to be.

"Ah, it's you!" he said on catching sight of me. "You've just caused me a nice bit of trouble."

"How so?"

"I've been rehearsing our first concert. When we began the Scherzo of the C-minor Symphony, I'll be hanged if our double-basses didn't start playing, and when I stopped them, they protested against my cutting them out of the passage, quoting your opinion."

"What!" I said. "Those wretches had the audacity to defy you and play the bass parts written by Beethoven! That cries out for vengeance!"

"Come, come, you are making fun of me. The basses just don't sound well there. I cut them out more than twenty years ago; I prefer the cellos by themselves. You know very well that when a new work is to be played, there are always some things the conductor has to change."

"That is news to me. All I know is that when they come to a work for the first time, the conductor and his performers should begin by trying to understand it, then should play it with scrupulous fidelity, combined with inspiration if possible. That is all I know. If you had written a symphony and asked Beethoven to correct it and he consented to touch it up from top to bottom to please you, that would be the most natural thing in the world. But to lay your hand on a Beethoven symphony without authority, without authorization, is the maddest form of brashness and irreverence that could be cited in the history of art. As to the effect produced by the double-basses in that passage, and which in your opinion is bad, that's no concern of yours or of mine, or anyone else's. The parts were written by the composer and they must be played. Anyway, not every conductor who follows your example of tampering will share your opinion. You like to hear the theme of the Scherzo played by the cellos; another will prefer the bassoons; one will want the clarinets, still another the violas. The only one with no say in the matter will be the composer. Isn't that the acme of confusion, universal disorder, the end of art? Wouldn't you cut a sorry figure were Beethoven to come back to life and on hearing his symphony rearranged in this way, ask who dared give him a lesson in instrumentation? Would you dare answer: I, sir, it was I? Lully once broke a violin over the head of an Opéra musician who did not show him proper respect. It would not be a violin that Beethoven, seeing himself insulted and defied in this way, would break over your head; it would be a double bass."

My man considered a moment, then struck his fist on the table: "No matter; the double-basses are not going to play."

"Well, as to that, people who know you will not doubt it for a moment. We can only wait."

He died. His successor[23] thought fit to reinstate the basses in the Scherzo. But that had not been the only change imposed on this splendid symphony. In the finale, a repeat mark calls for the first part of the piece to be played twice; this repeat had been cut on the ground that it made the piece too long. The new conductor, who had just decided in Beethoven's favor on the question of the double-basses, took his predecessor's view against Beethoven's repeat. (You see where the exercise of free choice leads? Wonderful, don't you think?) The new conductor died. If M. T—,[24] who has replaced him, now does full justice to Beethoven (as he probably will), he will reinstate the repeat. In that case, it will have taken three generations of conductors and 35 years of effort on the part of Beethoven's admirers to have his marvelous work performed in Paris as the greatest composer of instrumental music conceived it.

Surely, gentlemen, you would not approve of this delay.[25] Yet that is what comes of tolerating insubordination by performers and the incredible liberties they take in correcting composers. One of our most celebrated virtuosos had this to say on the subject: "We are not the nail on which the painting is hung, we are the sun that illuminates it." Granted. We accept this modest comparison. But when the sun shines on a painting, it reveals exactly its line and color; it does not grow trees or weeds, or make birds or serpents appear where the artist has not put any. It does not change facial expressions, making sad faces happy and happy faces sad. It does not widen some contours or flatten others. It does not change white to black, or black to white. In short, it shows the picture as the artist painted it. Who could wish for more! That is just what we are asking. Be then our suns, ladies and gentlemen; we shall be happy to adore you. Be suns, and try never to be just wax tapers or lanterns for rag-pickers.[26]

I was raging in my soul as I ascended with great strides the mountain to the old castle. I could not dispel the idea that great poets and great artists are inescapably destined to be insulted in a thousand ways. If they turn the *Iliad* into a vaudeville, and the *Odyssey* into a ballet, put a pipe in the mouth of the Farnese Hercules, draw moustaches on the Venus de Milo, correct the work of sculptors, and mutilate masterpieces of music, there is nobody to avenge the artists. Our rulers do not trouble themselves about such trivial matters.

The old castle of Baden is an enormous medieval ruin, a vulture's nest built on top of a mountain that towers above the whole valley of the Oos. In the midst of a forest of gigantic fir trees, there are bare walls, black and hard as rocks, and slabs of rock as upright as the walls. Ancient oaks preside in the courtyards, and inquisitive old beeches poke their leafy heads through windows. Interminable stairways and bottomless wells appear on every hand to surprise the explorer, who cannot help feeling a secret terror. Here, once upon a time there lived—we know not when (nor do we know their names)—landgraves, margraves, or burgraves; human birds of prey, men of plunder, robbery, and murder, whom civilization caused to disappear. What crimes must have been committed under these fearful vaults, what cries of despair, what orgies of bloodshed must have echoed through these panelled halls! Today, O prosiness, O dull utility! today these walls house a restaurant and resound only with the noise of huge kitchen ovens, the popping of champagne corks, the raucous laughter of German burghers and French tourists enjoying themselves. Nonetheless, if you have the courage to climb to the top of the ruined monument, you will gradually find solitude, silence, and poetry. From the top of the highest platform, you can see, in the plain on the other side of the mountain, cheerful little German villages, well-tilled fields, a luxuriant vegetation, and the Rhine, gloomy and silent, winding its interminable silver ribbon into the horizon.

There I arrived, still growling like an impatient locomotive. Little by little, I was restored to calm and indifference, listening the while to the mysterious voices that speak there with such indifference and calm of men and times that are no more.

The love of music seemed to revive in me at the ineffable sound of the aeolian harps[27] that some benevolent German had placed among the jagged ruins, where the wind draws from them poetic laments. These ethereal chords give an intimation of infinity; one cannot tell when they begin or end; one seems to keep hearing them even after they have stopped vibrating. They awaken buried memories of long-lost youth, of vanished loves and disappointed hopes. And one sadly weeps—unless one is too old; for then, one's eyes stay dry, they close, and one falls asleep.

Apparently, I cannot be classed yet as too old: I didn't fall asleep. Far from it; the sun came back after the shower and I began to think of a little work I am engaged in just now. Perched on the battlement, pen in hand, I began to write the verses of a nocturne that I shall soon try to set to music. Here it is:

> Nuit paisible et sereine!
> La lune, douce reine

Qui plane en souriant,
L'insecte des prairies
Dans les herbes fleuries
En secret bruissant,
      Philomèle,
      Qui mêle
Au murmure du bois
Les splendeurs de sa voix;
      L'hirondelle
      Fidèle
Caressant sous nos toits
Sa nichée en émois;
Dans sa coupe de marbre
Ce jet d'eau retombant
      Écumant;
L'ombre de ce grand arbre
En spectre se mouvant
      Sous le vent;
      Harmonies
      Infinies,
Que vous avez d'attraits
Et de charmes secrets
Pour les âmes attendries! [28]

Night, peaceful and serene!
The moon, gentle queen
That floats by smiling;
Insects of the meadow
In the grass flowering
Secretly rustling,
      Philomela
      Mingling
Her voice's splendor
With the forest's murmur;
      Faithful
      Swallow
Caressing like a mother
Your nestlings all aflutter;
From its cup of marble
The fountain springing,
      Foaming;
The shadow of an arbor
Like a specter stirring
      In the wind;
      Harmonies,
      Infinities,
Your charms will capture,
Secretly enrapture
Tender souls beguiling!

That was the point I had reached in my nocturne when one of these birds of passage now so common in Baden burst on the scene, plunging me back into the world of prose. "So it's you," he gabbled at me with the voice of those other birds that once saved the Capitol in Rome.[29] "What the devil are you doing up here by yourself, perched on this battlement? Ah, poetry. I bet you're working on the opera M. Bénazet has ordered from you for the inauguration of the Baden theater. Well, it's coming along, this new theater. It will be ready next year. It's true that the builder is getting on in years, but he's still spry. He's the man who used to work so enthusiastically in Paris in the 1820s to put up the Arc de Triomphe."

"Yes, my dear man, I am indeed writing that little opera,[30] but please do not use such unseemly expressions. M. Bénazet hasn't *ordered* me to do anything. One does not give orders to artists, you should know that. You can order a French regiment to go and get itself killed, and it will go; you can order a French ship to go and get blown up, and it will; you can order a French critic to go to a comic opera which he is to review, and he will listen to it, but that is as far as it goes. If you ordered certain actors to change their habits, to become simple, natural, and noble, to avoid both the trite and the overflorid; if you ordered certain singers to sing from their soul and to keep the rhythm; if you ordered certain critics to know what they are talking about, certain writers to respect grammar, certain composers to know the rules of counterpoint—well, artists are proud: they wouldn't obey. As for me, from the moment I am ordered to do something, you can be sure of the result. It paralyzes me and makes me lifeless and stupid. And since I believe that you are of a similar disposition, I beg you earnestly—it would be useless to give you an order—I entreat you to go back down to Baden and leave me to go on dreaming up here on my battlement." And the silly goose left, laughing derisively.

But I had lost the thread of my thoughts. After several useless attempts to find it again, I gave up and, mindless, I listened to the hymn to the Austrian emperor, played far away in the music shell by a Prussian military band, wafted to me by the south wind in bits and pieces from the depths of the valley. This melody of the good Haydn is so touching. From it emanates a sort of religious affection, truly the song of a nation that loves its sovereign. Please note that I do not say the *good Haydn* in any mocking way. God forbid! I am always indignant at Horace, that most Parisian of the ancient Roman poets, who dared to write *Aliquando bonus dormitat Homerus*[31] (Sometimes even the good Homer nods).

"The good Haydn" was not just a good fellow; he was a *good man*, and the proof of it is that he had an impossible wife, whom he never beat but by whom, they say, he sometimes let himself be beaten.

Finally, night began to fall and I had to go back down. "La lune, douce reine/Planait en souriant." I walked again through the forest of fir trees. It has more resonance, a better sonority than most of our concert halls; indeed, it would be a good place to play quartets. I have often thought what an excellent thing it would be to perform on a fine summer night the scene in the Elysian fields from Gluck's *Orphée*. In the half-light under this green dome, I can hear the chorus of happy Shades, with their Italian words adding to the charm of the melody:

> Torna o bella al tuo consorte,
> Che no vuol che più diviso
> Sia di te pietoso il ciel.

> Return, o beautiful one, to your husband,
> Whom heaven in its mercy
> Wishes to be parted from you no longer.

But when people get musical inclinations in the woods, it always happens after eating liver paté at lunch. And so they play fanfares, fanfares with hunting horns, which evoke nothing but dogs, hunters, and wine merchants.

Halfway down the mountain, I came across a softly murmuring fountain and sat by a pool. I could have listened to the peaceful sound until the next day, if it had not reminded me of the fountain in the inner corridor of La Grande Chartreuse, which I first heard 35 years ago (alas! 35 years!). La Grande Chartreuse made me think of the monks, who keep saying in their prescribed motto: "Brother, you will die!"

This gloomy phrase reminded me that I had to go to Karlsruhe early the next morning to rehearse the choruses of my *Requiem*, two of its movements being included in this year's program.[32] So I returned to my lodgings to get ready for the trip.

"What can he be thinking of," you will ask, "making these vacationing ladies and gentlemen come to Baden to listen to sections of a mass for the dead?" It was precisely this contrast that attracted me in making up the program. It seemed to me the musical embodiment of Hamlet's thoughts as he held Yorick's skull: "Now get you to my lady's chamber, and tell her, let her paint an inch thick, to this favour she must come. Make her laugh at that."[33]

Yes, let's make them laugh, said I to myself, all these crinolined beauties, so proud of their young charms, their ancient name, and their millions. Let's make them laugh, these imperious women who sully souls and break hearts; let's make them laugh, these merchants of bodies and souls, these abusers of the suffering and the poor; let's do it by singing the unknown poet's fearsome poem, whose barbarous rhymed Latin from the Middle Ages only adds to its terrifying menace:

Dies irae, dies illa—

Day of wrath, the day that will dissolve the world in ashes.
How great a trembling, what terror then, when the Judge will appear
and examine all things.
A book will be brought forth in which everything is written and by
its contents the world will be judged.
The trumpet, sending its fearful sound throughout the tombs of
every land, will gather all before the throne.
To the Judge seated in His place, whatever is hidden shall be made
manifest; nothing will remain unpunished.
Stupefaction of death and nature.[34]

Let's make them laugh at such ideas!

Since most of the audience know no Latin, I shall take care to have
these lines printed in the program in French. Let's make them laugh.

What a poem! What a text for a musician! I cannot express the upheaval in my soul when, conducting an immense orchestra, I reach these
lines: *Judex ergo cum sedebit.* Everything goes black around me, I can
see nothing; I feel as though I have fallen into eternal night.

"Ah, so you have an audience predestined for damnation?" you ask.

Yes, I can see that my apocalyptic tirade might give you that impression; I was carried away by a current of Shakespearean ideas. The fact is
that Baden's fashionable society is composed of decent people who have
no reason to fear when they think of the other world. There are only a
small number of scoundrels—those who do not go to the concerts.

You will also ask me how in so small a town I am going to find the
musicians necessary to perform my *Dies irae,* when it is so difficult to
muster the forces in Paris. How will they all fit into the festival hall
and how shall we stand the earth-shaking sound? First, you should know
that I have rescored the kettledrum parts for only three timpanists, and
as for the brass bands, *Mirum spargentes sonum,* they were formed easily enough by combining the musicians from Karlsruhe and those of
Baden, together with the Prussians stationed at Fort Rastadt near Karlsruhe.[35] The chorus was assembled by Messrs. Strauss and Krug, musical
director and choirmaster to the Grand Duke. The chorus has been working now for two weeks, while I have been rehearsing the instrumentalists three times a week. Everything has been going smoothly and with
perfect regularity.

On the two evenings before the concert I shall take our musicians to
Karlsruhe by train. They will rehearse there with those of the Grand
Duke's chapel. Early on the morning of the concert, M. Strauss will
bring the musicians from Karlsruhe, and they will rehearse with those
of Baden on a large platform that will have been built the night before
at one end of the Salle de Conversation. Gaming will be suspended for
the day. A rather large platform will be set up behind the orchestra,
where I shall place my battery of timpani and brass choirs. Our intelligent and devoted conductor in Baden, M. Kenneman, will direct them.

Those tremendous voices and thunderous sounds will not lose any of their musical power, I hope, for being projected from such a distance. In any event, the tempo of the *Tuba mirum* is so broad that the two conductors can use their eyes and ears to stay together without mishap.

As you can see, I shall have a rough day. From nine in the morning till noon, final dress rehearsal; at three, I put back in order the seating and the parts, which will be more or less in disarray after the morning rehearsal, a task I dare not entrust to anyone else. At eight o'clock the concert begins.

At midnight after such a day, I do not feel much like dancing. But the Princess of Prussia (now the Queen[36]) is usually present on these occasions. Often she condescends to detain me for a few moments to make observations on the principal works of the program, observations which, in spite of their subtlety, are unfailingly kind. She speaks with so much charm and displays such an intimate understanding of music, her sensibility is joined to such rare intelligence, and she is so adept at giving encouragement and confidence that, after five minutes of her charming conversation, all my fatigue vanishes and I would be ready to start again.

Now you know, gentlemen, what I am doing in Baden. There are other details I could supply, but God forbid that I go on further. I can see half your gathering from here—fast asleep.

THE RISE IN CONCERT PITCH[1]

Concerned about the ever more alarming way in which music is performed in our opera houses, shocked by the brevity of singers' careers, and believing correctly that the steady rise in pitch is one of the causes behind the ruin of some of our finest voices, the Minister of State for Fine Arts has just appointed a committee to look into the matter with care, ascertain the extent of the evil, and find a remedy.

While waiting for this gathering of experts—composers, physicists, and connoisseurs of music—to resume its work, which was suspended this past month, I shall try to cast some light on the facts of the case and, without prejudging the decision that the committee will eventually take, submit my own observations and ideas.[2]

Has Pitch Really Risen* during the Last 100 Years, and If So to What Extent?

Yes, there is no doubt about it; the rise in pitch is acknowledged as a fact by every musician and singer, indeed by the whole musical world. The progress of this rise seems to have been more or less the same everywhere. The difference today in the pitch of various orchestras in the same city and among orchestras separated by a considerable distance is generally slight; it does not keep those orchestras from merging their members and, as long as they take certain precautions, from forming a large instrumental ensemble able to play satisfactorily in tune. If there were, as is often said in Paris, a great divergence in pitch between the Opéra, the Opéra-Comique, the Théâtre-Italien, and the military bands, how would it have been possible to bring together seven or eight hundred performers and make up the orchestras that I conducted so often in the spacious halls of the Champs-Elysées after the exhibitions of 1844[4] and 1855,[5] and in the church of St. Eustache?[6] Those musical aggregations had to include nearly every instrumentalist from the many musical organizations in Paris.

In Germany and England, too, where the festivals often combine orchestras from several towns, differences in pitch are slight. Generally all

---

*I am using the terms in general use, *high* and *low*[3] sounds, and the verbs *rise* and *fall*—even though they lack real meaning. It is only by an absurd custom that they are employed in talking about music to distinguish between sounds made by rapid vibrations and those made by slow vibrations.

that has to be done is to adjust the slides of the wind instruments that sound too high, and the pitch differences vanish.

Nonetheless, these differences, however slight, do exist. We shall soon have evidence on this point, since the official committee has written to virtually all the choral directors, concertmasters, and conductors in the cities of Europe and America where the art of music is cultivated, asking them for a sample of the steel device which, under various names, they use just as we do to give the A to their orchestras and to tune their organs and pianos. When these contemporary tuning devices come to be compared with the old ones that we possess from 1790, 1806, and so on, the difference between our pitch today and that of the late eighteenth century will become obvious and precise.

Moreover, several old church organs, whose special function in the service of worship has kept them isolated, have never played with wind instruments from the theater world and have retained the pitch of the period when they were built. And this pitch is usually a full tone lower than that of the present day. They have on that account come to be known as organs in B-flat, their C being a whole tone lower than ours and in unison with our B-flat. Such organs are at least one hundred years old. The conclusion from those various facts, which tally with each other, is that our pitch has risen a whole tone in one hundred years, or a half tone in a half century. If it continues its upward march, in six hundred years it will have run up the twelve half tones of the scale; by the year 2458 it will have risen a whole *octave*.[7]

The absurdity of such an outcome is enough to show the importance of the measure taken by the Minister of Fine Arts. It is highly regrettable that none of his predecessors thought of taking it long ago.

To be sure, music has rarely been given enlightened official protection, although of all the arts it is the most in need of it. Almost always and almost everywhere, its fate has been put in the hands of officials who are insensitive to its power, its grandeur and nobility, and who are ignorant of its nature and the means it requires. Almost always and almost everywhere, the art has been treated like a gypsy girl who must sing and dance in the company of monkeys and performing dogs, similarly dressed in showy togs to attract the crowd, and who is expected to sell herself to any passerby.[8] But the action taken by the Minister gives us occasion to hope that music will soon have in France the protection it needs, and that other important reforms in the practice and teaching of music will closely follow the reform of concert pitch.

The Ill Effects of the Rise in Pitch

When dramatic music and operas were just beginning to be composed in France—in Lully's time, for example—concert pitch was established but not fixed (as we shall soon see). Singers of whatever kind found no difficulty in singing parts written within the limits then observed for the voice. Later, when the pitch level rose perceptibly, composers should have taken this change into account; it was both their duty and in their self-interest to write parts somewhat lower. They did not do it. Even so, the music composed for the Paris stage by Rameau, Monsigny, Grétry, Gluck, Piccinni, and Sacchini, in the years when the pitch was nearly a whole tone lower than ours, remained singable for a long time. Indeed, most of it still is, so cautious and restrained were these masters in writing for the voice. Exceptions may be found—passages by Monsigny, in particular—where the top of the melodic line, which was already a bit high for his time, is much too high for ours.

Spontini in *La Vestale, Cortez,* and *Olympie,* even wrote some tenor parts that singers nowadays find too low.[9]

Twenty-five years later, during which the pitch had risen rapidly, there appeared many more high notes for sopranos and tenors. High Cs began to be written for tenors in both head and chest voice, as well as the high C-sharp, as a head note to be sure, but one that earlier composers would never have thought to use. Tenors were required more and more often to lash out with a high B-natural in full force from the chest, which in the old pitch would have been a C-sharp, no trace of which can be found in eighteenth-century scores. Again, sopranos were expected to attack and sustain their high Cs, while the bass parts came to be strewn with high E-naturals. This last note was already used too often in the days of lower pitch under the name of high F-sharp; still, it appeared much less often than it does nowadays in the guise of E-natural.

In the end, there was such a proliferation of excessively high notes, notes that a singer could no longer produce but had to *extract* by main force as a dentist does a bad tooth, that on the evidence one must draw a curious conclusion: as the pitch rose in France, composers of grand opera wrote parts that rose higher still. This is readily confirmed by comparing the scores of the last century with those of our time.

The part of Achilles in *Iphigénie en Aulide* (one of the highest tenor roles Gluck ever wrote) goes no higher than B-natural, which corresponds to our A, and is thus a whole tone lower than our B of today. Only once did Gluck call for a high D, in *Orphée,* but that single note, the same as the C used three times in *William Tell,*[10] occurs as a head note in a slow vocalise, so that it is lightly touched rather than given with full voice. It is consequently neither risky nor tiring for the singer. Only one of Gluck's great female roles—Alceste—includes a high B-flat that has to be fully voiced and strongly sustained. This B-flat amounted to our A-flat. Who nowadays hesitates to ask a prima donna to sing a high A-flat, an A-natural, a B-flat or even a B, even a C?

The highest female role that Gluck ever wrote is Daphne in *Cythère assiégée.*[11] One aria, "Ah, quel bonheur d'aimer!" (Oh, what bliss it is to love) rises in a rapid run to C (our B-flat today). Looking at the part as a whole, one can see that it was composed for one of those exceptional sopranos found in every age, who have what are called light voices. These singers have an exceptional upper range. In our day there are Mmes Cabel,[12] Carvalho,[13] Lagrange,[14] Zerr, and a few others. And remember, Daphne's high C is our B-flat, now a commonplace. Mme Cabel and Mlle Zerr reach the high F above the staff; Mme Carvalho takes on high E without fear, and Mme Lagrange does not shrink from the high G of the flute.

When writing for Paris theaters, the older composers persisted—I do not know why—in continually forcing the deep voices upward. In their bass roles, virtually all the notes are in the baritone range. They never dared to make their basses sing below B-flat, and even this note was rare. As late as 1827, it was still received wisdom at the Opéra that the deeper notes lacked resonance and could not be heard in a large hall. The bass voices were thus denatured, and the parts of Thoas, Orestes, Calchas, Agamemnon, and Sylvain,[15] which I heard sung by the elder Dérivis,[16] sound as though Gluck and Grétry wrote them for baritones. These roles, therefore, though singable at that time by true basses, are no longer so today. Still, neither Gluck nor his peers ever dared to demand of tenors and sopranos the high notes I mentioned earlier, and which are overused today.

These excesses by even the most expert modern composers have certainly had unfortunate results. How many tenors have shattered their voices on the high Cs and Bs of the chest register! How many sopranos have given forth not song but shrieks of horror and distress, in a host of passages of the modern repertoire—far too numerous to be listed here![17] Add the fact that violently dramatic situations often give rise to energetic (if not strident) orchestration and that in such cases the excessive volume of instrumental sound drives the singers, without their realizing it, to yet fiercer efforts to be heard; they let out howls that no longer have any human quality. Some composers have been skillful enough to refrain from writing loud chords for full orchestra at the same point that the voice has a significant passage. They "uncover" the voice in a sort of dialogue with the instruments. But many others literally crush it under a heap of brass and percussion. And some of these have acquired a name as models of the art of accompanying the voice—what an accompaniment!

These crude, palpable, obvious flaws, when aggravated by the rise in pitch, were bound to bring about the deplorable results that now strike the least attentive of opera goers. But there is another grievous consequence of the rise in A: musicians who play the horn, trumpet, or cornet can no longer safely manage—indeed most of them can no longer even reach—certain notes that were in common use before; for example, the high G of the trumpet in D and the E of the trumpet in F (these two notes sounding to the ear as A); the high G of the horn in G, the high C of this same horn in G (a note used by Handel and Gluck and that has since become unplayable); and the high C of the cornet in A. At any moment, raucous, broken sounds, commonly known as squawks, burst out and spoil an instrumental ensemble whose performers may be among the best of musicians. And people wonder: "Don't the trumpet and the horn players have lips any more? What's happened? The human body is still the same." No, it is not humankind that has changed; it is the pitch. And many modern composers seem quite unaware that it has.

Causes of the Rise in Pitch

It now seems clear that the guilty ones are the makers of wind instruments; it is they who are responsible for what we deplore. In order to give their flutes, oboes, and clarinets a little extra brilliance, certain instrument makers have secretly raised their pitch. When the young virtuosos who came to own these instruments began to play in an orchestra, they found that they had to pull out the crook or slide a little to bring them into tune with the others. But since lengthening the tube (particularly in a flute) disturbs its proportions, it also spoils the intonation. Players therefore gradually gave up doing it, whereupon the whole band of string instruments followed the pitch upward, perhaps unconsciously, taking their cue from the high-pitched winds. By tightening their strings a bit, the violins, violas, cellos, and double-basses adapted easily to the new pitch.

The other musicians, the elders of the orchestra—bassoons, horns, trumpets, and second oboes—grew tired of not reaching, no matter how hard they tried, the pitch that had now come to prevail. They took their instruments back to the maker to have the tube deftly shortened, to have it *cut* (that is the term in use) and thus reach the new tuning. And now you have the higher pitch settled in that particular orchestra. Soon it also became the rule in recitals, the piano having been adjusted to match the pitch of tuning forks whose prongs had been shortened by filing down. The same thing—it is sometimes acknowledged, sometimes not—now happens more or less everywhere, every twenty years.

Today even the organ makers follow the trend and tune their instruments to the high pitch. Of course, we have no idea what the pitch was when St. Gregory and St. Ambrose composed the plainsong they bequeathed to the liturgy, but it is quite clear that the more the pitch rises in church while the organ continues to give (without transposing) the pitch to the singers, the more it distorts the whole system of plainsong and upsets the vocal economy of the sacred hymns. An organ tuned to modern pitch should transpose when it accompanies plainsong. Otherwise organs should be tuned to the old pitch, but fixed in some exact relation to modern pitch, so that by transposing, the organ can play with the instruments of the orchestra. For instance, if an organ is a tone and a half below our current pitch, orchestral instruments could still be perfectly in tune with it by playing, for example, in F when the organ plays in A-flat.

Unfortunately, some manufacturers choose the worst of all compromises: they build organs that are a quarter tone below orchestra pitch. I had a harrowing experience of this a few years ago in the church of St. Eustache, where for the performance of a *Te Deum*[18] it proved impossible by any lengthening of the wind instruments to bring them in tune with an organ that had been built barely three years earlier.

Should We Lower the Pitch?

In my opinion, lowering the pitch would bring nothing but good to music and especially to the art of singing. But I do not think it feasible that the reform can be extended throughout France. An abuse that has obtained for many years cannot be eradicated in a few days. The very musicians, singers, and others who would benefit the most from the lowering of the pitch would probably be the first to oppose it. It would upset their habits, and Lord knows if there is anything in France more immovable than a habit. Even supposing that some all-powerful authority were to impose the reform, it would cost an enormous amount of money to carry it out. Even without counting the organs, new wind instruments would have to be bought for all the theaters and military bands, and use of the old ones would have to be forbidden. And if France adopted the change and the rest of the world did not follow suit, we would find ourselves alone with our concert pitch, unable to carry on musical relations with other peoples.

Should We Then Do No More than "Freeze" the Current Pitch?

That, I think, is the wisest course; we have the means to achieve it. Thanks to the recently invented ingenious acoustical device known as the *siren,* we can now calculate with mathematical precision the number of vibrations emitted by a source of sound. If the A of the Paris Opéra, which I take to be 898 vibrations a second,[19] were to be adopted as the official standard, it would only be necessary to install an organ pipe of this designated pitch in all the theaters and concert halls. This pipe would become the sole point of reference for the A, and orchestras would no longer tune to the oboe or flute, which can so easily be given too high a pitch, the former by pinching the reed with the lips, the latter by slightly turning the embouchure outward.

The wind instruments will consequently be perfectly in tune with the organ pipe.[20] Between performances they will have to be locked up in the same room with it, this room being, like a greenhouse, maintained at the constant temperature of the hall when full of people. Thanks to this precaution, the wind instruments would no longer arrive cold and then start rising in pitch after an hour of playing, because of the performers' breath and the warmer air of the hall. To say all this means also that the wind instruments of a theater (at least one owned by the government) would never be allowed to leave the premises under any pretext whatever. They would stay in their "greenhouse," just as the scenery stays in the storeroom. If some player should take it into his head to remove his flute or clarinet to have it "cut," the misdeed would be found out without delay, since its A would differ from that of the organ pipe, which ought to be the only standard for tuning the orchestra.

Finally, once the A of 898 vibrations was officially adopted, any instrument maker who marketed a wind instrument, organ, or piano tuned above this A would be liable to certain penalties, like tradesmen who sell short measure or false weight. Once such actions had been taken, and the regulations were strictly enacted and enforced, the pitch would never rise again.

But the cure will prove useless for saving voices, if composers continue to demand the ruinously high notes mentioned earlier.[21] Therefore the authorities ought to step in again and prohibit composers (at least those who compose for the subsidized theaters) from writing those extravagant notes that have destroyed many a fine voice. At the same time, officialdom should *advise*—the censoring of scores must necessarily be ruled out—composers to heed appropriateness and to show more discretion in using the noisy instruments of the orchestra.

THE END IS NEAR[1]

The art of music is alive and well in Paris, and is being raised to high rank. It will be promoted Mamamouchi.[2] *Voler far un paladina. Ioc! Dar turbanta con galera. Ioc! Ioc! Hou la ba, ba la chou, ba la ba, ba la da!* After which, Mme Jourdain, that is to say, rational public opinion, will appear when it is too late to exclaim: "Heavens! it has gone mad!"[3]

Fortunately, when the art of music is not being dragged off to a lyric theater, it shows flashes of intelligence that are reassuring to its friends. We still have concerts in Paris where people make music; we have virtuosos who understand masterpieces and perform them as they deserve; audiences that listen with respect and worship sincerely. One must keep saying all this to oneself if one is to keep from jumping head first into a well.

Two days after the performance at the Opéra-Comique of an unspeakable work[4] that incensed the audience, I happened to be with a few friends in a musical household. We had just been discussing the dreadful new score we had heard, and we wondered for what Messiah its composer could be serving as John the Baptist. We were all thinking about the illness now afflicting the art of music, about the strange physicians attending the patient, the undertakers already knocking at the door, and the stonemasons cutting the epitaph on the tombstone, when it occurred to one of us to throw himself at the feet of Mme Massart[5] and beg her to play Beethoven's great F-minor sonata.[6] The virtuoso graciously acceded to his entreaties and soon the gathering succumbed to the sublime and terrifying spell of this peerless work. While listening to this Titanesque music, played with irresistible inspiration and disciplined ardor, we quickly forgot all the failings, the wretchedness, the shame, and the horrors of contemporary music. One felt shaken, one trembled with admiration in the presence of the profound thought and impetuous passion that animate Beethoven's work—a work greater than his greatest symphonies, greater than anything else he composed, and therefore superior to anything the art of music has ever produced.

As the performer, exhausted when she reached the final measure, sat panting at the piano, I took her hands, which had turned cold, and we all stood silent. What was there to say?

In that drawing room buried in the middle of Paris, where antiharmony never gained admittance, we were a group like the one in the painting of the *Decameron*,[7] which depicts beautiful young ladies and gentlemen breathing in the fragrant air of a charming villa, while all around that oasis Florence was being ravaged by the Black Death.

THE RICHARD WAGNER CONCERTS[1]

The Music of the Future

After an inordinate amount of trouble, enormous expense, and many rehearsals, though still far from enough, Richard Wagner has succeeded in having a few of his works performed at the Théâtre-Italien.[2] Excerpts from operatic works always lose something in being played outside their intended settings, but overtures and orchestral preludes gain from such performances, because they demand greater splendor and brilliance than can be mustered by the ordinary opera orchestra, which is much smaller and less favorably arranged than a concert orchestra.

The results of this experiment ventured by the German composer in Paris could be easily foreseen. Some of the listeners, whose minds were not closed by preconceived ideas, were quick to recognize the powerful qualities of the composer, as well as the regrettable tendency of his theories of composition. A larger number seemed to find in Wagner only his fierce determination, and in his music only a wearisome and irritating noise. The lobby of the Théâtre-Italien on the evening of the first concert was a curious sight.[3] People were raging and shouting, and arguments seemed constantly to be on the verge of turning into fisticuffs. In such situations the artist who has thus stirred up his audience would like to see things go even further, and would not mind witnessing hand-to-hand encounters between his supporters and his detractors, on condition, of course, that his supporters come out on top. This time there was little prospect of such a victory, God always being on the side of the big battalions. But the amount of nonsense, absurdity, and even outright lying that one hears on an occasion of this kind is prodigious—proof that, at least in this country, when we have to judge a type of music that differs from the run-of-the-mill, passion and prejudice hold the floor and keep good sense and judgment from speaking up.

Preconception, whether positive or negative, dictates almost all the judgments passed, even on works by masters who are already recognized and established. Should a composer who has been acclaimed as a great melodist write a work one day that is entirely bereft of melody, the work will nonetheless be admired by people who would have hissed had it been given under another's name. Beethoven's sublime and stirring *Leonore Overture*[4] is considered by many critics to be a work devoid of melody, even though it is full of melody—everything sings and weeps melodiously, no less in the *Allegro* than in the *Andante*. The same judges who disparage *Leonore*, applaud and often shout "encore" after Mozart's overture to *Don Giovanni*, in which there is no trace of what they call melody. But it is by Mozart, the great melodist!

In the opera *Don Giovanni* itself, they rave—as indeed they should—about its sublime expression of feeling, of passion, and of character. Yet when it comes to the *Allegro* of Donna Anna's final aria, not one of these critics, apparently so sensitive to expressiveness in music and so touchy about dramatic fitness, is shocked by the execrable vocalizing that Mozart, driven by some mysterious demon, had the misfortune to let fall from his pen. The poor injured and humiliated girl cries out: "Some day Heaven may again feel pity for me." And that is where the composer has written a series of high notes, with staccato runs, with cackling and jerky flourishes that lack even the merit of arousing applause. If anywhere in Europe there had ever been a truly sensitive and intelligent public, this crime (for that is what it surely is) would not have gone unpunished, and the guilty *Allegro* would have been expunged from Mozart's score.

I could cite a number of similar examples to show that, with rare exceptions, music is judged solely by preconception and under the sway of the most deplorable prejudices. This state of affairs is my excuse for taking the liberty of discussing Richard Wagner on the basis of my own perceptions, without taking any account of the various opinions that have been expressed about him.

He showed daring that first evening in presenting a program entirely made up of ensemble pieces, choral or symphonic. That was, to begin with, a gauntlet thrown down at the feet of the public, which, on the pretext of loving variety, is always ready to show the noisiest enthusiasm for a parlor song well sung, an insipid *cavatina* well warbled, for a violin solo well danced on the G-string, or for a set of variations well whistled on a wind instrument; whereas it gives a courteous but cool reception to some work of genius. This public thinks that a king and a shepherd are equal during their lifetime.

There is nothing like taking the bull by the horns. Wagner has just proved it. His program, devoid of the sugary confections that delight children of all ages at musical gatherings, was nonetheless received with close attention and keen interest.

He began with the overture to *The Flying Dutchman*,[5] a two-act opera which I saw in 1841 in Dresden, where the composer conducted and Mme Schroeder-Devrient sang the main role.[6] The overture made the same impression on me then as it did the other day. The piece begins with a thunderous orchestral explosion, which conveys straight off the howling gale, the shouts of sailors, the shrill cry of the rigging, and the sounds of a furious storm at sea. This opening is superb; it grips the

listener imperiously and carries him away. But as the device is repeated
again and again, tremolo succeeding tremolo, chromatic scales leading
only to more chromatic scales, with not a single ray of sunshine piercing through these dark, highly charged clouds that pour forth their tor-
rents without cease, not the slightest trace of melody to brighten the
black harmonies, the listener's attention begins to flag; finally he becomes discouraged and gives up. Already in this overture, whose development seems excessive, there appears the propensity of Wagner and his
school to disregard the senses and to see only the poetic and dramatic
idea that they wish to express, without worrying whether the expression
of the idea actually compels the composer to go beyond the conditions
of music.

The overture to *The Flying Dutchman* is powerfully orchestrated. For
the opening, the composer has shown what extraordinary use can be
made of the chord of the open fifth. Exploited in this way, the sound
takes on a wild and fierce aspect that makes one shudder.

The great scene in *Tannhäuser* with march and chorus is marked by
a superb brilliance and splendor, further enhanced by the special sono-
rousness of its B-major tonality. The rhythm, which is never blurred or
troubled in its progress by contrary rhythms, exhibits a proud, vigorous,
and chivalric character. One knows even without seeing it staged, that
this music goes with the actions of brave and stalwart men in shining
armor. There is also a melody, clear in design and elegant, though not
very original; its shape, if not its emotional tone, is reminiscent of a
famous theme in *Der Freischütz*.

The final return of the choral theme in the grand *tutti* has even greater
energy than all that went before, thanks to a bass line with eight notes
to the measure, in contrast to the higher melodic line of two or three.
There are perhaps some rather harsh modulations that follow each other
too closely, but the orchestra urges them with such vigor and authority
that the ear accepts them at once without hesitation. In short, one must
recognize this to be a masterly page, orchestrated like the rest of the
piece by an expert hand. A powerful impulse animates the winds and
voices, while the violins, scored with marvelous ease in their upper range,
seem to throw dazzling sparks over the whole ensemble.

In Germany the overture to *Tannhäuser* is Wagner's most popular orchestral work. Strength and grandeur are again dominant, but the effect,
at least on me, of the composer's chosen system is a feeling of great
fatigue. The overture begins with an *Andante maestoso*, a sort of chorale full of splendor, which returns toward the end of the *Allegro*, accompanied by an insistent figure high in the violins. The theme of this
Allegro consists of only two measures and is not in itself very interesting. The development that follows is treated, just as in the overture to
The Flying Dutchman, with bristling chromatic progressions, with mod-

ulations and harmonies of extreme harshness. When finally the chorale theme reappears, slow and broad, the violin figure that accompanies it to the very end repeats itself with a persistence that can only be very hard on the listener. He has already heard it 24 times in the *Andante;* now it is heard again 118 times at the peroration of the *Allegro.* This dogged, or rather relentless, motif thus figures altogether 142 times in the overture. Is this not excessive? It recurs several times again during the opera itself, which leads me to believe that the composer must attach to it some expressive meaning connected with the story, but I am unable to guess what it is.

The excerpts from *Lohengrin* shine by virtue of qualities that excel those of the preceding works. There is here, it seems to me, more originality than in *Tannhäuser.* The introduction that takes the place of an overture to this opera is one of Wagner's most striking inventions. An idea of it may be given to the eye by the figure < >. It is in fact a tremendous slow crescendo which, having reached the highest degree of sonorous strength, follows the reverse course to its point of departure and ends in an almost inaudible harmonious murmur. I do not know what connection there may be between this form of overture and the dramatic idea of the opera, but leaving the question aside, and considering the piece simply as a symphonic work, I find it admirable in all respects. True, there is no *phrase,* properly speaking, but the harmonic progressions are melodious and charming, and interest never flags for a moment, in spite of the slowness of the crescendo and decrescendo. Let me add that it is a marvel of orchestration, in the gentle shadings no less than in the brilliant colors. Near the end, one notices a diatonic bass line that rises steadily while the other parts descend, the plan of which is most ingenious. This splendid piece contains no harshness of any kind; it is as smooth and harmonious as it is lofty, reverberant, and powerful. In my opinion, it is a masterpiece.

The great march in G which opens the second act aroused in Paris the same kind of excitement that it did in Germany—this, despite the vagueness of the idea at the beginning and the frigid, undecided character of the episodic passage in the middle. Those colorless measures, where the composer seems to be groping, seeking his way, are but a sort of preparation for the monumental, irresistible idea which one must see as the true theme of the march. A four-measure phrase—repeated twice, each time a third higher—makes up this rousing declaration, to which perhaps nothing in music can be compared for vehement grandeur, strength, or brilliance. Pealed forth by the brass in unison at the start of each phrase, the strong accents on C, E, and G resound like cannon shots, shaking the listener to the core.

I believe the effect would have been still more remarkable had the composer avoided the harmonic conflicts that strike the ear in the second phrase, where the fourth inversion of the major-ninth chord and the suspension of the fifth by the sixth produce double dissonances that many people (I am one of them) find hard to bear.

The march introduces the chorus in duple time ("Freulich geführt ziehet dahin"[7]), which (coming at this point) causes dismay, because it is so feeble, not to say childish, in style. The effect it produced on the audience at the Salle Ventadour was rendered all the worse by the fact that the opening measures brought to mind a wretched number in Boïeldieu's *Deux Nuits*,[8] "La belle nuit, la belle fête" (What a lovely night, what a lovely fête), which has been making the rounds in the vaudeville theaters and is familiar to everyone in Paris.

I have not yet discussed the orchestral introduction to Wagner's latest opera, *Tristan and Isolde*.[9] It is surprising that the composer should have included it in the same program as the prelude to *Lohengrin*, for the two pieces are constructed on the same plan. Once again, we have a slow beginning, *pianissimo*, which gradually rises to a *fortissimo* and sinks back to the nuance of its inception. There is no theme other than a kind of chromatic moan, filled with dissonant chords whose long appoggiaturas in place of the true harmonic note further intensify the painfulness.

I have read and reread this curious work several times. I have listened to it with the most careful attention and a keen desire to understand, but I must confess that I still have no idea what the composer was trying to do.

This sincere account has, I trust, brought out Wagner's great musical qualities. One cannot but conclude, it seems to me, that he possesses that rare intensity of feeling, that inner fire and strength of will, that faith which stirs the emotions, conquers, and sweeps everything before it. But these qualities would shine with even greater luster if the composer were more inventive and less studied, and showed a more balanced appreciation of some of the constituent elements of the art of music. So much for Wagner's practice.

Now let us look at the theories said to be those of his school, the school generally called the Music of the Future.[10] It bears this name because it is deemed to be diametrically opposed to the musical taste of the present day, and certain to find itself perfectly in harmony with the taste of a future time.

For many years now, I have been credited in Germany and elsewhere with views on this subject that are not mine. I have often received praise that I could have taken as a virtual insult; I have kept silent throughout. Now that I am called upon to explain myself categorically, can I still stay silent? Or should I utter a profession of faith that is a lie? Nobody, I should hope, entertains that expectation.

Let me speak then, in complete frankness. If the school of the future says the following:

"Music today is in the vigor of her youth; she is emancipated, she is free; she does whatever she wishes to do.

"Many of the old rules no longer hold; they were made by inattentive observers, or by routine minds for other routine minds.

"New needs of mind and heart and the sense of hearing all demand new departures and even at times the breaking of old laws.

"Many forms of composition have been worn so threadbare as to be no longer acceptable.

"Moreover, anything may be good, anything may be bad, depending on the use of the thing and the reason for it.

"When combined with drama or with words to be sung, music should always be in direct rapport with the feeling expressed by the words, the character singing the role, and often even with the accent and vocal inflections that are felt to be most natural to the spoken word.

"Operas should not be composed for singers; on the contrary, the singers should be trained for the operas.

"Works composed for the sole purpose of showing off the talents of virtuosi can only be works of a secondary order, usually of little value.

"Performers are merely more or less intelligent instruments whose task is to bring out the form and inner meaning of the work; their despotic rule is over.

"The composer must remain the master; it is for him to command.

"Beauty of sound ranks below the idea; the idea ranks below feeling and passion.

"Lengthy and rapid vocal flourishes, ornaments, and trills, and many kinds of rhythms are all incompatible with the expression of most serious, noble, and deep feelings.

"Thus, it is absurd to write in a *Kyrie eleison*, the humblest prayer of the Catholic church, vocal figures that could be mistaken for the shouts of a crowd roistering in a tavern.

"It is no less absurd to compose the same kind of music for idolaters invoking Baal and for the children of Israel praying to Jehovah.

"It is even more reprehensible to take an ideal being, a creation of the greatest of poets, an angel of purity and love, and make her sing like a street-walker"—and so on and so forth.

If such be the musical code of the school of the future, then I belong to this school, I belong to it body and soul, with the deepest conviction and the most ardent fellow feeling.

But nowadays everyone professes these beliefs more or less openly, in part or as a whole. Is there a great composer who does not write just as he wants? Who is there who still believes in the infallibility of the academic rules, except a few timid souls who would be frightened of the shadow of their nose if they had one?

I go further: all I have said has been true for quite a while. Gluck himself in one sense belonged to the school of the future. In his famous preface to *Alceste* he said: "There is no rule that I was not ready to sacrifice for the sake of dramatic effect."

And what of Beethoven? What was he if not the boldest, the most independent of all composers, the most impatient of constraint? And well before Beethoven, Gluck had made use of high pedal-points (sustained notes in the high register) which are not part of the harmony and which produce double and triple dissonances. He used this daring device to sublime effect in the introduction to the Hades scene in *Orphée,* in a chorus in *Iphigénie en Aulide,* and especially in the immortal aria in *Iphigénie en Tauride:* "Mêlez vos cris plaintifs à mes gémissements"[11] (Mingle your plaintive cries with my groans).

M. Auber did the same thing in the Tarantella of his *Muette.*[12] And the liberties Gluck took with rhythm! As for Mendelssohn, who is considered a classicist by the school of the future, he readily ignored tonal unity in his fine overture to *Athalie,*[13] which begins in F and ends in D major, just like Gluck, who opens a chorus of *Iphigénie en Tauride* in E minor and closes in A minor.

Thus all of us, in these ways, belong to the school of the future.

But, if that school maintains:

"One must do the opposite of what the rules prescribe.

"We are tired of melody, of melodic figures, of arias, duets, trios, of pieces whose themes develop regularly; we are surfeited with consonant harmonies, with simple dissonances that are prepared and resolved, and with natural modulations artfully managed.

"We must concentrate only on the idea and ignore the senses altogether.

"We must scorn the ear, rubbish that it is; we must brutalize it in order to master it. It is not the purpose of music to please the ear. We must accustom it to everything, to series of ascending and descending diminished sevenths that are like a nest of hissing snakes that writhe and tear at each other; to triple dissonances that are neither prepared nor resolved; to inner parts that are made to keep in step without matching either harmonically or rhythmically, and which therefore rub each other raw; we must get the ear used to cruel modulations that bring in a new key in one part of the orchestra before the previous key has made its exit.

"Nor is the art of singing to be shown any consideration, nor should attention be paid to its nature or requirements.

"In opera we must do no more than set notes for declamation, to the point of using, if necessary, ugly, unsingable, outlandish intervals.

"No distinction need be made between music that is read by a musician sitting quietly in front of his stand, and that which has to be sung from memory, on stage, by a performer who must also attend to his acting and that of others.

"We need not concern ourselves over what is possible or impossible in performance.

"If singers find it as difficult to learn a role and commit it to memory, as to learn a page of Sanskrit by heart or swallow a fistful of nutshells— too bad for them. They are paid to do it; they are slaves.

"The witches of *Macbeth* are right: fair is foul, and foul is fair."[14]

If this is the new religion—very new indeed—I am very far from professing it; I never have joined it, I do not join it now, and never shall. I raise my hand and swear: *Non credo*.

I believe on the contrary and firmly, that fair is not foul, and foul is not fair. It is certainly not the sole purpose of music to sound pleasant to the ear, but it is a thousand times less its purpose to be unpleasant to it, to torture and murder it.

I am made of flesh and blood like everybody else. I want my feelings to be taken into account; I want my ear, that bit of rubbish, to be treated with consideration. Guenille si l'on veut; ma guenille m'est chère[15] [Call it an old rag, if you will, but my old rag is dear to me].

I will therefore repeat calmly, imperturbably, what I said one day to a lady of generous heart and fine mind who was rather captivated by the idea of freedom in art, even when carried to the point of absurdity. She asked me, concerning a noisy piece about which I had refrained from expressing an opinion, "But this is the sort of thing you must like, surely?"

"Yes, I like it as I like to drink vitriol and eat arsenic." Some time later, the same compliment was paid me by a famous singer[16] who is known today as one of the most violent opponents of the music of the future. He had composed an opera containing an important scene in which a Jewish rabble jeers at a captive. So as to depict the howling of the mob better, this realist had written for his orchestra and chorus a string of continuous dissonances. Carried away by his own daring, the composer one day opened his score at this cacophonous page and said to me (without a trace of malice, I am happy to say), "You must look at this scene, *you are bound to like it.*" I said nothing and mentioned neither vitriol nor arsenic. But since I am now speaking my mind and since that curious compliment still weighs on it, I shall say to him:

"No, my dear D――, I am *not* bound to like it. On the contrary, I dislike it intensely. You slander me when you assume that I am a rackety realist. I am told that you have declared yourself opposed to Wagner and his followers, but they have more right to include you among the rattlesnakes of the music of the future—you, a musician who is three-quarters Italian and yet capable and culpable of perpetrating this horror— than you have to rank me among the eagles of that school, me, a musician three-quarters German but one who has never composed anything of the sort. I repeat, *never*. Indeed, I challenge you to prove the contrary. So go ahead, invite someone likeminded, get some oxydized copper bowls, pour out the vitriol and drink. As for me, I prefer water, even lukewarm—or an opera by Cimarosa."

SUNT LACRYMAE RERUM [1]

It is not generally appreciated how much hard work goes into the composition of a full-scale grand opera, and how much additional and even more demanding work is needed to bring it before the public. Dependent as he is on two or three hundred middlemen, the composer is a man born to suffer. Neither moral principles nor real power, however disguised,

> Ni l'or ni la grandeur ne le rendent heureux,
> Et ces divinités n'accordent à ses voeux
> Que des biens peu certains, des plaisirs peu tranquilles.[2]

> Nor gold nor greatness can make him happy,
> And the gods respond to his pleas
> Only with uncertain rewards and unquiet pleasures.

Only the gifted virtuoso who is able to perform his own works is sheltered from the thousand and one torments that follow on the composition of a musical work. This amounts to saying that in one particular musical genre the composer is something of a paragon, and that in dramatic or symphonic or religious music, which requires the intelligent cooperation of a great number of people of good will, this paragon simply cannot exist. They say that Sophocles used to recite his poems at the Olympic celebrations in Greece, thereby easily exalting his huge audience to enthusiasm, moving it to tears. Now *there* is an example of the creator who is happy, strong, radiant, almost godlike. He was heard and applauded, and was so well understood that four-fifths of his audience applauded him even when they could not hear him.

Try nowadays to sing your new opera to some small audience of 6,000 (a number that would be trifling compared to the multitudes that attended the Olympic games)—in a time like ours, when composers are even worse singers than the professionals, in a time when we make fun of the four-stringed lyre, when we call for orchestras of 80 performers, choruses of 80 voices; in a period of unbridled communism, when every groundling who has or has not paid for his seat claims the *right* (how I love this old word, which is more comical than it is long) to hear everything that is said, everything that is sung or shouted on stage, everything that is strummed in the innermost recesses of the orchestra, all the bawling and wailing in the hidden corners of the chorus; in an age when faith in art no longer exists, when it is not only unable to enrapture human beings, but when even the mountains turn a deaf ear to its spell and respond to its most pressing appeals only by a most insolent inertia, a most blasphemous immobility.

No, nowadays one must pay hard cash to achieve a success, pay dear and often. Ask our great composers what their fame costs them year in and year out. They will not tell you, but they could. And once fame is attained, once it has become an undisputed and almost indisputable possession, do you suppose they can make it serve the spread of faith? Do you suppose the public will emulate the Athenians and say, amidst their applause, "I can hear nothing, but since it is Sophocles speaking, what he says must be sublime"? Quite the contrary. With each new work, a modern Sophocles must start again from scratch. Our modern Athenians, who scarcely listen, but who nevertheless hear with the full length of their ears, take care not to applaud with the connoisseurs in the stalls; they even laugh, the wretches, at the fervor of this knowledgeable applause. It is no use telling them: this piece is by Sophocles! They sit unmoved like the mountains, or else, should they scent a success, they take to gamboling around it like lambs. It is this frolicsome response that is the more to be feared. If I were a Sophocles, I would rather Mount Athos stayed firm and cold before me, deaf to my entreaties, than be the center of a lively dance by a flock of Parisian lambs. Suppose they turned out to be rams and goats?

Thus, the only compensation for all the care that artists take in creating, with no thought of the commercial value of their work, is their inner satisfaction and the deep joy they feel in measuring the distance they have traveled along the road to beauty. This one travels hundreds of miles, only to collapse just as he thinks he has won the prize. Another goes further, but still does not arrive, for the ideal can never be attained. A third goes a shorter distance. But all advance nonetheless, and they all prefer this march under the heat of the sun, with all the thirst and weariness it entails, to the cool shelters and the intoxicating liquors that popularity pours out for those other runners, who do not seek the unattainable and indeed turn their backs to it.

Let me add a rather sad remark about the current indifference of the fashionable public, I will not say to all of art, but to the most serious ventures undertaken by the Opéra. The holders of the best boxes are no more in their seats at the first performance of a work than at the hundredth, no more at eight o'clock than at seven.[3] Not even curiosity, that vulgar emotion which is so strong in most people, can these days propel them there. If a new opera were to be advertised as having a trio in the first act sung by the angel Gabriel in person, together with the archangel Michael and Saint Mary Magdalene,[4] the saint and the two angels would sing their trio to empty boxes, and those present would remain inattentive, just as if the cast were ordinary mortals.

Another, no less alarming, symptom is noticeable. Audiences used to spend the intermissions discussing a new work, always criticizing it severely. People would say, "It's dreadful; it's not music; it puts you to sleep"; and so on and so forth. Today nobody talks about the work at all, neither about the music nor about the drama. Instead, people chatter at random about the stock market and the races at the Champ de Mars, about table turning[5] and Tamberlick's[6] success in London, about Mlle Hayes's[7] triumph in San Francisco and the latest hospital built by Jenny Lind.[8] They also mention the spring and the budding leaves; they say, "I'm leaving for Baden, I'm going to England," or to Nice, or merely to Fontainebleau. If some primitive scatterbrain from the golden age should throw into the conversation the ridiculous question, "What do you think of it?" the answer would be:

"What do I think of what?"

"The new opera."

"Oh, I don't think anything about it—that is to say, I can't remember what I thought of it a moment ago. I wasn't paying much attention."

As regards the Opéra, the public seems to have sent in its resignation. It is like the drum major who became fed up with hearing the virtuosos under his command play *ra* instead of *fla*,[9] and turned in his baton to the Minister of Fine Arts.

Sometimes, however, the public resuscitates and even grows enthusiastic; and then it unleashes with passion all its prejudices, preconceptions, infatuations. At the première of Victor Hugo's *Hernani*,[10] when the hero cried, "Stupid old fool! He loves her!" a classicist leapt up in outrage and shouted, "What did you say? 'Stoop, you're awful!' Vulgar nonsense! You can't insult the public like that and get away with it." At which a romanticist who heard the words no better, jumped up in admiration, and retorted, "Yes, yes, 'Stoop, you're awful'. Nothing the matter with that! It's magnificent, it's human nature to the very life. I say, Bravo! It's superb!"[11]

That is exactly how music is judged at the theater.

THE SYMPHONIES OF H. REBER;
STEPHEN HELLER [1]

In this age of comic operas, operettas, salon operas, open-air operas, and water music—all useful works designed to comfort people who are wearied by making money—is it not a strange idea to bother with a composer of symphonies? But what is even stranger is that this composer ever took it into his head to write symphonies, for what does this sort of work do for a musician in this country? I am afraid even to think of the answer.

Here is what usually happens to an artist who has the misfortune to give way to the temptation of producing this type of music. If he has any ideas (and he absolutely must have some in order to compose music in which there are no words to suggest the likeness of phrases, no melodic platitudes, and no visual props to divert the spectator), if, I say, he has ideas, he must first spend time sorting them out, organizing them, and assessing their worth. Next, he makes a choice and, mustering all the artistry at his command, develops those that seem to him the most striking and most worthy of a place in his musical offering.

There he is at work, concentrating on the task of weaving his musical fabric. His imagination catches fire, his heart swells in his breast, he falls into strange reveries. When, late at night, after working all day, he feels the need for a breath of air, he is likely to go out without his hat and carrying a candle. He goes to bed but cannot sleep. The harmonious denizens of his orchestra frolic about in his brain, making sleep impossible. It is then that he finds his boldest and most original combinations, invents his freshest melodies, conceives the most unexpected contrasts. It is the hour of true inspiration.

It can also be the hour of misfortune. For if, when he has found a splendid idea, examined it from every angle, and unhurriedly ruminated upon it, he yields to the weakness of going to sleep and, relying upon his memory, puts off writing down his fine idea until morning, almost invariably he awakens to find that every trace of it has vanished. The wretched composer then experiences torments that defy description.[2] He strains to recapture the melodic or harmonic phantom that had so enchanted him, but to no avail. Even if he manages to remember a few bits and pieces, they are misshapen and disconnected; they seem the product of nightmare rather than of a poetic dream. He curses sleep: "If only I had got up and written it down," he says to himself, "the phantom would not have escaped me. Well, it can't be helped. Stop worrying; go out for a walk."

So there he is, strolling quietly not far from home. He no longer thinks about his symphony, he hums as he glances at the river flowing by, at the capricious flight of birds, when suddenly, the pace of his steps happens to coincide with that of the musical phrase he has forgotten; the phrase itself comes back to him. "Good God," he cries, "there it is! I shan't lose it this time!" Quickly, he slips his hand into his pocket but, confound it, he finds neither notebook nor pencil—he can't write it down. He sings the phrase, shaking with fear that it will vanish once more;[3] he sings it again and again, running and humming all the way home. He bumps into people, they call him names, dogs bark at his heels, he speeds on ever faster. At last he is home, still singing, his face haggard to the point of scaring the concierge; he flings open the door of his apartment, seizes a sheet of paper, and with trembling hand, scribbles down the accursed phrase. Overcome with fatigue and anxiety, but filled with joy, he collapses onto a chair. The idea is his at last; he has caught it and clipped its wings.

For it must be admitted, most composers feel they are only the amanuensis of a mischievous musical sprite within them, which dictates its ideas when it feels like it, and which the most ardent entreaties cannot move to speak if it has decided to keep silent. Hence the many capricious acts of the mind. There are times when the amanuensis cannot write fast enough, and others when the imp seems to taunt him by offering nothing but inanities that nobody would dare commit to paper.

I remember one occasion when I had the idea of writing a choral cantata on a short poem by Béranger entitled *Le Cinq mai* (The Fifth of May).[4] For the first few lines, the music came to me easily enough, but I was brought up short by the last two—the most important, since they are the refrain of every stanza:

> Pauvre soldat, je reverrai la France,
> La main d'un fils me fermera les yeux.
>
> Wretched soldier, I shall see France again,
> The hand of a son will close my eyes.

For several weeks I stubbornly tried to find the right melody for this couplet, but all I could think of were platitudes devoid of both style and expression. I finally gave up and dropped the cantata. Two years later, long after I had forgotten all about it, I was in Rome strolling about the steep bank of the Tiber known as Poussin's Walk.[5] I ventured too near the edge, slipped, and fell into the river. As I was falling, the thought that I was going to drown flashed across my mind; but when I saw that I had landed in mud with no harm but wet feet, I burst out laughing and clambered out of the Tiber, singing "Pauvre soldat, je reverrai la France," precisely to the tune that had eluded me two years earlier. "Yes," thought I, "that's it. Better late than never!" And so the cantata was completed.

To return to my symphonic composer. Let us suppose he has completed the work. He reads it through again, examines it with great care. He is satisfied with it; he, too, sees *that it is good.*[6] From that moment on, he is obsessed by the thought of getting the parts copied. He resists the temptation for a time, but sooner or later he gives in to it. He spends rather a large sum to get the copying done; after all, you must sow if you want to reap. Now to find a way of having the symphony performed. There exist musical societies that have courageous orchestras perfectly capable of giving such works a good rendering. But alas! the opportunity may never come. The symphony is not asked for; if the composer offers it, it is not accepted. If it is accepted, the musicians find it too difficult—and there is not enough time to rehearse it properly. If it is rehearsed properly and given a good performance, the audience finds the style too austere and fails to understand it. If, on the contrary, the public does receive it favorably, two days later it is forgotten, and the composer, like a loser, is back at square one.

If he takes it into his head to give a concert himself, things are even worse. He must spend huge sums for the hall, the musicians, the posters, etc., and in addition, take out of the receipts the sizable tax for the poor. His symphony, heard just once, is just as quickly forgotten. He has put himself to infinite trouble and all he has achieved is the loss of a great deal of money.

If he then dares to submit his score to a publisher, the latter stares at him in amazement, wondering if the man has lost his mind, and replies: "We have many important things to bring out—orchestral music doesn't sell very well—we cannot afford—etc., etc." Occasionally, an intrepid publisher who believes in the composer's future and is willing to run risks to save a fine work from oblivion takes a hand—such a publisher as Brandus or Richault.[7] He publishes the symphony, rescues it. Now it will not perish utterly. Some ten or twelve music libraries in Europe will give it room; five or six dedicated musicians will buy it; one day it will be scratched through by a provincial philharmonic orchestra, and then—and then . . . that is all!

Such are the reasons why there are fewer and fewer new symphonies. Haydn wrote more than a hundred; Mozart left us seventeen, Beethoven nine, Mendelssohn three, and Schubert one.[8] M. Reber[9] has been a bit more courageous than the latter two: he has composed four, just published in full score by the honorable house of Richault. These symphonies are in the classical mold used by Haydn and Mozart. Each has four movements—an *Allegro,* an *Adagio,* a scherzo or minuet, and a finale in fast tempo.

I must, however, point out that the third movement in each differs in type. The first symphony (in D minor) has a scherzo in duple time, lively, light, and sparkling, of the kind found in Mendelssohn. In the second symphony (in C) the scherzo is replaced by a somewhat animated move-

.

Henri Reber, by Pierre Petit. Bibliothèque de l'Opéra, courtesy
Bibliothèque Nationale.

ment in triple time that belongs to the species of minuet found in Mozart and Haydn. By contrast, the third (in E-flat) contains a slow minuet
of the same tempo and character as the dance music that originally bore
that name. Finally, the third movement of the fourth symphony (in G
major) is a scherzo in fast triple time, similar to those of Beethoven. M.
Reber has thus produced in his symphonies examples of the various types
of third movements used in turn by the four great masters, Haydn, Mozart, Beethoven, and Mendelssohn. He has also restored to the symphony (and I congratulate him for it) the slow minuet, the true minuet,
which differs essentially from the fast minuets of Haydn and Mozart,
and for which the one in Gluck's *Armide* remains the splendid model.[10]
It is said concerning this piece that when *Armide* was in rehearsal, Vestris asked Gluck, "Tell me, Chevalier, have you written my minuet?"

To which Gluck replied: "Yes, but it is of so broad a style that you will have to dance it on the Place du Carrousel."[11]

M. Reber's melodic style is unfailingly distinguished and pure. Some passages of his trios for piano and strings show his penchant for archaic forms, recalling early masters such as Rameau or Couperin, but with a fullness and wealth of development unknown to those composers. His symphonies are more modern. His harmonies are bolder than those of Haydn or Mozart, but without the least inclination toward brutal discords and the systematic hurly-burly introduced in the last four or five years by some German musicians, whose reason is not entirely sound and who are today the bane and terror of musical civilization.[12]

As for the orchestration in M. Reber's symphonies, it is polished, subtle, often ingenious, and entirely free of coarse effects. Each part is written with delightful skill and care. The orchestra is made up as in Mozart: there are no trombones or other instruments of large volume, no percussion except the timpani, no modern wind instruments. Needless to say, the hand of the skilled contrapuntist is displayed throughout. The various parts cross, pursue, and imitate each other with an ease and freedom of movement that never endangers the clarity of the whole. Finally, it seems to me that one of Reber's most obvious merits lies in the general ordering of the movements, in his control of the effects and in his knowledge—so rare—of when to stop. Without confining himself to narrow proportions, Reber never goes beyond the point where the listener might tire of following him; he never seems to lose sight of Boileau's maxim: "Qui ne sut se borner ne sut jamais écrire"[13] (He who does not know to stay within bounds, does not know how to write).

I do not recall whether all four of Reber's symphonies have been played at the Conservatoire concerts. A few years ago I heard two of them at one of those public ceremonies to which admission is not easily obtained; both of them enjoyed a brilliant success.

Stephen Heller[14] also seems to me to belong to that small family of resigned musicians who love and respect their art. He has a great deal of talent, a fine mind, unfailing patience, modest ambitions. He also has convictions, which his studies, his common sense, and his experience of life have rendered unshakable. An accomplished pianist, he also composes for the piano, but never promotes his own works—in fact, never plays in public. Nor does he give them the kind of glitter, coupled with a loose and insipid facility, that ensures success in so many pieces composed for the salons. His works, which exploit all the resources of the modern art of piano music, nevertheless show none of the unmanageable intricacies that make people buy certain *études*, of which they cannot play four measures, but which they exhibit on their pianos to make others believe that they can.

Indeed, Heller cannot be accused of charlatanism of any kind. In recent years, he has even given up teaching, thus denying himself the advantage (more profitable than people suppose) of having students to promote his fame. He composes, quietly, fine works that are rich in ideas, usually gentle in coloring, though at times also very lively. They are gaining ground little by little wherever the art of piano playing is seriously cultivated; his reputation is growing. He lives quietly, and the absurdities of the musical world merely raise a smile. Ah, happy, happy man!

ROMEO AND JULIET[1]

Opera in Four Acts by Bellini
Its Première at the Opéra
Madame Vestvali's Debut

There are now five operas in existence bearing the name *Romeo and Juliet*, their subject supposedly furnished by Shakespeare's immortal play. Yet nothing could be further from the English poet's masterpiece than the librettos, for the most part misshapen, paltry, and sometimes inane to the point of idiocy, that various composers have set to music. All the librettists claim to have taken their inspiration from Shakespeare, to have fired their torches at his burning sun of love. Pale torches, these texts. Three are at most little pink candles. Only one manages to emit some light amid a lot of smoke, and another can only be compared to a rag-and-bone man's candle end.

What these poetasters who have supplied texts in French and Italian have done with Shakespeare's work is childish and brainless beyond imagination (except for M. Romani,[2] who is, I believe, the author of Bellini's opera[3]). Not that it is possible to turn a play into an opera without modifying, upsetting, and spoiling the original in greater or lesser degree. Everybody knows that. But there are so many intelligent ways of carrying out the work of desecration required by the exigencies of the music. For example, even though it is not possible to keep all of Shakespeare's characters, why didn't any of these author-arrangers think of keeping at least one of the characters they all left out?

In the two French operas that have been performed in places where *opéra-comique* is the rule, why not keep either Mercutio or the nurse? These two characters are very different from the principals and could have given the composer the opportunity to fashion some striking contrasts in the score. To make up for the deficit, in those two operas of such unequal merit, a number of new characters were gratuitously introduced: there is an Antonio, an Alberti, a Cébas, a Gennaro, an Adriani, a Nisa, a Cécile,[4] among others—but to what end, and to achieve what result?

The two French operas have happy endings: at that time the unhappy kind were excluded from our opera houses. The spectacle of death was banned, out of consideration for the delicate sensibilities of the public. In the three Italian operas, on the contrary, the final catastrophe is ac-

Vincenzo Bellini, by Desjardins. Bibliothèque de l'Opéra, courtesy Bibliothèque
Nationale.

cepted. Romeo poisons himself; Juliet gives herself a little stab with a
pretty little silver-gilt dagger. She sits down gently next to Romeo's body,
sighs a charming little "Ah!" which is supposed to represent her last
gasp, and that's it.

Of course, neither the French nor the Italians, no more than the English themselves on their legitimate stage, have dared to keep the character of Romeo as it is, or give so much as a hint at his first love for
Rosaline.[5] For shame! To think that the young Montague could have
loved anyone before Capulet's daughter! It would be unworthy of everybody's idea of this paragon of lovers. It would take all the poetry out of
him. The public, of course, consists entirely of such pure and constant
souls.

And yet how profound is the lesson that the poet wished to teach!
How many times do we imagine we are in love before coming to the
real thing! How many Romeos die without ever knowing it! And how
many others have felt their heart bleed during many long years for a
Rosaline who was in fact chasms away from their inmost being! Chasms
whose depths they refused to see! How many have said to a friend: "I
have lost myself; I am not here; This is not Romeo, he's some other-
where. O! Teach me how I should forget to think!"[6] How many times
does Rosaline's would-be lover hear Mercutio say to him: "We'll draw
thee from the mire, of—save your reverence—love, wherein thou
stick'st"![7] He replies only with a smile of disbelief to the cheerful phi-

losopher, who, weary of Romeo's sorrow, departs muttering: "That same hard-hearted wench, that Rosaline, torments him so, that he will surely run mad."[8] And so it goes—until Romeo catches sight of Juliet among the splendors of the ball given by the wealthy Capulet. Hardly has he heard a few words from that voice charged with feeling than he recognizes the being he has so long been seeking. His heart leaps and swells as he breathes in the poetic flame, and the image of Rosaline vanishes like a ghost at break of day.

After the ball, in the throes of a divine distress that foreshadows the tremendous upheaval he will undergo, Romeo wanders aimlessly outside the Capulet house. He overhears the noble girl confess her feelings; he thrills with joy and amazement. Then begins the immortal dialogue, worthy of the very angels in heaven:

> JULIET: I gave thee mine [heart] before thou didst request it;
>   And yet I would it were to give again.
> ROMEO: Wouldst thou withdraw it? for what purpose, love?
> JULIET: But to be frank, and give it thee again.
> ROMEO: O blessed, blessed night! I am afeard,
> Being in night, all this is but a dream,
> Too flattering-sweet to be substantial.[9]

But they must part. Romeo feels a pang of intense grief and says to his beloved: "I cannot think we must be separated, that I must leave you, even for only a few hours. Listen, above the music that resounds in the distance, do you hear that heart-rending cry? I think it issues from my breast. Behold the splendor of the sky—all these sparkling lights. You would think fairies have lit up their palace to celebrate our love."[10] And the trembling Juliet replies only with her tears. A true grand passion is born, vast and unutterable, reinforced by all the powers of the imagination, the heart and the senses. Romeo and Juliet, who up to then had only existed, now fully live: they love each other.

Shakespeare! Father!

When one comes to know this marvelous poem, written in letters of fire, and compares it with the grotesque librettos taken from it that are passed off as operas, these frigid rhapsodies written with pens dipped in cucumber juice, one is impelled to exclaim, "Shakespeare! God!" Happily he is beyond the reach of such outrages!

Of the five operas I mentioned at the outset, Steibelt's *Romeo*,[11] first performed at the Feydeau Theater on September 10, 1793, is vastly superior to the others. It has a score, it really does exist as a work; it has style, feeling, invention, and even some rather remarkable innovations in harmony and instrumentation that in those days must have seemed daring. The overture is well designed and expertly managed, full of vigor and feeling. There is a very fine aria preceded by a beautiful recitative:

"Du calme de la nuit tout ressent les doux charmes"[12] (Who but must feel the charm of this still night). Its *Andante* has an expressive and elegant melodic line, which the composer had the amazing courage to end on the third of the key without rehashing the final cadence, as most of his contemporaries used to do.

The subject of this aria is from Act III, scene 2 of Shakespeare's play, where Juliet, who has been married to Romeo earlier that day, is waiting alone in her bedchamber for her young husband.

> Spread thy close curtain, love-performing night!
> That runaway's eyes may wink, and Romeo
> Leap to these arms, untalk'd of and unseen!
> Lovers can see to do their amorous rites
> By their own beauties; or if love be blind,
> It best agrees with night. Come, civil night,
> Thou sober-suited matron, all in black,
> And learn me how to lose a winning match,
> (Play'd for a pair of stainless maidenhoods:)[13]

I should also point out in Steibelt's work the aria with chorus for old Capulet, which moves briskly in its fierceness:

> Oui, la fureur de se venger
> Est un premier besoin de l'âme![14]
>
> The passion for revenge
> Is a primal need of the soul

the funeral march, "Grâces, vertus, soyez en deuil!"[15] (Ye graces and virtues, go into mourning!); and the aria Juliet sings when she is about to drink the potion.[16] It is dramatic, it is even quite moving; but how far (ye gods!) is the musical inspiration, however well it sustains our interest to the end, from Shakespeare's stupendous crescendo—he was indeed the inventor of the crescendo. The one in this play has no parallel, unless it be in the fourth scene of Act III of *Hamlet*, at the words, "Now mother what's the matter?"[17] What a rising tide of terror in this long monologue of Juliet's:

> What if it be a poison, which the friar
> Subtly hath minister'd to have me dead,
> Lest in this marriage he should be dishonour'd
> Because he married me before to Romeo?
> I fear it is: And yet, methinks, it should not,
> For he hath still be tried a holy man.
> I will not entertain so bad a thought.
> How if, when I am laid into the tomb,
> I wake before the time that Romeo

Come to redeem me? there's the fearful point!
Shall I not then be stifled in the vault,
To whose foul mouth no healthsome air breathes in,
And there die strangled ere my Romeo comes?
Or, if I live, is it not very like,
The horrible conceit of death and night,
Together with the terror of the place,
As in a vault, an ancient receptacle,
Where, for these many hundred years, the bones
Of all my buried ancestors are pack'd;
Where bloody Tybalt, yet but green in earth,
Lies festering in his shroud; where, as they say,
At some hours in the night spirits resort:
Alack, alack! is it not like that I,
So early waking, what with loathsome smells,
And shrieks like mandrakes' torn out of the earth,
That living mortals, hearing them, run mad:
O! if I wake, shall I not be distraught,
Environed with all these hideous fears,
And madly play with my forefathers' joints,
And pluck the mangled Tybalt from his shroud?
And in this rage, with some great kinsman's bone,
As with a club, dash out my desperate brains?
O, look! methinks I see my cousin's ghost
Seeking out Romeo, that did spit his body
Upon a rapier's point. Stay, Tybalt, stay!
Romeo, I come! this do I drink to thee.[18]

Music, I am confident, is capable of reaching such a peak, but *where* it has actually done so I cannot say. Whenever I see these two terrifying scenes on stage, I feel my brain spin in my skull and my bones split in my body. I shall never forget the overwhelming cry of love and anguish, "Romeo, I come! this do I drink to thee."[19]

Do you expect that when one has come to know such works and has experienced such moments, one can take seriously your tepid passions, your little wax figures of love made for display under glass? You expect that those who have spent their whole lives in lands where great oceanic lakes lie dreaming, where primeval forests of art rise up proud and lush, will put up with your little flower beds, your boxwood hedges clipped square, your goldfish bowls, or your pools which are merely the stagnant haunt of toads! Miserable concocters of tiny operas!

The other French score bearing the title *Roméo et Juliette* is almost forgotten today. It was composed—unfortunately for our national self-esteem—by Dalayrac; the author of the execrable libretto had just enough sense not to give his name.[20] It is appallingly flat and stupid throughout and in every way. It seems the work of two idiots who know neither passion, nor sentiment, nor common sense, nor French, nor music.

In the two operas I have mentioned so far, the part of Romeo was at least written for a man. The three Italian *maestri*, on the contrary, wished Juliet's lover to be played by a woman. It is a hangover from the old musical customs of the Italian school, due to its perpetual preoccupation with a puerile sensualism. They wanted a woman to sing the lover's part, because in love duets a pair of feminine voices will produce more readily those successions of thirds that are so dear to Italian ears. In the early operas of that school, there are scarcely any bass parts to be found; deep voices were abhorred by these voluptuaries, who were as fond of sweet sonorities as children are of sugar candy.

Zingarelli's[21] opera enjoyed a fairly lasting vogue in France and Italy. It is tranquil, graceful music, with not a trace of Shakespearean characters. It makes no more pretense at expressing the passions of the principals than if the composer had not understood the language he was setting to music. One of Romeo's arias, "Ombra adorata," is often mentioned; for a long time this famous number was sufficient to lure Paris audiences to the Théâtre-Italien and allow them to endure the frigid boredom of the rest of the opera. It is a graceful piece, elegant, and well put together. The flute plays pretty little runs that carry on a pleasant dialogue with fragments of the vocal line. Indeed this aria is almost all smiles. Romeo, about to die, expresses his joy at soon finding his Juliet again, and he looks forward to tasting the unalloyed pleasures of love in the abode of the blessed:

> Nel fortunato Eliso
> Avrò contento il cor.[22]
>
> In happy Elysium
> I shall have a happy heart.

Juliet sings numbers in which true expression is mixed with musical buffoonery. For example, in one long aria, she cries out that there is not another soul so crushed with misfortune as hers: "No v'e un alma a questo eccesso/Sventurata al par di me."[23] Then she reflects for a moment and launches *con brio* into a wordless vocalise in which long series of triplets convey the most cheerful effect, while jolly outbursts from the first violins heighten still further her *allegria*.

As to the final duet, that terrible scene where Juliet thinks she is on the brink of happiness, finds instead that Romeo has been poisoned, watches his agony, and finally expires on his body, nothing could be more tranquil than her anguish, nothing more charming than her convulsions. No better occasion can be imagined for saying with Hamlet: "They do but jest, poison in jest."[24]

Vaccaï's *Romeo*[25] is hardly ever performed, except for the third act, which is usually described as full of passion and of high dramatic force.

I heard it in London,[26] but have to confess that I noticed in it neither passion nor drama. Again the two lovers despair in a completely relaxed fashion. (They do but jest, poison in jest.) I do not know whether or not it is true that this third act is the one that now serves as the fourth act of the Bellini opera, just staged at the Opéra; I did not recognize it.[27] A few weeks ago, so it was said, Bellini's last act was found to be *too weak*; the poison seemed to be too much *in jest*, whereas it should be something—well, prodigious. I heard the opera in Florence twenty-five years ago[28] and of the dénouement I do not remember a thing.

This *Romeo*, fifth of the name,[29] although it is one of Bellini's weakest scores, contains some pretty things as well as a spirited finale, in which the two lovers sing a beautiful phrase in unison. The passage struck me when I heard it for the first time, at the Pergola theater.[30] It was very well performed in every way. The two lovers are forcibly torn apart by their enraged parents, the Montagues holding Romeo, the Capulets Juliet. Then, at the last return of the lovely passage: "Nous nous reverrons au ciel!" (We shall meet again in heaven!), they both break free of their persecutors, throw themselves into each others' arms, and kiss with a quite Shakespearean frenzy. At that moment one began to believe in their love. Our Opéra took good care not to risk this act of daring. It is not considered seemly in France that two stage lovers should embrace each other in so reckless a fashion. Think of the proprieties.

So far as I can remember, in his *Romeo* the gentle Bellini used only a moderate orchestra with neither ordinary drums nor the big bass drum. At the Opéra, of course, his orchestra was supplied with these two auxiliary devices of prime importance. Since there are scenes of civil war in the play, can the orchestra really do without a side drum? And can one dance and sing nowadays without a big bass drum? When Juliet prostrates herself at her father's feet, uttering cries of despair, the bass drum, unperturbed, booms on the downbeats with pompous regularity and produces—who could deny it?—an irresistibly comic effect. As its noise outtops everything, the audience forgets all about Juliet and thinks it is listening to a military band leading a battalion of the National Guard.

The dance tunes introduced into Bellini's score are not of a particularly high quality; they lack charm and spirit. One *Andante* did please the audience; its theme comes from an aria in *La Straniera:*[31] "Meco tu vieni, o misera" (Come with me, you unhappy thing), one of Bellini's most touching inspirations. They dance to it. But what then—we dance to everything now, we do everything to everything.

The costumes are quite ordinary; only Lorenzo's[32] was particularly noticed: it is a great overcoat lined with fur—the good friar is dressed like a Pole. It must have been cold in the Verona of those days. Marié,[33] who filled this fur-lined role, was suffering from a cold ("it is the cause"[34]) and had several vocal mishaps. Gueymard[35] was a very energetic Tybalt. Mme Gueymard[36] sang the part of Juliet with her golden voice and fine musicianship. The newcomer, Mme Vestvali,[37] is tall and handsome, with a contralto voice of extensive range in the deep register but lacking luster in the middle. Her vocalizing is not facile, and her attack, especially in the high octave, is sometimes not quite in tune. She played Romeo with a great deal of—shall I say?—dignity.

The tomb scene, as performed by great English actors, will always be the most sublime wonder of the art of theater.[38] When Juliet, coming back to life, feebly whispers the name Romeo, young Montague is struck dumb for a moment and stands transfixed. A second call, more tender this time, draws his attention to the bier. Juliet stirs, dispelling his doubt. She is alive! He leaps up to the funeral couch, snatches up the beloved body, tears away veil and shroud, and carries it downstage, upright in his arms. Juliet looks around languidly, her eyes dull. Romeo asks questions, presses her to him in a wild embrace, brushes back the hair that hides her pale brow, covers her face with frenzied kisses, bursts out in convulsive laughter. In his wild joy, he has forgotten that he is going to die. Juliet is breathing. Juliet! Juliet! But a terrible pain gives him warning: the poison is working and burning at his vitals! "Oh, potent poison! Capulet! Capulet! Mercy!" He goes down on his knees in supplication, deliriously believing he sees Juliet's father, come to take her from him again.

That same scene, in the new opera, goes like this:

Broad steps have been constructed on each side of the bier, so that Juliet may descend from her tomb conveniently and decently. She does in fact descend them so, and walks with measured tread toward her transfixed lover; whereupon they begin to talk over their little concerns, calmly explaining to each other a number of things:

ROMEO: What do I see?
JULIET: Romeo!
ROMEO: Juliet alive!
JULIET: From apparent death
I wake *this day*
And thus return to your love!
ROMEO: *Is this true?*
JULIET: Did Lorenzo not inform you?
ROMEO: Knowing nothing, understanding nothing,
I believed, unfortunately for me, that I had lost you forever.[39]

"Are there no stones in heaven?"[40]

No, there are no stones in heaven. Othello's question is pointless here. No, there is no beauty, no ugliness, no truth, no falsehood, nothing sublime or absurd—it is all one. The public knows this very well—hence its imperturbable indifference.

But let us cool down. From the standpoint of art—well, art has nothing to do with it. From the standpoint of business—the Opéra's financial interests—I believe that in engaging Mme Vestvali and putting on Bellini's *Romeo,* the director of this fine big theater will be out of pocket.

Let us sleep!

I can no more . . .

CONCERNING A BALLET BASED ON *FAUST*

A *Bon Mot* of Beethoven's [1]

The idea of having Faust dance[2] is the most extravagant that ever entered the brainless head of one of those men who meddle in everything, who desecrate everything without meaning the least harm, like the blackbirds and sparrows in our public parks who make perches of the finest statuary.[3] The composer of a *Faust* ballet seems to me far more amazing than Molière's Marquis, who was busy writing "the whole of Roman history in madrigals."[4]

As for the musicians who have made singers of the characters in this illustrious poem, they must be forgiven a great deal because they loved a great deal;[5] and also because these characters belong by right to the realm and art of dreams, of passion, the art of the vague, the infinite, the limitless art of sound.

How many dedications were inflicted on Goethe the Olympian![6] How many musicians wrote to him: "O thou!" or simply "O!" to which he replied, or should have replied: "I am very grateful, Sir, that you have deigned to adorn a poem that otherwise would have remained in obscurity." He liked a bit of raillery, this god of Weimar, whom someone—I don't know who—misnamed "the Voltaire of Germany."

Once only did Goethe meet his match in a musician. For it seems now proved that the art of music is not so besotting as the literati have long wished us to believe; indeed, it is said that during the past hundred years, there have been almost as many musicians blessed with wits as there have been men of letters without.

And so, Goethe once came to spend a few weeks in Vienna. He liked the company of Beethoven, whose music[7] had just truly adorned Goethe's tragedy *Egmont*. One day as the poet strolled on the Prater with the melancholy Titan, they received respectful nods from the passersby, but Goethe alone responded to their greetings. Finally, becoming impatient at being forced to tip his hat so often, Goethe said: "My, these good people are tiresome with their eternal bowing and scraping."

"Don't be annoyed, *Excellence*," Beethoven replied gently, "perhaps I am the one they are saluting."

TO BE OR NOT TO BE
A Paraphrase[1]

To be or not to be, that is the question. Whether 'tis nobler in the mind to suffer third-rate operas, ridiculous concerts, indifferent performers, mad composers, or to take arms against this sea of troubles and by opposing end them? To die, to sleep—no more; and by a sleep to say we end the assaults on the ear, the torments of heart and mind, and the thousand natural shocks inflicted upon our intelligence and our senses by the practice of criticism. 'Tis a consummation devoutly to be wished. To die, to sleep, to sleep, perchance to have a nightmare. Ay, there's the rub. For in that sleep of death, what tortures may come in dreams when we have shuffled off this mortal coil, what mad theories shall we have to examine, what discordant music to hear, what idiots to praise, what indignities to see inflicted on masterpieces, what absurdities to hear applauded, what windmills to see taken for giants?

All this must give us pause; there's the thought that makes *feuilletons* so numerous and prolongs the life of the wretches who must write them.

For who would bear this senseless world, the sight of its madness, the scorn and errors of its ignorance, the injustice of its justice, the icy indifference of its rulers? For who would whirl in the wind of the lowest of passions, the pettiest of motives masquerading as the love of art; who would stoop to discuss the absurd, to be a soldier and teach one's general to command, to be a traveler and guide one's guide, who will get lost anyway, when one could be released from these humiliations by a flask of chloroform or a steel bullet? For who would bear to see in this base world despair grow out of hope, weariness inaction, and rage patience, were it not for the dread of worse beyond death, the undiscovered country from whose bourn no critic has ever returned? That is what puzzles the will . . .

But come, it's not allowed to meditate even for a few moments. Here comes the young prima donna Ophelia, armed with a score and a wry smile.

"What do you expect from me? Flattery, isn't it? It's always flattery."

"No, my lord, I have a score of yours that I've long wanted to return to you. Please take it."

"No, not I. I never gave you aught."

"My honoured lord, you know right well you did, and with it words of so sweet breath composed as made the gift more rich. Take it back, for to a noble heart the most precious gifts lose their value when he who gave them feels nothing for us but indifference. There, my lord."

"Ah! So you have a heart?"

"My lord?"

"You're a singer, are you not?"

"What means your lordship?"

"Then if you have a heart and you're a singer, let your heart admit no discourse to your voice."

"Could the voice, my lord, have better commerce than with the heart?"

"Ay, truly. A talent like yours would sooner pervert the noblest impulses of the heart than the heart would ennoble the aspirations of talent. This was sometime a paradox, but now the time gives it proof. I did admire you once."

"Indeed, my lord, you made me believe so."

"You were wrong to believe me. My admiration was not real."

"Then I was all the more deceived."

"Get thee to a nunnery. What is your ambition? Fame, money, the applause of fools, a titled husband, the rank of Duchess. They all dream of marrying a prince. Why wouldst thou be a breeder of idiots?"

"Help him, you sweet heavens!"

"If thou dost marry, I'll give thee this dismal truth for thy dowry; be a singer as chaste as ice, as pure as snow, she will not escape calumny. Get thee to a nunnery. Farewell. Or if thou wilt needs marry, marry a fool, for wise men know well enough the torments you reserve for them ... To a nunnery go, and quickly too. Farewell.

"O heavenly powers, restore him."

"I have heard enough of your vocal affectations, your ridiculous pretensions, your stupid vanity. God has given you one voice and you make yourself another. You are entrusted with a masterpiece, and you distort it, you change its character, you deck it out with cheap ornaments, you make insolent cuts, you add grotesque roulades, absurd arpeggios, and ridiculous trills. You insult the master, people of taste, art, and common sense. Go to, I'll no more on't. To a nunnery, go." [Exit.]

Young Ophelia is not totally in the wrong. Hamlet may indeed have lost his mind. But in our musical world, where everyone is completely mad, no one will notice. Besides, the poor Prince of Denmark has his moments of sanity. He's mad only north-northwest; when the wind is southerly, he certainly knows an eagle from a silly goose.[2]

Appendix
The Lapdog School

[By a strange whim, Berlioz reprinted the following paragraph from his *feuilleton* of March 30, 1862 as the last "essay" of his book, under the title "The Lapdog School." Since it repeats what he said earlier, adds nothing new, and spoils by anticlimax the fine Shakespearean close, I have made it an Appendix, for completeness' sake. Berlioz himself supplies a justification for so doing when he writes of the omission of the final chorus of Gluck's *Alceste:* that it was done "out of respect for the man of genius," by preventing "the conclusion of his masterpiece . . . from being a page unworthy of him." (See above, p. 128.)]

The Lapdog School is a school of singers whose range extends upwards to extraordinarily high notes, enabling them to let forth high Es and high Fs at any moment. As to the effect and the pleasure these afford the listener, they resemble the yelping of a King Charles spaniel when someone steps on its paw. It is only fair to add that when Mme Cabel practiced this vocal system, she always reached her destination. If she aimed at an E or an F or even at the dizzy height of a high G, it was indeed a G, F, or E that she reached. Yet nobody seemed much obliged; whereas her pupils or imitators, who generally reach only as far as D-sharp when they aim at E, or E when their goal is F, always excite frenzied applause. This injustice, and this unjustness, have ended by turning Mme Cabel against her own school of singing. It was bound to happen. Now she is content to sing like the charming woman she is; she has given up trying to imitate the birds and the little dogs.

Notes

The Art of Music

1. Ernest-Wilfrid Legouvé (1807–1903), French playwright and poet, was a close friend of Berlioz, with whom he shared a passion for music. In their youth both men were fanatical devotees of the Opéra and the music of Gluck. Legouvé was a friend to other musicians, including Liszt. He was music critic for *Gazette Musicale* (hereafter *G.M.*). He wrote the lyrics for *La Mort d'Ophélie*, the ballad for voice and orchestra that Berlioz composed in 1842. He also collaborated with Scribe on the play *Adrianne Lecouvreur*, which was later to become an opera by Cilea. Legouvé was elected to the Académie Française in 1855, a year before Berlioz. In 1836, Legouvé lent Berlioz 2,000 francs to allow him to complete *Benvenuto Cellini*. (See *Memoirs*, translated by David Cairns [New York: Norton, 1969], p. 246.) Legouvé's books include *Eugène Scribe* (1874), *Maria Malibran* (1880), and *Soixante ans de souvenirs* (1886). The last contains a lively portrait of Berlioz, which Cairns describes as fascinating but not always dependable.

2. *Voyage musical en Allemagne et en Italie* (hereafter *V.M.*, 1844).

3. The article "Musique" (The Art of Music) appeared in *G.M.*, September 10, 1837, pp. 405–409, under the title "De la musique en général." It was written for the *Dictionnaire de la conversation* (1837; 2d ed., 1863). Berlioz included it in *V.M.*, Vol. I, pp. 241–260, where, as here, it preceded *Etude analytique des Symphonies de Beethoven*.

4. "Music can be defined as the art of combining sounds so as to touch the emotions." (François-Joseph Fétis, *La Musique mise à la portée de tout le monde* [Music for Everyone] [Paris: Mesnier, 1830], translated by B. Perkins as *Music Explained to the World* [Boston, 1842; New York: Da Capo Press, 1987].)

5. These first two sentences and the entire paragraph seem to be a riposte to Fétis's work, whose title alone must have exasperated Berlioz. See below, "Lines Written Soon after the First Performance of *Orphée*," p. 85 and note 15.

6. Horace, *Ars poetica*, verses 408–410.

7. See *Correspondance générale*, Vol. I, 1803–1832 (Paris: Flammarion, 1972), for the touching anecdote about Rouget de Lisle that Berlioz related to his sister, Nanci (letter of August 4, 1830, pp. 346–348), and the letter to Rouget de Lisle (December 29, 1830, p. 394), which is included in chapter 29 of *Memoirs*.

8. "The writers of antiquity had divergent opinions on the nature, object, scope, and elements of music. On the whole, 'music' had a far more comprehensive meaning for them than it does for us today. As we have observed, the word embraced dance, pantomime, poetry, and even the whole collection of the sciences." (J. J. Rousseau, "Musique," *Dictionnaire de musique*.) Berlioz undoubtedly had this article before him as he wrote. He cites it later.

9. Timotheus, a musician from Thebes, was a flute player in Alexander's retinue. Rousseau mentions him in the article cited above.

10. Berlioz more or less copies this passage from Rousseau's article. The story may derive from the career of King Erik XIV of Sweden.

11. After listening to the *Adagio* of Beethoven's Piano Sonata in C-sharp minor, played by Liszt at Legouvé's house, "we all shivered in silence and, after the last chord had died down . . . we wept." (*V.M.*, Vol. I, p. 365.) See below, "Trios and Sonatas of Beethoven." See also the October 6, 1829 issue of *Le Correspondant* for the effect on Berlioz of the performance of Beethoven's String

Quartet in C-sharp minor by the Baillot Quartet (English translation in Jacques Barzun, *Berlioz and the Romantic Century*, 3d ed. [New York: Columbia University Press, 1969], Vol. I, p. 99).

12. The subject of the twelfth evening, "Suicide from Enthusiasm," in *Les Soirées de l'orchestre* (translated by Jacques Barzun as *Evenings with the Orchestra* [Chicago: University of Chicago Press, 1956; Phoenix edition 1973]).

13. Maria Felicità Malibran (née García, 1808–1836) was a celebrated Spanish mezzo-contralto, famous for the color and unusual range of her voice as well as her excitable temperament. She was a sister of Pauline Viardot. See below, "Gluck's *Orphée*," note 3.

14. *Expression:* "Quality through which the musician feels keenly and conveys vigorously all the ideas he must convey and all the feelings he must express." (Rousseau, *Dictionnaire de musique.*)

15. A few years later a series of articles by Berlioz entitled "On Instrumentation" appeared in *G.M.* (November 21–December 19, 1841 and January 2–July 3, 1842). In 1844, they were published as the famous *Grand Traité d'Instrumentation et d'Orchestration.*

16. These debates on the music of the ancients, notably that of the Greeks, and their comparison with modern music, as well as the quarrel between the ancients and the moderns, became a tradition in France in the seventeenth century.

17. Jean-François Lesueur, or Le Sueur (1760–1837), was a prominent French composer of church music and opera during the Revolution, the Empire, and the Restoration. His *Ossian ou les Bardes* was one of the greatest operatic successes of the first half of the nineteenth century. In 1818 he became professor of composition at the Conservatoire, where his pupils included Berlioz, Gounod, and Ambroise Thomas. Today he is best known as Berlioz's teacher. Lesueur was also a mentor and friend to Berlioz and an important influence on his development. They shared an insistence on expressive integrity and an interest in acoustics, the contrast of timbres, and the liberation of rhythm. As David Cairns says, it was a poetic injustice that Lesueur should have died a few months before the performance of Berlioz's most Lesueurian work, the *Requiem.*

18. Guido of Arezzo (991–after 1033) was a Benedictine monk, music theorist, and pedagogue who had legendary status in the Middle Ages. He developed a method of sight-singing based on the syllables ut, re, mi, fa, sol, la, which he adapted to the hexachord. The fingers of the "Guidonian hand" demonstrate the hexachordal positions. Guido has also been credited with developing a system of precise pitch notation by means of lines and spaces.

19. Sappho lived in Lesbos around 600 B.C. She left odes, epithalamia, elegies, and hymns, and may have invented the four-line stanza form known as "sapphic."

20. Olympus (seventh century B.C.) is said to have composed a number of instrumental and vocal melodies. He introduced into Greece the Phrygian "auletic," a piece of music played on the aulos—a double-reed instrument—and invented certain rhythms. He is mentioned by Alcibiades in Plato's *Symposium.*

21. Terpander was born in Lesbos and probably lived near the end of the eighth century B.C. According to Plutarch, he won the prize for poetry and song at the Pythian Games four times in a row. Airs for cithara and flute and the invention of the seven-string lyre are ascribed to him.

22. Aristoxenus, the most famous Greek music theorist, was born in Tarentum, now Taranto in Italy, about 354 B.C.

23. This impressive list was borrowed from the article "Instruments" in *Le Dictionnaire de musique*, which Rousseau may have borrowed from an earlier work.

24. This work was mentioned many times by Lesueur himself and, after his

death, by his wife and heirs. As late as 1880, in his *Supplément* to Fétis's *Biographie universelle des musiciens*, Arthur Pougin wrote: "Finally, Lesueur left an important work on Greek music, *Traité de la musique des anciens*, which he had intended to publish since 1822, but which has remained unpublished to this day. This work recently caused a lawsuit between Lesueur's heirs, and eventually one of his sons-in-law, M. X. Boisselot, was authorized to publish it. As a result, *Le Traité de la musique des anciens* [also known as *Histoire générale de la musique*] will be published soon." Alas, Boisselot did not publish it, and after his death in 1893, the manuscript seems to have disappeared. The question is thoroughly discussed in Jean Mongrédien, *Le Catalogue Thématique de l'Oeuvre Complète du Compositeur Jean-Francois Le Sueur* (New York: Pendragon Press, 1980).

Modern scholars have doubts about Lesueur's scholarship and even wonder whether the lost manuscript might in fact have damaged Lesueur's reputation had it ever appeared. Even in the nineteenth century, Fétis, in commenting on other articles by Lesueur, says that he did "music history as he would wish it to be . . . replacing almost everywhere the real historical facts by his own views."

Lesueur seems to have been exceptionally unlucky with his manuscripts. Many other books and articles apparently disappeared from the libraries of Paris, even as late as the twentieth century. What are left now for us are mostly works of his old age. Like Fétis, however, Berlioz would have had access to articles written by Lesueur, and he would have heard his teacher speak often of ancient music. (See Barzun, *Berlioz and the Romantic Century*, Vol. I, pp. 144–145. See also David Cairns, *Berlioz* [London: André Deutsch, 1989], pp. 120–122.)

25. See "Twenty-first Evening" of *Evenings with the Orchestra*; and, below, "Musical Customs of China."

A Critical Study of Beethoven's Nine Symphonies

1. In *Le Correspondant* of August 4 and 11, and October 6, 1829, Berlioz had published a biography of Beethoven and a study of his works entitled "Beaux-arts, Biographie etrangère.—Beethoven." The analyses that follow appeared in the *G.M.* of April 9, 1837 and January 28, February 4, February 11, February 18, and March 4, 1838. They were reprinted in *V.M.*, Vol. I, pp. 261–355, with their variants.

2. The Paris Opéra.

3. François-Antoine Habeneck (1781–1849) was a violinist, conductor, and composer. As conductor of the Conservatoire concerts, he was instrumental in making known the symphonies of Beethoven. He was as well chief conductor of the Opéra; thus, for two decades he was the most powerful conductor in Paris and certainly a force to be reckoned with. Berlioz's relations with him were sometimes strained. (See *Memoirs*.)

4. It was at concerts of the Paris Conservatoire (established in 1828) that Beethoven's symphonies were revealed to the Paris public. Habeneck played them regularly every year. Wagner, who attended the concert series of 1839, said that they were the best performances of the Beethoven symphonies he had ever heard. (See Barzun, *Berlioz and the Romantic Century*, Vol. I, p. 88 and note.)

5. The Viennese nobleman and ballet composer Graf Robert von Gallenberg (1783–1839) is known to us chiefly for having married Beethoven's beloved Giulietta Guicciardi, the dedicatee of the "Moonlight" Sonata. The couple lived in Vienna and Italy, where Gallenberg composed some fifty ballets. His *Alfred le Grand*, a ballet in three acts, was performed at the Paris Opéra on September 18, 1822.

6. Pierre Gaveaux (1760–1825) was a singer and composer of romances and thirty opéras-comiques. See below, *"Fidelio,"* p. 41 and note 4.

7. Rodolphe Kreutzer (1766–1831), the famous violin soloist and composer, preceded Habeneck as conductor of the Paris Opéra. Beethoven's "Kreutzer" sonata, for violin and piano, is dedicated to him.

8. Berlioz wrote an article to the glory of the Académie royale de musique, the Société des Concerts du Conservatoire, and their conductor, Habeneck, in the *Berliner Allgemeine Musikalische Zeitung* of July 18, 1829. See also Antoine Elwart, *L'Histoire de la Société des Concerts du Conservatoire* (Paris, 1860); *Memoirs*, XX; and Wagner's *Mein Leben*. Berlioz's reviews in *G.M.* and *Le Rénovateur* of the Concerts du Conservatoire began to appear in 1834.

Symphony No. 1 in C

9. Measure 50. Breitkopf & Härtel edition.
10. On timpani, see *Traité*, pp. 263–264.

Symphony No. 2 in D

11. Measure 73.

Symphony No. 3—The *Eroica*

12. Berlioz inserts here the section on the *Eroica Symphony* from his article in *G.M.* of April 9, 1837; he also devoted several lines to it in *G.M.* of March 17, 1839. In his *Traité*, he cites two examples from this symphony, one on the disconsolate mood the oboe can create (p. 115), the other on the stopped notes of the three horns in E-flat in the Scherzo (p. 174).

13. *Sinfonia eroica.* The symphony was originally entitled "Bonaparte" as a tribute to the young hero of revolutionary France who was almost exactly Beethoven's age. According to a well-known story, on hearing that the Consul had proclaimed himself emperor in May 1804, Beethoven was enraged and tore up the title page. On its publication in 1806, the symphony was given its present title.

14. Measure 128.
15. Measures 276–279.
16. Measure 394.
17. Ferdinand Ries (baptized 1784–1838), a pianist and composer born in Bonn, came from a family of German musicians. His father, Franz Anton Ries, had taught Beethoven the violin. Ferdinand studied piano with Beethoven and composition with Albrechtsberger. Later he lived by turns in several countries, and from 1813 to 1824 in London. (See Barzun [trans.], *Evenings with the Orchestra*, p. 323.)

18. *Aeneid*, XI, verses 78–79 and 89–90.
19. Measure 238.
20. For example, the funeral of Patroclus and the games celebrated in his honor (Book XXIII).
21. Measures 36–37.
22. Measure 349.
23. Here ends the excerpt from *G.M.*, April 9, 1837. The next few pages are from *V.M.*, Vol. II, pp. 285–288, after which follows the *G.M.* article of January 28, 1838.

Symphony No. 4 in B-Flat

24. In his *Traité* Berlioz quotes two passages from this symphony to illustrate the use of *pizzicato* in the strings (p. 27) and *pianissimo* by the timpani (p. 263).

25. Measure 238. The dominant-seventh is based on F-sharp.

26. Fifth Canto of the *Inferno*. It is the subject of the opera by Della Viola in the "First Evening" of *Evenings with the Orchestra.*

Symphony No. 5 in C minor

27. In his *Traité*, Berlioz uses four examples from this Symphony to illustrate violas playing in unison with the cellos so as to reinforce the latter (pp. 31 and 38), a bassoon effect (p. 129), and a timpani *pianissimo* (p. 264).

28. Horace, *Ars poetica*, v. 269, quoted also below in "*On Church Music* by Joseph d'Ortigue," p. 175, note 10.

29. When Beethoven was about twenty, according to Fétis, "he conceived a passion for the great German poets, as well as for the works of Homer, Virgil, and Tacitus."

30. Berlioz is presumably referring to Napoleon. See above, "Symphony No. 3," p. 13, note 13.

31. Beethoven's *Andante con moto.*

32. Measures 98–101.

33. Measures 49–52.

34. Measures 133–143. The flute and oboe are in thirds; the two clarinets are also playing in thirds, in contrary motion to the first two instruments.

35. Measures 185ff.

36. *Faust*, Part I, Walpurgis Night, the Blocksberg scene.

37. Measure 293. See also *Traité*, p. 128.

38. This is also virtually the first time that trombones appear in symphonic music.

39. In *Armide*, Act IV, scene 3, Ubalde warns Renaud. Berlioz cites this passage and writes about it at length in *G.M.*, June 8, 1834, p. 183.

40. Here ends the *G.M.* article of January 28, 1838.

Symphony No. 6—The *Pastoral*

41. Here begins the second article from *G.M.*, published on February 4, 1838. Three examples from the *Pastoral* Symphony appear in *Traité*, pp. 57, 112, 160.

42. Louis-Sébastien Lebrun (1764–1829) was a singer, teacher, and composer. *Le rossignol*, his one-act opera of 1816, was often performed in Paris. Berlioz reviewed it in his *feuilletons* of May 17, 1845 and October 24, 1857. (See also Berlioz, *Grotesques de la musique* [Paris: Gründ, 1969], pp. 28, 215–216.)

43. *Le Devin du village* (Paris, 1752), opera by Jean-Jacques Rousseau, the famous French writer and philosopher (1712–1778), who published his *Dictionnaire de Musique* in 1767.

44. See "La scène aux champs" of Berlioz's *Symphonie fantastique*. Berlioz says: "Sensations douces qu'inspirent l'aspect d'un riant paysage" for "Erwachen heiterer Gefühle bei der Ankunft auf dem Lande," which, rendered literally, is: "Awakening of exalted sentiments on arriving in the country."

45. Measure 129.

46. Measure 91.

47. *Traité*, p. 112.

48. Measure 165.

49. See the end of the "Scène aux champs" of *Symphonie fantastique.*
50. Measure 95.
51. Measure 106.
52. Beethoven calls it: "Hirtengesang—Frohe, dankbare Gefühle nach dem Sturm" (Shepherd's song—Happy and thankful feelings after the storm).
53. Measure 21.
54. 'Measure 5 of the *Allegretto.*
55. The excerpt from *G.M.* ends here. The dialogue that follows comes from *V.M.,* Vol. I, p. 311.
56. Virgil, *Georgics,* III, v. 1–2.

Symphony No. 7 in A

57. This section appeared in *G.M.,* February 11, 1838. Three examples from the Seventh Symphony appear in *Traité:* the oboes, p. 114; the stopped notes of the horn, p. 178; and the trumpets playing *piano,* p. 190.
58. Berlioz himself calls it *Andante* in two different passages of his earlier work.
59. It was the custom of the time to applaud after each movement of a symphony.
60. It is proven today.
61. *V.M.* and the *A Travers Chants* edition of 1862 has *"tenus"* (sustained), but the text of *G.M.,* Guichard informs us, has *"ténus"* (thin, tenuous). As he says, it is not easy to decide between the two readings.
62. Measure 57. Actually, flutes with oboes.
63. Measure 160.
64. Measures 401ff.
65. Measure 133.
66. Measure 27. Berlioz mentions only the cellos, but the violas are also playing the lament.
67. Measure 102. Shakespeare, *Twelfth Night,* Act II, scene 4, line 116—"like Patience on a monument smiling at grief."
68. Verse by the Irish poet Thomas Moore (1779–1852), which Byron used as an epigraph to *The Giaour.*
69. Measure 255.
70. The last words spoken by Hamlet (Act V, scene 2, line 347).
71. Measures 188–206.
72. *Armide* (Paris, 1777), opera by Gluck on a libretto by Quinault.
73. Measures 388ff. The bass line consists of alternating E's and D-sharps in quarter notes, with the E's on the strong beats.
74. Here ends the third article in *G.M.,* that of February 11, 1838.

Symphony No. 8 in F

75. Here begins the fourth article in *G.M.,* that of February 18, 1838.
76. Measure 38.
77. Measure 52; the chord is F-sharp, A, C, E-flat.
78. *Allegretto scherzando.*
79. It was the custom in Italian opera to use such a repeated motif to close an act.
80. Measures 161–162.
81. Measure 17 and again at measure 178.
82. Measure 372.

Symphony No. 9—*Choral* Symphony

83. This article was published in *G.M.* on March 4, 1838.

84. In a letter to Liszt in which he evokes his visit to Weimar, Berlioz was moved by Schiller's fate: "Did those two small windows really light the garret where Schiller lived? Was it in that wretched abode that the poet of the noblest passions of the human heart wrote *Don Carlos, Mary Stuart, The Robbers, Wallenstein?* He lived there like a mere student! I do not like Goethe for allowing that. He, a rich man, a minister of state, could surely have transformed his friend's existence. Schiller! Schiller! I cannot take my eyes from the narrow windows, the obscure house, the mean black roof. One in the morning, a brilliant moon, the cold intense; all quiet in that city of the dead. As I stand watching, my heart swells, a trembling seizes me. Overwhelmed by respect and regret and by that infinite sympathy that genius can inspire from beyond the grave in the lowliest of the living, I kneel by the humble threshold and repeat over and over again in love, grief, and admiration, Schiller! Schiller!" (*V.M.*, Vol. I, pp. 65–66; quoted in *Memoirs*, translated by David Cairns [New York: Norton, 1969], pp. 288–289.)

85. Measure 513.

86. Measures 216–217.

87. Measure 177. The score reads *Ritmo di tre battute,* i.e., a three-measure pattern, one beat per measure.

88. Measure 454.

89. Jean Paul Egide Martini (born Johan Paul Aegidias Schwartzendorf; 1741–1816) was a German organist and composer. He served at the court of the Duke of Lorraine in Nancy. In 1764 he went to Paris, where he wrote marches, church music, and operas. His opera *Sapho* was performed at the Théâtre Louvois in 1794. His only famous work is the song "Plaisir d'amour."

90. One of the four registers of the clarinet, between the medium and the low (*Traité,* p. 137). Today it is the lowest of three registers: the top—altissimo, the middle—clarion, the low—chalumeau. Chalumeau was also the name of an instrument from which the modern clarinet developed.

91. Beethoven gives the same rapid notes to the contra bassoon as well. About rapid runs in the double-bass, see *Traité,* pp. 55 and 57. "Beethoven in this example (the Storm from the *Pastoral* and in many other passages) gave the double-basses low notes that they cannot play" (p. 57).

92. Translation © Deutsche Grammophon, 1963. Recording by Berlin Philharmonic, conducted by Herbert von Karajan.

A Few Words about the Trios and Sonatas of Beethoven

1. Article published in *Débats*, March 12, 1837, taken up again in *V.M.*, Vol. I, pp. 357–365, under the title "Trios and Sonatas."

2. *Fidelio*, three successive versions: 1805, 1806, 1814. See Berlioz's article in *Le Correspondant* of August 11, 1829 and the next essay in the present book.

3. *The Creatures of Prometheus,* 1801.

4. *Egmont,* 1810, incidental music to Goethe's tragedy. One scene (Egmont's Dream) is a melodrama, i.e., music accompanying spoken words.

5. *Coriolan,* 1807, play by Heinrich von Collin.

6. *The Ruins of Athens,* 1811, incidental music for a play by Kotzebue.

7. *Mass in C,* 1807, and *Mass in D,* 1822.

8. *Christ on the Mount of Olives,* 1803.

9. There is only one such work, the Quintet, Op. 16, for four wind instruments and piano.

10. Translated from the German by Fétis as *Etudes de Beethoven, Traité d'harmonie et de composition,* 2 vols. (Berlin: Schlesinger, 1833). Berlioz published an article entitled "Le Traité de composition de Beethoven," in Le *Rénovateur,* January 27, 1834.

11. Horace, *Ars Poetica,* v. 359: "Indignor quandoque bonus dormitat Homerus."

12. The "Moonlight" Sonata, Op. 27 (1801).

13. In 1832. See the remorse expressed by Liszt in his "Lettre d'un bachelier ès-musique, un poète voyageur," *G.M.,* January 1837.

14. Perhaps "Agathe's sublime aria" in the second act. See *Evenings with the Orchestra,* pp. 53ff.

15. It was very likely Legouvé. See "The Art of Music," note 1.

Fidelio

1. This article was published in *Débats,* May 19 and 22, 1860. On reading it, Wagner wrote to Berlioz with "a thousand thanks" and of the "special kind of joy" afforded him by "an intelligence which understands so perfectly . . . the most intimate secrets of a creation by another hero of art." (See Jacques Barzun, *Berlioz and the Romantic Century,* 3d ed., 2 vols. [New York: Columbia University Press, 1969], Vol. II, p. 174.)

2. February 17, 1798. Berlioz uses the revolutionary calendar here, no doubt to remind readers that the play was written during the revolutionary period.

3. Jean-Nicolas Bouilly (1763–1842) was a French writer and administrator of the department around Tours during the Reign of Terror. Bouilly was perhaps the best-known writer of librettos for "Rescue Operas," which became popular after the French Revolution of 1789 and were sometimes based on real events. In addition to *Léonore,* Bouilly wrote the libretto for Cherubini's opera *Les Deux Journées* (1800), also known as *The Water Carrier,* and in another genre, Méhul's *Le Jeune Henri* (1797).

4. Pierre Gaveaux (1760–1825) was a French tenor and composer. He became known in Paris about 1790 as an opera singer, appearing as Floreski in Cherubini's *Lodoïska* (1791) and as Romeo in Steibelt's *Roméo et Juliette* (1793). During the Revolution, he wrote patriotic songs. His own operas include *Sophie et Moncars* (1797), in addition to *Léonore ou l'Amour Conjugal* (1798), in which he sang Florestan. In 1793, he and his brother founded a music shop called A la Nouveauté, in the Passage Feydeau, where he published his own and others' works.

5. Claudine-Angélique Legrand (1770–1807) was the wife of Etienne Scio, a composer and violinist at the Théâtre Feydeau. Both of them were hired in 1792. She specialized in trouser roles.

6. Ferdinando Paër (1771–1839) was an Italian composer who spent most of his career writing Italian operas in other countries. He settled in Vienna (1798), Dresden (1803), and finally Paris (1807), where Napoleon appointed him *maître de chapelle.* His *Leonora o L'Amore Conjugale* was produced in Dresden in 1804. In the 1820s he taught composition to the young Liszt. Berlioz had as little respect for Paër's music as for what he considered his scheming personality. (See *Revue européenne,* 1832; *V.M.,* Vol. II, p. 87; and *Memoirs,* trans. Cairns, p. 105.)

7. This anecdote must have impressed Berlioz, for he also included it in his *Evenings with the Orchestra* (trans. Barzun, p. 325).

8. The première took place in Vienna on November 20, 1805; this first version was in fact called *Leonore.* Beethoven seems to have always preferred this

title; he changed it to *Fidelio* for the 1806 performances only under pressure from the management of the Theater an der Wien, who wished to avoid pre-empting the name of Paër's *Leonora*, which they intended to produce later. The 1814 production again used the name *Fidelio*. (Today the title *Leonore* is often used to distinguish the 1805 and 1806 versions from the more familiar 1814 *Fidelio*.)

9. It was performed on November 20, 21, and 22, 1805. It failed, and Beethoven was persuaded to make drastic cuts.

10. *Fidelio* appeared again for two performances on March 29 and April 10, 1806, with *Leonore* No. 3 as the overture. *Leonore* No. 1 had already been laid aside before the 1805 performances, replaced by Overture No. 2.

11. It was not the second, but the third attempt that finally met with a complete triumph in Vienna in 1814, when it was played 22 times. It was also produced in Prague, where it was conducted by Weber in November of that year. But according to John Warrack, it was received coolly, to Weber's indignation (*Carl Maria von Weber*, [Cambridge: Cambridge University Press, 1976], p. 164).

12. Romain Rolland, *Beethoven the Creator*, translated by Ernest Newman, (New York: Dover, 1964), p. 182.

13. Berlioz wrote two reviews: "*Fidelio* à Covent Garden," *Le Rénovateur*, June 29, 1835; and "Grand succès de *Fidelio* au Théâtre de la Reine," *Débats*, May 31 and July 1, 1851.

14. These performances took place in 1829 and 1830, not 1827. (See *Correspondance générale*, Vol. I, letters of June 3, 1829, p. 257; and May 13, 1830, p. 328.)

15. Anton Haizinger (1796–1869), an Austrian tenor, made his debut at the Theater an der Wien in 1821. The great Florestan of his day, he first sang the part in Vienna in 1822, at a performance that Beethoven attended. Berlioz heard him in Paris in 1829–30. In 1823, Haizinger created the part of Adolar in *Euryanthe*, a role Weber wrote for him.

16. Wilhelmina Schröder (1804–1860) was a German soprano, famous for her dramatic singing. See below, "*Oberon*," note 13.

17. See Rolland, pp. 218–226.

18. Now known as *Leonore* No. 2. What is now called No. 1 was published posthumously in 1832 and does not figure in Berlioz's numbering. Hence, in this paragraph and the next, "first" or "original" means *Leonore* No. 2; "second version" is *Leonore* No. 3.

19. It was during the 1847–48 season that Berlioz conducted *Leonore* No. 2 in London. "We began the concert with Beethoven's splendid overture . . . superbly played." (*Correspondance générale*, Vol. III, p. 483, letter of December 8, 1847.)

20. Now known as *Leonore* No. 1, because it is generally believed to have been first in order of composition.

21. This fourth overture, *Fidelio*, was not ready for the first night, May 23, 1814. It was played at the second performance, on May 28.

22. Léon Carvaille, dit Carvalho (1825–1897), a singer, was director of the Théâtre-Lyrique and the Opéra-Comique. He staged *Les Troyens à Carthage* in 1863. See below, "*Oberon*," note 16.

23. What Berlioz does not say (or did not know) is that Bouilly, who was associated with Mirabeau and Barnave, as well as being a judge in a civil court and a public prosecutor during the Revolution, had already made a different substitution, moving the action from France to Spain. The real "historical event" which inspired Bouilly had taken place during the French Revolution. (See Rolland, p. 190.)

24. This remark had already been cited in Berlioz's *Les Grotesques de la mu-*

sique (1859), p. 240, where Berlioz disparaged Grétry for making it. Berlioz no doubt took it from the article on Grétry in Fétis' *Biographie universelle*.

25. Very likely that of 1806.

26. *Leonore, Oper in zwei Akten* (Leipzig: Breitkopf & Härtel, 1851).

27. The Italian poet Count Vittorio Alfieri (1749–1803) was celebrated in his time for his classical tragedies, satires, and political writings.

28. For a fuller account of the trials and tribulations of *William Tell*, see *Les Grotesques de la musique*, pp. 209, 212–213.

29. An Aristarch is a severe critic. The name comes from Aristarchus (220?– 150 b.c.), a Greek critic and grammarian.

30. Nicolas Boileau, *L' Art poétique* (1674), Vol. I, p. 174.

31. Rolland (p. 197) observes that the vocalized development of this quartet in canon "was not lost on the young Berlioz in his *Benvenuto Cellini*."

32. Rossini, *Mosè in Egitto* [later *Moïse*] (Paris: Launer, 1841), No. 11.

33. The Czech baritone Johann Baptist Pischek [Pišek] (1814–1873) is highly praised in the *Memoirs* and in *Evenings with the Orchestra*, where his voice is described as "the finest in quality of any male singer that I know." Pischek was a popular singer in England in the late 1840s and early 1850s. In his *Memoirs*, Berlioz says of him: "Pischek is an artist. He has obviously studied hard, but nature has richly endowed him. He has a magnificent baritone voice, penetrating, flexible, true and of good range, a noble face and a tall, commanding figure, and he is young and full of fire and energy. It is a great misfortune that he knows only German." (*Memoirs*, trans. Cairns, p. 270.)

34. Here ends the *feuilleton* of May 19, 1860.

35. It was sung by Clara Novello at the celebrations in honor of Beethoven in 1845. (See *Evenings with the Orchestra*, p. 341.)

36. In France, the Festival of the Epiphany on January 6, also called The Day of Kings, or Twelfth Night, is a holiday as popular with children as Christmas. It commemorates the recognition of Jesus by the three kings (Magi), and the small figure hidden in the cake brings good luck to the child in whose slice it turns up.

37. The basset horn is an eighteenth-century instrument akin to the clarinet, but with its own characteristic timbre, evidently much prized by Mozart. It was pitched in G or, more usually, in F. Its range extends some four tones below the normal clarinet, and at least two tones below the basset clarinet, which was also used by Mozart. It owes its name "horn" to the curved shape of its original eighteenth-century form. Some modern versions are straight. (See *Traité*, p. 149.)

38. *La Clemenza di Tito, opera seria in two acts* (Prague, 1791). See *Traité*, p. 150.

39. Act II, scene 2, no. 8. On *La Vestale* and Gaspare Spontini, see *Evenings with the Orchestra*, pp. 152ff.

40. *Lucia di Lammermoor* (1836). Berlioz had conducted this opera at Drury Lane in London in 1847, with Mme Dorus-Gras and John Sims Reeves in the principal roles. Mme Dorus-Gras was a French singer who made her debut at the Opéra in 1830 in *Le Comte Ory*. She sang at Drury Lane, where Berlioz conducted in 1847–48. The English tenor John Sims Reeves (1818–1900) sang Faust in *La Damnation de Faust* in its first performance in English. Reeves also sang the title role in Gounod's opera.

41. *Iphigénie en Tauride*, Act II, scene 1.

42. Partial quotation from Dante, of the words inscribed on the gates of Hell.

43. At the performances of the German company in Paris in 1829–30.

44. The now current expression was coined by Hamlet in Act I, scene 2, line 185: "In my mind's eye, Horatio."

45. Adolphe Nourrit (1802–1839), a French tenor, made his debut in 1821 at

the Paris Opéra, where he became principal tenor five years later. He created roles there in Rossini's *Siège de Corinth* (1826), *Moïse* (1827), and *Le Comte Ory* (1828) and in Meyerbeer's *Robert le Diable* and *Les Huguenots*. See below, "Current State of the Art of Singing," note 8.

Beethoven In the Rings of Saturn

1. This is an excerpt from the *feuilleton* of November 24, 1860.
2. A mountainous island of the Lesser Sundas, now ruled as part of Indonesia.
3. During the quarrel between the Gluckists and the Piccinnists, the jokers of Paris put it about that Gluck lodged at the rue du Grand Hurleur (Street of the Great Shouter), Piccinni at the rue des Petits-Chants (Street of the Small Songs), and Marmontel, his librettist, at the rue des Mauvaises-Paroles (Street of Bad Words).
4. According to Guichard, there is no trace of an Englishman bearing this name. But there is an explorer with a somewhat similar name, William Henry Giles Kington (1814–1880). Berlioz doubtless indulged his taste for distant lands and travelers' tales in this parody.
5. The vogue for spiritualism in Europe in the nineteenth century is notorious—witness Victor Hugo with his seances of table-turning in Jersey.
6. The Kärtnertor (Carinthian gate) is only a few minutes' walk from the Hofburg Palace.
7. *Zémire et Azor* is a ballet-opéra in verse, in four acts, with music by Grétry. It was performed at Fontainebleau on November 9 and at the Comédie-Italienne in Paris on December 16, 1771. It was revived at the Opéra-Comique. Berlioz reviewed it in *Le Rénovateur*, on December 23, 1834, and in the *feuilletons* of July 18, 1846 and September 27, 1862.
8. This is sung by Ali in the first act.
9. Three styles or periods are traditionally distinguished in Beethoven's work. See *Evenings with the Orchestra*, pp. 315ff.
10. Pallas, an asteroid, was discovered in 1802.

The Emoluments of Singers

1. This is an excerpt from the *feuilleton* of November 24, 1860. See also in the *feuilleton* of October 29, 1862, "Les tenors sont fort chers" (Tenors are very dear).
2. In Act III, scene 3, of *Robert Macaire*, the hero rings his handbell and announces, "Starting tomorrow, the till will be open."
Everyone: "Ah! Ah!"
M. Magloire: "We'll be paid?"
Macaire: "No. It will be open to receive the funds of the new shareholders of the Society Against Robbery."
Robert Macaire was a favorite of Berlioz. See also p. 247 note 5.
3. The Danaïdes, sisters in Greek mythology, murdered their husbands at the command of their father, Danaus, a king of Argos. They were condemned to carry water in leaking jars throughout eternity.
4. See *Evenings with the Orchestra*, pp. 70–71.
5. Grandgousier is Gargantua's father in Rabelais' *Gargantua and Pantagruel*.
6. Berlioz is playing with a phrase from the Game scene at the end of Act I of Meyerbeer's *Robert le Diable:* "Gold is but a dream."

The Current State of the Art of Singing

1. This article appeared in *Débats*, February 6, 1853, a propos of Verdi's opera *Luisa Miller*.

2. Berlioz means the French (or Italian) vowels *i* and *a*, sounding something like *ee* and *ah*.

3. To fit his argument, Berlioz slightly adapted some lines from Auguste Barbier's *Iambes* (la Curée, III).

> . . . Se plaît aux cris du peuple, aux sanglantes mêlées,
> Aux longs roulements des tambours.

> . . . Delights in the cries of the people, in bloody frays,
> In the long roll of drums.

Barbier was co-author, with Léon de Wailly, of the libretto for Berlioz's *Benvenuto Cellini*.

4. *Othello*, Act V, scene 2, line 1.

5. On the phenomenon of the claque, see the "Seventh Evening," from *Evenings with the Orchestra*.

6. In the October 6, 1829 issue of *Le Correspondant*, Berlioz describes the effect on people listening to Beethoven's C-sharp minor Quartet played at one of Baillot's musical evenings. (Jacques Barzun, *Berlioz and the Romantic Century*, 2 vols. [New York: Columbia University Press, 1969], Vol. I, p. 99.)

7. His first experience of Gluck was in 1821, the year Berlioz arrived in Paris. (See *Correspondance générale*, Vol. I, p. 36; and *Memoirs*, chap. V.)

8. The French tenor Adolphe Nourrit (1802–1839) made his debut at the Paris Opéra in 1821 in Gluck's *Iphigénie en Tauride*. *Orphée* was revived in 1824 especially for him. He was principal tenor of the Opéra from 1826 till 1837; he left when Duprez was engaged as first tenor. Nourrit committed suicide some two years later. (See also "Fidelio," note 45, above.) For Nourrit's late career, see Barzun, *Berlioz and the Romantic Century*, Vol. I, p. 275.

9. The première took place on February 29, 1836. Berlioz reviewed it in *G.M.*, in the issues of March 6, 13, and 20, 1836.

10. The excerpt from the February 6, 1853 issue of *Débats* ends here. The next three paragraphs are taken from the *feuilleton* of March 26, 1861.

11. The *feuilleton* of February 6, 1853 resumes here.

12. Also in Milan.

13. See *Memoirs*, p. 208.

14. Henriette Sontag (1806–1854) was one of the most successful German sopranos of the first half of the nineteenth century. Beautiful, possessing a lively, brilliant voice, she was said to be technically equal to any singer of the day, including her rival Maria Malibran. Berlioz had a high regard for Sontag.

15. Jan Kritel Pischek (Pišek) (1814–1873) was a Bohemian baritone with a rich and expressive voice encompassing two octaves. Berlioz thought highly of his talent, calling him "perhaps the greatest dramatic singer of the age." Pischek sang a great deal in Germany and was also popular in England. (See above, "Fidelio," note 33.)

16. Joseph Tichatchek (Tichaček) (1807–1886), a Bohemian tenor whose beautiful and brilliant voice brought him widespread acclaim, was also the prototype of the Wagnerian *Heldentenor*, having created the title roles of *Rienzi* and *Tannhäuser*.

17. Jenny Lind (1820–1887), nicknamed the "Swedish nightingale," was a very

popular soprano throughout Europe. In 1850 she was brought to the U.S. on a successful concert tour by P. T. Barnum. (See "Eighth Evening," in *Evenings with the Orchestra*.) She sang mostly recitals and oratorios; her operatic career lasted less than five years.

18. *Iphigénie en Aulide*, Paris production, 1774. No. 7, final chorus, *Andante maestoso* (Breitkopf & Härtel edition, p. 429).

19. The Italian composer Gaspare Luigi Pacifico Spontini (1774–1851) lived in Paris between 1803 and 1820. He wrote his most-celebrated works—*La Vestale, Fernand Cortez*, and *Olympie*—for the Opéra. These works are characterized by grandeur and spectacle. Berlioz was an enthusiastic admirer, especially of *La Vestale*, and he considered Spontini one of the three masters (the other two being Beethoven and Weber) who most influenced his own style of expressive orchestration.

20. *La Vestale*, Act I, scene 5, No. 6, Finale (Triumphal procession), pp. 103ff.; and Ballet, No. 1, pp. 153ff. (J. Delahante edition, 1820s or '30s).

21. Berlioz must be thinking of the march in Act I of *Fernand Cortez* (Bologna edition, 1869, p. 247).

22. In October 1826.

23. In 1823.

24. Adolphe (Antoine-Joseph) Sax (1814–1894), a Belgian, was the inventor of the saxophone and related instruments. Berlioz was among his first supporters and the first to employ the saxophone at a public concert. (See *Evenings with the Orchestra*, index; and *Traité*.)

25. *La Magicienne*, opera in five acts, performed at the Théâtre-Lyrique in 1858. (See Berlioz's *feuilleton* of March 24, 1858.)

26. See *Traité*, p. 280.

Good Singers and Bad

1. This article is an excerpt from *Débats*, June 2, 1856. Berlioz omitted his discussion of the claque when he published *A Travers Chants*.

2. In the original, "liaisons dangereuses," an untranslatable allusion to Choderlos de Laclos's eighteenth-century novel of cynicism and amorous adventure, *Les Liaisons Dangereuses*.

3. See Appendix, "The Lapdog School."

4. This is an adaptation of a line from Victor Hugo's poem "Napoleon II," from *Les Chants du Crépuscule:* "Les canons monstrueux à la porte accroupis" (The monstrous cannon squatting by the gate).

5. *Hamlet*, Act III, scene 2, lines 8–11. Hamlet's instructions to players in the play within the play.

Gluck's Orphée

1. This article appeared in the *Débats*, Nov. 22, 1859. Berlioz had announced the project of reviving *Orphée* in his October 8 *feuilleton*. The part Berlioz played in this revival is well known. (See Barzun, *Berlioz and the Romantic Century*, Vol. II, pp. 165–168.) It was this task, as Berlioz calls it, that enabled him to discuss Gluck's scores with such precision. *Orphée* was performed no fewer than 138 times at the Théâtre-Lyrique between 1859 and 1863. In the *Débats*, March 17, 1839, Berlioz had already had occasion to speak of *Orphée*, comparing it with the earlier Italian version, *Orfeo*.

2. A style of singing characterized as broad, declamatory, and plain, that is, without added ornamentation.

3. Pauline Viardot (née Michelle-Ferdinande-Pauline García, 1821–1910), a sister

of Maria Malibran was born in Paris. She married the French impresario Louis Viardot in 1841. Though no beauty, she was admired for her mezzo-soprano voice and excellent acting. An intelligent and cultivated woman, she was a friend of many of the leading artists and intellectuals of the day in Paris (including Turgenev, with whom she lived for many years). Berlioz had at first judged her art severely (see, for example, his *feuilleton* of March 17, 1839), but he later came to appreciate it highly. During their collaboration on the revival of Gluck's *Orphée* in 1859, they seemed to have conceived a passion for each other, though there is no evidence that this was consummated (see her letters to Julius Rietz in *The Musical Quarterly*, Vol. I, 1915). (See also p. 76, and notes 21, 22, and 26 of this chapter.)

4. In fact, it was October 5, 1762, in the presence of the court at the Burgtheater. The same cast is said to have taken part in a special coronation performance of *Orfeo* at Frankfurt in 1764.

5. *Orfeo* was performed in Parma in August 1769 as the third part of a spectacle called *Le Feste d'Apollo*, put together by Gluck for the wedding of Maria Amalia of Austria and Don Ferdinand de Bourbon. Giuseppe Millico, one of the best castrati of the time, sang the role of Orpheus, Antonia Maria Girelli Aguilar that of Euridice, and Felicita Suardo that of Cupid. Gluck later chose Millico to teach singing to his beloved niece Marianne.

6. Gluck composed the roles of Telemaco and Orfeo for Gaetano Guadagni (1725?–1797). In 1776 Guadagni had a resounding success in Bertoni's *Orfeo*.

7. Gasparo Angiolini (1731–1803), of Milan, was choreographer, dancer, and later composer of ballet music (see Alfred Einstein, *Gluck*, translated by Eric Blom [New York: Collier Books, 1962], p. 110). Giovanni Maria Quaglio (c.1700–c.1765) was one of a famous family of Italian-German scene painters and stage designers.

In the 1760s, Angiolini and Quaglio were key figures in the reform of the ballet and opera, working in Vienna with Gluck and later also with his librettist Calzabigi, under the patronage of the court theater director, the Conte Durazzo. "It was out of this group of men that first of all the new ballet, and then the new opera, arose to startle Europe . . ." (Martin Cooper, *Gluck* [London: Chatto & Windus, 1935], p. 78). Their chief works were the ballet *Don Juan* (1761), the operas *Orfeo ed Euridice* (1762) and *Telemaco* (1765), and the ballet *Semiramide*, (1765), all with music by Gluck. See also Gluck's Preface to *Alceste*, p. 101 of essay on *Alceste*.

8. The première of *Orphée* took place on August 2, 1774 at the Académie Royale de Musique, that is, the Paris Opéra.

9. Pierre-Louis Moline (1739–1820), born in Montpellier, was a lawyer at the high court in Paris. He later became secretary-clerk of the National Convention. He began writing early and prolifically for the theater. Gluck composed new melodies in 1762 for his comedy *L'Arbre Enchanté* [The Magic Tree]. In 1801 Moline translated the libretto of *Il Matrimonio Segreto* [The Secret Marriage], the opera-buffa by Cimarosa.

10. See Cooper, pp. 109 and 204.

11. Joseph Legros (1739–1793), French tenor and concert manager, made his debut at the Paris Opéra in 1764, singing in Rameau's *Castor et Pollux*, *Zoroastre*, *Hippolyte et Aricie*, and *Dardanus*. He became Gluck's principal tenor, creating roles in *Alceste* and both *Iphigénies*. He was also Orphée.

Haute-contre is an abbreviation of *tenor haute-contre*. France has a tradition of these high tenors, who are not *falsetti*, i.e., the chest voice predominates and is present to some degree throughout, except possibly for the very top of the range. For some *haute-contres* (though apparently not Legros), this range is virtually the whole compass of the contralto voice. The English term "countertenor" also applies to male voices of high tessitura, but is often used to refer to singers using mainly head voice *(falsetto)*.

12. A letter to Ferrand, dated June 10, 1824 *(Correspondance générale*, Vol. I, 1803–1832), refers to these performances of *Orphée.* Berlioz knew these works by Gluck from fragments he discovered in his father's library (see *Memoirs*, trans. Cairns, p. 47).

13. Jules Janin (1804–1874) was one of the most influential French literary and theater critics of his day, and a leading writer of *feuilletons*, especially in the *Journal des Débats.* He was a supporter and friend of Berlioz.

14. In *Hamlet*, Act II, scene 2, line 490, Hamlet says of Polonius who finds an actor's speech too long: "He's for a jig or a tale of bawdry, or he sleeps. . . ."

15. The Second Empire, established by Louis Napoléon (Napoléon III) in 1852, was a period of unusual expansion in French commerce and industry. In his *Europe Since Napoleon* (London: Longman, 1957), David Thomson says the 1850s and 60s were characterized by "the consolidation of conservative governments in Europe. . . . France sent a great deal of capital abroad. . . . Like Britain, France became a world colonial power. . . . The Second Empire was an era of organization and depended on capital accumulation and investment, which Napoleon encouraged."

16. Molière has Dorante say this in scene 7 of *La Critique de l'Ecole des Femmes* (Critique of the School for Wives).

17. *Georgics*, IV, verses 465–466.

18. Ferdinando Giuseppe Bertoni (1725–1813), an Italian composer, was a pupil of Martini and also an organist and chorus master in Venice. His *Orfeo ed Euridice*, set to the same libretto by Calzabigi, was performed in 1776 and sung by the same singer, Guadagni. His *Tancredi* was composed in 1766.

19. Marie Marimon, born in 1836, was a pupil of Duprez. She made her debut at the Théâtre-Lyrique in 1857. She went on to sing at the Opéra-Comique in 1860 and returned to the Théâtre-Lyrique in 1868.

20. Marie-Constance Sass (1838–1907), a Belgian singer born in Ghent, was a pupil of Madame Ugalde. She was engaged in 1860 by the Opéra, where she became the leading soprano for a long time. She had to give up the name Saxe, with which she had made her debut, as a result of a lawsuit brought against her by the famous inventor and maker of musical instruments, Adolphe Sax (see *feuilleton* of November 24, 1860).

21. The range of Mme Viardot's voice, according to Reynaldo Hahn (1874–1947), French composer and critic, extended from F-sharp below the treble staff to D above (*Notes: Journal d'un Musicien* [Paris: Plon, 1938], p. 8).

22. Mme Viardot protested to the young Reynaldo Hahn: " 'But I didn't do anything that wasn't absolutely approved by Berlioz and Saint-Saëns. This famous cadenza, for which people gave me the honor of a reproach and which I sang in the great bravura aria, was composed by *all three of us!'* She went to the piano and, without sitting down, leaned over and played for me the bass line slowly, stopping to explain the role played by each of them. [What follows is Hahn's judgment.] The first part (by Berlioz) was good; the second, by Saint-Saëns, was a bit facile; the little run, composed by the singer, was a little too 'operatic'; and the last part, by Berlioz, could have been written by a concierge" (ibid., p. 8). Caveat: Hahn disliked Berlioz.

23. Erebus, one of the two divisions of the Underworld (Hades), was the place where the dead passed as soon as they died. Tartarus, the deeper of the two, was the prison of the sons of the Earth. But Tartarus was often the name used for the entire lower regions.

24. *Aeneid*, VI, verses 306–307.

25. In his dedicatory letter to *Paride ed Elena*.

26. Berlioz was not always of this opinion. Twenty years earlier, on February 3, 1839, he heard the future Pauline Viardot sing with Duprez a duet from *Orphée* in the salon of the piano manufacturer Pape. Berlioz wrote to Victor Schoelcher: "Mlle Pauline Garcia has greatly disappointed me. It was not worth making such a fuss about this would-be talent. She is a failed prima donna, and I loathe prima donnas. These creatures are the death of real music and musicians. How she ruined this sublime duet of Orphée's with Duprez. To do Gluck justice, singers must have a voice, soul, and genius." (She would have only been eighteen at the time.) See Jacques Barzun, *New Letters of Berlioz* (New York: Columbia University Press, 1954). See also *Débats*, March 17, 1839; and *Correspondance générale*, Vol. II, p. 531.

Victor Schoelcher (1804–1893), was a French left-wing politician and journalist who battled for the abolition of slavery. As under-secretary of state in the government of the Second Republic (1848), he issued the decree emancipating blacks. Also a music lover, he wrote a book on Handel.

Lines Written Soon after the First Performance of Orphée

1. Excerpt from the *feuilleton* of December 9, 1859. Berlioz is referring to the first performance of the revival of *Orphée* in 1859.

2. See above, "*Orphée*," note 1.

3. (Joseph) Prud'homme, a character invented by Henri Monnier in 1852, was given to uttering sententious platitudes, personifying the pompous and empty-headed bourgeois.

4. Les Bouffes-Parisiens, established on the Champs-Elysées in 1855; Offenbach's opéra-bouffe *Orphée aux Enfers* was performed there on October 21, 1858.

5. A line from Robert Macaire, lead character in a series of plays of the 1820s and 30s by Benjamin Antier and others. The actor Frederick Lemaître made his name as Macaire, changing him from murderer to impudent rogue.

6. Berlioz liked to quote the Athenian general and patriot Phocion, who asked, when his fellow citizens applauded him, "Have I said something stupid?"

7. In his article of February 6, 1853. See above, "The Current State of the Art of Singing."

8. Berlioz has adapted lines from Molière's *Amphitryon*, where Mercury says of Sosie:

> Comme avec irrévérence
> Parle des dieux ce maraud!
>
> With what irreverence
> This rogue speaks of the gods!

9. Francesca Cuzzoni refused to sing the aria "Falsa immagine" from the opera *Ottone*, in 1723. It seems, however, that a threat from Handel was enough to persuade the lady.

10. Marie-Antoinette was only the Dauphine (wife of the future Louis XVI) when she invited Gluck to come to Paris. She became queen of France after the death of Louis XV, on May 10, 1774.

11. Gaëtan-Apolline-Balthazar Vestris (1729–1808), a ballet pupil of Dupré, was nicknamed "the handsome Vestris" to distinguish him from his brothers. He joined the Opéra in 1748, became a solo dancer in 1751, ballet master in 1761, choreographer-ballet-master in 1770, and resigned in 1776. He had the highest regard for himself, taking over the appellation "god of the dance," which was previously accorded to Dupré. "There are only three great men in Europe,"

he said, "the king of Prussia, Voltaire, and me," which prompted Berchoux to write the following epigram:

> Ses yeux ne daignaient voir de son temps sur la terre
> Que trois grands hommes: lui, Frédéric et Voltaire;
> Quand il fallait entre eux determiner son choix,
> Il se mettait toujours à la tête des trois.

> In his time on earth, he deigned only to be aware
> Of three great men: himself, Frederick, and Voltaire;
> When he had to make a choice among the three,
> He'd say: "The greatest of the three is me."

12. François-André Danican, known as Philidor (1726–1795), was a famous chess player and the inventor of Philidor's defense. He composed several opéras-comiques between 1759 and 1788.

13. *Le Sorcier*, a lyric comedy in two acts with libretto by Poinsinet, was performed at the Comédie-Italienne on January 2, 1764 and at Versailles before the king on March 21 of the same year.

14. Charles-Louis de Sévelinges (1768–1832) wrote biting reviews of play-wrights, composers, and actors in Paris. They are collected in *Le Rideau Levé, ou Petite Revue de Nos Grands Théâtres* (Curtain Up, or Short Survey of Our Great Theaters) (Paris: Maradon, 1818). He also wrote biographical articles on musicians for Michaud's *Biographie Universelle*.

15. This passage can be found under "Philidor" in *Biographie Universelle des Musiciens* by François-Joseph Fétis (1784–1871), the Belgian musicologist, critic, editor, teacher, administrator, and composer. In spite of inaccuracies, his eight-volume *Biographie* is still a basic work of reference. As an influential critic and arranger active in Paris, Fétis had many ups and downs with Berlioz. In the end, they were reconciled by Gluck's *Alceste*. (See D. Kern Holoman, *Berlioz* [Cambridge: Harvard University Press, 1989], p. 580; see also above, "The Art of Music," p. 1 and notes 4 and 5.)

16. In *France Musicale*, November 27 and December 4, 1859. Jacques-Hippolyte-Aristide Farrenc (1794–1865), a flutist, composer, and musicologist, was an ardent advocate of early music. He helped edit and revise Fétis' *Biographie Universelle* and corrected the proofs of the second edition, where *Orfeo* is given its correct date—Vienna, 1762.

17. "He offered to correct the mistakes *gratis* and examine the engraving of the work," wrote Favart (librettist, playwright, and impresario, 1710–1792) to the Conte Durazzo on April 19, 1763. (Farrenc, *France Musicale*, 1859.)

18. In this one sentence, Berlioz sums up Fétis' reasoning. A contrary view was put forth as early as 1773 by Louis Petit de Bachaumont (1690–1771) in *Mémoires Secrets*, in which he analyzes plays, books, and vaudevilles; tells anecdotes; and praises artists, scholars, and men of letters. Bachaumont pointed out that "the music of *Orphée* was printed in Paris eight or ten years ago, but has stirred so little excitement that up to now the printer has sold no more than twelve copies. Nevertheless, it seems that not everyone ignored this treasure house of harmony; it was very surprising to find at the performance [of Orphée] that Messieurs Philidor, Gossec, Floquet, et al. had helped themselves freely from it and that entire numbers of their works could be rediscovered there, which made them a little embarrassed."

19. According to *Grove's Dictionary*, "Philidor's notorious plagiarism of Gluck damaged his reputation in the nineteenth century; an air in *Le Sorcier* and the overture and first duet in *Ernelinde* certainly use the music of *Orfeo* which Philidor had seen through the press in 1763."

20. Claude-Philibert Coquéau (1753–1794) was an architect who also wrote about music: "The very Italian arietta 'L'espoir renaît dans mon âme' is very beautiful, but let us not forget it is by Bertoni" (*Entretiens* [Conversations] [Amsterdam, 1779], p. 66).

21. For a reasoned twentieth-century denial, which appeared in Max Arend's biography of Gluck (Berlin, 1921), see Martin Cooper, *Gluck* [London: Chatto & Windus, 1935], pp. 117, 124–125, and 204.

22. This follow-up letter, which appeared without date or place (it was in Paris) contained: *A Notice, A Reply to the First Excerpt of M.S.* in *Le Mercure* of August 14, 1779, *Reply to M.S.'s Letter* in No. 237 of the *Journal de Paris*, and *Reply to the Second Excerpt of M.S.*, followed by a postscript.

Jean-Baptiste Antoine Suard (1773–1817), a journalist and critic, became a member of the Académie Française in 1774. In *Le Mercure de France*, he commented on Coquéau's *Entretiens*.

23. Godefroid Engelbert Anders (1795–1866) was born in Bonn and settled in Paris in 1829. He was appointed to organize the music division of the Library in 1833. He, too, wrote for *G.M.*

24. See above, "*Orphée*," note 5. It is probably the same singer.

25. Fétis, Grove, and other authorities mention only an *Ifigenia in Aulide* by Bertoni.

26. The aria in question is for Amenaïde in scene 4 of Bertoni's *Tancredi*.

27. Fétis gives 1778 as the date, in which case the French *Orphée* would have preceded *Tancredi* not followed it. Later scholarship prefers 1766–67 as the correct date.

28. The correct date for Bertoni's *Orfeo* is 1776.

29. Berlioz translates freely the "Note to the Reader" that Bertoni placed at the head of his printed score; it reads: "It is not without apprehension that I have accepted the task of setting to music the *Orfeo* of the famous Calzabigi, after the well-deserved success M. Gluck obtained throughout all the nations of Europe. . . . I should consider myself happy if I were able, not like M. Gluck to win the applause of other nations, but only to find from you the indulgent welcome which was accorded me in Venice. . . ."

30. This conjecture is consistent with the date given in the 1862 edition of *A Travers Chants* for the first performance of Bertoni's *Orfeo*, i.e., 1766. It can be ruled out, however, if this date is corrected to 1776.

31. According to Quicherat (*A. Nourrit*, Vol. I, p. 17), it was in 1824 that the opera *Orphée* was revived for this young tenor, who proved to be a tremendous success.

32. Paris, 1779, libretto by Baron Tschudi.

33. Bärenreiter edition, 1953, p. 153. The text has: "O combats, o désordre extrême." (See *G.M.*, June 8, 1834, p. 185.)

Alceste

1. Berlioz did not wait for the revivals of *Orphée* (1859) and *Alceste* (1861) to express his admiration for Gluck, which had not cooled since the performance of *Iphigénie en Tauride* he had seen at the Opéra in 1821, when he was seventeen (*Correspondance générale*, Vol. I, pp. 36–37). He had already published two articles on Gluck in *G.M.*, June 1 and 8, 1834; four under the title "*Iphigénie en Tauride*," *G.M.*, November 9–December 7, 1834; "Du répertoire de Gluck à l'Académie royale de musique," *Le Monde Dramatique*, July 18, 1835; "Du système de Gluck en musique dramatique," *Débats*, October 2, 1835; and "Des deux 'Alcestes' de Gluck," *Débats*, October 16 and 23, 1835. In addition, he had discussed *Armide* in *G.M.*, February 26, 1837, and "*Iphigénie en Tauride* à

Londres" in *Débats*, July 19, 1840. He had already reprinted his articles of October 2, 16, and 23, 1835 in *V.M.*, Vol. II, 1844, pp. 263–307. He reorganized, cut, recast, and expanded his various articles for publication in *Débats*, October 12, 15, and 20, November 6, 23, and December 8, 1861, and used them ultimately for the present essay. Other articles on Gluck exist but were not collected in this book. On Berlioz's affinity for Gluck, see Hugh Macdonald, *Berlioz* (London: Dent, 1982), chapter on Berlioz's style, especially pp. 184–185.

2. *Alceste ou le Triomphe d'Alcide*, tragedy in music by Quinault and Lully, was first performed at the Palais-Royal on January 11, 1674.

3. Raniero di Calzabigi (1714–1795) was an Italian poet who worked with Gluck in Vienna to reform opera. Gluck used his librettos for *Orfeo ed Euridice* (1762), *Alceste* (1767), and *Paride ed Elena* (1770).

4. Christoph Martin Wieland (1733–1813) was a German poet, dramatist, translator, and editor. He also wrote the verse epic *Oberon*, on which Planché based his libretto for Weber's opera.

5. Anton S. Schweitzer (1735–1787), a German composer, played a significant part in the emergence of German opera. His *Alceste* was composed in 1773.

6. By the Bailli du Roullet (Marie-François-Louis-Gand) (1716–1786), who was Gluck's first and foremost advocate in Paris. Though not the first to use Racine for a libretto, he started the fashion of adapting seventeenth-century tragedies for the opera with Gluck's *Iphigénie en Aulide* in 1774.

7. This took place on October 21, 1861.

8. Jean-Antoine-Anne Mandelart (1791–1841?), known as Bobêche, was famous as a Paris street performer in his own farces, especially in the second decade of the century. Euripides' play in fact developed out of satyric drama and is moving and comical by turns.

9. *Aeneid*, IV, verses 328–329. When Berlioz made his own free version of this passage for his opera *Les Troyens* (1856–58), he omitted "playing in my court." Dido says to Aeneas (Act V, scene 1), "If a son of Aeneas were smiling at my breast, his proud, sweet face reminding me of you, I would feel less abandoned. . . ."

10. Paul Jérémie Bitaubé (1732–1808) was born of a Protestant family that had escaped to Germany. He translated the *Iliad* (1780) and the *Odyssey* (1785) into French, and settled in Paris in 1786.

11. Abbé Delille (1718–1813), a prolific poet on themes drawn from nature and from the practical arts, also translated the *Georgics* (1769) and the *Aeneid* (1804).

12. Père Brumoy (1688–1742), a Jesuit, was known primarily for his *Théâtre des Grecs*, 3 vols., 1730.

13. From here until "command our joy and wonderment" (p. 92), Berlioz is summarizing Brumoy's text with more or less exact quotations. He does not always follow the order of scenes and dialogue.

14. Chrysalis in *Les Femmes Savantes* (The Learned Ladies), Act II, scene 7.

15. This is the last line of La Fontaine, *La Mort et le mourant* (Death and the Dying Man).

16. Eurystheus, king of Argos, ordered Hercules to undertake twelve labors to atone for having killed his wife and children in a fit of madness. Tiryns was a territory of Argos, a city in the Peloponnesus.

17. Diomedes, king of the Bistones, in Thrace, kept fierce war-horses who ate human flesh. Capturing these horses was Hercules' eighth labor.

18. Alcmene was the wife of Amphitryon; Hercules was her son by Zeus.

19. *Julius Caesar*, Act IV, scene 3, lines 148–151: "Brutus: She [Portia] is dead. . . ./ Cassius: How 'scap'd I killing when I cross'd you so?"

20. Philippe Quinault (1635–1688), the French dramatist and librettist, pro-

vided Lully with the text of *Cadmus et Hermione* (1673), *Armide* (1686), and *Alceste* (1674).

21. "Je suis roi de Scyros et Thétis est ma soeur" (I am king of Scyros and Thetis is my sister), Act I, scene 5 of Lully's *Alceste.*

22. These last two sentences substantially repeat Quinault's stage directions at the head of the first act.

23. Stage directions for the end of Act III, scene 3.

24. Alcides is another name for Hercules.

25. In Greek mythology, one of the three Eumenides or Furies.

26. Nicolas Boileau (1636–1711) was a poet and the leading critic of his time. His *Art Poétique* also influenced eighteenth-century English poets, including Dryden, Pope, and Dr. Johnson.

27. Boileau, *Satire*, X, pp. 141–142.

28. Alizard, a bass at the Opéra, sang Friar Laurence in Berlioz's *Roméo et Juliette* in 1839. Berlioz knew him and thought well of him.

29. This view was not peculiar to Berlioz. Jules Janin also criticized these musical divertissements in *Débats* and reproached the Théâtre-Français for performing them.

30. Sébastien Erard (1752–1831), French piano and harp maker and music publisher, founded a long-lasting firm under his name. John Broadwood (1732–1812) was a leading piano maker in London.

31. Here ends the article of October 12, 1861. The article of October 15 follows.

32. Berlioz is poking fun at the titles printed in Lully's scores, as published by Ballard.

33. Most of these librettos are by Metastasio.

34. *Telemaco* (Vienna, 1765).

35. It is Iphigénie who is singing. Berlioz observed that Gluck also used this piece in *Antigono*, a three-act opera with libretto by Metastasio (Rome, 1756) and said that almost all of it can be found in outline in a sonata by Bach (*G.M.*, June 8, 1834, pp. 184–185).

36. Berlioz had already quoted and discussed Asteria's aria in *G.M.* June 1, 1834, p. 174.

37. *La Clemenza di Tito* (Naples, 1751).

38. *Paride ed Elena* (Vienna, 1769).

39. "Fortunately, the libretto suited my purposes marvelously well; the famous author . . . had replaced flowery descriptions, superfluous comparisons, and sententious and cold moralizings with the language of the heart, strong passions, interesting situations, and a constantly changing scene."

40. See note 1 above.

41. See *Memoirs*, chapter 36, as well as *Harold in Italy.*

42. This is the way Berlioz described Marcello's psalm *I cielo immenso* (see *Les Grotesques de la musique*, 1969 Gründ edition, p. 251).

43. Johann Joseph Fux (1660–1741) was an Austrian composer and music theorist. His *Gradus ad Parnassum* is a well-known textbook on counterpoint.

44. Johann Georg Albrechtsberger (1736–1809) was an Austrian composer, organist, and theorist. Beethoven was one of his pupils.

45. Also told in *Evenings with the Orchestra*, pp. 323–324.

46. Victor Hugo.

47. Here the article of October 15, 1861 ends, and that of October 20 begins.

48. She had to retire from the stage the next year (*Evenings with the Orchestra*, pp. 147, 165–166, 255).

49. Berlioz defines it as the "alto of the oboe" (see *Traité*, pp. 122–127).

50. Gluck himself composed a *Demofoönte* (Milan, 1742), but Berlioz is referring here to Vogel's opera, performed posthumously in Paris in 1789.

51. Johann Christoph Vogel (1756–1788), a German composer active in France, was a pupil and imitator of Gluck (see *G.M.*, June 1, 1834). His chief operas are *La Toison d'Or* and *Démophon*.

52. See above, "Gluck's *Orphée*," note 11.

53. The Commendatore's words come in the Finale: "Parlo, ascolta, più tempo non ho" (Listen to what I say, time is running out).

54. "It should not be a flight in haste, as when one is escaping from an enemy, but a flight of dismay, which should be, so to speak, ashamed and secretive rather than blatant and quick. If the composer had wished to make this chorus express an exhortation to joy, he could not have done better." (Jean-Jacques Rousseau, "Fragments d'observation sur l'*Alceste* italien de M. le chevalier Gluck," in "Ecrits sur la musique," *Oeuvres* [1819], Vol. XI, p. 405.)

55. Here the article of October 20, 1861 ends, and that of November 6 begins.

56. *Tremoto* (appoggiato) = *vibrato*. The term *tremoto* seems to be Gluck's own coinage, perhaps a combination of two Italian words of similar meaning, *tremolo* and *tremito*.

57. See *G.M.*, June 8, 1834, p. 182, where Berlioz reproduces both the original Italian text and its French translation underneath the notation.

58. Sharp-timbre = high pitch. Berlioz is using his own recommended terminology. See below, "High and Low Sounds."

59. See above, "The Current State of the Art of Singing," note 18.

60. Here the article of November 6 ends, and that of November 23 begins.

61. This melodious lament is given to the flute, while the second violins and violas play arpeggios.

62. See note 6 of this essay.

63. François Arnaud (1721–1784), Abbé de Grandchamp, a man of letters and a member of the Académie Française, was a classical scholar and a translator. He was one of the Encyclopédistes and a supporter of Gluck's operatic reforms.

64. The Marchese Caraccioli (1711–1789), the Neapolitan ambassador to the French court, was a wit and a friend of the Enlightenment philosophers. He helped bring Piccinni from Naples and promoted his work against Gluck's to "raise the level of opera."

65. Marianne died of smallpox on April 21, 1766, on the eve of the première of *Alceste*.

66. François-Joseph Gossec (1734–1829) was a Walloon composer active in France before, during, and after the French Revolution. From 1775, he was maître de musique at the Opéra. He supported Gluck in his rivalry with Piccinni.

67. Alfred Einstein says: "and it is probable that the aria 'C'est en vain que l'Enfer' is not by Gluck, but by Gossec, who furbished it up from an old aria from Gluck's *Ezio*, 'Ecco alle mie catene.'" (*Gluck* [New York: Collier Books, 1962], p. 121.)

68. *Coriolan* Overture, Op. 62, composed in 1807. See *feuilleton* of November 19, 1862.

69. "Of all the instruments of the orchestra, the horn is the one for which Gluck composed least skillfully. . . . Nonetheless, the three-note horn call imitating Charon's conch shell in the aria in *Alceste*, "Caron t'appelle" [Charon is calling you] has a touch of genius." (*Traité*, p. 183.)

70. Here the article of November 23 ends, and that of December 8 begins.

71. Acheron is one of the rivers of Hades.

72. The text has "Je suivrai *ses* pas" (I shall follow *her* footsteps).

73. See the following essay, "The Revival of Gluck's *Alceste* at the Opéra."

74. *Banquettes* are theater seats in general. As spectators leave hurriedly, the seats snap back noisily.

75. It was the *Alceste* of Pietro Alessandro Guglielmi (1728–1804) which was performed in Milan in 1769, two years after Gluck's. In his own time he was highly esteemed and was judged the equal of Cimarosa and Paisiello.

76. Giovanni Paisiello (1740–1816), one of the most successful opera composers of the eighteenth-century, wrote over 80 operas. His *Barber of Seville* was performed at St. Petersburg in 1782 and in Paris at the Théâtre de Monsieur in 1789. Rossini's *Barber of Seville* was produced in Rome in 1816.

77. Jean-Baptiste Lully (1632–1687), composer, dancer, and violinist, was born in Florence. He became the leading composer in France through his important contribution to theater music, including the creation of "tragédies en musique." His *Armide* was produced in 1686.

78. See above, *"Fidelio,"* p. 41 and notes 4 and 6.

79. First performed 1791. Rossini's oepra also came out in Paris, in 1829.

80. Parthenia is Alceste's sister in this opera.

81. That is what Fétis says. But the work was first performed on May 28, 1773 in Weimar, and it was only later that Schweitzer replaced Benda at the court of Gotha.

82. See above, "Good Singers and Bad," and Appendix, the "Lapdog School."

83. Handel's *Admeto* was first performed at the Royal Opera, London, in 1727. The libretto was by A. Aureli. In 1750, Handel also composed incidental music for an *Alceste* that was not performed.

84. *Giulio Cesare* (London, 1724), *Tamerlano* (London, 1727), *Rodelinda* (London, 1727), *Scipione* (London, 1727), *Lotario* (London, 1730), *Alessandro* (London, 1727). As with *Admeto*, Berlioz gives English or Latin names for most of these operas, and these have been kept in the text.

85. Giovanni Buononcini, or Bononcini (1670–1747), was an Italian composer and cellist whose rivalry with Handel lasted from 1720 to 1727.

86. Handel's *Admeto*, "Se un cor e contento" (The heart is contented).

87. In the Leipzig edition of 1877, in addition to the overtures to the first and second acts, there are two *Sinfonias*, one toward the end of the first act and another immediately following the overture to the second act.

88. Francesco Bernardi (c. 1680–c. 1758), celebrated alto castrato, known as Senesino.

89. Faustina Bordoni (1697–1781), Cuzzoni's famous rival, later married Hasse (see note 93).

90. Francesca Cuzzoni (1696–1778). See above, "Lines Written Soon after the First Performance of *Orphée,* " p. 84 and note 9.

91. The *duetto* is actually sung by Admeto and Antigona.

92. Benedetto Marcello (1686–1739), Venetian composer of instrumental and church music, including 50 settings of psalm-paraphrases.

93. Johann Adolf Hasse (1699–1783) was, in his day, the most widely admired composer of *opera seria* in both Italy and Germany. Fétis observed, however, that few composers have been as famous as Hasse and as quickly forgotten.

94. "Sad or wretched unknown."

95. Exactly forty years: Handel's opera dates from 1727, Gluck's from 1767.

96. The pasticcio *Piramo e Tisbe* (London, 1746). Pasticcios were pot-pourris made up of arias taken from various operas by different composers, to which a few new numbers and a new text were added.

97. *La Caduta de' Giganti* (London, 1746).

Revival of Gluck's Alceste

1. From *Débats*, October 24, 1861. Berlioz was in charge of preparing the music for this production. (See D. Kern Holoman, *Berlioz* [Cambridge: Harvard University Press, 1989], p. 551.)

2. *Paride ed Elena* was produced in Vienna in 1769 and published in 1770.

3. Alphonse Royer (1803–1875), formerly director of the Théâtre de l'Odéon, was General Director of the Opéra from July 1, 1856 to December 20, 1862.

4. Yet in 1825 the orchestra was conducted by Habeneck.

5. This is the moral of Fable I, in Book II, "Contre ceux qui ont le goût difficile" (Against people who are hard to please), in La Fontaine, *Fables* (1668).

6. Letter of dedication for *Paride ed Elena.*

7. *Memoirs,* trans. David Cairns, p. 394.

8. The Cocytus is one of the rivers of Hades. Geographically, it is a tributary of the Acheron in Epirus in northwest Greece.

9. Rosalie Levasseur (1749–1826), a French soprano, made her debut at the Opéra in 1766, as Zaïde in Campra's *L'Europe Galante,* and sang there until 1785. Gluck's friend and favorite performer, she sang the title roles in *Alceste* (1776), *Armide* (1777), and *Iphigénie en Tauride* (1779).

10. Antoinette Cécile Clavel, Mme de St. Huberti (1756–1812), a French soprano, made her debut as Melisse in Gluck's *Armide* (1777) and later became principal singer at the Opéra.

11. Marie-Thérèse Davoux, dite Mlle Maillard (1766–1818), was first a dancer, then a singer at the Opéra.

12. Rose-Timoléone Caroline Chevalier de Lavit (1780–1850) was married to Branchu, a dancer at the Opéra. She created the title role in *La Vestale* in 1807. Berlioz, who heard her in Gluck and in Spontini's *Olympie,* confessed to a "passion admirative" (*Corréspondance générale,* vol. IV, p. 660) for her "talent pathétique." He knew her well enough to attend the marriage of her daughter in 1825 (ibid., vol. I, p. 97). See also *Evenings with the Orchestra,* trans. Barzun, pp. 165–166.

13. In operas by Gluck (*Alceste* and the two *Iphigénies*) and by Spontini (*La Vestale* and *Olympie*).

14. Dominique-Pierre-Jean Garat (1762–1823), a French tenor and baritone, taught at the Conservatoire, where he stressed interpretation and expression rather than technique.

15. "Style large" or "chant large," the grand style, is without ornamentation and derives from French theatrical declamation.

16. *Sylvain,* by Marmontel, music by Grétry, is a comedy interspersed with ariettas; it was performed at the Comédie-Italienne in 1770.

17. "At that time, the musician Gluck arrived from Germany so strongly recommended to the young queen by her brother Emperor Joseph that the success of German music took on the importance of an affair of state" (Marmontel, *Mémoires* [1804], Book IX, p. 160).

18. See above, "The *Alceste* of Euripides," note 64.

19. Jean François Marmontel (1723–1799), a man of letters and an academician, collaborated with Grétry on works for the Opéra-Comique. A supporter of Piccinni, he was Gluck's *bête noir.*

20. Jean-François de La Harpe (1739–1803) was a playwright and later a famous critic. He and Marmontel, who sided with the Italians against Gluck, also proclaimed the superiority of Lully's *Armide* over Gluck's. Berlioz acknowledged that "Gluck's defense was as shrill and biased as La Harpe's attack had been witty and moderate" (*G.M.,* June 1, 1834, p. 175).

21. See *Evenings with the Orchestra*, p. 158.

22. She retired in March 1826. She sang the role of Statira for the last time in the revival of *Olympie* on February 27.

23. The French tersely implies that she had changed, Berlioz had changed, but unfortunately the musical world had *not* changed.

24. See *feuilleton* of March 26, 1861.

25. See above, Gluck's *Orphée*, note 26.

26. Berlioz reported Michot's debut in his *feuilleton* of June 2, 1856.

27. Louis Nourrit (1780–1831), a pupil of Garat, was an understudy for Lainez (1805), whom he replaced at the Opéra in 1812. He retired in 1826.

28. Mlle Lefrançois de Taisy; see *feuilleton*, April 24, 1861.

29. Grizy (b. 1833) was a composer and organist. He was hired as second tenor by the Opéra in 1861.

30. Victor Massé (1822–1884), a French composer, replaced Dietsch as chorus master at the Opéra.

31. It was Berlioz himself who introduced the electric metronome to the Paris Opéra, after first using it at a concert he conducted at the Paris Exhibition of 1855 (in the Palace of Industrial Productions): "I had called in an inventor of my acquaintance [the Belgian Verbrugghen], and he had come to Paris and set up an electric metronome with five separate arms. By simply moving one finger of my left hand, while holding the baton in my right, I could indicate the time to five different and widely spaced points in the huge area which the performers occupied; the electric wires transmitted my tempo to five sub-conductors who straightway gave it to the forces under their direction. The ensemble was marvellous. Since then, most opera houses have adopted the electric metronome for use with offstage choruses in cases where the chorus-master can neither see the beat nor hear the orchestra. The Opéra alone rejected it; but when I was directing rehearsals of *Alceste* I managed to get this valuable device introduced there, too." (*Memoirs*, trans. Cairns, p. 483.)

32. Pierre-Louis-Philippe Dietsch (1808–1865), French conductor and composer, became chorus master at the Opéra in 1840. He succeeded Girard as conductor in 1860.

33. Vincent-Joseph van Steenkist (1812–1896), known under his wife's surname, Dorus, was long a soloist at the Opéra and at Conservatoire concerts. He composed a large number of works for flute.

34. Joseph-Henri Altès (b. 1826), a flutist and a composer, was a pupil of Tulou. He replaced Dorus as professor of flute at the Conservatoire in 1868, and was the author of a textbook still in use.

35. Lucien, one of three famous dancers and choreographers of the Petipa family, was *premier danseur* and choreographer at the Opéra. His brother Marius was the despot of the Russian imperial ballet beginning in 1847. His father, Jean, taught at the Russian Imperial Academy of Dance.

36. This may be Eugène Cormon (b. 1811), a playwright who wrote librettos for comic operas.

37. See above, *Alceste*, note 63.

38. Here ends the *feuilleton* of October 24, 1861.

39. Berlioz summarizes here the responses of Goneril and Regan to their father in *King Lear*, Act II, scene 4.

40. Berlioz paraphrases from *King Lear*, Act III, scene 2.

41. *Hamlet*, Act III, scene 2, lines 8–10.

42. *Hamlet*, Act II, scene 2, lines 488–490. See also "Gluck's *Orphée*," note 14.

43. Paraphrased from *Hamlet*, Act III, scene 2.

44. Probably Meyerbeer, who was always very exacting about the proper per-

formance of his works. Possibly Verdi, whom Berlioz praises for his demands at the Opéra in 1855.

45. These ideas are also set forth elsewhere, notably, in "Euphonia," the "Twenty-fifth Evening" of *Evenings with the Orchestra*.

Instruments Added by Modern Composers to the Scores of Old Masters

1. Excerpt from *Débats*, April 7, 1861.
2. Act II, scene 2, pp. 72–82 (Paris: Deslauriers, 1777).

High and Low Sounds

1. Excerpt from *Débats*, July 3, 1861.
2. Concerning the system of figured notes, see the *feuilleton* of February 19, 1861.
3. Berlioz would have been pleased to read the following passage in Donald Grout, *A History of Western Music* (New York: Norton, 1960), p. 13: "In Greek [musical] terminology the words 'low' and 'high' are used with meanings opposite to ours. This is because the names were taken from the relative position of the strings of the lyre; the instrument was held by the player so that the low-pitched strings were farther from the ground than the high-pitched ones."
4. See above, "The Revival of Gluck's *Alceste* at the Opéra," p. 144.

Der Freischütz

1. *Débats*, June 16, 1841. The original German title of Weber's work, *Der Freischütz*, is normal usage in the English-speaking world. It should be noted, however, that Berlioz generally writes about productions in French and refers to the opera as *Le Freyschütz*.
2. Measures 96ff. Berlioz quotes this musical passage in his article on the clarinet, (*Traité*, pp. 138–148). It is also mentioned in *Evenings with the Orchestra*, p. 38.
3. It was produced in 1841. (See John Warrack, *Carl Maria von Weber* [Cambridge: Cambridge University Press, 1976], p. 238.)
4. Berlioz's music for the recitatives is considered an amazingly Weber-like piece of work. Berlioz also orchestrated Weber's *Invitation to the Dance* for the ballet.
5. In 1829–1830. See above, "*Fidelio*," p. 41. They performed *Fidelio*, *The Magic Flute*, *La Dame Blanche* (by Boïeldieu), as well as *Der Freischütz*.
6. These performances took place while Berlioz was traveling in Germany in 1842–43. (See Warrack, p. 238; and Jacques Barzun, *Berlioz and the Romantic Century*, Vol. II, p. 77.)

Oberon

1. *Débats*, March 6, 1857.
2. At Covent Garden, London.
3. James Robinson Planché (1796–1880), an English man of letters of Huguenot descent, was the author of many plays. He used a translation by Sotheby (1798) of Wieland's *Oberon* published in 1780, as well as the medieval tale *Huon de Bordeaux*. According to John Warrack (*Carl Maria von Weber*, p. 323), Wieland based his poem on the prose version of *Huon de Bordeaux*, published, like the source used for *Euryanthe*, in Louis de Tressan's *Bibliothèque Universelle des Romans* (1778).

4. John Braham (1774–1856) was very popular in England. He was known for his powerful voice and wide range (A to e″).

5. *Euryanthe*, with libretto by Helmina von Chézy, was first produced at the Kärtnertortheater in Vienna in October 1823. It was performed at the Théâtre-Lyrique in 1857 with little success. Berlioz reviewed it in his *feuilleton* on September 3, 1857. (See *Correspondance générale*, V, pp. 487–488.)

6. According to Warrack (p. 306), at a dress rehearsal that lasted from 10 A.M. to 2 P.M., Weber is reported to have said: "I'm afraid my *Euryanthe* will become *Ennyante*."

7. *Jubel-Kantata*, for soloists, chorus, and orchestra, was composed in 1818. Weber himself arranged it as *The Festival of Peace* for this occasion.

8. Sir George Smart (1776–1867) was a conductor, organist, and composer. In 1825, he traveled throughout Europe and noted his observations on musical practices in his journal, a record comparable to Burney's 50 years earlier. Smart became one of the directors of Jullien's enterprise at Drury Lane in 1847–48, and thus came to know Berlioz (see *Memoirs*, p. 448).

9. *Hamlet*, Act I, scene 2, lines 187–188. Hamlet, referring to his father, says, "He was a man, take him for all in all/I shall not look upon his like again."

10. This was *Robin des Bois* (i.e., Robin Hood), an arrangement by Castil-Blaze (1784–1857), who made a practice of producing such pastiches, combining music by several composers to borrowed libretti. Berlioz attacked the practice in *Lélio* (see David Cairns, *Berlioz: The Making of an Artist* [London: André Deutsch, 1989], pp. 181–184.) Castil-Blaze also figures as a critic; he was one of Berlioz's predecessors at *Débats*.

11. The first concert of the Société des Concerts du Conservatoire took place on March 9, 1828; the overture to *Oberon* was performed on March 29. Between 1829 and 1857 (the date of Berlioz's *feuilleton*), it was performed 27 times, including a concert at the Tuileries. Berlioz was often on his travels during those years; this may explain why he was not aware that Weber, like Beethoven, was well served by the Société des Concerts.

12. See above, "*Der Freischütz*," note 5.

13. Wilhelmina Schröder-Devrient (1804–1860), a German soprano, was famous for dramatic singing, particularly as Donna Anna, Euryanthe, Rezia, Norma, Desdemona (in Rossini's *Otello*), and the title role in Gluck's *Iphigénie en Aulide*. Her Leonore won praise from Beethoven. Weber is said to have considered her the best of Agathes. Berlioz found her acting exaggerated and her style of declamation too vehement. Wagner thought "she sang more with the soul than with the voice," and credited her Leonore as having roused him at the age of sixteen to his sense of vocation as a dramatic composer.

14. "Reiza" in the original London version of the opera, but "Rezia" in German, French, and even some later editions in Britain.

15. An allusion to a fable by La Fontaine, "Le Coq et la Perle."

16. Léon Carvalho, né Carvaille (1825–1897), was born in Mauritius. He was successively director of the Théâtre-Lyrique (1856–1868), chief producer at the Opéra (1869–1875), and then director of the Opéra-Comique from 1878. At the Théâtre-Lyrique his repertoire included *Oberon*, *Orphée*, *The Pearl Fishers*, *Figaro*, and the last three acts of *Les Troyens* (1863). David Cairns describes him as the "most enlightened operatic impresario of his time." But Berlioz (in his *Memoirs*) was not the only one to complain of Carvalho's high-handed way with composers.

17. *Oberon* was revived in 1858 and in 1863 at the Théâtre-Lyrique. See *feuilletons* of November 8, 1858 and May 14, 1863.

18. By Nuitter, Beaumont, and Chazot.

19. "Et vogue la nacelle/Qui porte *mes* amours" is the refrain of the Barca-

rolle, sung by Lisette and Lubin in the first act of *Marie,* a comic opera by Hérold, with libretto by Planard (1826).

20. *Hamlet,* Act IV, scene 5, lines 183–184.

21. Barcarolle in the second act.

22. Virgil, *Eclogues,* VIII, 75.

23. La Fontaine, *Fables,* "La Montagne Qui Accouche" (The Mountain that Gives Birth, i.e., to a mouse), Book V, Fable 10.

24. Mme Juana Rossi-Caccia (b. 1818) was a pupil of Bordogni. She made her debut at the Opéra-Comique in 1836 in Hérold's *Le Pré-aux-Clercs.* She was engaged by the Opéra for Halévy's *La Juive* in 1846.

25. Caroline Girard (b. 1834) studied under Révial at the Conservatoire. Although she won the premier prix d'opéra-comique in 1853, she preferred to enter the Théâtre-Lyrique, where she made her debut on September 3. See *feuilletons* of April 7, 1861 and July 23, 1863.

Abu Hassan; The Abduction from the Seraglio

1. Excerpt from *Débats,* May 19, 1859.

2. Weber was in fact about 24 when he wrote this comic opera in Darmstadt. It was performed in Munich on June 4, 1811.

3. Weber was indeed close to Meyerbeer at the time—1809–10—in Darmstadt, but Meyerbeer was eighteen or nineteen years old.

4. The French lyrics were by Nuitter and Beaumont. Auguste-Alphonse Meillet (1828–1871) won the prix d'opéra-comique in 1848, made his debut at the Opéra in 1850, and sang with success at the Théâtre-Lyrique in 1851. Berlioz often spoke of Meillet and his wife, also a singer, in his *feuilletons.*

5. *The Abduction from the Seraglio* was composed and performed in Vienna in 1782 when Mozart was 26.

6. Alexander Dimitrievich Ulibishev (1794–1858) was an amateur musician and writer on music. His three-volume work on Mozart appeared in Moscow in 1843. He disliked Beethoven's late works and attacked Lenz's book on the subject; this aroused Berlioz's ire (see *Evenings with the Orchestra,* pp. 314–326).

7. In the score, Constanze loves Belmonte, and Blonde, Pedrillo.

8. This is not the situation in the original libretto; Belmonte turns out to be the son of the pasha's Spanish *enemy.* When the pasha (a real Turk) lets his captives go free, he says to Belmonte: "Tell your father, it gives pleasure to repay an injustice with good deeds." Curiously, the version given by Berlioz comes very close to the events of the last scene of Mozart's other "Turkish" opera, the unfinished "Zaïde" (K. 344), which Berlioz is unlikely to have known.

9. Presumably the piece known as *Rondo alla Turca,* finale of the Piano Sonata in A, K. 331.

10. The aria was taken from Constanze's role and given to the soubrette (Blonde). Presumably it is the famous "Martern aller Arten."

11. See below, "The Rise in Concert Pitch."

12. Osmin and Pedrillo (bass and tenor).

13. It is the romance sung by Pedrillo.

14. After this duet, the score contains a number in which each of the main characters sings a verse in turn, and all of them join in the refrain. This "vaudeville" (see below, *"On Church Music,"* note 5) leads into a final chorus in praise of Pasha Selim.

15. Mme Meillet, née Mayer in 1829, was the wife of Auguste-Alphonse Meillet (see note 4 above).

16. See note 10 above. Mme Delphine Ugalde, née Beaucé in 1829, was one

of the most famous singers of her time. She first sang at the Opéra-Comique. See the *feuilleton* of February 9, 1855.

17. These comments may have prompted the editor of the score, Legouix, or perhaps the director of the Théâtre-Lyrique, to write this prefatory note: "The requirements of the French stage forced us to compress into two acts what was originally divided into three, thus bringing about new conditions in the order of numbers. But that was a mere matter of arrangement; it does not affect the music. The score was treated with all the respect that it merits; we did not follow the Italian translation, where textual errors are numbered in the hundreds, but Mozart's own scoring. As everybody knows, *The Abduction from the Seraglio* was composed to a German libretto." Paris, May 1859.

The Method Discovered by M. Delsarte for Tuning Instruments

1. Excerpt, *Débats*, December 30, 1859.
2. François-Alexandre-Nicholas Chéri Delsarte (1811–1871), a teacher of singing, was also a follower of St. Simon. His device for tuning, exhibited in 1855 at the Paris Exposition universelle de l'industrie, was called *Guide-accord* or *Sonotype*.

On Church Music

1. Excerpt from *Débats* of January 7, 1862. Joseph-Louis d'Ortigue (1802–1866) was a critic, musicologist, and close friend of Berlioz. He was an ardent advocate of Berlioz's music, despite differences of opinion on religion and religious music. A disciple of Lamennais (the nineteenth-century Catholic socialist thinker), d'Ortigue contributed to many Catholic journals. Aside from *La musique à l'église* (Didier, 1861), he wrote a substantial *Dictionnaire liturgique, historique et théorique de plainchant et de musique religieuse* (1854, 1860). He wrote for *Débats* in Berlioz's absence and replaced him there on his retirement in 1863.
2. D'Ortigue's preface could well be a description of *A Travers Chants*.
3. *L'Homme armé* (the armed man) is an old secular song. The tune was used by fifteenth- and sixteenth-century composers such as Dufay, Tinctoris, and Josquin Desprez as the *cantus firmus* for their masses, which then came to be known by this name.
4. See *Memoirs* (trans. Cairns), pp. 180ff.
5. *Vaudeville* is a French term of varying meaning and uncertain origin. By the late nineteenth century, vaudevilles had become songs sung at the end of spoken stage pieces or even operas, for example, Rousseau's *Le Devin du Village* and Mozart's *Abduction from the Seraglio*. The vaudeville tune was sung verse by verse by each of the characters in turn and sometimes by the chorus. However, the nineteenth-century vaudeville referred to by Berlioz was a skit—half dialogue, half song, on a semicomic, semisentimental subject. Yet another usage was an entire program of light music stage entertainment. From this, the term *vaudeville* came to denote a series of variety turns with no link or plot and only occasional music; as such, it survived in the United States into the twentieth century.
6. The Concerts spirituels were founded in Paris in 1725 by Anne Danican Philidor, oboist and elder half-brother of François-André (Danican) Philidor, the chess master and composer. The concerts consisted mainly of sacred music, but later they expanded to include symphonic pieces and became an important fixture in French musical life.
7. See above, "*Oberon*," note 10.

8. D'Ortigue, *La musique à l'église,* pp. 329–330.

9. Berlioz himself used modes in several compositions, such as *La Damnation de Faust* (Marguerite's *chanson gothique* "The King of Thule"), *Les Troyens* (Hylas's song), and *L'Enfance du Christ* (the orchestral passage which opens Part II and Herod's air "written in the Phrygian mode of plainsong after an introductory recitative ends on a Dorian cadence"). (Jacques Barzun, *Berlioz and the Romantic Century,* Vol. II, p. 92.)

10. Horace, *Ars poetica,* verse 269.

Musical Customs of China

1. Excerpt from *Débats,* December 29, 1860.

2. On December 19, 1860, *Débats* had reported a peace treaty with China, concluding some twenty years of war. On December 27 it published the main articles of the Treaty of Tientsin, which opened China to European trade.

3. On December 23, 1860, *Débats* related the capture of the Summer Palace.

4. See *Evenings with the Orchestra,* pp. 246–250.

5. Jean-Madeleine Schneitzhoeffer (1785–1852), born in Toulouse, was a composer of ballets and the chorus master at the Opéra from 1823. This French composer with a German name is best known for composing the original score of the ballet *La Sylphide* (Paris Opéra, 1832).

6. During Berlioz's first journey to Russia, in March–June 1847.

7. See *Memoirs* (trans. Cairns), pp. 111–113. Berlioz is lampooning the voting system used by The Academy of Fine Arts when he was a candidate for the Prix de Rome. (See Barzun, *Berlioz and the Romantic Century,* Vol. I, p. 95.)

8. An obsolete Chinese punishment, known as *kia* or *ka* ("cang" or "cangue" in English), in which the offender is incapacitated by a chain around his neck and wrists, and a sign telling the nature of his crime is hung from his neck.

Letter to the Academy of Fine Arts of the Institute

1. From *Débats,* September 11 and 12, 1861. Berlioz was elected to membership in the Académie des beaux-arts in 1856. It is composed of 40 members, elected for life, among them painters, sculptors, engravers, and musicians.

2. The Institut de France is composed of the Académie française and four other organizations: Académie des inscriptions et belles-lettres, Académie des sciences, Académie des beaux-arts, and Académie des sciences morales et politiques.

3. Eugène Guinot was the author of *Eté à Bade,* illustrated by Tony Johannot, E. Lami, Français and Daubigny (Paris: Bourdin, 1857). It was cited in the *feuilleton* of September 24, 1857.

4. *Bade et ses Environs,* drawn from nature by Jules Coignet, with text by Amédée Achard (Paris: Hachette, 1858).

5. Paul de Kock (1794–1871) published many popular novels concerning the manners of the common people and the bourgeoisie.

6. See above, "Lines Written Soon after the First Performance of *Orphée,*" note 11.

7. Berlioz is alluding to Crispin's famous retort in Regnard's *Le Légataire universel* [The Sole Heir], Act V, scene 6: "It's your lethargy!"

8. Baden-Baden is a German spa town near the French border. It became an important musical center in the nineteenth century, drawing virtuosos such as Liszt, Thalberg, and Paganini. Berlioz conducted summer festivals there from 1856 to 1863. In 1861, he assisted the rediscovery of Pergolesi by reviving *La serva padrona.*

9. Edouard Bénazet was born in 1801 in Paris and died in 1867 in Nice. In 1848 he succeeded his father, Jacques Bénazet, as director of the Casino in Baden-Baden. From the mid-1850s Bénazet organized annual music festivals each August, with performances in the Casino itself and later in the new Theater am Goetheplatz, which he had built and which opened in 1862 with the first performance of the opera he had commissioned from Berlioz, *Béatrice et Bénédict.* Berlioz sings his praises in the *feuilleton* of September 24, 1857.

10: Famous aria from Grétry's *Richard Coeur-de-Lion.*

11. The Concert of Europe was the consensus among the monarchies of Europe during the post-Napoleonic era to maintain the political and territorial status quo. The great powers assumed the right to impose their will on states threatened by internal rebellion.

12. See *Les Grotesques de la musique*, "Petites misères des grands concerts" [Small annoyances at great concerts], pp. 145–149.

13. Renard, a singer of the Paris Opéra, sang an aria from *La Juive* (*G.M.*, September 1, 1861).

14. Jacques-François Fromental Halévy (1799–1862) was a popular and prolific opera composer. *La Juive* was his masterpiece and greatest success.

15. Stephen de la Madelaine (1801–1868) was a singer and writer on singing. Berlioz refers to his book *Théories complètes du chant*, which was approved by the Academy.

16. *Traditore* (It. traitor).

17. Berlioz reviewed Renard's début at the Opéra, in *William Tell*, in the *feuilleton* of June 3, 1857.

18. In December 1842. Cf. *Memoirs* (trans. Cairns), p. 271.

19. The French two-act opera, *Le Sylphe* (1856) was composed by Antoine Louis Clapisson (1808–1866). The libretto was by Jules-Henri Vernoy de Saint-Georges, a prolific librettist and director of the Opéra-Comique.

20. The rotund Clapisson won a place in the Academy in 1854 with his popular opéra-comiques.

21. Philinte was a character in French theater. His manners were affected and precious.

22. François Habeneck, who introduced Beethoven's symphonies to Paris. See above, "A Critical Study of Beethoven's Nine Symphonies," notes 3 and 8.

23. The French conductor Narcisse Girard (1797–1860) succeeded Habeneck in 1847.

24. Théophile (Alexandre) Tilmant (1799–1878), French conductor and violinist, had been deputy conductor at the Société des concerts since its establishment in 1828. He replaced Girard in 1860 and served until 1863.

25. Here ends the *feuilleton* of September 11, 1861.

26. Berlioz employs a similar image to express his disdain for certain opera texts based on Shakespeare. See below, "*Romeo and Juliet*," p. 219.

27. An aeolian harp is a string instrument sounded by natural wind. It is interesting as much for its symbolic significance as for its musical importance. See *Evenings with the Orchestra*, p. 36; *V.M.*, Vol. II, p. 160; and *Memoirs* (trans. Cairns), p. 184.

28. This is the nocturne sung by Hero and Ursula which ends the first act of *Béatrice et Bénédict.*

29. Geese saved the Capitol in ancient Rome from the attacking Gauls by making their usual barnyard noise, which alerted the Romans.

30. *Béatrice et Bénédict.* The première took place on August 9, 1862.

31. "Quandoque bonus dormitat Homerus," *Ars Poetica.*

32. The program included the *Dies irae, Tuba mirum*, and *Offertorium.*

33. *Hamlet*, Act V, scene 1, lines 185–187.

34. The text of the *Dies irae,* the sequence of the Mass for the Dead, is ascribed to Thomas of Celano (d. circa 1250). "Since Berlioz's *Symphonie fantastique,* a rich and productive symbolism has grown up round the ancient melody, embracing not only death and the fear of death, but also the supernatural" *(Grove's Dictionary).*

35. See the *feuilleton* of September 24, 1857; and *Les Grotesques de la musique,* p. 181.

36. Queen Augusta of Prussia (1811–1890) was born in Weimar, a daughter of Grand Duke Karl Friedrich. Her husband, Wilhelm, had just acceded to the Prussian throne in 1861. A decade later he became Kaiser of the new German Empire. The queen's presence at this concert and her admiration for Berlioz were reported in *G.M.* and *France musicale.*

The Rise in Concert Pitch

1. *Débats,* September 29, 1858, reprinted in *G.M.,* October 3, 1858. See also *G.M.,* February 27, 1859: "Du Diapason Normal" (Concerning Normal Pitch), based on the report of a committee of twelve members (including Berlioz) to the Minister of State (*Moniteur,* February 25, 1859).

2. Berlioz modestly omits mentioning that he himself was one of the composers named to the committee, along with Meyerbeer, Auber, Rossini, Ambroise Thomas, and Halévy, who was *rapporteur.*

3. See above, "High and Low Sounds."

4. On the mammoth concert of August 1, 1844 to close the Exhibition of Industrial Productions, see Barzun, *Berlioz and the Romantic Century,* Vol. I, pp. 443–445.

5. On the three concerts organized by Berlioz for the closing of the Great Exhibition of 1855, see ibid., Vol. II, pp. 112–113.

6. For the opening of the Exhibition of 1855 on April 30, Berlioz conducted his *Te Deum* in the church of St. Eustache with 800 performers, see ibid., pp. 108–109).

7. It now seems established (see, e.g., *Grove's Dictionary,* article on "Pitch") that the rise in pitch from the late eighteenth century (Mozart and Gluck) to the mid-nineteenth century *(A Travers Chants)* amounted to about one half tone. But since most of the rise occurred after about 1820, the rate of increase during the following three decades was probably even higher than Berlioz's half a tone in half a century!

8. See "Tenth Evening," *Evenings with the Orchestra,* pp. 118ff.

9. See "Thirteenth Evening," ibid., pp. 152ff.

10. Rossini's opera, based on Schiller's play, composed in 1829.

11. First produced in Mannheim in 1759; a second version was performed in Paris in 1775.

12. Marie-Josèphe Cabel (1827–1885) was born in Liège. She sang at the Opéra-Comique in 1849, then in Brussels, Strasbourg, and Geneva before going to the Théâtre-Lyrique in 1853. The "young Cabel" (her son?) gave a much-admired rendition of Hylas' song in the first production of *Les Troyens* (see *Memoirs* [trans. Cairns], p. 491).

13. Caroline-Félix Carvalho (née Miolan) (1827–1859), a pupil of Duprez, married one of her colleagues at the Opéra-Comique, Léon Carvalho, and followed him to the Théâtre-Lyrique when he became its director. See *G.M.* and the *feuilleton* of July 20, 1858.

14. Anna-Caroline de Lagrange was born in Paris in 1825. A pupil of Bordogni, she sang in Italy with great success before coming to Paris in 1848. See *feuilletons* of November 25, 1854 and February 17, and July 20, 1858.

15. In *Iphigénie en Tauride* and *Iphigénie en Aulide* and in Grétry's opera *Sylvain* (1770).

16. Henri-Etienne Dérivis (1780–1856) was the leading bass of the Opéra at this time. Berlioz probably heard him in 1823 as the High Priest in Spontini's *La Vestale*, as well as in Gluck and Mozart operas. See *Memoirs* (trans. Cairns), pp. 47, 54, 84, and 581.

17. Berlioz returned to this theme in a brief page, "The Lapdog School of Singing" (see Appendix), which he appended—unsuitably—to this volume of essays.

18. It was Berlioz's own *Te Deum*. See note 6 above.

19. Equivalent to 449 vibrations for the A one octave lower, and thus slightly higher than standard modern pitch (A = 440). The French government's committee actually went beyond Berlioz and recommended a reduction in the pitch level to A = 435; this became law in France in 1859 and was adopted voluntarily elsewhere, for example, by Covent Garden Opera in London in 1880. However, the problem still had not been solved. By the 1940s, "normal" pitch had generally shifted up to 440, despite some resistance, notably in France. New efforts were then made to stabilize it at this level, by the BBC in London and the Smithsonian Institution in Washington, D.C., then by a resolution of the Council of Europe in Strasbourg (1970–71), culminating in the 1975 proclamation that A = 440 by the International Standards Organization in Geneva. This standard was widely approved but is not legally binding. Indeed, Berlioz might again be sounding the alarm, were he aware of recent trends. "The hunt for increased brilliance would appear to have been re-initiated during the past few decades, as many symphony orchestras are now tuning to pitches several Hz (frequencies) above the normal international standard." (Cary Karp, article on "Pitch," in *Performance Practice*, eds. Howard Mayer Brown and Stanley Sadie [London: Macmillan, and New York: W. W. Norton, 1989]. See also *Grove's Dictionary*, article on "Pitch," p. 785.)

20. From this point on, the tone suggests that Berlioz is no longer seeking to make practical proposals. He is only exercising his imagination to indicate his exacting standards of performance. In another context he wrote, "Approximation in music is torture."

21. It should be noted that Berlioz himself had just completed writing the role of Aeneas, which many would consider full of those "ruinously high notes." For whatever reason, it seems to be one of the most difficult of operatic roles to cast, now that *Les Troyens* is at last becoming part of the repertoire. High tenor parts occur also in *Cellini* and the *Sanctus* of the *Requiem*, although the slow tempo of the latter makes the tenor's part more manageable. Of course, in Berlioz's time singers expected such notes in order to show off their powers.

The End Is Near

1. Excerpt from *Débats*, January 2–3, 1861.

2. "Mamamouchi" is a pseudo-Turkish honorific invented by Molière for M. Jourdain in *Le Bourgeois Gentilhomme*. The words in italics also come from the "Turkish" ceremony in the fourth act of the play. Some seem to be pure nonsense, but those of Latin origin come from a kind of pidgin spoken along the Mediterranean coast.

3. In Act 5, scene 1 of *Le Bourgeois Gentilhomme*, Mme Jourdain says: "Good Heavens, my husband has gone mad."

4. This is most probably *Barkouf*, an operetta by Offenbach, which had its première at the Opéra-Comique on December 24, 1860. Berlioz was not fond of Offenbach, being out of sympathy with his debunking of the classics, which

Berlioz found silly. On his side, Offenbach respected and admired Berlioz and his music. (See Barzun, *Berlioz and the Romantic Century*, Vol. II, pp. 84, 211, and 241.)

5. Louise-Aglaé Masson (b. 1827) won the first prize for piano at the Conservatoire at the age of thirteen. She married the violinist and teacher Joseph Massart, concertmaster of the Société Philharmonique. On M. and Mme Massart, see *Correspondance générale*, Vol. IV, p. 549; and the *feuilletons* of February 3 and September 24, 1857.

6. The "Appassionata," Op. 57. See the *feuilleton* of February 16, 1862.

7. Winterhalter's painting, exhibited at the Salon of 1837 and popularized by Girard's engraving.

The Richard Wagner Concerts

1. Wagner's theatrical agent, Giacomelli, organized these concerts to draw the public's attention to the composer and his music before *Tannhäuser* was put on at the Opéra. Berlioz had already heralded Wagner's coming to Paris in his *feuilleton* of December 9, 1859. On the relationship of Berlioz and Wagner, see Barzun, *Berlioz and the Romantic Century*, Vol. II, pp. 170–174, 176–202.

2. See Léon Guichard, *La Musique et les lettres en France au temps du wagnérisme* (Paris: Presses Universitaires de France, 1955), p. 31 and notes.

3. It took place on January 25, 1860. The two others were on February 1 and 8, 1860.

4. See above, "*Fidelio.*"

5. *The Flying Dutchman* (1841) was staged at the Dresden Opera on January 2, 1843.

6. Berlioz was in Dresden, February 7–19, 1843, to give two concerts. It was then that he saw *The Flying Dutchman*. See *Débats*, September 12, 1843, reproduced in *V.M.* and *Memoirs* (trans. Cairns), pp. 300–307.

7. The famous bridal chorus or wedding march, Act III, scene 1 ("*Treulich geführt ziehet dahin*").

8. Comic opera with a libretto by Scribe and Bouilly, first performed May 20, 1829.

9. The score of *Tristan* was finished in 1859. Four days before his first Paris concert, Wagner sent a copy of his work to Berlioz with the following note: "Dear Berlioz, I am delighted to be able to present you with the first copy of my *Tristan*. Please accept and keep it out of friendship for: Yours, Richard Wagner. January 21, 1860" (Julien Tiersot, *Lettres françaises de Richard Wagner* [Paris: B. Grasset, 1935], p. 188).

10. See Wagner's reply to this article, published in *Débats*, February 22, 1860, and included in his *Lettres françaises*. Berlioz's review (abridged) and Wagner's published reply are reproduced together in H. Barth, D. Hack, and E. Voss, eds., *Wagner: A Documentary Study* (English translation, London, Thames & Hudson, 1975), pp. 189–193.

11. It is Iphigenia's own aria, "O malheureuse Iphigénie" see *G.M.*, June 8, 1834, p. 184; and *Evenings with the Orchestra*, pp. 253–255, where Berlioz cites this same aria.

12. *La Muette de Portici (Masaniello)*, Paris, 1828.

13. Composed and first performed in Berlin in 1845.

14. Berlioz loved to quote this motto. See *Evenings with the Orchestra*, p. 252; *Les Grotesques de la musique*, p. 252.

15. This is what Chrysalis says to Philaminte in Molière's *Femmes savantes*, Act II, scene 7.

16. It may be Duprez, who is hinted at further on by the symbol D—. He composed several operas.

Sunt Lacrymae Rerum

1. *Aeneid*, I, verse 462. When Aeneas is first in Carthage, he is moved at seeing the sorrows of the Trojan wars depicted on the walls of a temple in Dido's new city. He exclaims: ". . . *they weep here / For how the world goes, and our life that passes / Touches their hearts*" (trans. Robert Fitzgerald [New York: Random House, 1983], lines 628–630, p. 20).

2. Line from La Fontaine in *Philémon et Baucis*, somewhat altered.

3. See "Les Dilettanti du grand monde," in *Les Grotesques de la musique*, p. 265.

4. Ibid., p. 266.

5. See above, "Beethoven in the Rings of Saturn," note 5.

6. Enrico Tamberlik (Tamberlick) (1820–1889), a famous Italian tenor, sang the role of Benvenuto Cellini at Covent Garden in June 1853. "I have the best tenor [Tamberlick] that it is possible to wish for, who sings and understands the role admirably. . . " (Correspondance générale, Vol. IV, p. 326).

7. Catherine Hayes (1825–1861), an Irish soprano, studied with Manuel García (father of María Malibran and Pauline Viardot) in Paris and with Ronconi in Milan. According to Mendelssohn, she was one of the three greatest female singers of her day.

8. Jenny Lind (1820–1887), the celebrated Swedish soprano, also studied with García in Paris. She sang in London, at first in operatic roles and later in concerts; toured the world; and practiced philanthropy. She was known in the English-speaking press as "The Swedish Nightingale." See also above, "The Current State of the Art of Singing," note 17.

9. Two ways of beating the (snare) drum are indicated in French by *ra* and *fla*: *ra* = ruff (three notes preceding an accented note); *fla* = flam (first note played unaccented before the beat and joined quickly to the second).

10. Berlioz was one of Hugo's defenders at the first night of *Hernani* at the Théâtre Français, February 25, 1830. On Berlioz, *Hernani*, and the Romanticists, see Barzun, *Berlioz and the Romantic Century*, Vol. I, pp. 127–131; and David Cairns, *Berlioz* (London: André Deutsch, 1989), Vol. I, pp. 323–324.

11. Act III, scene 7. The text begins "Vieillard stupide . . . ," which is already disrespectful, but some of the spectators apparently heard it as "Vieil as de pique!" Literally, this means "Old ace of spades," but colloquially it meant "chicken rump" (parson's nose)—a worthless character, a chump. Whether the spectators misheard or the actor mispronounced, the furor was such that Victor Hugo had to change the acting version to "O misérable." In the translation I have tried to approximate the confusion, at the cost of altering the expression, though not its intent. What Berlioz is saying is that judgments about music—both favorable and unfavorable—often mistake or disregard what the composer actually wrote.

The Symphonies of H. Reber; Stephen Heller

1. *Feuilleton* of July 23, 1861.

2. See *Memoirs* (trans. Cairns), pp. 470–471, concerning the "Symphony in A minor," which Berlioz dreamed and forgot, in his case intentionally.

3. "In Prague, I got up in the middle of the night to set down a tune that I

was afraid of forgetting, the angelic chorus in the scene of Margaret's apotheosis: 'Remonte au ciel, âme naïve, que l'amour égara' " (ibid., p. 415).

4. Cantata for bass and chorus on the death of Napoleon, composed in the summer of 1835 to "les mauvais vers de Béranger" (*Corréspondance générale,* Vol. II, p. 279) and performed for the first time at the Conservatoire on November 22, 1835.

5. The painter Nicolas Poussin lived in Rome, next to Salvator Rosa and opposite Claude Lorrain.

6. Genesis, seventh day of creation.

7. Brandus and Richault, among the leading publishing houses in Paris, were the two main publishers of Berlioz's works. Brandus brought out the first editions of *Harold in Italy, Roméo et Juliette,* the *Te Deum,* and a piano-vocal score of *Béatrice et Bénédict.* Brandus also published works by Chopin, Meyerbeer, Offenbach and Liszt.

Richault was the first publisher of *La Damnation de Faust, L'Enfance du Christ, Lélio,* four overtures, several vocal works, and a collection of *mélodies* with piano accompaniment by Berlioz. Richault also published Alkan and Reber, as well as Beethoven, Weber, and Schumann, among others. (See also Cecil Hopkinson, *Bibliography of the Musical and Literary Works of Hector Berlioz* [Edinburgh, 1951].)

8. This list understates the number of symphonies by Mozart, Mendelssohn, and especially Schubert.

9. Henri (Napoléon) Reber (1807–1880), a French composer, was, like Berlioz, a pupil of Lesueur and Reicha. Berlioz often discussed him in his *feuilletons.* Reber is remembered chiefly for his *Traité d'harmonie* (1862). He also composed operas and chamber music.

10. The minuet is in Act V.

11. Gluck is telling Vestris that the minuet is of such a broad style that Vestris will need all the room of the Place du Carrousel to dance it in. The Place du Carrousel was built by Louis XIV opposite the Tuileries palace for shows of jousting without actual fighting—symbolic parades and evolutions of horsemen in costume. On Vestris, see above, "Lines Written Soon after the First Performance of *Orphée,*" note 11.

12. Wagner and Offenbach?

13. Nicolas Boileau, *Art Poétique* (1674), Vol. I, p. 63.

14. Stephen (István) Heller (1813–1888), a Hungarian pianist and composer, spent his youth in Augsburg. Schumann gave Heller's work enthusiastic reviews in *Neue Zeitschrift für Musik* and included him among his Davidsbundler, a fictitious society of friends whose mission was to tease and oppose the Philistines of art. This society also included Berlioz. In 1838, Heller moved to Paris, where he lived for the rest of his life. He wrote a large number of compositions for piano, which occupy a transitional position between late German Romanticism and French Impressionism.

Romeo and Juliet

1. *Feuilleton* of September 13, 1859. In this article, Berlioz chooses to make no mention of his own dramatic symphony "Roméo et Juliette" (1839). Gounod's opera of that name was premièred in Paris in 1867, five years after the publication of *A Travers Chants.*

2. Of the ten opera librettos set to music by Bellini, seven, including *Norma* and *La Sonnambula,* are by Felice Romani.

3. Vincenzo Bellini (1801–1835) was the composer of *I Capuleti ed i Montecchi* (Venice, March 11, 1830). The Paris production used a translation of Ro-

mani's libretto by Nuitter. In his short life, Bellini became one of the most successful opera composers of the nineteenth century. His works still in the repertoire are *La Sonnambula* (Milan, 1831), *Norma* (Milan, 1831), and *I Puritani* (Paris, 1835).

4. Antonio, Alberti, Cébas, and Cécile are characters in Steibelt's *Romeo*. The others are in the opera by Dalayrac.

5. Rosaline is first mentioned by Mercutio in *Romeo and Juliet*, Act II, scene 1, line 17.

6. Berlioz condenses Act I, scene 1, lines 198–199 and 226.

7. Act I, scene 4, lines 41–42.

8. Act II, scene 4, lines 4–5.

9. Act II, scene 2, lines 129–132, 140–142.

10. This passage does not appear in Shakespeare's play. It seems to be a sort of fantasia by Berlioz on themes from *Romeo and Juliet*.

11. Daniel Steibelt (1765–1823), a German pianist and composer, made his career in Paris, London, and St. Petersburg. The libretto of his opera in three acts (1792) is by the Vicomte de Ségur. It was recast and successfully produced at the Théâtre Feydeau on September 10, 1793.

12. Act I, scene 3, Juliet (alone).

13. Act III, scene 2, lines 5–13.

14. Steibelt, *Romeo*, Act I, scene 10, pp. 108–131 (the end of Act I).

15. Ibid., Act III, scene 1, pp. 261–283.

16. Ibid., Act II, scene 8, Juliet alone, pp. 178–195.

17. *Hamlet*, Act III, scene 4, line 9.

18. *Romeo and Juliet*, Act IV, scene 3, lines 24–59.

19. Berlioz has "Romeo! Romeo!—Here's drink!—I drink to thee!" In combining the original English with a translation, Berlioz unwittingly misquotes.

20. Nicholas-Marie Dalayrac (D'Alayrac) (1753–1809), a French composer, wrote sixty opéra-comiques, including *Tout pour l'amour, ou Roméo et Juliette*, in four acts, which was performed at the Théâtre Favart on July 7, 1792. Berlioz wrote a review of the revival of his *Nina, ou la Folle par l'amour* (Nina, or the Woman Made Mad by Love) in his *feuilleton* of January 7, 1852. He followed it up on January 13, 1852 with *Quelques notes sur Dalayrac* (A Brief Note about Dalayrac). The libretto of Dalayrac's Romeo was by Jacques-Marie Boutet de Monvel (1745–1811), an actor at the Comédie-Française and a playwright.

21. Nicola Antonio Zingarelli (1752–1837) was an Italian composer of operas and, after 1804, of church music. His first opera, *Montezuma*, was produced by Haydn at Eszterháza. Zingarelli was the last major composer of opera seria. *Giulietta e Romeo* (1796), his best-known opera, became a favorite vehicle for Maria Malibran. It was first produced at La Scala on January 30, 1796 and was performed at the Théâtre des Tuileries on March 9, 1809. According to the preface *(argomento)* to the libretto published in 1804, Zingarelli (or his librettist, Foppa) took the story directly from a source earlier than Shakespeare, *Histories of Verona* by Girolamo dalla Corte.

22. Berlioz has "avrà" (= he/she) will have a happy heart. This may derive from the original printed libretto of 1796, which reads "avrà (contenti!)." Later versions of the libretto, from 1804, have "avrò contento." According to Guichard, this aria was published separately several times in nineteenth-century France, "words in Italian or French."

23. This passage does not appear among the few words Juliet is given to sing in the printed librettos of 1796 and 1804. By 1829, she had acquired a full-scale aria: its words are not as Berlioz gives them but its sentiments are somewhat similar. In 1859 Berlioz may have had access to a still later version of the libretto.

24. *Hamlet*, Act III, scene 2, line 229.

25. Nicola Vaccaï (1790–1848) was an Italian composer and teacher. His *Giulietta e Romeo* to a libretto by Romani was first performed in La Cannobiana (Milan) on October 31, 1825.

26. In London, the scene with the aria "Ah! se tu dormi" often replaced the last act of Bellini's opera. A quarrel between Vaccaï and Romani played its part in the decision by Romani and Bellini to write *I Capuleti ed I Montecchi*, which then eclipsed Vaccaï's slighter opera. However, at Rossini's suggestion, Maria Malibran interpolated the tomb scene of Vaccaï's opera into that of Bellini. Her example was so widely followed that in many scores of *I Capuleti ed I Montecchi*, Vaccaï's scene was given in full as an appendix.

27. There exists a score of *Roméo et Juliette* by Vincenzo Bellini, "opera in four acts, French translation by C. de Charlemagne, edition augmented with the *Grande scène des tombeaux* of the same opera, music by Vaccaï" (Paris: Aulagnier, no date).

28. It was in March 1831.

29. *I Capuleti ed I Montecchi* (see Note 3 above). Berlioz saw Bellini's opera in Florence early in 1831. Its shortcomings may have helped focus his thinking about his own project of a dramatic symphony on *Romeo and Juliet*. (See Cairns, *Berlioz*, Vol. I, p. 409.)

30. *Memoirs* (trans. Cairns), pp. 160–162.

31. First performed at La Scala, February 14, 1829.

32. Friar Laurence.

33. Marié (b. 1814) was a pupil of Alexandre Choron (1771–1834) and later sang at the Opéra-Comique. In 1840 he replaced Duprez at the Opéra.

34. *Othello*, Act V, scene 2, line 1.

35. Louis Gueymard (b. 1822) joined the Opéra in 1848, and there, until 1868, he sang the roles of heroic tenors.

36. Pauline Lauters, mezzo-soprano born in Brussels in 1834, had her debut at the Théâtre-Lyrique in 1854 and at the Opéra in 1857 (see *feuilletons* of October 11, 1854 and February 3, 1857). She married Gueymard, her second husband, in 1858 (see the *feuilleton* of April 24, 1861).

37. Felicja Vestfali (Felicité Vestvali) (1824–1880), a Polish contralto and tragic actress, studied under Romani and Mercadante in Naples. She was known for her acting in Shakespearean roles, notably in *Hamlet*. See the *feuilleton* of July 13, 1859, where Berlioz announces her arrival in Paris.

38. This is the well-known Garrick ending, not Shakespeare's, as Berlioz is perfectly aware. "Garrick's denouement to *Romeo and Juliet*, which he substituted for the less striking ending that Shakespeare wrote, is an inspired invention, incomparable in its pathos" (*Memoirs* [trans. Cairns], p. 91). Garrick's version was the one Berlioz saw performed in Paris in 1827, when the English players triumphed over the anti-Shakespeare prejudices of the French. It was during this season, too, that Berlioz first saw his future wife, Harriet Smithson; she was a sensational success as Ophelia in *Hamlet* and aroused in Berlioz one of the most famous grand passions in music history.

39. This may be a translation from Romani's libretto. Guichard says that the words quoted by Berlioz are not from the Charlemagne translation, and that Fétis does not name the translator for the version made for the performance at the Opéra.

40. *Othello*, Act V, scene 2, line 234. Often quoted by Berlioz.

Concerning a Ballet Based on Faust

1. Excerpts from *Débats*, March 26, 1859, in which Berlioz reviewed Gounod's opera *Faust*. The ballet he discusses was presumably that by Adolphe Adam (1833); the first production of Gounod's *Faust* (1859) did not contain a ballet.

2. In 1828, while composing *Eight Scenes from Faust*, Berlioz himself was apparently approached by the Opéra about writing ballet music to a scenario on *Faust* by Victor Bohain, the editor of the new *Figaro* (Cairns, *Berlioz*, Vol. I, p. 275.)

3. The vivid image of birds fouling statues occurs also in Berlioz's *Lélio*.

4. Mascarille in Molière's *Précieuses ridicules*, scene 10.

5. Berlioz's "excuse" here is drawn from *Faust* itself, in which Gretchen is forgiven her sin because her love was great. With his usual reverence for masterworks, Berlioz felt he too needed an excuse, since he had used the drama again for his *Damnation de Faust* (1846).

6. Berlioz sent Goethe his *Eight Scenes from Faust* in 1829. Goethe passed it on to his composer friend Zelter, who called it "a series of grunts, snorts, and expectorations" (see Barzun, *Berlioz and the Romantic Century*, Vol. I, p. 97).

7. Overture and incidental music (nine pieces), composed in 1810.

To Be or Not To Be

1. *Débats*, March 13, 1861. This essay is a paraphrase of Hamlet's famous soliloquy and of the following scene with Ophelia, Act III, scene 1, lines 57–149.

2. Paraphrase of "I know a hawk from a handsaw," Act II, scene 2, lines 371–372.

Index

Achard, Amédée, 180, 260n4
Adam, Adolphe, 269n1
Albrechtsberger, Johann Georg, 104, 251n44
Alexander the Great, 2–3
Alfieri, Count Vittorio, 45, 241n27
Alizard, Adolphe, 96, 251n28
Altès, Joseph-Henri, 145, 255n34
Anders, Godefroid E., 86, 249n23
Angiolini, Gasparo, 72, 245n7
Antier-Chevrillon, Benjamin, 247n5
Apocalypse, 180
Arend, Max, 249n21
Aristarchs, 45, 241n29
Aristexenus, 6, 233n22
Arnaud, Abbé François, 122, 146, 252n63
Auber, Daniel-François-Esprit, 208, 264n12

Bachaumont, Louis Petit de, 248n18
Baden, 180, 182, 187, 189–192 (passim), 212, 260n8
Baldi (singer), 134, 135
Barbier, Auguste, 59–60, 243n3
Barzun, Jacques, 233nn11,12, 234n24, 239n1, 243nn6,8, 244n1, 247n26, 256n6, 260n9, 262n4, 264n1, 265n10, 269n6
Bataille (bass singer), 168
BBC London, 263n19
Beethoven, Ludwig van, 9–56, 104, 125, 148–149, 185–186, 200, 208, 228; mentioned, 162, 215, 216; Coriolan, 38, 125; Egmont, 38, 228n4, 269n7; Fidelio, 38, 41–52, 129, 148, 167, 182–183, 202–203, 238n2; late quartets, etc., 52, 258n6; sonatas and trios, 38–40, 52, 60, 61, 97, 200, 232n11, 258n6
—Symphonies: I, 11–12, 29; II, 9, 10, 12–13, 17; Eroica, 13–17, 26, 235nn12,13; IV, 17–19, 20; V, 3, 18, 19–22, 149, 185–186; Pastoral, 22–25, 26, 28, 29; VII, 10, 20, 25–29; VIII, 29–31; IX, 16–17, 31–37, 52
Bellini, Vincenzo, 219, 225, 227, 266n3, 268nn26–29
Bénazet, Edouard, 180, 181, 189, 261n9
Benda, Georg (Jiři), 253n81
Béranger, Pierre-Jean de, 214 (quoted), 266n4
Berlin Grand Opera, 64, 140
Berlioz, Hector, 232nn1,11, 234nn24,1, 244nn19, 24, 260nn6,7; on Mme Branchu, 254n12; on Carvalho, 257n16; on Freischütz, 154; on Gluck, 244n1, 249n1, 254n1; on modes, 260n9; on pitch, 262nn1,2, 263nn20,21; on Schröder-De-

vrient, 257n13; on Viardot, 244–245n3, 246n22, 247n26; on Victor Hugo, 265nn10,11; Béatrice et Bénédict, 187–188 (quoted), 189, 261nn9,28,30; Benvenuto Cellini, 232n1, 263n21, 265n6; Damnation de Faust, 241n40, 265–266n3, 269nn2,5,6; La Mort d'Ophélie, 232n1; Requiem, 190–192, 261n32, 263n21; Roméo et Juliette, 251n28, 266n1, 268n29; Symphonie fantastique, 262n34; Te Deum, 198, 263n18, 262n6; Troyens, 240n22, 250n9, 257n16, 262n12, 263n21; Evenings with the Orchestra, 256n45, 258n6, 260n4, 261n27; Grotesques de la Musique, 240n24, 241n28, 261n12, 265nn3,4; Memoirs, 232n1, 239n6, 261n27, 265n2; Traité d'Instrumentation, 233n15, 235n12, 236nn24,27, 238nn90,91, 241nn37,38, 256n2; A Travers Chants, 259n2; Voyage Musical, 232n2
Berlioz, Nanci, 232n7
Bertoni, Ferdinando, 76, 86–87, 129, 246n18, 249nn20,25–30
Bertrand. See Schneitzhoeffer
Bitaubé, Paul Jérémie, 89, 250n10
Bobêche (Mandelart, known as), 88, 250n8
Boïeldieu, François Adrien, 206, 256n5, 264n8
Boileau, Nicolas, 45 (quoted), 96 (quoted), 217 (quoted), 251nn26,27, 266n13
Borchardt (bass-baritone), 144–145
Bordogni, Giulio Marco, 258n24, 262n14
Borghèse, Mlle (contralto), 164
Boschi, Giuseppe (bass singer), 134
Bouilly, Jean-Nicolas, 41, 44, 129, 239n3, 240n23, 264n8
Braham, John, 156, 257n4
Mme Branchu, 105, 140, 142, 252n12, 255nn22,23
Brandus (publisher), 215, 266n7
Breitkopf & Härtel (Leipzig), 45, 241n26
Broadwood (piano), 97, 251n30
Brumoy, Père, 89, 250nn12,13
Buononcini, Giovanni, 133, 253n85
Burney, Charles, 257n8

Cabel, Marie Josèphe, 196, 231, 262n12
Cairns, David, 232n1, 234n24, 257nn10,16, 265n10, 268n29, 269n2
Calzabigi, Raniero di: Alceste, 88, 99–100, 121–124 (quoted passim), 128, 129 (quoted), 132, 250n3; Orfeo, 71, 72, 87, 190 (quoted), 245n7, 246n18, 249n29

ELIZABETH CSICSERY-RÓNAY, based in Brussels, Belgium, makes English translations of novels, plays, short stories, and articles written in French and in Hungarian. She also writes music reviews and articles, which have appeared in *Berlioz Society Bulletin, Opera News, Musical America,* and *La Revue Musicale Suisse,* among other periodicals.